Three Lives of a Warrior

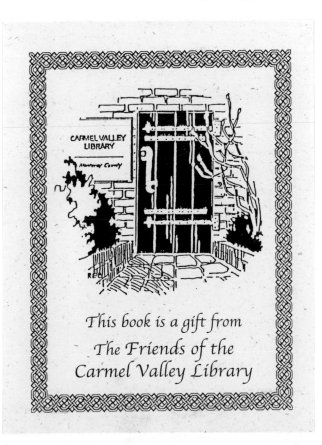

THREE LIVES

OF A WARRIOR

Phillip Butler

A CAMELOT PRESS BOOK

Dedication

Three Lives of a Warrior is dedicated to all warriors who never got the chance to live their third lives.

Contents

Foreword

It was a cold, gray day in March 1973. I was standing on the tarmac at Andrews Air Force base, waiting for the arrival of several men who had recently been released from prison in Hanoi. Some of these American POWs had been held for years.

It was a conflicting situation for me, though I didn't know it until I was ready to leave. I had been vocal in my opposition to the war we had waged in Vietnam since 1965, when I had first researched our involvement in their country for a lengthy paper I wrote in prep school. American involvement went back to the Second World War, when President Roosevelt had promised Ho Chi Minh that in honor of his fighting against the Japanese the United States would support his bid for independence against the French.

But that policy changed under Truman, and then Eisenhower and Nixon. In fact, when the French were about to fall at Dien Bien Phu in 1954, Nixon persuaded Eisenhower to let him offer nuclear weapons to the beleaguered French garrison. It was too late for them, however. But the U.S. then inserted itself into the post-war Geneva negotiations that determined the political settlement which paved the way for the Ho Chi Minh government to take control the country in 1956.

That plan was thwarted unilaterally by the United States, as we built a puppet government in the southern part of Vietnam, headed first by Bao Dai, a minion from the French era, and then others named Diem, Ky and Thieu. The U.S. poured billions of dollars into the south, to prop up the government and to militarize their effort against the north. Much of the design was promulgated by the Dulles brothers – John Foster as Secretary of State and Allen at CIA – and heavily weighted by the anti-communist, red scare politics of the time.

The behind-the-scenes activities continued into the Kennedy and Johnson administrations. Some historians say that at the time Kennedy was killed in 1963 – three weeks after the Diem assassination – he was planning to wind down our involvement there, but Johnson went the other way, sending in hundreds of thousands of troops backed by the Air Force and Navy.

This policy shift was made possible by a public relations gambit. The military reported attacks by North Vietnamese patrol boats against the *Maddox* and *Turner Joy* in the Gulf of Tonkin in August of 1964. One of these reports wasn't true, and the other was greatly over blown, but the Congress was persuaded to authorize war against the North Vietnamese, and so began the full-fledged tragedy we refer to today as the Vietnam conflict.

During the course of the Vietnam war, more than 58,000 Americans were killed and three times that many were wounded. Many thousands of returning military came back home with serious emotional problems and addictions. There were more than 60,000 Vietnam veteran suicides.

The North Vietnamese reported 1,100,000 million killed while the South said it lost 184,000 military. The estimates of civilian deaths throughout the country range up to 4,000,000.

It took some time for the extent of the horror of that war to be learned. The release of the Pentagon Papers in 1971 illuminated a political conspiracy by the military to sustain and expand their murderous adventurism. They were abetted by Henry Kissinger, who kept the war going much longer than it need have been, with his "Peace is at hand" remark just before the 1972 presidential elections, and then the Christmas bombing of the North a month later.

Public outrage at those bombings forced a different posture at the seemingly-endless peace talks, and finally an agreement was made that winter.

So the American war in Vietnam was essentially over by that March day in 1973. The American-made regime in the South would continue the battle for another two years before falling. Their fate had been inevitable for two decades. There would be more unnecessary bloodshed, but at least, for all of our culpability in the killing, it wouldn't be Americans who were dying 12,000 miles away.

Personally, I was angry with my government and the people who had supported this tragic war that created a permanent scar on our nation's reputation. Professionally, though, I was stoic, standing there in the drizzle, producing the coverage for ABC News. It was a simple assignment. The camera crew filmed the arrival of the plane, the door opening, a man climbing down the steps, his family rushing toward him.

That's when I started to cry.

The number of Americans captured in that war was relatively small, 730, and 664 were returned alive. Others who were listed as missing might also have been captured. We don't know what happened to them.

Recently I met one of the men who'd been captured by the North Vietnamese. Phillip Butler was a 26-year-old U.S. Navy pilot when he was shot down. He was imprisoned in the Hanoi Hilton and spent almost eight years in prison. I interviewed Phil twice on a radio program called "America Back on Track," and later we became friends.

More to the point, I was interested as a journalist in his story. It is an important story. Few in the military are willing to admit they were wrong, especially those who killed, and those who suffered. Phil Butler's story is one of courage and insight. It is of considerable value to a nation, and a world, that needs to shift course; to recognize that war is a primitive exercise, and that we must all be warriors for peace to bring about our evolution.

There is more to be added to this introduction, now that I've spent three months with Phil's story, through hours of interviews and editing the lengthy debriefing that followed his release from the Vietnamese. Phil Butler is a mensch, which is a term I don't use often. He's a man of integrity, character, and purpose, as you shall see in the following pages. He lays fair claim, too, to the term warrior, and in this book he recounts what have been three separate lives as a warrior, and the threads that have run through them.

TONY SETON
Monterey, California
June 2010

Preface

Warrior (n)
One who is engaged in or experienced in battle.
One who is engaged aggressively or energetically in an activity,
cause, or conflict: *neighborhood warriors fighting against developers.*

This book is about my life transition. It has actually been a journey through three lives. My self perception is clear about those lives. I even like to call them my "before, during and after" lives. They are the three lives of a warrior. Of course I'm the same guy with the same body, heart and brain. But in each case there existed a totally different Phil Butler.

In the beginning, becoming a warrior took some socialization and training. During the first life Phil goes through the experiences of growing up to maturity and learning to be a warrior, a killer of other humans. In the second life the warrior has to not only survive the North Vietnam hell holes as a POW, but to do it in such a way as to return with honor. In the third life, the warrior returns home to eventually focus warrior skills on a more circumspect life. Now the warrior turns away from killing and survival to making a contribution to earth and humanity. But in each case I believe there has been a warrior within me that pushes forward.

For years I considered writing a book about my eight year experience of being a Prisoner of War in Vietnam. But somehow that never seemed to be quite right for me. Countless people have encouraged me to write one, especially during the 20 years I was a professional speaker. Many of my fellow POWs have written books about their experiences, probably numbering close to 50 by now. And several documentaries on our trials there are now available. So that subject, in itself, is pretty well covered, albeit always from the viewpoints and biases of each individual writer. And as I've often told friends: Why should I just write another "hair, teeth and eyeballs" story about our POW experience? At least those have been the excuses for my procrastination.

So why wait until I'm 71 to write this book? One reason is I find myself in a very different life space from most of my fellow POWs, Naval

Academy shipmates and veterans. So how did that come about? Why am I a committed environmental, peace and justice activist, dedicated to the welfare of our earth and to all of those less fortunate than myself? How and why did I become a warrior in my first life, make war in my second, and want to be of service as a warrior for peace, justice and environment in the third?

Now that I am 71 the time seems right to tell about my life experiences. Maybe it's my time to look back and analyze it all. But more than that, I want this book to have a forward trajectory for readers. I want other warriors, veterans or non-veterans, to see how and why my life dedication has changed from *destruction to construction*. Nevertheless, I don't want the book to be preachy or advisory. I have meant throughout for it to be *descriptive, not prescriptive. Three Lives of a Warrior* is simply my legacy for family, friends, supporters, detractors, military and non-military readers, workers, searchers, volunteers, students and anyone else who cares to find out about all the stuff that has happened to this guy.

I want to thank my Naval Intelligence debriefer, Brian Kelly, who met me first when I came home and stayed to support me. Our official Navy debriefing took a total of 36 hours and was recorded on reel to reel tapes in 1973. The transcripts I gained later and edited for clarity form the "Second Life" section of this book. It is the harsh and graphic truth about my experiences as a POW in North Vietnam, as related by a very angry man.

I am grateful for the counsel and expert assistance of Tony Seton for helping make this book a reality. I must confess that book writing is just not something I enjoy doing. I managed to get it done the first time with my PhD dissertation. That agonizing process took three years of data gathering and then the better part of two years to write. Unfortunately completing that task left me with enough negative memories to remain in a procrastinating mode for over 25 years. But with Tony's encouragement and invaluable expert assistance, I have been motivated to carry this project to completion.

I had never wanted to write "just another POW book" because there are enough of those out now to satisfy any casual reader or serious scholar engaging in research. But with Tony's help, I began to visualize a book that made more sense to me. The concept, a book about my three lives and the life transitions I've experienced, seemed more important and worth the effort. I was interviewed on the experiences of my first and third lives for over 24 hours by Tony. He got them transcribed and then put all that data into categorical and chronological order for me. That made writing those two life stories easier, to show how they flow together with my second life-story from my returned POW debrief.

Tony has lived a full and diverse life. He is a writer, journalist, producer, professional speaker, radio host, TV personality and quintessential communicator. He is also exceedingly patient and soft spoken, great skills to have when working with a warrior-spirited man. Above all Tony is one of the most generous men I've ever met. I am fortunate that Tony Seton has become a good friend and colleague. Who knows? We may yet collaborate on another story. But the next one will for sure have to be fiction, not another agonizing autobiography.

I want to thank some expert and persistent people who edited my manuscript. They are Phyllis Cleveland and Jean Stallings, who along with my wife Barbara made literally hundreds of typographical and grammatical corrections. I also greatly appreciate Kedron Bryson who professionally formatted the book for publication.

I have been blessed in life to have a wonderful sister, Linda, who stood by me always, even during those terrible eight POW years. I have great love for her and we share the powerful bond that only siblings who have suffered parental abuse together can know.

Now I have another "brother and sister," Barbara's brother Chuck and his wife Terry. We are both family and close friends who truly enjoy each other's company on a regular basis. I married well and got a new brother and sister in the bargain.

Most of all I thank my wife, Barbara Baldock, for loving, supporting and always being there for me. She is ever the consummate voice of reason, my business partner, my sounding board, my best friend and the love of my life.

PHILLIP BUTLER
Monterey, California
June 2010

THE FIRST LIFE OF A WARRIOR

Introduction

I had to learn how to be a warrior. It probably doesn't come naturally for most people, as I believe it did not for me. But like many kids who grow up in our United States, I was taught early on that our service men and women, and the wars they fight, are to be held in utmost honor.

People of my generation, born before or during World War II, grew up with first-hand accounts from relatives and friends of combat, service and self sacrifice. Unlike the wars and military interventions our country has engaged in since, that was a war of national salvation. There was no question after the Japanese attack on Pearl Harbor and German invasions of European countries that we had to fight for our very way of life.

So my childhood and youthful socialization to serve my country were powerful. I learned about "Fidelity and Obedience" years before I would enter the U.S. Naval Academy at Annapolis. And I aspired to "Duty, Honor, Country" before I would ever find out about the U.S. Military Academy at West Point.

I was indoctrinated, one might even say imprinted, on flying from a very early age. Aviation was almost in my genes because the man I revered most, my father, was crazy about flying. Some of my earliest memories are of airplanes and flying because of him. And he was even my first instructor.

But that's all in my first story here. It's about how I learned to be a warrior during my first life.

1. Early Lessons on War

1938 - 1945

I was born on a hot day in Oklahoma, August 11, 1938. Of course it was hot. It was Tulsa, Oklahoma in August.

My earliest recollection wasn't until I was about four. It was probably just a typical childhood event. I was on the front lawn of somebody's house. I'm not sure if it was our house or the house of an aunt and uncle. I was with a couple of cousins; girls who were each a year older than I. The lawn was filled with clover and there were bees all over the place. One of my neat cousins told me to catch a bee with my hands. I did and it stung me, indelibly etching my earliest memory in my hand and my mind. I remember that it really hurt but it probably served as an early lesson - about reactively doing whatever people tell you to do.

I was born two years before the "Last Good War." Oklahoma, like much of the nation, was climbing out of The Great Depression. I think by and large Oklahoma, and most of the United States for that matter, was pretty much isolated within itself as the result of the massive financial dislocation. What may surprise some readers is the degree of that isolation. In Oklahoma, as in many parts of the country, there was a lot of labor and anti-war protest in 1938, '39 and '40. The Communist Party was active as was the Workers' Party and Socialist Party. It was a very tough time for ordinary people.

I learned from my mother and father later on, when I was old enough to understand what they were saying, that 1938 was still the Depression where we lived. We didn't really come out of it until things turned around when the government under Franklin Roosevelt began to flood the economy with jobs and money. He had started many public works projects, which helped tremendously the people who were trying to dig themselves out. Then in 1941 the build-up for World War II started. But 1938, from what they told me, was still pretty much a tough year for people. My family was acutely aware of the dust bowl hardships people in our area suffered. So I was raised and encouraged to appreciate all that I had, so I wouldn't take my relatively good life for granted.

My father, R.B Butler, was the son of Baptist minister who had complicated his family's lives with philandering and by being abusive to his

2

children. Dad's birth name was Roy Bertram Butler, Jr. But he disliked my grandfather, "Pappy," so much he always went by "R.B." and he even claimed that was his legal name. Dad graduated from Oklahoma Agricultural and Mechanical College in 1936, two years before I arrived. It later became Oklahoma State University. He was a hail-fellow-well-met, President of his Pi Kappa Alpha fraternity. I got the sense that academics were not very rigorous in those days for a business major like my father. But it was tough finding enough money to complete college during the Depression. Nevertheless he graduated with a Bachelor of Arts Degree in Business and went on with his life from there.

After graduation he married his high school sweetheart, Mae, who was a year younger. My mother had two years of secretarial training at Tulsa University. They started life working for businesses in Tulsa and after being married for about two years I came along. I was their only child until my sister was born in 1949, almost eleven years later. Unfortunately, they had my sister in a vain attempt to save their marriage. It's the very last thing you want to do to save a marriage, but that's what they did, and it didn't save their marriage.

During the early years R.B. and Mae were loving parents. My mother doted on me as an only child. My father was a very nice guy. He was a man you could immediately warm up to. He had an outgoing personality. One of the most important things to R. B. Butler, a lesson he repeated frequently, was to be liked by other people. I think he worried about me. He wanted to make sure I knew that the most important thing for me to do in school was to be liked. But I didn't always quite see it that way because very early on I saw that some people didn't like me and sometimes I didn't like them.

But they were very good parents in those early years. For instance, when I was five years old my mom convinced dad to buy a cheap upright piano. Then she sat me down and began to teach me scales and a little bit of piano that she knew. She spent about a year teaching me what she knew about the basics of reading music and then she arranged for piano lessons. I loved the piano and took lessons for about six years before I quit. Regrettably I didn't take it up again until thirty-five years later at age 56.

I quit for two reasons. One was I got really interested in playing neighborhood sports with my friends. Typically, for all the kids in those days it was football in the fall, basketball in the winter, and baseball in spring and summer. Sports seemed to always interfere with my piano practicing. And I was forever banging up my fingers, strategically just before a recital. The other reason is that my parents began to have their own problems, both individually and with each other. They started paying less attention to me. They weren't telling me what I needed to be doing and so I did what I wanted. That started with quitting piano and playing neighborhood sports with my pals when I was twelve and in the seventh grade.

My father used his B.A. in business by going into accounting. Though it doesn't seem like accounting would have fit him, because he was never very good at math. But I guess he did understand the fundamentals of accounting so that's what he was doing before the war broke out. As I was told later, at the beginning of 1941 he and his best friend found out that the U.S. government was gearing up for war and they needed aviators.

The Battle of Britain had shown how important the air war would be. So our government put out the word to anybody who had a private pilot's license that they could train to become a civilian instructor for the Army Air Corps. My dad and his pal jumped on this opportunity. They got some quick flying time to qualify for a private pilot's license. My dad loved to say they even got some "P-51" flying time. He would laugh and say that meant "Parker 51," a common fountain pen of the day. They went to the Spartan School of Aviation in Tulsa for training to become civilian instructors for the Army Air Corps. About mid 1942 my dad qualified to be an instructor and we moved to a little town south of Oklahoma City called Chickasha – there are lots of town with Indian names in Oklahoma – where there was a small Army airfield.

If you've ever flown down low over Oklahoma and Texas, everywhere you look there are the remnants of air fields. There were literally hundreds of airfields throughout the Midwest that the Army Air Corps built and used during World War II. My father's job there was to train Army Air Corps Cadets in PT-19s. They were the primary trainers of the day. They were fabric-covered, low-wing, tandem-seated, airplanes with conventional landing gear.

That's really how I started getting interested in being a pilot. My dad preached flying to me from the time I was born. I think I knew about flying when I came out of the hospital. I have an airplane picture I drew with crayons in kindergarten. I found it among my mother's things after her death in 2006. Flying was dad's true life love. I can still remember being there in the house during the time my father was instructing. He would finish up with a class of students, usually eight or ten of these guys, and he'd have them over to the house. They would all sit around on the floor and what little furniture we had and, I guess, talk aviation and stuff. It was kind of their little going away party.

My dad had a little yellow model of a PT-19 and he would bring me out into the middle of the group, much to my terror, hand me the model and have me go through the various parts. "Now what is this Phil?" And with each question I would reply "This is the wing, aileron, propeller, rudder and so on." I still remember how this produced peels of laughter from his students, that this four year old kid had memorized all of this stuff on the airplane. My dad worked diligently with me to get me to memorize the parts of the airplane. I remember it wasn't easy.

Dad got another opportunity in 1943 or '44. This was what amounted in those days to become a military air transport pilot. It meant that we moved to Dallas, Texas so he could be a co-pilot in a DC-3 for Braniff Airlines. Braniff, like other airlines in those days, was not really civilian. The airlines had pretty much been nationalized for the war effort. They were working for the military, transporting people and supplies in DC-3s. My dad was a co-pilot for Braniff Airlines until the end of the war in August of 1945.

Then my dad was faced with a life-changing decision. He could stay in Dallas as an airline pilot, or move back to Tulsa and go into business with his mother in real estate. Grandma Butler had separated from Pappy some years before and had started her own business. She was an independent and powerful woman, the matriarch of our family. He opted to return to work with his mother. It was a mistake, one that he recalled vocally for the rest of his life. Many times I heard him say that he wished he stayed in Dallas as an airline pilot.

The culture of Oklahoma and the South was very patriotic. During the post-war era America was the world's savior while at the same time we were bursting out of the Depression era mentality. My family was patriotic. I grew up with this notion of patriotism. When my dad went to Dallas to be a Braniff pilot in 1944, we lived right across the street from Love Field in a prefab duplex. I remember sitting on our porch, watching them firing and sighting in the guns on P-51 aircraft. It was very exciting.

So at the early age of five or six I wanted to be a fighter pilot in the military, and be a hero. My uncle was a bomber pilot in the Army Air Corps. He came out of the war a Colonel, and he was a hero with a chest-full of medals and great stories. Early on I had the notion that it was important to serve, and to serve when I was growing up meant going into the military. That's the way young men served their country. There were other ways that were less esteemed but to really serve meant the military.

5

That was the belief I had growing up and going to the Naval Academy. I viewed becoming a naval officer a lot like becoming a priest or a peace officer. I was serving my country and that was very important. It seemed like a calling, an avocation, something over and above just an ordinary job.

2. R.B.

My father was an acute alcoholic and he became a severe binge drinker. He would go for anywhere from a month to as short as a week or two in sobriety and then he would binge drink. When he'd binge he would find a place to be alone, sometimes our living room, one of the houses that he was building or even a closet. Then he would just up-end the bottle, open his throat and pour a quart of bourbon, gin or whatever he had down his throat. Then he would pass out.

Towards the end of his life he was drinking himself almost into a coma. I would take him to the hospital on these many occasions. There was a ward at Hillcrest Hospital in Tulsa called Forty-Two North, a place for alcoholics to dry out.

I would have to carry my father to the car, take him there and they would bring him in on a stretcher. Then three or four days later I would go pick him up. He would always be terribly embarrassed and contrite. And he would also be going through the delirium tremens, shaking uncontrollably. I would take him home and try to help take care of him.

I could almost always tell when he was going to go on a bender because he would get depressed and start speaking negatively. He would begin to say things like, "Oh, I don't know if it's worth it Phil. I don't know if life is worth it. I don't even know why I'm here." He'd start to talk like that and I'd know that he was about ready to start drinking again. Today we know more about such behavior and hindsight would indicate that my dad was suffering from depression. But in the 1950s I doubt they had identified that problem completely and they certainly didn't have medications for it like they do now.

We always got two weeks of annual leave to go home for Christmas at the Naval Academy. During my second class year in 1959, I went home to Tulsa. When it came time for me to return after Christmas, we sat down in the living room and talked. He was acting depressed again. I just pleaded with him. I said, "Dad, don't start drinking. Please don't start drinking after I'm gone." He said, "Oh, okay, all right. I won't do that." Of course I knew he was going back to the bottle, but I couldn't stay with him.

I got on an airplane, flew back to the Naval Academy and reported in about January 2nd, 1960. Two days later I got an emergency notice to report to the main office at Bancroft Hall and I knew something bad had happened. When I got there, the officer of the day informed me that my father was dead. He had drunk himself into a coma. When they found him in his bedroom, he was dead. He had finally abused his body to the point where his heart just couldn't take it anymore and it quit.

I was absolutely devastated. I had just lost probably the most important person in my life. Going through high school and college, he had been a combination of my dad, my son, my brother and my best friend. I could hardly maintain a sense of self that day, waiting for the opportunity to go to Washington DC and get on an airplane to fly back home. I didn't have any money but the Naval Academy had an emergency fund for things like that. So I was given enough money to buy an airplane ticket and a few extra dollars to come home.

I went home and found myself in the midst of my family, naturally, but not pleasantly. Ironically and sadly it turned out that my Aunt Mary, my dad's sister who was also an alcoholic, had drunk herself to death seven hours before my dad drank himself to death. It was almost like they had a kind of simultaneous suicide pact, though I couldn't imagine it. At the time I thought it had to be just coincidental. The word in the family was that they had been drinking together the day they both died.

A nurse who had gone to the house to look after my father found him. The family sent her there after Mary died and she found him dead too. My father and my aunt had been very close. In fact Dad was pretty close to all three of his sisters. Two of them were older and one younger. My grandmother was shattered. I don't think she ever really recovered from the suicides, emotionally or physically.

We wound up burying my dad and my aunt in a dual funeral and burial ceremony. I was with my little sister. Linda was only ten years old and I had to go back to the Naval Academy, leaving her with our mother who was psychologically unbalanced. I constantly worried about Linda's well-being after I left.

I was the executor of the estate and I saw to it that from what little money Dad had there was some set aside for Linda's care until she was eighteen, at which time she got the majority of the money that was left over. That was the story of my dad's death. I've lived many years now, looking back and missing him terribly. To this very day my sister and I really miss the guy because in truth he was a very sweet man. It was hard for me to think that he was so proud of me being a midshipman at the Naval Academy and that he missed my graduation, my marriage, and the birth of his granddaughter, Diane. He missed so much and his life ended so prematurely at just age 44.

Dad had been really depressed about his divorce. He was supposedly madly in love with my mother all those years. He dated after he split with my mother. He had girlfriends, but he always seemed to be able to find things to be depressed about. It could be anything, like our dog being sick, or a house that wasn't selling.

I think that psychologically he probably had depression for a long time and might have been compensating for it by being the hail-fellow-well-met and wanting to be liked. But I think my dad never really liked himself all that much. He had some insecurities. At least that's what I surmise these many years later.

3. Mae

Effie Mae Butler, called Mae because she hated the name "Effie," was my mother. Growing up until I was about 14 years old, she was "Mom" to me but after that age she became "Mother." That's because "mom" seemed to carry more the feeling of a loving closeness than "mother."

Mae was a loving and doting mom until sometime in my early puberty. She was very affectionate, caring and responsive to whatever I got interested in or wanted to do. She started giving me piano lessons at age five and hired a piano teacher for me at age seven. She taught and gave me a lifetime appreciation for music and art. I remember attending classical concerts with her at the Tulsa Convention Center when I was a child.

But things really started falling apart for me sometime when I was about 12. She became abusive toward my father and often depressed. She never had many friends but sometime in the early 1950s, while still in her late 30s, she became confrontational and angry towards our family members, friends and acquaintances. It seemed that dad's alcoholism and her abusive personality fed off each other, each making the other more acute. I was young then and can't say for sure which caused the other. But in retrospect they seemed to bloom together.

Then mother started seeing her doctor who, after the medical style of the day for women patients, gave her sedatives. These were called "sleeping pills" back then and he prescribed them in unending quantities. I believe they were Seconal and drugs of that kind. She obviously became hooked on her prescription drugs. And she became more abusive, angry and profane year by year.

She came after dad with kitchen knives on numerous occasions. She was prone to throwing things, whatever there was at hand; plates, pots, pans, a vase or whatever. Then she began doing the same to me, saying, "You are just like your father." She came after me twice with a butcher knife. In both cases my life was in danger. The second time she did it happened in our garage, where I finally defensively struck her with a forceful slap, knocking her down on the garage floor. On another occasion, she drove to a baseball game my dad and I were attending and began to entertain the crowd with screaming, slapping and profanity. Dad and I beat a hasty retreat up the stands and out onto the passageway. There was a guard rail protecting people from a four story drop where we stopped when she caught up with us. I had my back turned to her when she ran with all her force and tried to shove me over the guard rail. My dad grabbed me, preventing the fall, and saved my life.

I left her when she and dad divorced, thus escaping her at about age 14. But my poor sister Linda had to endure her for yet another 10 or 11 years. I think my sister went through far more than I did with our mother because she had to live with her all that time. While I was still living there, my mother would spank and later she would slap and hit. Linda was abused and persecuted, emotionally and physically, until she was about fourteen or fifteen and could defend herself. That's when all the physical abuse stopped because Linda could fight back and she stopped my mother the same way I had.

Obviously our mother was sick. She was manic, abusive and paranoid. But after the divorce it was too late for us to do anything about it. Dad could no longer legally mandate treatment for her because he wasn't married to her any longer. We even tried to get her parents to help by having her committed to treatment but they refused to interfere.

It was emotionally draining to have such a mother. You are supposed to love and respect your mother first, above all other people in your life. She is the woman who gave you life. So you feel you owe her all of that. But it takes more than just giving birth to qualify as a true mother. A real mother doesn't curse, embarrass, torment and abuse her children. As it turned out, this woman, our birth-mother was to live yet another 50 years to age 90. And she never changed her vicious behavior. Linda and I both have the emotional scars to prove it.

4. Growing Up

1945 - 1956

We returned to Tulsa after the war and I entered second grade at Sidney Lanier grade school. Many people were returning to their home towns and their roots at this time. Men and women who had served in the military came home. Many of my school mates were kids whose families had returned to make a living in Tulsa.

In the beginning we moved into the house with my grandmother Butler and I was reunited with my cousins, aunts and uncles. Shortly after that we moved into a small house dad had built. He was taking over the home building part of grandmother's business. Businesses were booming after the war and people were buy homes on the G.I. Bill by the millions. Dad had a successful new business going in no time.

Mother didn't work. She was a homemaker. She took care of me and my father, and later my sister. In those days, the mode was for the man to work and the woman to stay home and take care of the hearth and children, and that's pretty much the way it worked in our family. Most of the thousands of women who had worked for the war effort were now without jobs and relegated to returning home. It wasn't until years later that the culture shifted and women joined the workforce in large numbers. We lived more modestly back then. We listened to the radio and television didn't appear in our house until the early 1950s. There was no television blaring all the time about what people should buy, so we didn't need two incomes to afford what we didn't need. Back then we didn't hunger for a washer, dryer, second cars, bigger homes and things like that. That came later.

I don't really know what caused the rift between my parents. I was young, so I'm not sure. I know there were fatal flaws in both of them. My father had an extreme sensitivity to alcohol. He could drink one beer and become pretty happy and mellow. Alcohol affected him dramatically and by the time I was around twelve or thirteen he had become an alcoholic and then a binge drinker. He tried to stay away from booze and would manage to do so for maybe a month or two, then later on for only for a couple of weeks.

At the same time my mother began to have psychological problems. Her behavior changed and she began to react to people with wild temper

12

outbursts. She would use incredible profanity. She became physically abusive to my father and to me. Later she also became abusive to my sister.

So my mother was addicted to prescription drugs and my father to alcohol. But before their problems fully bloomed, around the time I was in fifth grade, they decided that what they needed to keep the marriage together was another child. So they had my sister in February 1949, But of course that didn't do any good at all. In fact it made things even worse. Their relationship got worse and worse, their own problems became more and more severe, until they got a divorce.

They split up in 1952 when I was in eighth grade. I felt loyal to my father because I thought he needed somebody to be with him and help take care of him. So I requested that the judge allow me to live with my father who had moved a few blocks away to an apartment. The judge agreed and I moved in with my father. Unfortunately my sister had to stay with mother, which meant that my baby sister and I were split up. She was only two or three then and I was worried about her. I did everything I could to continue to see her as much as possible and my father got to have her on weekends. At least we had the weekends together.

Aside from the personal trauma the divorce caused, it was compounded by the fact that it wasn't nearly as common as it is today. Not only was it unusual, but it was really looked at in a very negative way. So I pretty much kept it a secret from people that my parents were divorced. It was something that wasn't talked about because it was a very bad thing. It was a social blight to be from a divorced family. I had little choice but to internalize my problems so by the time I got to high school I became a pretty angry kid. I remember acting out in wild driving, on my motorcycle and later in my car.

There were times when I wondered, rhetorically, if I had been mistakenly switched at birth. I was very shy growing up. I have a cousin, C.J. Luton, who was like an older brother to me. He was five years older and to this very day he tells me, "You know when we were kids, and we had the family get-togethers people hardly knew you existed." He said, "Nobody heard boo from you Phil. You were always the quietest kid in the world and you always seemed to be observing and not saying anything."

I think he was right. I didn't feel as though I fit in. I always felt better off observing from the sidelines. I remember my experience going through grade school, junior high and high school was similar. I was shy and never wanted to get up in front of people to speak or anything like that. I think I lived a quiet introspective life though I didn't realize what I was doing at the time. It seems clearer to me now, and I have friends from high school days who tell me that I was an introspective kid.

But it wasn't like I was alone or a loner. I had friends in grade school; a cadre of three or four or five guys. In junior high school, I think I had fewer friends. But in high school there was a group of five or six guys I ran around with. We hunted and went fishing together. One of the guy's parents owned a cabin on Grand Lake which was a couple of hours from Tulsa. We boys would go up there and stay for three or four days, getting drunk while hunting, fishing and swimming. We had a good time. We also often had a poker game going. One of the guy's parents had taught us all to play poker when we were about thirteen years old. Poker has been an abiding hobby of mine since then. It was great to learn the game as a kid.

Some of these guys were very good friends. In fact, I'm still in touch with several of them. One, Upton Hudson, went to Yale, graduated and ultimately became an executive for US Steel. He's very right wing in his political views but I'm still working on twisting his brain around, though unsuccessfully so far. Upton and I shared many experiences together as paper boys, double dating, hunting, fishing, playing poker and underage drinking. We are still good friends. Nick Fate, Upton's cousin and our pal, died before reaching 40 of a brain tumor. Wally Davis and I bowled, ice skated and caroused together during my senior year. Other friends to this day go all the way back to the beginning of grade school. Leonard Krisman and Dave Shoemaker have been my pals for over 60 years.

Then there were airplanes and girls. Girls and airplanes. One of my earliest memories is from 1943 when I was five at Kindergarten in Dallas, Texas. I still have the airplane drawing I did that year. And I still remember the little girl who sat at our table and pulled her pants down to give us boys a look. Not much else sticks in my mind from kindergarten.

I had girl friends after that, even in grade school and junior high school. But my relationships with girls were pretty platonic until high school. I remember "it" happened when I was just 16 and Sue (last name with-held) was 15. I put this in just in case someone from a much younger generation might be reading this book. Young people always seem to think they invented early sex. I know I did, until my dad questioned me one day about my relationship with Sue. I admitted the truth to him because I trusted him. And would you believe? He admitted to me that he had his first sexual experience at age 16, back in 1931. I was astounded! Did they really do that way back then? But even more impressive was the next day when he gave me a package of condoms and said, "Always have one of these in your wallet son." He was a wonderful father and friend in many ways.

As a kid growing up in Oklahoma I was outside most of the time when I wasn't in school. Life for us kids, boys at least, was very physical. We were always running around in the neighborhood, playing cops and robbers, playing military war games, football, basketball, baseball or riding our bicycles. Kids then had roller skates that hooked onto our shoes and we roller skated around on the sidewalks and streets. We also played in fields and woods that were nearby; running around in nature. Sometimes we would go out into the woods, make a fire and camp overnight with just a blanket, some hot dogs, our guns and dogs.

Our bikes were important to us. That's how we got around. I can recall riding my Schwinn; no gearshifts, of course, just a straight fat-tire bicycle. Going up hills on that thing was really exhausting work, especially if the basket in front was full of newspapers when I delivered my paper route. It was certainly good exercise. I was a "paper boy" for the Tulsa World and Tulsa Tribune a total of five years. It was wonderful training for life experience in business and how to deal with customers. My boss, Charlie Beach, was our route manager. He was a great early mentor and teacher of good values and work ethic.

My dad loved dogs and I inherited that love too. The only time I remember not having a dog or two was at the Naval Academy and in prison. I had a small female Boxer when I was a paper boy. She followed me on my bicycle to my route every day. Then when I got a Cushman Eagle motorcycle she learned to ride on the seat. I'd put her in front of me, between my arms, and her head stuck up above mine so I had to look around her to drive. We would pass cars and get incredulous stares, smiles and frequent honks.

I didn't play sports at Will Rogers High School because I worked all the time instead, but I was still in good physical condition. Sports or working, I was able to build a strong body like we did in those days. There was no sitting in front of a television set or doing video games. It was a very active outside kind of growing up that I remember. I did learn two "sports" from dad. They were pool and shuffleboard, excellent skills to have even today. Shuffleboard earned me a few extra bucks when I worked in a beer bar at Oklahoma University for extra money.

I mentioned that we played cops and robbers. There were some cowboys and Indians, too, but since it was right after World War II, the favorite conflict in our neighborhood was playing at war with each other.

15

At some point, we took it to a higher level because we all had Red Rider, lever action BB guns and would occasionally shoot each other. Actually, the BBs could be quite painful but we had our own war rules in the neighborhood, one of which was you couldn't shoot anyone above the waist. Since we were all wearing blue jeans it stung like hell but no one was going to seriously injure anybody.

In regards to the cowboys and Indians playing, that was really less of a genre for us because even though Oklahoma was still pretty rugged and cowboy in nature, there were Indian folks everywhere and they were pretty well integrated into our society at the time. I know there was a lot of intermarriage. There was even some intermarriage with Indians in my own family. My aunt married a man who was half Cherokee. My mother's family passed down that our great grandmother was half Choctaw. So if that's true, despite growing up a blond with blue eyes, I must be one sixteenth Choctaw.

Guns were also an important part of the culture, partly because it was Oklahoma and also because it was pretty rural. My father bought me a .22 caliber rifle and taught me how to shoot when I was eight or nine. I remember it fondly, a little Remington, bolt action .22 rifle. We would shoot at targets. Then we would go home and he taught me how to clean it after firing. But when we were finished, he kept the gun.

Then when I was ten he just gave me the gun and said I could go target practice or hunting when I wanted to, telling me to just be safe like I had been taught. I had other friends around the neighborhood that also had guns by that time. We lived on the outskirts of Tulsa near open fields, so we kids would go out and shoot target practice. We also shot at rabbits and squirrels.

A bunch of us kids got interested in hunting rabbits on winter mornings when the snow was on the ground and it was easier to track them. I talked my father into buying me a shotgun. He got me a Mossberg .410 gauge shotgun. I remember that it had three different chokes with it that I could screw on to the end of the barrel. I would put on the "open," "modified" or the "full" choke according to what I was hunting and what range I was shooting. (The chokes would modify the shot pattern.)

It might seem strange today, but back then, on a Sunday some of us would go out at four o'clock in the morning and throw our paper routes. We'd bring our shotguns with us and when we finished our routes we would ride off to some farmer's field, leave our bicycles, and go hunt rabbits. I would be home by nine or ten o'clock in the morning with a couple of rabbits, which I would skin and prepare for cooking. My mother always hated me bringing home the rabbits. Basically she didn't like the idea of killing things. But I had been taught that it was a normal thing and no big deal to kill animals or to catch fish.

I must admit that I became a pretty angry guy during my high school years because of all the problems with my mother and father. When I was old enough to buy a motorcycle, a Cushman Eagle, I drove it fast and started hanging out with other motorcycle guys. I even raced motorcycles on dirt tracks. When I bought my first car at age 16 I became a relentlessly reckless driver. When dad was drunk I would take his Oldsmobile out and drive it over 100 mph. No seat belts or safety equipment in those days. I got numerous tickets for speeding and even was once thrown in jail for reckless driving. Dad had to come bail me out. I made up my mind then to never get put in jail again. That resolution held up until 1965.

I got in trouble numerous times in high school for doing stupid pranks. Each time I would be sent to see our Will Rogers High School principal, Doctor Raymond Knight. This man was an angel in disguise. He would always tell me to hang in there, that I was going to be something really good in life because I had the stuff to achieve. He meant a lot to me back in those days. He believed in me, and I think he even convinced me to believe in myself.

5. Always an Okie

It may surprise some people that I still consider myself an Okie, at least in part. That's where I was born and brought up. That's where I grew up. Oklahomans are proud of that name. It means you are tough and can survive hardships, like our forbearers did during the dustbowl days. Maybe that's the origin of my warrior spirit, as later it began to appear when it was called up by necessity.

My grandparents on both sides reinforced that Oklahoma heritage. All of them migrated there in the late 1800s, even before Oklahoma was a state. The grandparents on my father's side came from Tennessee and on my mother's they came from Missouri. So they were all second or third generation Americans themselves. On my father's side I have an English-Irish heritage and on my mother's side English and "Pennsylvania Dutch" (German) heritage. But I know my genealogy includes much more, with probably some Native American Indian, so I really think of myself as just a mutt in terms of genealogical heritage.

My family on both sides spent their lives in and around Tulsa. Also both sides were staunch Southern Baptists. So I was a product of my heritage and my culture. I didn't know a lot about the outside world. I did, however, have an abiding curiosity about it, something that didn't seem to come with my genes. There was one incident in particular that provoked – or revealed – my interest in what was happening outside of my home state.

My aunt Marguerite, one of my dad's three sisters, was a fiery woman. She had been married four or five times and I guess nobody in the family was quite sure. But at the end of one of her divorces she went to live in Los Angeles, California. I think it was with a boyfriend or new husband or maybe just by herself. Anyway, she got into clothes designing and selling there, where she was fairly successful at it. One Christmas she came back to Tulsa for our family reunion when I was around ten years old.

Aunt Marguerite talked about California and I was amazed and intrigued at the notion of what California was like. She kept saying how free it was there and how it was so different. She said there were so many different kinds of people and ideas there. It was incredibly appealing to me, and probably to no one else in the room. But at that moment it was so compelling I made the decision that when I grew up I wanted to go live in California. So I had the notion very early on of wanting to get away from

Tulsa and find something else.

It wasn't that I didn't like Oklahoma at the time, but rather that there was something more, unknown, and I wanted to know about it. A few years later this feeling would be reinforced. The turmoil in my family and the southern culture itself became factors that increased my determination to leave.

Still, I've enjoyed going back to Tulsa on occasion. It's changed since I was growing up there more than a half-century ago. For instance, Tulsa used to be the oil capital of the world where all of the major oil companies had main offices. The big oil tycoons of the early 20th century built residential mansions and office buildings in Tulsa. But that's not true anymore as they have all relocated elsewhere. There is still some residual oil being pumped out of wells and the area is rich in natural gas but it's nothing like the heyday of the 1920's with Glen Pool, the big oil and the big homes that oil built in Tulsa back then. When I was a kid in high school it was still known as the oil capital of the world and it was a big part of the economy. Oklahoma University, which I attended for one year, was known worldwide for their petroleum engineering studies.

Tulsa was also really a Southern City at the time I was growing up there. It still basically is a Southern city. The culture is Southern as is the food, the accent, the language, and the attitudes. Curiously, when I was growing up, there was plenty of discrimination against African Americans, Jews, Mexicans and anyone from a foreign country.

But oddly enough, American Indians were not thought of that way. They were by and large thought of as part of us and as I said there was a tremendous amount of intermarriage. The word "Oklahoma" is a Choctaw word meaning "Home of the Red Man." Our state was "Indian Territory" where many tribes were contained after having their native lands stolen from them. Several tribes today receive royalties from oil that was discovered on their assigned reservations. But that wasn't the usual case for our Native American Indians then and it still isn't. A much too high percentage of them suffer grinding poverty, lack of education, alcoholism and hopelessness on reservations where they didn't get a fair shot at the good life.

6. A Broken Crutch

Religion was and still is a very important part of life in The American South, and Oklahoma culture has deep roots in religious fundamentalist ways of thinking. It's no wonder they refer to our Oklahoma area as "the Bible belt." My grandparents on both sides were devout Southern Baptists. My dad's father was a Southern Baptist minister and my grandfather on my mother's side was a deacon in the Southern Baptist Church in Cleveland, Oklahoma. They were very religious so as a kid I was regularly sent to Baptist Sunday school and church.

But when I was about eleven, I started having serious problems with Sunday school. I got into arguments with some of my Sunday school teachers about things that didn't make sense to me. There were things like who could go to Heaven. I could not figure out for the life of me why a Baptist was going to Heaven and a Methodist, Catholic, Muslim or Animist wasn't. Why did being born into a Baptist family and then being baptized entitle you to that? That just didn't make a whole lot of sense to me. Or, for that matter, why someone who even had no religion would not be allowed into our Heaven? What kind of "merciful God" was that?

Maybe I was rebelling in part because of the trouble brewing at home between my parents, but mostly I remember it as offending my notion of common sense. Then I also began to question the concept of heaven. It seemed kind of silly to me. I asked my teachers what they really knew about Heaven. Where did it come from? Hell also seemed pretty ridiculous to me. So there I was, beginning to question some of the major tenants of the Baptist Church.

I was also really bothered about the racism of the Baptist ministry. According to the church, blacks had the "Mark of Cain" on them. God had made them to be the slaves, servants and all that nonsense. When I raised questions about what seemed so absurd to me, the answer came back that it was God's will and we shouldn't question any of that. Even then I saw it as a perfect alibi for racism and racial prejudice.

Then one Sunday I was in Sunday school when we had a youth minister visiting our class of some 30 students, all of us about thirteen years old. This guy did the usual Baptist rant about "dedicating your life to Jesus, come on down, take Jesus as your personal savior" and that sort of thing. He got everybody in the room whipped up and all these kids were signifying their commitment by standing up for Jesus. But there I was, sitting for Phil.

Adults came over and pushed on my shoulders and said, "Come on, stand up and dedicate your life to Jesus." Finally, it was so intense that I got infuriated, jumped up, and ran out of the Sunday school. I didn't go to church that day. I went to a bus stop and caught a bus home. My mother and father were there at home. They hadn't gone to church either and my parents said, "What's the deal? How come you came home early?"

To which I replied, "I left and I'm never going back again." My mother said, "Well, you certainly are! You're going to go back next Sunday. You're a Baptist and you're going back."

But my father came through for me again. My dad said, "Now wait a minute, Mac. I think the boy has made his own decision. I think we'll have to leave it up to him. We're not going to force him to do anything."

And I didn't go back to the First Baptist church of Tulsa again. I think on rare occasions I might have gone to church when I was visiting with my grandparents in Cleveland, Oklahoma. I did it because it would have made them feel badly if I hadn't, especially since my granddad was a deacon. I loved them very much and didn't want to worry or offend them so I kept my beliefs and objections to myself. But my heart certainly wasn't in it. Religion was never again a strong part of my belief system and I eventually grew into being an atheist.

There were no repercussions from my decision, certainly not among my friends. Kids that I knew went to different churches so it was not a big deal. I remember that in high school we had the student bible thumpers that would go around with a Bible under their arm. Most of the guys I knew and hung out with saw them as village idiots, to be ignored. They were also thought of as weak and sissy.

I have to say that I started life believing what my parents did, that there was a god and heaven and hell, but that was just buying in to what they said was so. When I got old enough to seek answers for myself, they weren't there. An independent mind was, if you'll pardon the expression, a cross I had to bear. It was part of being a warrior. I could have my allegiances, but they had to be my own. I couldn't take anything on faith, from anyone, including faith.

I didn't make a wild jump out of religion. First I broke with the Baptist church. And then later on, occasions arose when I learned more about other beliefs. When I went to OklahomaUniversity and got in contact with foreign students, I began to have really serious discussions with other people about this concept of god, heaven, hell, afterlife and different ways of looking at life, where we came from and where we are going.

So at Oklahoma University I really started to seriously think about it. But when I went to the Naval Academy I had to attend church every Sunday. (They changed that regulation later.) But when I arrived at Annapolis in 1957, I was under orders to attend a church or religious service of my choice every Sunday. I didn't have the latitude I'd had to rebel against my parents. At least we got to choose what church. We had a Naval Academy Chapel that most guys went to. When I was a plebe, my first year, I went to the Chapel too for lack of anything better.

But in my second year I found out about a Presbyterian Church in town from some other guys who said it was a pretty neat thing, and that the minister was a good guy. Besides they got to go out into town. We could leave the Naval Academy and march out to church in town. I did that my second and remaining years at the USNA.

The minister there was Reverend Hudnutt, and he was really a good guy. He was supportive of anybody's religion. And he was open to anything and everything. In my junior year, I became our "church party" (as it was called) leader. It was my responsibility to assemble everybody, take roll and march us out to the church in Annapolis. We had our own Sunday school discussion group.

Reverend Hudnutt's ideas embodied a Christian religion. But he also encouraged freedom of thought and individual introspection. He taught a philosophy of tolerance, that everyone's gods were good and true if their values were humane. His teaching embraced peace and justice.

One Sunday I asked him, "Would you mind if instead of just doing the normal Sunday school thing, we begin talking about different world religions each Sunday?" He said, "Absolutely not. I think that's a great idea Phil. Why don't you take that on? You lead that and if you want me to come from time to time and join in the discussion or offer any ideas, I'll be glad to."

And that's what I and we did. I led our church party out to the Presbyterian Church Sunday School throughout my last two years at the Naval Academy, where we studied and discussed the world's different religions.

Just before my graduation at Annapolis in 1961, I asked Reverend Hudnutt to officiate my marriage to my high school sweetheart Karen. We went to him for the usual premarital counseling and to talk about the wedding. On one occasion when I was alone with him, Reverend Hudnutt looked at me and said, "Phil, let me ask you something. Are you a Christian?"

I said, "Well, I'm not sure. I don't know."

He said, "What do you mean you don't know? Do you believe that Jesus Christ died on the cross to save you?"

And I said, "No."

Then he got a satisfied smile and said, "There! You've got it! You're not a Christian. Good for you Phil. Now you know."

And that was the first time in my life that I realized I didn't have to say that I was a Christian.

7. What's the Difference?

If I sometimes thought I might have been switched at birth, it wasn't with another Tulsa baby. There was much about the southern culture I found myself at odds with, and I rose against it in such a way that some of my relatives may have thought my parents came home with the wrong baby. Racism was a particular point of contention for me.

I think my relatives thought I was an intelligent and good looking little boy. But they also thought I was a little bit screwy, and not in sync with everybody else. I grew up in an apartheid society with black and white schools, churches, restaurants, bus seats, restrooms and even drinking fountains. I could never understand what was happening to black people. It surfaced at the Southern Baptist Church I attended. Black people were said to be doomed by God to an inferior existence. That was the biblical excuse for racism when I grew up, at least in the Baptist Church and probably other southern evangelical churches then and now.

Anyway, it bothered me and one of the first times I remember speaking up about it was with my family members. I remember my grandmother Butler using the term "nigger" in the house at a family gathering and I asked her not to do that. Everybody thought I was a bit crazy, but I was pretty insistent about it and after a while they quit doing it, at least in front of me.

My grandmother was a very bright, independent woman and a politically active Democrat. She was an early feminist in some sense in that she started a real estate and home building business in the1920's. She was also one of only a handful of women who graduated from college at the turn of the century. My dad took over the home construction part of the business and he named it "Butler Personality Homes."

Our carpenters were three Czechoslovakian brothers who were really neat guys. Then there was the black guy who carried the lumber around and toted the bricks and did the other heavy lifting. And he was simply known as "the nigger." I worked for my father a couple of summers during high school, as an apprentice carpenter under John Bejeck, our foreman. I tried to make friends with the black man but he was fearful because I was white and the boss' son. He was always standoffish but we did talk. And we carried boards, bricks and stones together too. I should also note that our white carpenters always treated him with some respect and they never referred to him in that way.

A few years after my parents divorced, dad hired a black woman to come clean our house and cook for us about three days a week. Her name was Iola Haywood. Iola became much more than our house cleaner and cook. She actually became my surrogate mother. I loved her dearly, like a mother, and she loved me and my sister Linda like her own children. She would berate and lecture my dad when he recovered from a drunk. When I left for college, in a tearful parting, Iola told me "Phil, if you wasn't so white, I'd sweah you was my own son." I think at that moment I wished I wasn't so white.

That was the way it was back then. When we needed day labor, you picked up a couple of "niggers." I think it was the same thing people do now in California when they go down to the big hardware store at the curb where there are a group of Mexicans looking for work. Black people did all the brute force work back then. But I think the purported racism was less about skin color and really more about class. No matter where it occurs, there is always something underlying the whole exchange that is about benefit for one party and exploitation of the other. The exploited ones usually don't have many other options.

Also, from my experience, religion is frequently used as the basis for discrimination, like skin color, but those are the superficial reasons and the real reasons probably boil down to class. The fact that in Oklahoma the Indians were more or less integrated into the social structure is an indication that it was less about skin color.

I never understood why people hated Jews so much. It seems pervasive, certainly across our country, and we know about other parts of the world where it is out in the open and much more virulent. It was huge in Oklahoma when I was growing up. My father would talk about some guy buying one of our ranch style houses, saying, "He's a rich Jew. Look at the Cadillac he drives. He can afford this house." The Jews were always the rich guys to him.

When I was growing up in Tulsa I had a friend named Leonard Krisman who is Jewish. He was a really good friend from second grade through high school and is now today, over 60 years later. It's odd but my parents sort of went along with this. I mean, he was a friend and when I had kids over in the back yard to play ball, or throw a basketball or whatever, Leonard was always one of the bunch. He lived about four blocks from my house, so we would walk or ride our bicycles to each others house.

I went to Leonard's bar mitzvah and Leonard's mother, who was always very funny, told my parents it was the most wonderful thing in the world to look down the men's side of the room and see that little blond-haired boy with a yarmulke on his head, watching his friend go through his stuff for his bar mitzvah. All that stuff he had to memorize. Oy.

I remember one day when we were in fourth or fifth grade, before home room started, Leonard and I were sitting in the classroom when a guy who was a school bully came in. He walked to the back of the room and looked at my friend Leonard and said, "You dirty Jew." I piped up and said, "Hey! You can't call my friend that. You stop that." Like my take-no-prisoners attitude when it came to my family using the word "nigger." The bully didn't react as well. Instead of backing off, he came over and pasted me. It was an important learning lesson in life for this Butler kid — to fight my own battles and not somebody else's. But then later I found myself fighting lots of other people's battles.

8. Paperboy

I think like many American boys at the time, a paper route was part of life. We had *Tulsa World* which was the morning paper and *Tulsa Tribune* which was the afternoon paper and then the two shared a Sunday paper. So the *Tulsa World* Sunday paper was shared by both the *Tribune* and the *World* paper boys on a given route. They were pretty much the same company, as I recall, but they published different newspapers.

I lived in a middle class neighborhood with mostly wood frame-type houses. These houses, which are still there to this day, were usually two-bedroom houses, one bath, sometimes three bedrooms and one bathroom. Most were not more than a thousand square feet. They were pretty typical homes for the time. Most had just a single-car garage because people then only had one car. Each house would have a front and back yard, many of them with a chain link fence around the back yard so they could have a dog or two. I'd say the houses were usually about twenty feet apart. That was also the setting for my two paper routes.

For those of us who had the morning route we would be at the paper stop about 4:30am to get our papers, and those who had the afternoon route would be there after school around 3:30 or 4:00. In the eighth grade through high school I had both kinds of paper routes, morning and afternoon and sometimes both at the same time. I would ride my bicycle to my paper stop about three miles from home. It was a steel box that was about six feet by six feet where the papers were delivered for the guys who had routes in that area. There were about six or seven of us paperboys who got our newspapers at my route box.

I would load up my bike basket and deliver to my customers all year 'round. For the most part, I would walk or ride down the street and throw the newspapers onto people's porches. In our day, it was pretty much the law of the land that we had to "porch" the newspapers. Besides, we got better tips at the end of the month when we went around to collect.

The tough one was the early morning route, especially in the winter time when there was snow and ice and it was maybe ten or fifteen degrees below zero. It was quite wicked then. A kid could get frostbite in a hurry those days. Some days I would beg my father to take me to the route box, but he would rarely ever do that. I was usually on my own, regardless of the weather, making my way out to my route box, getting my newspapers and delivering them to my customers. Sometimes it was tricky getting my bicycle down the street when there was ice. Sometimes I had to get off and just push it through the snow.

But it was a wonderful training, in various ways, including in public relations. I learned how to get along with customers, and I learned to appreciate the people who did nice things. I had several women on the route who would occasionally give me a pie or cake and I might even get a small tip from a customer at the end of the month too. In a good month I would make about forty bucks on my paper route, which was good money in the 1950s, especially for a kid.

Another thing about a paper route, and most kids back then would say this, was that we learned responsibility. We couldn't skip out because we always had our route manager looking over our shoulder. My route manager was a guy that I've remembered all my life. He was a wonderful role model for us paper boys, on top of being a terrific leader. His name was Charlie Beach. Charlie would be there to help, and also to see that we fulfilled our responsibilities. I got to see Charlie years later when I came home from Vietnam. I'm glad because I had the opportunity to thank him for his leadership later in life when I understood how important he had been to me.

In addition to responsibility, we learned money management, an invaluable lesson. I quickly learned where money came from, that it didn't grow on trees, and that I had to use it cautiously and save what I could.

The flip side of our learning responsibility was that we had very few customers who tried to skate on us. It was their responsibility to pay when we came around to collect every month. I had trouble with one man who I think had mental problems. He wouldn't want to pay when I came to collect so I had to come back, again and again. On one occasion, the last, for some reason he erupted in a fury at me. He started swearing at me, and then he came thundering out of his front door onto his porch where he spit at me.

I ran away and told my trusty route manager, Charlie Beach, what happened. Charlie put me in his car and we drove back to the guy's house. Charlie had me stand at the bottom of the porch steps, and then he walked up and knocked on the door. The guy answered and Charlie faced him down. He said, "I know what you did to my paperboy and guess what, you will never receive another newspaper from this company as long as you live. You can go buy your newspapers. You will not get them from any of our paperboys." He really stood up for me. Charlie Beach was like a god to me that day. It was a very important lesson in leadership for me.

You think about today, I don't know what the situation is in most neighborhoods, but now you see a grown up delivering papers from a car. Sometimes it's a mother or father driving around and the paperboy or girl is tossing the paper from the car, but now I guess a lot of the delivery people are adults earning money. They put the newspaper, if we're lucky, in the tube next to our mailbox. There's no "porching" of the newspapers anymore like in the days of old.

Not to wax too nostalgic, but I think delivering newspapers was great training for kids. I think kids today are missing something by not having a paper route.

9. Baby Sister

Linda was born February 25, 1949. I wasn't even eleven, but my parents gave me the responsibility to take care of my little sister. I did everything from change her diapers to playing with her and later reading to her. I enjoyed her, and confess that I teased her in the way an older brother would do with a little sister.

A few years after she was born, when I was thirteen, we had a great experience together. Unlike most middle class families or couples at the time, my parents had two cars. My mother's car was a 1950 Plymouth, with a stick shift on the column. One night when my parents went to a movie, I found the keys to the Plymouth and went out and fiddled around with the car. I had watched my mother carefully and essentially learned to drive it just by paying attention. That night I just practiced a little in the garage. Then I got brave enough to back it out and drive it around the neighborhood. Later, when my parents went to the movie I would get my little sister and put her in the seat next to me. Linda would be asleep in no time and I would drive us around town in my mother's Plymouth.

One night, of course, as it is written into every kid's life, my parents came home ahead of me. No car and no kids so my mother was frightened and absolutely furious. As she was prone to physical displays, she was going to whip me for it. My father was pretty pissed off, too. But, and this is etched deeply in my memory, he said, "You know what, Mae? The good part of this is he didn't abandon his little sister. He took her with him." My mother responded, "Yeah, but my God, he doesn't know how to drive. He could have killed them both." So that became a family joke. I didn't abandon my little sister and I did know how to drive.

As my parents problems got worse – my mother with her addiction to pills and my father's to alcohol – my responsibility for Linda grew. By the time I was in high school and later at the Naval Academy I had become a father figure to my sister. This became even more important, to both of us, when my father put himself into his last alcoholic coma. He died in January of 1960; when I was a 20-year-old Second Classman (Junior) at the Academy, and Linda was not yet 11. It was a huge shock for both my sister and me because we were very close to our dad.

For the next five years, Linda and I were each other's family. Then my airplane exploded over Vietnam when she was only 16 years old, and I

30

didn't come back to her for eight very long years. And for the first five or six weeks, she didn't even know I was alive because I had been reported as killed in action.

Growing up with our mother was very tough for Linda. They didn't get along at all and for that matter no one got along with our mother. Neither one of us got along with her, but Linda couldn't get away and mother abused her terribly.

10. Born to Fly

Flying would have been my father's life if he had followed his heart, and I learned to fly and loved it because of him. Dad would fly when he was sober and sometimes I think he flew when he wasn't quite sober. He was able to give me my initial flying lessons because he was a licensed flight instructor. We owned a little two-place Ercoupe. He gave me seven hours and 30 minutes of training just before my 16th birthday. Then on my birthday he hopped out and said, "Make a couple of tours around the field, give me three touch-and-go landings and then a full stop." And that's what I did. I soloed on my sixteenth birthday.

I have to say that in the beginning I didn't care about flying that much. Maybe I did it because my father had such a passion for it. Also I had a thing about motorcycles. I loved riding motorcycles and I think that distracted me from flying. But it didn't take long before I really began to love flying.

We drove away from the airport where I had just gotten my student pilot's license and he drove me to the DMV where I then got my driver's license on the same day. But I got my pilot's license before my driver's license and my dad thought that was very cool.

I had acquired a smoking habit about two years before this. We kids thought smoking was grownup and cool in those days and I easily got hooked by smoking with some paper route pals early in the morning before other people were up. I carefully hid my cigarettes and smoking from dad, or at least so I thought. But on that wonderful day of my 16th birthday, with dad driving us to the DMV, he looked over at me and shook his head. Then he said, "Oh hell, I know you smoke, so here have one of mine." I took it and lit up. Then he said, "I guess you are about grown up now." I believe from that moment on my dad and I became more like brothers and good friends than father and son.

I worked at Brown Airport summers and on weekends and whenever I could. The job I had was widely known in the day as the "airport flunky." I washed, gassed and put oil in airplanes. I "propped" airplanes that didn't have an electrical starter. I cleaned out the office spaces and the hanger. I pushed airplanes here and there and parked them for customers. I mostly worked for flight time rather than getting paid anything. I got money from my paper routes but got flight time by working at Brown Airport. I managed to get about 45 hours the next year with a different instructor, an old aviator named Jimmy Gosney, who was there at the airport. Then I got my private license on my seventeenth birthday, which was the minimum age.

I flew a lot that following year. I took people illegally for airplane rides over Tulsa. It was five bucks for a fifteen minute airplane ride in a two-seat Cessna 140. That enabled me to accumulate over the required 200 hours flight time for the next level.

Then I went to the Spartan School of Aviation in Tulsa, through ground school and more flight training. Then Mr. John Guthrie, the Chief Pilot and instructor gave me flight instructions and my final check ride on August 11th, 1956, my eighteenth birthday and I got my commercial license. Mr. Guthrie was a well-known aviator. He was a former crop-duster, barnstormer and early aviator who held Private Pilot's license number 222. I was very proud to be the youngest commercial pilot in the United States.

Flying was clearly an important part of my early life, but my interest in it took a considerable – and understandable – downturn after my final mission over Vietnam. But getting up there was great fun. Of course it was my dad's love of flying and my love of him that kindled the interest in aviation.

I really had the best of flying when I was growing up in Oklahoma. Everywhere was designated an "elsewhere area" where you could fly as low as you wanted. I could go out and fly all over Oklahoma. I would fly down to twenty-five feet over the Arkansas River. I flew pipelines for people. I had great fun flying. Some other pilots and I even clowned around trying to fly formation. All my flying was VFR, visual flight rules not needing instruments, and just wide open. I got to fly lots of interesting airplanes like a Stagger-Wing Beach, a Stearman, a conventional landing gear, radial engine, Cessna 190. I flew a Swift which was like a little fighter airplane. And I flew all the "air knockers." The Aeroncas and Piper Cubs.

When I got my appointment to the Naval Academy, I had no interest in boats or ships, but very much wanted to be a naval aviator. That was much to the chagrin of my Air Force Colonel Uncle who was absolutely insistent that I go to the Air Force Academy and not the Naval Academy.

The Air Force Academy was brand new. The first class graduated in 1959. I took the test for the Air Force Academy when I was a senior in high school and came in second in the state of Oklahoma for the class of 1960. I was an alternate at a time when only one person was allowed to go from our state because they had such a small class. So I missed the Air Force

Academy, but qualified for and took an NROTC scholarship to Oklahoma University. The following year, while at O.U., I took qualifying exams and got appointed to the Naval Academy.

Preparing for catapult takeoff, USS Midway in the Pacific, 1963.

Phil firing rockets; taken by F-8 photo aircraft, 1963.

R.B. Butler, Phil's dad, 1943
Army Air Corps PT-19 flight instructor.

Mae Butler, Phil's mother, 1937.

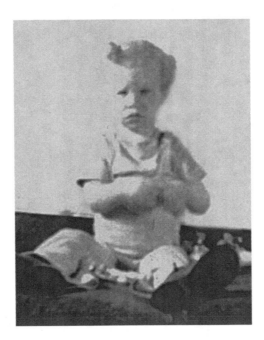

Phil at age two.

Phil with sister Linda in New Mexico, 1954.

Sidney Lanier grade school buddies, 1948.

USNA battalion in President Kennedy's inaugural parade, January, 1961. Phil in the lead, behind battalion staff, ready to give the command "Eyes Left" as they pass the president.

Navy Light Attack Squadron 22, VA-22 pilots, 1964, displaying Navy squadron award "E" for excellence. Phil, standing, second to right of the squadron flag.

11. College, Of Course

There are those remarkable moments in life when something happens or someone appears who gives you a hint or a shove in a new direction and it makes all the difference in the world. Call it fate or luck or coincidence, looking back on those times you can sometimes see a real sparkle in the moment.

I went to good public schools. I look back at my public school education and I think it had things going for it in the fifties that public school education doesn't have today. I attended Sidney Lanier grade school where we had good fundamental training in reading, writing and arithmetic. We also had great classes in science, history, music, physical education, speech and drama. We continued to advance in all these areas at Woodrow Wilson Junior High School.

At Will Rogers High School, grades 10 through 12, we could choose a pre-college curriculum or a technical skills curriculum for those who did not want to attend college after graduation. All of us remarkably made friends across these curriculum boundaries so choosing one or the other didn't seem to affect your social life. But if you were in the pre-college program it was pretty much assumed that you were going to go to college. My father and mother were very insistent that I go to college.

I remember one summer before my junior year in high school I was working as an apprentice carpenter and laborer for my father. It was a confusing time for me, with all my family problems. One day we were sitting next to the work site, having our 30-minute lunch break eating our sandwiches. John Bejeck, dad's construction supervisor, looked at me and said, "Phil, what are you going to do when you get out of high school?"

I answered, "Well, I don't know John. I haven't really decided for sure."

His immediate response was: "Bullshit! You're going to college. You're not going to be out here doing what we're doing. Don't kid yourself! You're going to college, young man."

So the push for college even came from the carpenters. I knew we didn't have much money. By the time I got to high school my father's drinking had pretty much submerged our income. I was working to make my own money. So I knew I had to have some help with college. That's the main reason I saw an opportunity and took the test to get an NROTC (Naval Reserve Officers Training Corps) scholarship.

Because of circumstances at home, I chose Oklahoma University. The reason was that I thought I wouldn't be too far from my father if he got into trouble. It was only 100 miles back to Tulsa to help dad if I was needed. In a sense, it was a big mistake because it de-focused me from my studies at O.U. Speaking truthfully; I was still trying to hang on to my father to save his life. It was a while longer before I understood that no one can cure an alcoholic but the alcoholic.

Since I had this abiding need to help my father and help him get off the booze, I had chosen Oklahoma University on the basis of its proximity to Tulsa. And I was unhappy with my choice.

My father always proudly reminded me that he had been the president of his college fraternity, Pi Kappa Alpha. So of course, being a fraternity "legacy," and to honor my father, I pledged Pi Kappa Alpha. After the first semester of being a pledge I was made a member. I didn't really care for fraternity life. I thought some of my fraternity brothers were pretty immature and that the whole idea of life around the "Pike" house seemed to revolve around drinking. I had a couple of friends in the fraternity but the rest of them I really didn't care for. At the end of my first semester when I made my grades and was initiated, I immediately moved into a University dormitory named Whitehand Hall.

Whitehand was a very inexpensive place to live in those days. I think I paid about twenty-five bucks a month for a room I shared with another fraternity brother friend. Our dorm was filled with international students. For me, that was a very big draw. I thought mixing with people from other countries was very stimulating. I spent much of my free time during that second semester at Oklahoma University making friends with many of them. I remember spending late evenings talking with guys from Canada, Indonesia and other countries. Many of them had been sent there by their countries for petroleum engineering. They were very bright guys, very fluent in English and smart. I just soaked up their culture and what their world views were.

One day in my second semester, in my Naval Science class, my instructor, Lieutenant Mayo, called me to his desk after class. I still remember him so clearly, his face, bearing and the way he gave the lectures to us. As I was walking out of the room, he said, "Mr. Butler, step over here please." He was standing behind his lectern and I thought, "Uh Oh. What have I done now?" He must have been close to psychic because then he said "Mr. Butler, how do you like being here at Oklahoma University? How do you like your studies?"

I said, "Well sir, I really don't like it here very much."

He asked, "Why? What's the problem?"

I said, "I guess I just don't like what Oklahoma University is all about. I'm not really very crazy about my engineering classes." I added, not gratuitously, "I like this class probably more than the others."

Then he said, "Well, the reason I ask you is because have you ever thought about going to the Naval Academy?"

"I'm not sure what that is," I replied.

He explained what the United States Naval Academy was and then he told me, "In two weeks, when we have spring break, if you go to the Naval Air Station in Dallas you can take a battery of tests that will last for four days. It consists of medical, physical fitness, and two days batteries of mental examinations. Why don't you go take those tests? You might qualify to go to the Naval Academy." And I told him, "Sounds like a good idea. I'll do it. Why not?"

So, two weeks later I went to NAS Dallas. I think he called ahead and got me into the program to get into testing, and I went through the four days of examinations. There was also an interview with a Senior Naval Officer, as luck would have it, a naval aviator. He asked me about my extra-curricular activities and I told him I had a commercial license. That was probably a knockout because he really loved that.

After the school year, a couple of months later, I was at home and actually getting ready to go on my first midshipman cruise with my NROTC classmates. It was to be a South American cruise aboard the USS Wisconsin. But late that afternoon the phone rang and my father answered. He talked a little bit and then he turned to me. With tears running down his face he said, "My God son! You're going to the Naval Academy. Incredible!" I had been given one of two hundred nationwide presidential appointments to the United States Naval Academy.

Dad handed me the phone and I talked to the Naval Academy officer who told me when and where to report.

I think my admission to the United States Naval Academy meant more to my father at the time than it did to me. He was very emotional about it. He knew, at some level, what an extraordinary ticket this was for me, out of Tulsa and into the wider world. I suspect it reflected back on his own decision to come back to Tulsa and work for his mother, rather than stay with Braniff as an airline pilot. To him it meant staying in Tulsa and becoming an alcoholic. Despite the alcohol and the problems with my mother, he had always had my best interests in his heart.

As he was digesting the incredible news that I had been admitted to the Naval Academy, he said to me, "Well, we'll drive there. We'll drive there from Tulsa. I'll drive and we'll take your little sister and we'll go with you and watch you get inducted into the Naval Academy."

And that's what we did. At the end of that June we drove across the country to Annapolis, Maryland. I was still 18 at the time, and my sister Linda was only seven. I vividly remember walking around the Naval Academy grounds and looking out at the Severn River. I was thinking to myself that it was the first time I had ever seen the ocean and I was going into the Navy.

I was sworn in as Midshipman at the U.S. Naval Academy on June 30, 1957 with 1,300 classmates. My proud dad and sister were in the crowd watching the ceremony.

12. United States Naval Academy

Dad and Linda stayed with a family near the main gate of the Naval Academy grounds. It was the home of Mister J.W. Crosby and his wife. They turned out to be very good friends of mine as a midshipman and Karen would stay with them when she visited me later on. The Crosbys ran what was called by Naval Academy people a "drag house." Your "drag" was the young woman you were dating for a weekend and the rooms in homes that many Annapolis people rented out for those occasions were called drag houses. It turned out that J.W. Crosby had been the choirmaster at the Naval Academy for many years and he was the author of our Alma Mater song "Navy Blue and Gold." Mister Crosby was also a veteran of the Spanish American War in 1898. That life legacy amazes me today. To think I had a friend who fought in a war over 110 years ago. The chain will continue when some young midshipmen now at the Naval Academy will someday remember they knew a Vietnam veteran.

I was inducted as a Midshipman, Fourth Class into the USNA class of 1961. My sister and father drove back to Tulsa, and I was left in a brand new world. We immediately began what was called "Plebe Summer." That was where we new civilian kids were brought in off the streets for some fundamental training. We were guys who had qualified to come to the school but most of us were clueless about what we were actually going to be doing there.

My plebe class, about thirteen hundred of us, went through two months of training before the brigade of upper-class Midshipmen came back and we all started the academic year in September. So July and August was called Plebe Summer. There was a select cadre of second classmen (juniors) who served as our leaders and also a select group of new Ensigns who had just graduated from the Naval Academy. They assigned us to companies and we started learning everything from how to wear a uniform, shine our shoes, march, and execute the manual of arms and all kinds of things about the Naval Academy itself. There were no academics; it was orientation to the Naval Academy and to becoming a Midshipman.

We had a lot of training to develop physical fitness. We trained in swimming, boxing, wrestling, gymnastics, obstacle courses and the like. We learned how to stand with proper military posture and to march and do manual of arms with an M1 rifle. We learned how to sail several types of boats and we made trips across the Severn River to the firing range where we qualified in rifle and pistol shooting.

We learned discipline, too. We were taught to always reply "Yes sir," "No sir," or "I'll find out sir." No excuses allowed, ever. We were all given a little book called "Reef Points." That little 300 page blue book was a bible for Naval Academy Plebes. It was filled with information about the Naval Academy and becoming a Midshipman. Much of it was based on tradition and a lot of it was history. There were also canned answers to questions that we had to memorize. We were pretty much required to memorize everything in the book so that we would be able to answer anything and everything between the covers when questioned by the returning Upper Classmen. I still have my Reef Points book and can recite a lot of the stuff I memorized over 50 years ago. Now that's training.

At the end of the summer we were sent out to other wings of Bancroft Hall to join our assigned companies. The Brigade of Midshipmen consisted of 24 companies, divided into 6 battalions at that time. I was assigned to the Seventeenth Company, which was in the Fifth Battalion of the Brigade of Midshipmen.

When the academic year started and the Upper Class men came back the shit really hit the fan because they were there to run us ragged; to give us what they considered to be a sufficient plebe year. It was very intense and designed to separate out the wheat from the chaff. There was an awful lot of running around and hazing and memorizing things and finding things out. Plebe year was a tough, tough time. It was really a test, and it was a time when a lot of guys didn't make it. I think our class had boiled down from thirteen hundred or so to probably around nine hundred by the end of that first year.

The academics were very difficult, too, because in those days every Midshipman was required to undergo the same study to get a Bachelor of Science degree in Marine Engineering. This was done in four years. So on top of all the military stuff, to get a Bachelor of Science in Marine Engineering meant we were taking 145 units of courses by the end of four years. In engineering it meant in our last two years sometimes carrying 22 units and with many of them having labs because we were engineering students. So it was very tough. Being a Midshipman at the Naval Academy was like trying to drink from a fire hose.

The purpose was to weed out those who weren't going to be able to make it, but you also have to understand that all of the guys there were pretty much super achievers. I was amazed when I met the other guys in my company to find that practically everybody had been a captain of some football or sports team, or valedictorian of his high school class, or president of his high school class. These were the typical guys that you met there. Also almost everybody already had some either college or preparatory school before coming there. Not too many guys came there straight out of high school. I thankfully had had a year at Oklahoma University which prepared me for this onslaught of academic requirements so I could also simultaneously manage the military requirements of being a Plebe. I seriously doubt I could have made it coming straight out of high school.

For those who are not aware of the way people are selected for the military academies, each member of Congress has two appointments, which totals almost 1100, and there are an additional 200 presidential appointments, which I was one of. My grandmother had been friends with Congressman Paige Belcher who represented my area in Tulsa, and she had sought to have him make me one of his appointments. I was already at the Naval Academy going through Plebe Summer when I got a Western Union telegram congratulating me on his having appointed me to the United States Naval Academy. I called my grandmother and told her to thank him and to appoint somebody else because I was already there.

That system of appointments meant that men from all over the country came together. It was wonderful, a great experience to find out things from other guys. It was one of the really nice things about being at the Naval Academy. All of your friends were from all over the country and some from all over the world. Some had come from Navy families or military families that were in Germany and other American military bases around the world. One of my best friends, Ted Fenno, was the son of a Navy vice admiral and he had lived all over the world. It was really interesting to talk with him and hear about his experiences in growing up as a Navy junior. It was very valuable part of our education, I think, to live with people from all over the country.

The scope of the education and the pressure was a great leveler. All these guys were super achievers in some aspect of their lives or another. My claim to achievement was that I had a commercial pilot's license. I think when they were deciding whether or not to admit they also had given me credit for working while I was in school.

The Naval Academy suited me very well. I think I longed for the structure. I had lived through high school with my family situation with no structure. I was glad to get into a situation where my life was structured. My academic courses I had to take were laid out in front of me. What I needed to accomplish as a Midshipman was clear within the regulations of the Naval Academy. I also slipped right into the system that fed me three terrific meals a day at exactly the right time, called for me to fall into formation, and to march to class or parades on Saturday or whatever. It was all highly regulated and structured. I had longed for more order in my life. It was at a time when I needed it.

The rebel in me wasn't entirely gone. I earned quite a few demerits my first year. We were allowed 300 and I picked up over 100. I had a hard time being the perfect Plebe Midshipman. My recalcitrance was less about the Naval Academy and more about some upper class men. It was the Second Class men – "Segundos" we called them – who were the ones that rode the Plebes the hardest. And there were a couple of them living down the hall that took a special interest in me. They found many ways to give me demerits so I got lots of "extra duty" time that meant I had to do either calisthenics or march around the parade ground at five in the morning.

There was a lot of physical hazing. The upper class men would have us running around in four or five pairs of sweat gear to make us sweat and they used paddles on our rear ends. There were a lot of physical hazing rituals that later became illegal. But in those days there was quite a bit of it.

One interesting feature of my time in 17th company at the Naval Academy was, as fate would have it, I lived in a room with two roommates directly across the hall from two First Class men. One of them was John McCain. I got to know John very well that year. He took a special interest in me but always from the standpoint of razzing, joking and messing around. He had a special style. He would do the usual, brace me up against his bulkhead (wall) which is what you did when you were a Plebe.

But his style was he liked to scream and yell, and he liked to get his face close to yours. In fact, sometimes he would take great delight in pressing his nose against my nose while he yelled things like "Butler, you dumb shit!" He seemed to get great joy out of that. Actually my fellow plebes and I thought if was funny too.

I guess I had been a Plebe for maybe a couple of months when I had to come around to John's room one night after evening meal. When I went in, I got braced up against the wall as usual and he said to me, "Butler, I want you to dress up in night gear. Do you know what night gear is?"

I didn't know so dutifully said, "I'll find out, Sir." That was the only reply you gave upper classmen when you didn't know the answer.

"Oh bullshit Butler, you dumb shit. I'm going to tell you what night gear is," he said. "Night gear is everything that you have that is Navy blue.

You're going to wear a Navy blue work shirt, your gonna wear service dress blue, you're gonna make sure you have a blue cap cover, you've gotta make sure you have gray gloves, black shoes, black socks. That's night gear." Then he said, "Guess what? You're gonna report to my room in night gear at zero one hundred (1 A.M.) tonight. Now get outta here."

I went back to my room across the hall and told my roommates what was going on but none of us could figure out what McCain had in mind. Of course, we just obeyed orders that first year, so I set the alarm clock for twelve forty-five, and when it rang, I jumped out of bed, got into night gear, went racing across the hall, threw open the door and bounced in the door ready to sound off, "Midshipman Butler, Fourth Class, Sir."

But McCain was waiting for me. He grabbed me and he shoved his hand across my mouth before I could sound off and he said, "Shush. Follow me."

That was when I noticed he was in night gear. We were on the fourth deck, or fifth floor, of Bancroft Hall, and he led me in the dark down the hallway, down all the "ladders" (stairs), and out into the yard. We made our way in the dark to the wall that separated the Naval Academy from the town of Annapolis. We sneaked our way along the wall to a place near the main gate where the wall was only about four or five feet high. He climbed over the wall and waved me to follow. Over I went.

Being over the wall was huge. It was a Class A punishment, very serious. And here he was leading me. We walked out to the street where a taxi cab was waiting. The driver got out of the taxi cab, walked around his car and said, "Hey Johnny, how're ya doin?" We got in and drove about five miles to a bar outside of Annapolis. We went inside the bar and sat down. John ordered two beers, and I thought, "Oh boy, I'm going to get a beer."

But John put both in front of his place and said; "Now Butler, you're not allowed to drink. You're not going to get anything to drink. I'm showing you how to get over the wall but I'm not going to be responsible for giving you an illegal alcoholic beverage." After he drank beers, we went out, got in the cab and rode back to the Naval Academy.

I experienced some of John McCain's early leadership. He taught me how to go over the wall. It was an excellent and useful lesson.

John was a hell raiser and he had a very quick temper which I saw him lose with classmates numerous times. His military dress was always the worst. He would try to get away with anything he possibly could. And if he had not been the son and grandson of Admirals he would have been in trouble.

McCain got special dispensation from the Superintendent of the Naval Academy at that time because he was from such a famous family. He just barely managed to graduate. His class standing was so bad that he was actually fifth from the bottom person in his class of more than 800.

He went to flight training after graduation and became a naval aviator. He crashed several airplanes before becoming a POW later. So my impression was that he was fairly irresponsible, prone to quick bursts of temper, and that he made spontaneous off-the-wall decisions that lots of times weren't healthy.

I formed life-long friendships and bonds with eight of my 17th Company classmates. Tom Case was my best man at my first marriage, Ted Fenno and Dick Gill were my second class roomies and close friends. Jay Savage, Larry Lubbs and Wally Guthrie were three fellow hell-raisers. And Dana French is the only one of the bunch who to this day always agrees with my progressive politics and crazy ideas. All of these guys would back me in a pinch, and vice-versa. That's a rare and valuable gift in life.

When I was a First Classman, during my second semester, we chose the service specialty we wanted to go into. It could be NavyLine (a ship driver,) nuclear submarines, Marine Corps, Naval aviation or other choices that came in accordance with your class standing. Of course I was going to choose Naval Aviation. One evening I got a phone call, which was quite unusual, to report to a battery of phones at one place in Bancroft Hall. I was told that a Colonel Howard was on the phone and wanted to talk to me.

I ran to the phone and said, "Uncle Jim. Hi, how are you doing?" He was the Director of Operations at nearby Pease Air Force Base.

He said, "So, I know that you're choosing what service you're going to go into, and I know that you have a pretty high class standing."

"Yeah, well," I responded, "I did alright."

"Well, you're gonna choose Air Force, right?"

There was a small quota for Naval Academy graduates who could choose to go into the Air Force. Just as there were small groups at the Air Force Academy and West Point who could choose to go Navy. Maybe only 30 or 40 guys out of a class of 800 could choose to change services.

"No Uncle Jim," I said, "I'm going naval air."

He said, "Oh, no! You don't want to do that. You're going to go Air Force and fly some real airplanes. I'll see to it that you get a good assignment if you go Air Force. You'll love it."

"I'm sorry, Uncle Jim. My mind's made up and I'm going Naval Air."

He said, "Oh God! I was afraid of that. You went to that school and there you go."

I was loyal to the Navy when I graduated. After four years at USNA I felt part of the Navy and Naval Aviation sounded exciting. I wanted to fly jets off carriers. We had fighters and the kind of airplanes I wanted to fly. It also looked like an interesting thing to do, and it turned out to be pretty interesting after all.

13. High School Sweetheart

I met Karen Olson in my junior year at Will Rogers High School. She had just moved to Tulsa from Chicago. She made a huge impression on me but we really didn't start to date until our senior year in 1955. After graduation I went to Oklahoma University and she went to Northwestern University in Chicago for nurse's training. We continued to correspond and see each other when we could. She went through a three-year program to qualify to be an RN. After a year at OU, I went to the Naval Academy where everyone spends four years, no matter how much college or preparatory school education you had before.

We continued to correspond and I would make my way to Chicago during leave periods, mostly by hitchhiking and sometimes by riding the train. We continued together that way until we were engaged. In my senior year, after my father had died, I had his car so I brought it to Annapolis for her to drive. She moved into an apartment in Washington, D.C. nearby, with two other women who were also dating buddies of mine, Larry Lubbs and Wally Guthrie, at school. We were all planning to get married after graduation.

Karen got a job as a nurse in Washington for that last year. Since I couldn't be married at the Naval Academy, it was against regulations; we had to wait until the day after I graduated for the wedding. We had a military ceremony in the Presbyterian Church with the crossed swords and full dress uniforms. People from her family came from Chicago and people from my family from Tulsa. The saddest part for me was the absence of my father. He never got to see me graduate from the Naval Academy or get married. After the wedding we left on a honeymoon trip through the Smokey Mountains on our way to Naval Air Station, Pensacola, Florida, where I was to be stationed.

Karen and I had a loving marriage for almost four years. We moved from my first duty station, Pensacola, to Meridian, Mississippi, then back to Pensacola, then to Kingsville, Texas where I completed flight training. Flight training was intense and stressful for both of us but we soldiered through it. I graduated first in my class of student aviators so had my choice of several duty stations. I picked the Naval Air Station at Lemoore because the call of California still resonated so strong within me. She pinned my Naval Aviation Wings on my uniform in a ceremony at Kingsville on

November 2, 1962. Then I received orders to report to NAS Lemoore, California where we were stationed until I went down over Vietnam in April of 1965.

14. Southern Racism

Karen and I seemed perfectly aligned in our values, socially and politically. Karen grew up in Chicago where Southern racism was pretty much unknown to her. She went to integrated schools, but her family moved to Tulsa for her junior and senior high school years. There she discovered a completely different culture, one I described earlier, as Southern and very racist.

Karen and I thought alike on this issue, that discrimination was really wrong, narrow-minded and stupid. We moved to my first assignment in Pensacola after we married where it was the real South and we encountered racism head on. The first incident I can recall happened one day when we went out to a McDonald's hamburger stand; one of the very first ones. When we parked we saw two drinking fountains on the wall outside with signs. One said "white" and the other said "colored." We looked at each other and said, "Oh yeah, really?" Then we got out of the car, went over and both of us drank out of the "colored" fountain. This earned us some catcalls, yelling and threats as we got back in the car.

Another experience happened at the first place we lived in Pensacola. The house had been separated front and back into a duplex, and our landlady lived in the back part of the house. One evening when I was still going through flight training ground school, a friend, Mack Johnson, came over for dinner. Mack was one of only two black midshipmen in the class of 1961. He had been a fabulous light-weight boxer in our class. He had also selected Naval Aviation so we were going through flight training together.

He was a bachelor, living in the BOQ, Bachelor Officers' Quarters. So it was natural for me to say one day, "Hey Mack, come on over tonight. You can meet Karen, have some dinner and we can talk."

He said, "Sure. Okay." and so he did. About five o'clock that evening he came, had dinner with us and then left later in the evening to return to his BOQ room.

The next evening our landlady came marching around and knocked on the front door. Her name was Mrs. Newsom. Karen and I referred to her as "Mrs. Nuisance" because she was always snooping around our side of the duplex. But the place was a bargain – $85 a month and we couldn't pass it up. We had two bedrooms, one bath and it was furnished. She was standing on the porch with her hands on her hips when I opened the door and she said, "It's my understanding that you had a Negro in your house, in my house, here last night."

I said, "Yeah, I guess so."

She said, "Well, that may be okay up North where you come from, but that's not okay here and you can't do that."

I said, "Are you aware that the man who was here is a graduate of the United States Naval Academy? That he's an officer in the Navy and he's going through flight training with me? Are you aware of that?"

She said, "Well, it doesn't make any difference. He's a Negro, he can't be here."

I said, "Okay," whereupon I turned around and I yelled back at Karen, "Karen, come out here."

Karen came to the door with me and I said, "Start packing things up. Mrs. Newsome doesn't want us to have Negroes in our house. So pack everything up and we'll leave tomorrow."

Karen said, "Absolutely! Okay. Good!"

Then Mrs. Newsome quickly said, "Well, well, alright, I didn't know you were going to take it like that, so never mind." And she turned around and stormed off.

We, of course, made it a point to have Mack over again several times after that.

Months later we were sent to Meridian, Mississippi for my first jet flight training at the Naval Air Station there. That place was really bad. It was evil. It was the worst of the Old South. It was like antebellum South right after the war, a hideously racist place.

One day after flying at the base, which was north of town, I drove home and remembered I was supposed to pick up something at a drugstore to take home. I got out of the car and was walking down the sidewalk to the store when I saw a woman coming towards me, carrying packages in both hands. She turned to go into the store after me. So I stepped back, held the door open and motioned for her to go in. She walked in and I followed after her. The proprietor of the store came up to me and said, "What did you just do?"

I said, "What do you mean what did I do?"

He said, "You opened the door for that "nigger." We don't do that around here. Get out of here. I'm not going to serve you."

The poor woman heard all this and of course she was terrified. She turned and ran out the door with her packages. So I just walked out, got in the car, drove home and told Karen what had happened.

There were local elections going on while we were there and we would hear political ads for people who were running for sheriff, mayor, and the like. Their consistent election themes were things like, "You can rest assured that Sheriff Joe Blow will protect all of our white women from the 'niggers'." It went on and on like this. Meridian, Mississippi was a horrible, ugly place in 1961.

There was another incident in Meridian that shook us to our cores. It had to do with my dear friend and classmate Terry Murphy and his wife, Claire. They were in Meridian the same time Karen and I were, so the four of us got together a lot. We played cards and drank Kool Aid together some evenings. Terry and Claire lived in a little house they had rented out in the countryside.

Terry and I both thought the Meridian area was kind of a wild west. So we thought it would be a good idea to we get our wives some kind of protection. We went to the local gun shop together one day and each of us bought our wives little .25 automatic pistols and some ammunition. We took Karen and Claire out and taught them how to shoot. Then we felt a bit safer, that they had some protection when we were gone and they were alone at home.

One evening Terry was flying a night flight and I was home with Karen. The phone rang and it was Claire. She sounded terrified. She was screaming and yelling, completely panicked. I said, "Okay Claire, calm down and I'll be right over there." Karen and I jumped into the car and raced out to their house. When we walked in she was standing in the living room, holding her pistol. She kept saying, "I shot somebody, I shot somebody!"

So I called the sheriff. He came quickly and looked around the property. Pretty soon one of his deputies drove up with a man in the back of a squad car. The sheriff had his deputy bring the man to the door outside, and said, "Is this the man you shot?" The man had some bleeding from his left cheek.

Claire said, "Yes."

We had gotten her calmed down by then and had learned from her what had happened. This guy had been naked and he had come to her door and was banging on the screen door, terrifying Claire. She got her gun and when it looked like he was going to come through the front screen door she shot at him. Luckily she only grazed his face and had taken a piece out of his cheek.

The man was black, as you might have inferred from the thread of this chapter, and more to the point, he was obviously mentally incompetent. The poor fellow was a nutcase. He wasn't trying to do anything at all to her, but he certainly had scared the bejesus out of poor Claire. But here's the kicker.

The Sheriff said, "Well, you know, the only thing I could say Mrs. Murphy is it's just a darn shame that you didn't kill him. We would have liked it if you'd just killed him instead of just grazing him. But anyhow, thanks for shooting him missus."

I said, "Well, she's injured a guy. What if she had killed him?" Is there anything in the law?

The sheriff responded, "Oh hell, he's a "nigger." It doesn't matter if you kill a "nigger" around here. This guy's crazy. We've known about him for years. He's always running around naked and doing stupid, crazy things like that. He doesn't have much of a mind, but it would have been a relief for us if she'd just killed him and we'd a been rid of that 'nigger'." We waited with Claire until Terry came home, about an hour later. He was completely panicked when he heard the whole story, but it ended safely for them.

15. Navy Flight Training

Graduating from the Naval Academy meant a four year obligation to serve. But for Naval Aviators obligated service was calculated after completion of flight training. I felt part of the Navy and Naval Aviation sounded good...flying off carriers. I knew we had fighters and the kind of airplanes I wanted to fly, so it looked like an interesting thing to do. It turned out to be pretty interesting after all.

It's obvious, of course, but the difference between the flying I did before the Navy and what I learned while in the Navy were as different as night and day.

Flying something like a jet fighter at 500 or 600 knots requires a very sensitive touch to maintain altitude. For Navy pilots, maintaining altitude means maintaining 10,575 feet and not 574 feet or 576 feet. Airspeed at any given moment requires the same. It's supposed to be pegged at the exact speed. That's the kind of precision naval aviation requires. Flying on and off carriers during day, night, good weather and bad requires the ultimate precision of any flying in the world.

That kind of flying also requires a certain mentality, one that is based on discipline and a sense of responsibility. It's built into the pilot as part of the 18 months of intense training. A lot of guys washed out in flight training along the way and never made it through. The training was that demanding. Naval aviation also requires a lot of self confidence. Fighter pilots are especially known for being confident and egocentric, but it's for a reason. They have to be in order to meet the many momentary challenges and close calls with death in order to stay calm and survive.

Pensacola is a spiritual place to all Naval Aviators. It's where naval aviation began at the turn of the 20th century. It is known to all Naval Aviators as "The Cradle of Naval Aviation."

The first eight or ten weeks, for all of us who were already commissioned officers, was ground school. For those who hadn't gone through the Academy or NROTC, ground school ran for sixteen weeks.

Next we received primary flight training at Saufley Field, near Pensacola NAS, in the T-34, a two place, propeller-driven aircraft. There was a lot to learn, even though I already had a commercial license. It must have been like drinking from a fire hydrant for all the guys who had never flown before. We were to get ten to twelve dual flights with our instructor before flying solo in the T-34. My instructor sent me out solo after three flights. But he agreed to let me have the same number of total flights as the other guys because I was really having fun in the T-34. We flew some dual flights together where we would fly formation with another T-34 out to one of the practice areas. The instructors did all the formation flying because we hadn't been taught that yet. But my instructor, Lieutenant Eiebert, let me take the controls for formation and he would delight in holding his hands in the air so the other instructor could see I was doing the flying.

Upon completion of primary flight training, those of us who qualified for jet training went on to intermediate flight training at NAS, Meridian, Mississippi. You had to have top grades in primary to qualify for jets. There we received instrument, acrobatic, and formation training in the T2J-1, a dual place, single engine, jet trainer.

Then it was back to Pensacola again for air-to-air gunnery and our first carrier qualification in the T2J.

Every naval aviator who gets his wings has to make a carrier landing. Even those who are trained to fly helicopters or fixed-wing propeller driven aircraft must make a carrier landing. Carrier landings are extremely challenging, especially in jet aircraft, and that was where a lot of people didn't cut it. Our carrier training was off Pensacola, Florida and in my day we did it on the USS Antietam. Our initial carrier training was in squadron VT 4 at the same base where the Blue Angels are based and practice.

First we did a lot of field carrier landing practice with an "LSO" – landing signal officer. First we did it with an instructor in the back seat and then solo, listening to the LSO standing on the runway below. We learned to fly on a lighted glide slope that is projected up off a mirror. It's called "the meatball" on a Fresnel lens. At the same time we must keep our aircraft on a precise speed, attitude and direction. Finally, after all this instruction and practice, the appointed day came and we launch off from Pensacola Naval Air Station to fly out, solo, for our first carrier landings. I was excited and terrified all at the same time.

The Navy has a tradition that all aviators make their first carrier landing solo. Nobody wants to be in the backseat and get splattered. So you're all by yourself. It's a very profound experience and I think a very good thing to do. The only thing I can remember about my first carrier landing was how small that carrier deck looked and that I was terrified I was going to crash.

It was just an amazing experience! That flight deck sure looked small. But my training paid off and it happened. They told us to make sure our kneeboard checklists were not loose and that we had everything clipped down. Mine weren't. So when I caught the arresting cable everything flew up from my kneeboard and all over the cockpit. There were loose papers and stuff flying all over the place. Then I came to a stop, raised my arresting hook to release the cable and began taxiing forward for my first catapult shot. While taxiing I tried to collect the papers and stuff them back under the kneeboard clip.

The next thing I knew was bam! I was being flung off the bow on my first catapult shot! The Antietam was an old carrier and so it had a hydraulic and not a more modern steam catapult. Those old hydraulic catapults gave us a huge slam right at the beginning instead of building up acceleration to throw us off the ship. It felt like somebody kicked me hard in the back and gave me a permanent headache. I made the required four landings and catapult takeoffs that day. And I did it all by myself.

After successfully completing intermediate jet training in the T2J I was sent to NAS Kingsville, Texas in June of 1962. There we received training in the F9F-8T and F9F-8B Grumman "Cougar" for the first part of advanced jet training. The "T" model was a tandem, two seat version that was used for dual instructor/student training. The "B" model was single seat. Both were late 1950s fighter jets that were now being used for advanced jet training. We learned more instrument flying, formation, low-level and high level navigation and air to ground weapons delivery tactics.

The final 13 flights in my Navy flight training were the cream on top of the entire experience. We flew the F11F-1, a fighter with afterburner that just a few years before had been the Blue Angels demonstration team aircraft. The F11 was a single-seated, supersonic, FUN airplane to fly. We flew gunnery, firing 20 mm canons at a target that was towed by an instructor in another F11. He had to be brave. We would begin our run on the "rag" at 40,000 feet, descending on the target in afterburner at a speed of 1.2 to 1.3 mach, beyond the speed of sound. We also practiced air-to-air combat with our instructors, during which they would of course always kick our butts and "shoot us down."

But my final two flights in the F11 were the most amazing and unusual. They were both on October 29, 1962 during the "Cuban Missile Crisis." That day we were ordered to fly combat air patrol over the ocean, east of Kingsville, Texas, in case there might be Cuban or Russian aircraft attempting to attack the U.S. We were loaded with 20 mm high-explosive ammunition and Sidewinder, air to air missiles. I flew wing on my instructor a Marine Captain. My briefing with him was hilarious. He said, "Ensign

Butler, you make damn sure your master armament switch is OFF and furthermore, you keep your fucking hand away from the gun trigger. Do you understand me?" I said, "Aye, aye sir!" This guy was no fool. He didn't want to be a victim of "friendly fire."

16. Naval Aviator

I received my Navy wings of gold, on November 2, 1962 and got an assignment to the Naval Air Station at Lemoore, California, about 30 miles south of Fresno in the central valley.

The movers packed up our belongings and we filled our little Volvo full of stuff for the trip to California. After a few stops along the way we drove into the San Joaquin Valley. As we drove to Lemoore, Karen burst into tears. She said, "I thought California was beautiful and this is so ugly." I agreed and almost felt like crying myself.

We arrived in Lemoore and after a few days found a nice house to rent near the air station. Karen got a nursing job at a nearby hospital and we settled down as the happy young Navy couple we were.

I began my training there with Navy survival school. All navy pilots and flight crew that might be dispatched to combat are required to go through survival school. It took a week and included training in how to survive off the land and how to evade capture. The final two days were a mock POW experience to teach us what that might be like. Honestly, it wasn't very close to the real thing, but at least we did receive valuable information about the importance of communication and maintaining group cohesion and military structure.

Next was instrument qualification in the TF-9J. After completing that course I went to the replacement air group where I trained to fly the A-4 Skyhawk, the Navy's single place, jet, light attack, carrier-based aircraft. After a couple of months I was assigned to VA-22, Attack Squadron 22, at NAS Lemoore. Our squadron was part of Carrier Air Group 2, based on the USS Midway for carrier deployments. The Midway was home-ported at NAS Alameda, California. Whenever the Midway would go out, we would fly our planes out of Lemoore and land aboard the ship in the Pacific Ocean.

Our operational training was intense. We flew constantly, both out of Lemoore and in operations off the coast on the Midway. We often trained at sea near the San Clemente Islands and west of there. Sometimes we went on short mid-Pacific cruises to Hawaii and back so it meant that I was away from Karen a lot. It was challenging, both mentally and physically, to be a squadron pilot. It's a tough job. And I know it was tough on her too.

I was deployed on a six-month, West Pacific cruise in November of

1963. This was a peacetime cruise so we didn't experience any actual combat operations, though we trained constantly for that. During our deployment we visited Japan, Hong Kong and the Philippines while conducting flight operations day and night at sea. Karen and some other squadron wives were able to fly over for a couple of months and see us when we would come into port. That part was a wonderful experience for us.

But naval carrier aviation is a very dangerous occupation. We lost 11 aviators and flight deck people on that "peacetime" cruise. Those deaths put a lot of stress on us, as it certainly did on our families.

17. Bass Lake

We flew a lot of low level, practice combat missions out of NAS Lemoore. We frequently flew practice navigation and bombing missions over the deserts of California and Nevada. Typically we would fly, while simultaneously navigating, at only 50 feet above the ground and at speeds of 300 to 500 knots. The A4 pilot's mantra for these missions was, "Don't sneeze!" Any twitch could put you into the ground, which was very unhealthy.

We also flew lots of combat tactics, especially air to ground at various targets that were near Yuma, California or Fallon, Nevada. We practiced dropping bombs, firing rockets, 20 mm gun strafing, and nuclear weapons delivery. We had a nuclear weapon capability for which we spent hundreds of hours with target planning, loading drills and simulated weapon deliveries. We also had a secondary air-to-air mission so we practiced fighter tactics with each other all the time.

I thought of myself as a really hot pilot back then, flying A4s on carriers and around Lemoore. I was 24 to 26 years old, a qualified Naval Aviator and full of myself. So I, and we, also did some irresponsible and dopey stuff that could have gotten us canned. One of those nutty things figured with Bass Lake.

Bass Lake is in the Sierra Nevada Mountains, south of Yosemite National Park. It was a very sparsely populated area back in the early 1960s. Two of us young Lieutenant, Junior Grade pilots were pretty good flyers so our commanding officer had designated us as squadron test pilots. Squadron aircraft would need a test flight after coming back from a major overhaul. The test procedure was very complex and it took the better part of 45 minutes to accomplish. We got to take an A4 out with just internal fuel – clean, with no external stores or weapons – so it was a really nice, fast airplane when configured that way.

We took it up for a 45-minute test which amounted to departing NAS Lemoore, climbing immediately to 40,000 feet, and then taking the aircraft through the specified test procedures. We had many systems to check out so the flight kept us really busy. Then we descended back down to 20,000 feet where we had more things check out.

Then one of the things we had to do at the very end, which was kind of unique to the A-4C, was executed when we were within 25 to 35 miles of

NAS Lemoore. We slowed down to 250 knots and disconnected the hydraulic control system, to fly the airplane manually. This checked that the mechanics had rigged the airplane properly. Flying manually, with no hydraulic boost, made the airplane very stiff and difficult to fly. But it was the only way we could tell whether they had rigged it properly. So if the plane suddenly went into a roll, or flipped upside down, we would probably be heading towards the ground and gaining speed, which would necessitate the need to eject! Once that last test was safely completed we landed the airplane in manual because there was no way to reengage the hydraulic system while flying.

I had flown all over Oklahoma as a kid and had a lot of time, quite frankly, "flat-hatting." That's an aviator's term for when you are flying down at ground level in places where you're not supposed to be. One of the things that I did as a kid when I was in high school was fly about 50 to 100 feet above the ground over to Will Rogers and buzz my high school. A lot of my classmates and friends would come outside and wave at me. I wasn't too far from the municipal airport, but they couldn't see me in those days if I stayed very low, so I never got caught.

One day this other Lieutenant (jg), Bill (last name withheld) and I were talking about test flights and we devised an illegal variation.

We boomed up to 40,000 feet and hurriedly completed our high altitude checks. All this time we were talking to FAA air controllers who were guiding us around the airspace at safe distances from other aircraft. After going quickly through our procedures, we called the controllers and told them – because they didn't have us on radar exactly – that we were now at low altitude, below APC (area of positive control) and that we were flying VFR (visual flight rules) in clear skies. Then the APC center controller handed us off to a lower altitude control facility. Then, and here's the tricky part, we made a position report to Monterey radio, telling them we were overhead. But - we were actually over Bass Lake and still at 40,000 feet.

So at this point, in clear skies, and not under anybody's control, we would do a "split-s" maneuver over Bass Lake. A split-s maneuver meant that we would roll over on our back and pull straight down into a vertical dive. We then went straight toward the ground at full power, through mach 1.0 at over 600 miles per hour. Then we made a nice "6G" – that's six times the force of gravity – pullout over Bass Lake, leveling out at about 50 feet above the water.

Now we were blasting across Bass Lake at close to mach 1.0. It was great fun because we could look in our rear-view mirrors and see the rooster tail that we were making. Water was flying up from the lake behind us. Plus there were incredible reactions from the boaters who were out on the lake.

Then after having our fun we would warp around towards NAS Lemoore, climb back to 10,000 feet, do the disconnect procedure to test the rigging, and come in to land. Back safely in our squadron spaces, we filled out our paper work and of course reported in to the "skipper," our commanding officer, that we had a successful test flight with a good airplane. All of this could have cost our wings if we'd been caught. But we never got caught. Thinking back on it all, I just hope those boaters are OK.

18. Becoming a Father

The experience of becoming a father was profound for me as I imagine it is for most new fathers. There's nothing quite like that experience of holding a child that you helped create. In 1965, just before I was to deploy on the USS Midway, Karen was pregnant. Sadly she had two miscarriages before Diane was born. It turned out there was nothing wrong with the babies but she was diagnosed with an "incompetent cervix," meaning the downward pressure of the fetus caused the miscarriage. This third time she had undergone a special operation which involved sewing her cervix to reinforce it so she could hold this baby and not lose it in a spontaneous abortion. They first had to be sure that the baby was okay for this procedure and she was.

Because of the procedure, Karen needed to deliver through a Caesarean. So she went into the hospital about February 28th, and Diane was born March 2nd 1965. I was there when she was born. I got to see my baby daughter and hold her for two days, until March 4th, 1965.

The experience of holding that little girl with the blue eyes was something beyond words for me. I remember saying to the nurse, "Boy, she's got blue eyes like mine." The nurse smiled and said, "Well, Mr. Butler, I hate to tell you this, but all babies are born with blue eyes and they change color later." And I said, "Oh, well yeah, but she really has blue eyes. I'm sure of that." It's so vivid to me still, just looking at that kid, especially her tiny hands and feet. As I compared them to my own it seemed like they were exact miniature copies. It was an incredible life experience and I felt an instantaneous and powerful connection with my daughter.

Then, just two days later on March 4th, Karen's sister, Judy Olson, drove me to the squadron so I could fly an airplane to Alameda and report aboard the Midway for our second cruise to the western Pacific. But this cruise was not peacetime. It was a deployment for combat in Vietnam. I didn't know it then but I was not to return until eight years later, when this little infant girl was eight years old.

19. Bombing Snakes and Monkeys

The first four or five of the thirteen combat missions I flew were over South Vietnam. Then the carrier moved to a station up north and we started flying missions into North Vietnam. I also flew one or two rescue missions over Hainan Island. Terry Murphy, who was a very close friend of mine through the Naval Academy and flight training, had gotten shot down over Hainan Island in an F-4, so we A-4 pilots were sent out for a low level search to see if we could find the crash site where the aircraft had gone in. He had actually had been shot down at 30,000 feet or so.

(You, the reader, will recall that Terry and his wife Claire were with Karen and me in Meridian, Mississippi when Claire shot the mentally deranged vagrant.)

The first information that came out was that he and his back-seat radar intercept officer were shot down by an enemy missile. Then the truth came out that his own wingman shot him down with a Sidewinder missile. It was a horrible mistake, brought about when the aircraft that was responsible for radar control for that flight mission got confused and told another F-4 to fire a Sidewinder missile at an "enemy" aircraft. They did this without first sighting the other aircraft. So TerryMurphy and his backseater were killed by friendly fire. Sadly it was his own wingman that mistakenly killed them.

That was pretty typical of the scatterbrained things that went on out there at that time. Everybody was really hopped up and excited about getting into a war. A lot got screwed up and it was Catch-22 all over the place. Anyway, we never saw the wreckage of Terry's airplane and nothing was ever found. They probably went down in the ocean.

But to show you just how crazy it all was, Hainan Island is part of China. And there we were in A-4s doing search and rescue over China, unauthorized in their airspace. We were flying at low speeds and altitudes, 250 knots and 500 feet, so we could see clearly what was below. It was a miracle that none of us got shot down by Chinese air defenses.

I went on two of those search missions, and then a half dozen more combat missions over North Vietnam. All but two of my missions over North Vietnam were at night. Night was a dangerous environment to fly combat formations and bombing runs. Also at night you could see flak that was coming up at you. In the daytime you couldn't see it. You were fat, dumb, and happy not seeing what was being thrown at you. But the truth is the day missions were more dangerous.

The combat missions we flew over South Vietnam were ridiculous. We would go out in flights of four and be directed to the target by a forward air controller who was an Air Force pilot, usually in an L-19 or an L-5, or sometimes a forward air controller who was on the ground. They would direct our fire. Basically all we could ever see was jungle below us. There might be smoke billowing up and some guy was saying, "You see that smoke coming up over there? Drop your bombs 500 yards west of that."

Every Air Group was assigned an Air Intelligence officer. The Air Intelligence officer in my Air Group was assigned to my squadron on the Midway. He was really a neat guy named Bill Bond. One of his jobs, besides combat intelligence briefings for Vietnam, was to work with us to develop our top secret strip charts and our attack modes for delivering nuclear weapons if the call came from the President. We had top secret targets in China and the Soviet Union in those days. It's a miracle our world is still here after those decades of living through that global nuclear standoff.

The USS Midway Intelligence Center that all the pilots used was close to our Ready Room. We went there to get intelligence and to receive briefings on the targets we were assigned before we were sent out on a mission.

We used to say we were bombing snakes and monkeys because we almost never saw what we were after. We would always come back to the ready room and debrief our mission with Bill, the AIO. Most of us thought the whole thing was insane and stupid because we didn't know where the bombs were going. Who knows how many innocents we killed down below us?

Even in the very beginning of the air war, we thought these missions over South Vietnam were crazy. The more sensible missions were the ones I flew over North Vietnam when I was trying to interdict and bomb the trucks that were coming down Highway 1. The North Vietnamese were running trucks down Highway 1 to the DMZ where they were supplying the South Vietnamese, the so-called Viet Cong.

Actually, they were supplying their own troops. So at night we would try to stop them on the way by blowing them up with bombs and rockets. In those days, we could actually see them from 20,000 feet. We could see them coming down the highway because they had their headlights on. Even though they had shielded headlights, like eyelids over the top of the headlights, we could still see the lights down below. The game was to see if we could roll in and get on them with bombs or rockets before they heard us, turned off their lights and got off the road into the jungle.

Once they turned off their lights, there was nothing to see. We didn't know where they were at that point so if we hit anything it was just luck. Sometimes we dropped 250- or 500-pound bombs and we were also using rockets. The 2.75 inch and Zuni rockets we fired had high explosive charges. We also had twin 20mm guns for strafing and I did have some missions that involved strafing. I never carried napalm but sometimes our guys were dropping that stuff, too.

One strafing mission I remember was on a large barge that was crossing a river near Vinh City. As I was making my gun run down the road toward the barge, I started to squeeze the trigger on my 20mm guns, strafing up the road into the barge. Suddenly some guy down there must have lost his nerve and he ran across the road. It was a huge mistake. The high explosive 20mm shells were exploding as they walked down the road and he just completely disappeared. I will never forget that image. It still haunts me to this day.

20. The Last Mission

I remember that I probably started my briefing for that last mission in the ready room about 1800 hours, 6 PM. This mission was to involve tanking (mid-air refueling) on the way to the target. After the normal briefing with our flight of four aircraft we preceded to the air intelligence spaces. There we met with the guys who were flying the A3B that would be our tanker. Their crew consisted of a pilot, his bombardier and a radar navigator. We coordinated our mission, planning the rendezvous with them. We were to in-flight refuel just short of our coast-in point over North Vietnam.

It was to be a night launch somewhere around 2000 hours. As I remember I don't think there was any specific information given that night on any radical changes in the enemy's defenses. It was pretty much standard, as it had been for the last few days. In other words we were not expecting to encounter much flack or trouble from enemy air defenses. In early 1965 the Vietnamese didn't have as much anti-aircraft defense as they did later in the war. And since they were driving their trucks down Highway 1 with their headlights on it was pretty easy to spot them. But usually they'd turn their lights off and get off the road by the time we rolled in for the run. So as you were coming down to shoot, you'd lose them.

They did have the trucks though. I remember several missions before where from 20,000 feet we could see literally thousands of trucks. They were backed up bumper to bumper up and down Highway 1 for just as far as you could see. It was incredible.

I went back to the Ready Room where we completed our last minute debriefs where I found out what the weapons on my aircraft were to be. I was carrying six 250 pound, VT (proximity) fused, Mark 81 bombs. This time I received second briefing from my Weapons Officer and was told that it was my option to have them set on single or ripple fire. I chose ripple fire, all at once, because our mission was to roll in, in pairs and we would not get another opportunity to attack again. It was to be a one-time run on the target.

I was also briefed that the fusing system installed in my aircraft was new. It was an electrical system, armed from the cockpit by the pilot, that would arm the bombs some distance below the aircraft after being dropped. The bombs were set to detonate six feet above the ground. The detonations were triggered by the shock waves coming back up from the ground to the nose of the bomb. Exploding the bombs above the ground made them much more devastating to personnel and light vehicles.

We had masked our wing lights so that just the small after portion was showing and this would be enough to fly formation on the lead aircraft yet keep people on the ground from seeing the aircraft. We were to fly over Highway 1 at 20,000 feet and look up ahead of us. When we saw trucks ahead we would do a two aircraft formation modified "split-s" maneuver into a 45 degree dive toward the targets. We had been practicing this night maneuver together as a squadron for sometime beforehand and all of us were pretty skilled at flying night formation and acrobatic type maneuvers at night.

We would "pickle," press our bomb-release buttons, together at 3,000 feet. The lead aircraft would do the tracking and when he pickled, then wingman would also pickle. Lead was given rockets and the wingman was given bombs. The purpose was to lay a stream of weapons fire along the road which we were running directly down and to knock out as many trucks as possible because they were bumper to bumper behind each other.

I went up on the flight deck and everything was normal in the pre-flight. I told my plane captain to insure my bombs were set on ripple fire which they were and I moved to the catapult. Fred Spellman was my lead and I was flying number two as his wingman. Another squadron mate, Dick Cherba had the section lead. His wingman was Joe Jamison. Joe was also carrying the same bombs I was. But Joe's aircraft went down. He had a hydraulic problem and so he could not launch.

The three of us launched off the catapult. I went last. I remember flashing my lights to the catapult officer and then the tremendous acceleration of being shot down the catapult track. But then, just as I launched into the air, my main attitude-gyroscope went to the inverted position and some of my other basic flight instruments went out. I experienced a partial electrical failure. I was able to go to my standby gyro and maintain a normal climb attitude into the muck, the night fog and clouds.

The AJB3's main attitude gyroscope was the primary instrument for maintaining correct flight attitude at night or in weather. I also lost my engine tachometer and my ASM 19 navigational computer. None of my primary engine instruments went out and they all seemed to be okay. Essentially I had a standby gyro and compass to fly by. As I started to climb out through the overcast on partial panel instruments, I went through several layers of cloud formations until I got to about 10,000 feet, which was the pre-briefed flight rendezvous altitude.

When I got to 10,000 feet I could see the blinking anti-collision lights of my lead A4 off in the distance and I kept making my way towards him. At the same time I called back to the ship and informed them of the failure of my instruments. I later received a recommendation from my commanding officer down in the Ready Room to hold overhead the ship at 20,000 feet rather than proceed to the target in company with my leader because of the loss of the instruments. That was because that night was primarily an IFR, instrument flying required, situation.

However, I decided that my aircraft was flying well, the standby gyro was working fine, and so I joined up with my lead and proceeded to the target area. The other section lead, Dick Cherba, flew in loose formation off to our right. We proceeded towards the "feet dry" coast-in point (point at which we would first fly over dry land) in conjunction with the A3B. Just before we reached the feet dry location we all plugged in to the A3 and got a drink – we topped off our internal fuel tanks.

We unplugged and by this time Dick Cherba was drifting behind and he became more or less detached from the two of us. He coasted in at a different point and my flight lead told him that since he had become disjoined and did not have a wingman that he should dispense his ordinance in a "safe" mode, not armed so they would just drop harmlessly into the ocean. He was directed to do that and then to proceed back to the ship, which I assume he did.

We two A4s then coasted in over North Vietnam, just north of Vinh City. I was flying formation on the right side of Spellman's aircraft. As soon as we coasted in I was looking left and at his aircraft and left down onto Highway 1. I had marked on my map the place we coasted in and it had been at the place we planned. At that time we were only bombing up to the 20th parallel of North Vietnam. Later in the war all of North Vietnam became a target area.

Suddenly I saw a line of trucks below, traveling south. I didn't think Fred saw them so I called him to tell him we had a line of trucks at 9 o'clock. He looked over and said, "Roger." Then we continued on for a little bit and then I radioed, "Let's roll in Fred." At this point he gave me a "roger" and we started to roll in.

My switches were armed as we coasted in and as soon as I saw the trucks, I put the master arm switch to "on." I checked the station selection switch to "all." Everything was set up correctly to the best of my knowledge.

We rolled into a left diving bank. I don't believe we had the 45° dive angle; it might have been just a little bit shallow. However, this wasn't really too important because we were going to lay a stick of ordinance down the highway.

I could see the lights of the trucks and we had slipped up on them as we had planned. This time our tactics had worked. They did not have a chance to get their lights out. It seems to me that some of the trucks were just beginning to turn their lights off when we reached the pre-briefed pickle (weapon release) altitude. Then Fred's rocket pack went off with a blinding flash of light in front of me. As soon as that happened I pickled off my bombs, and then BOOM!

THE SECOND LIFE OF A WARRIOR

"Now these are the laws of the Navy,
  Unwritten and varied they be;
And he who is wise will observe them,
  Going down in his ship to the sea.
On the strength of one link in the cable,
  Dependeth the might of the chain.
Who knows when thou may'st be tested?
  So live that thou bearest the strain!"

"The Laws of the Navy"
ADMIRAL R.A. HOPWOOD, Royal Navy
First and fifth of 27 verses

Introduction

This time in my life is about the warrior in Vietnam. Most of it is based on the debriefing I did with my intelligence officer, Lieutenant Brian Kelly, during the three weeks after my return from Vietnam on February 12th 1973. They were conducted with all returning military POWs to get a record of what happened to each of us. The purpose was not only to gather current military intelligence, but also to chronicle lessons learned that could be applied in future training for warriors who might be in harm's way.

But that wasn't the entire story of what happened to me during my attempted escape and succeeding captivity. There are some pieces I didn't describe in my debriefing. It wasn't to intentionally leave anything out of the official report, but because I either didn't remember or at that time I didn't think they were relevant to what the Navy wanted to know.

I could have inserted them into the account drawn from the debriefing, but I didn't want to interrupt either the flow or the tone. I have made some minor changes to the original transcripts in order to clarify terms that wouldn't be understood by non-Naval aviator readers and to

73

eliminate verbal repetitions. I have also eliminated Brian Kelly's questions for the sake of telling the story.

I was a different person then from who I am today. I was a man just returned from hell and I had a lot of anger stuffed away in my psyche from those eight long years of torture and abuse. I think it's important to keep the debriefing, as I delivered it more than 36 years ago, as true to the original as possible in order to show the warrior, Phil Butler, at that time. So in these following chapters, written in 2009, I attempt to maintain that snapshot of myself.

I was 34 years old, a returning prisoner of war and a man who'd missed eight very important years of my life. I was still very angry and had not yet found any acceptance in my heart for the way my comrades and I had been treated.

I say this to explain some of the language that appears in the succeeding chapters. There is plenty of swearing, appropriate to the circumstances I was relating. And my language was given for the audience of one, my fellow Navy officer and debriefer.

It might be offensive to some readers that I constantly used the word "Gooks" in my debriefing. I thought about changing this writing to another term, but then the narrative wouldn't have given you the true me at that time. My use of that dehumanizing and racist term reflects the intense hate I was still carrying.

Even though we were prisoners in Vietnam we were still fighting the war. This was part of our training and is an essential part of what it means to be an American fighting man. We were dealing with an enemy who considered us criminals, not prisoners of war. This was a completely pragmatic action on their part which they frequently told us gave them the right to treat us any way they wanted.

My behavior towards them in response was hard-lined hostility. We had to maintain this posture in order to prevent the Vietnamese from getting any propaganda value out of us. They constantly intended to use us as a propaganda weapon to fight the war. They believed that propaganda is as important a weapon in war as a bullet, grenade or bomb. And they were absolutely correct because it was their consistent political propaganda, combined with their bravery and tenacity as a people that enabled them to win the Vietnam War.

We POWs were combatants too. If they ever sensed weakness on the part of any POW that guy's fate would be to suffer even more intense pressure for propaganda. We also had to keep up our stiff resistance in order to keep up our morale. We were still warriors, after all, and in the most close up and personal terms. Calling them "Gooks" served to objectify them. It's one necessary piece in the puzzle of getting normally good people to make war and kill each other, the disgusting nature of war.

Some of our early senior officers came up with a powerful motto that helped sustain us through the most difficult times. When you were in an interrogation, harassed, tortured and abused, there was no one else there to watch you perform. So we needed something compelling to keep in mind. That motto was "Return With Honor." It meant that you would need to give it your all, no matter what they were doing to you. This was so that in those days and years that would come after all this was over, you would be able to "look into the mirror every morning while you shaved" and be proud of the guy looking back at you.

1. The Tragedy of Friendly Fire

BOOM! And then my beautiful first life was over forever. Now hell was in session.

As my luck would have it, I was the Navy's first "test pilot" for this Mark-81 "VT" electrically-fused bombing system. The Navy had come up with this new electrical fusing system that was designed to allow the bombs to detonate six feet above the ground, instead of on impact. Mine was probably the first airplane to ever take this new electrical fusing into combat. They briefed me on the carrier about the new devices, that I had a new arming-mechanism box in my cockpit.

But instead of integrating a new bomb with the fusing system that was already built into the airplane, they decided to "jerry-rig" to make use of the bombs they already had. We had literally millions of 250, 500, and 1,000-pound iron bombs that were left over from World War II and Korea. So when the Vietnam air war began they shipped these old surplus bombs out to the aircraft carriers for us to deliver.

My mission was called "road reconnaissance," the intended targets being supply trucks, light armored vehicles and personnel traveling south on Highway 1, the main route down the coast from North to South Vietnam. I was flying wing on Lt. Fred Spellman who had Zuni rockets. My main attitude gyro had gone out on takeoff so I only had limited instruments to fly by that night.

The "test" that night resulted in disaster for me. When I "pickled" the bomb release button I just blew myself right out of the sky. It was instantaneous. My six 250 lb. bombs were set to drop off in "ripple," together. I think what happened was the bombs went off because they ranged in on each other instead of the ground, and they must have detonated prematurely. They were set to detonate six feet above the ground and instead they detonated six feet below me. That's my best guess.

I saw an instantaneous flash of fire warning lights and then all my instrument lights went out and everything went black. I remember seeing red-hot bomb fragments coming up through the floor boards and the side instruments panels. As my brain went into slow motion, they looked like fireflies. The only bomb fragment that actually hit me, and I didn't even know it until I got on the ground, was a piece that came up through the left instrument panel and went into my left hand that had been on the throttle.

Out of my peripheral vision I saw both wings immediately separate as well as obviously the tail empennage of the aircraft. The control stick I was holding in my right hand immediately turned to lead. I was now just in a cockpit that immediately started a forward tumble, at 500 kts, more than 600 mph airspeed.

My head was immediately slammed into the canopy. I had strapped myself in quite loosely, as was my poor habit, prior to taking off on any mission. Luckily I had my gloves on that night but I'll have to say that in looking back had it been warmer weather, I probably would not have. I was pretty lax on those sorts of things. As I started this forward tumble I experienced lots of negative "G" forces, all the blood being pulled toward my head. When I say lots, I mean the most negative Gs I've ever been in. My best guess is that it was somewhere around $3\frac{1}{2}$ to 4 negative Gs. So my head and neck were plastered against the canopy.

I'm six-foot-two and there was no way to get to the face curtain for ejection. I think I remember myself saying into my dead mask, "God this is it." Then another flash went through my mind, "No it's not." My training kicked in and I remembered the auxiliary emergency ejection handle on the seat between my legs. I reached down between my legs, grabbed that beauty and pulled. Then I got a tremendous slam in the butt as the ejection seat rockets fired and punched me out of the cockpit of the aircraft.

Unfortunately my fanny was about six inches away from the seat when it went off. I guess I'm very fortunate that I experienced only compression fractures in my spine and a rupture of one muscle in my back. I was lucky that it didn't break my back. The ejection seat in the A4 was a "Douglas Rapek seat" that gave a rocket assisted, smoother and softer ride. In other words, I only experienced 12 "Gs," 12 times the force of gravity, instead of 18 from some of the other ejection seats of that time.

Bam! I was slammed out into the cold night air. I don't know what altitude but I must have been very low at this point. The next thing I remember was a snap as the ejection seat bladder automatically inflated and threw me away from it. Then there was a snap and jerk as my parachute automatically opened. I remember a sound of rushing air from the chute, meaning it might have been partially shredded from the force of 600 mph wind.

Either it partially shredded or my chute didn't have time to fully deploy, but what chute there was snagged on a canopy of trees and slowed my final descent. They also helped break my fall as I went ripping through a high canopy of trees that that must have been about 100 feet tall. My parachute shroud lines tangled in the trees as I came streaming down, saving my life. When I hit the ground, I hardly had any time to get into a good parachute landing position. I had just barely gotten my legs into position together and knees slightly bent when I hit the ground. I had my seat pack on and it crashed down onto the back of my legs and onto my ankle. I sustained a sprained ankle from this.

Later in the POW camps I found out that several other Navy pilots had been killed because of this same electrical fusing problem before they finally figured it out. At least one other crew I knew of, Commander Jerry Denton and his side seat guy in a Navy 86 light attack aircraft had the same thing happen to them. Their airplane was blown apart, but they survived too. So at least three of us became prisoners of war and several others were probably killed because of this malfunctioning system.

In any event, I was surely a victim of friendly fire. The ugly truth is that in war sometimes as many casualties and deaths come from friendly fire as from enemy fire. It's inevitable, when you get all those people out there in situations of complex coordination with all the dangerous equipment that's required. Then add in the chaos of warfare. No wonder there are so many deaths, casualties and damage from friendly fire.

2. Beefeater Four

I hit the ground and got snapped back up towards my entangled parachute by the nylon shroud lines. There I was, dangling about six feet above the ground. I knew I had to get out of that situation quickly so I unsheathed my survival knife and cut some of the tangled lines. That enabled me to drop to the ground.

My actual arrival in North Vietnam was probably about nine o'clock that night of April 20th. I had landed about 100 yards east of Highway 1. After I hit the ground I could hear horns beeping out on the road. I could look through the brush and actually see trucks. It was a fairly moonlit night and I could see them moving up and down the road. I could also see a lot of excitement amongst the Gooks. No doubt they were looking for me.

The first thing that came to my mind was to just get up and run like hell. However, I quickly found that I was so wound up in parachute lines and briar bushes that I couldn't go anywhere. This helped to settle me down a bit. I figured out that I had to get out of some of this paraphernalia before I could start running. I took out my survival knife and started cutting away the parachute riser cords that had me all tangled up. I got myself free and then got out of the brush. I cut a few risers off, rolled them up and stuck them into my survival kit.

I was wearing a survival vest we had previously prepared in the squadron. I will have to say that I had just about everything in that vest that I had a need for and of course some more too. I stood there in the dark and resisted my first inclination to start running. I knew that wasn't going to do any good. I had to get my bearings. I pulled out my compass and stood still for just a few seconds while I figured out which direction was what. Then I pulled my survival radio out of my seat pack and turned the beeper off. It was making a lot of noise, enough so if there had been someone near they would have heard it and come to investigate. I understood that later on in the war the beepers disconnected upon ejection so they didn't make any noise.

Then I started off in an easterly direction through the brush, thinking about going towards the ocean. Then I remembered a briefing we had received a couple of days before where some Air Force guys came out to the ship and briefed us on rescue and pickup in North Vietnam. They said it was impossible to pick someone up in the Vinh area at this time. They told us we would have to try to make it to Laos and get picked up there. The Navy rescue helicopters couldn't pick us up in the ocean either because the ship didn't have the capability, or was not using their helicopter facilities for pickup of downed pilots at this time.

There was another thing that I had received in a briefing and I can't remember exactly when. But I remember it stuck in my mind that someone had mentioned, probably my intelligence officer, that the North Vietnamese did use German shepherd dogs. They had dog units for tracking down people who went down in North Vietnam. This popped into my mind as I started to head out with all my survival equipment.

I continued trekking on to the east for about 200 yards and stopped. Everything seemed very quiet and it was obvious that no one was coming after me. I walked on and again I stopped and thought for a while about just how I was going to successfully evade capture.

After thinking it over I decided that going toward the water was not going to do me any good. Because when I got to the water, finding a boat would be a tough problem and getting a rescue would be very unlikely. So then I decided to reverse direction and travel west to get into the foothills near the Laotian boarder. From there I could follow them south until I reached a point where I could cross into Laos.

I was thinking of one of the passes through the mountains that led from North Vietnam into Laos. Particularly one pass which was west-southwest of Vinh. So I stopped about 200 yards east of where I'd landed and began to make a plan. I figured that they would probably have dogs after me so I decided as a diversionary maneuver to leave my flight helmet, seat pack and torso harness there. I took the survival items out of the seat pack that I thought I would need and tied them onto me securely. I left my G suit on, which would turn out to be invaluable to have in my trek. I also left my gloves on. Then I started back towards the west, retracing the steps that I first taken, in hopes that if they brought dogs into the area, they would go in my original direction. I was pretty familiar with how dogs operate from hunting with them as a kid in Oklahoma.

I had no thought that anyone except maybe my lead, Fred Spellman, was looking for me. My plane had virtually disintegrated. If he saw it he probably wouldn't have thought I could have survived. Also it was at night so seeing my parachute, which would have been visible only for a few seconds even during the day, was not likely. In fact I later learned that Lieutenant Spellman had returned to the ship and reported that there was not a chance that I could have gotten out of the aircraft. He reported that my aircraft had exploded in the air.

Heading back to the west I got back to my original downed position where the chute was all tangled up in the briar brush. By this time things had settled down on the highway and all I noticed was an occasional truck driving by. I think anyone who was investigating the explosion of my plane had probably gone off looking for the wreckage of the aircraft, wherever that might have been. There were fires in the area that I could see and a number of them were on the highway. I'm pretty sure those fires were from parts of my wrecked aircraft and also from Lieutenant Spellman's rockets.

I started to the west through very heavy brush towards the highway. As I got to the edge of Highway 1 I discovered that it was actually just a dirt road. This was the main supply route from the north to the fighting in the south. The good news was that there were long intervals when no one came by so I was able to just skip across the highway and head west toward safety in Laos.

I walked for two or three hours, until about midnight, without stopping so I could put some distance between me and the crash area. With the initial adrenaline rush finally tapering off, I stopped in heavy brush jungle. Secondary growth I guess you'd call it. I was also beginning to feel some pain in various parts of my body. One of the more painful was my hand. I got my flashlight out, took off my gloves, and that's when I found that I'd taken a piece of flack. I took out my survival pocket knife and dug a piece of metal out of the palm of my hand. It was an inch-long sliver about a quarter of an inch wide and maybe a 32nd of an inch thick. I rubbed some sulfa powder into the wound.

I got out a bandage and had this moment of humor when I started unrolling it and discovered that it was long enough to reach from there to New York City. I wrapped my hand up in it and then put my glove back on. After digging around in my survival kit a little bit more, I came up with some tetracycline pills and gobbled a couple of those down to prevent any infection. While digging I saw some little pills that said "malaria." I thought that was probably a good thing to avoid getting so I took one of those too.

I started out again and I hadn't gone for another thirty minutes or so when I had to stop. I don't know if it was the malaria medicine I had taken for the first time or just the excitement and fear that I was experiencing, but I found a likely spot and released a wild case of diarrhea. Anyway I think that would be a normal thing for a guy to expect almost right off the bat after he's gone down into hostile territory.

Then at this place I took my large survival knife and dug a hole in the ground, probably about 8 to 10 inches deep, and I buried all the kneeboard cards I was carrying in my G-suit. These were Marshall (aircraft recovery) flight patterns, radio frequencies and other pilot information that we carried with us on missions. There was also a set of classified-secret authenticator cards and some other stuff that I realized I didn't need.

I buried them in the ground, pushed brush back over them again and went on my way. I wasn't using my flashlight because there was bright moonlight that night. Using my compass, I knew I was heading northwest. My ankle was sore. I had bound it and though it was painful it wasn't hampering me. This first night I did quite a bit of zigzagging around, fighting the brush, and running into a blind alley or two where I discovered that it was better to retrace my steps and go around. I covered probably ten miles, traveling on until about 3:30 or 4 o'clock in the morning when I found a good spot atop a little knoll where I could stop.

I settled down on this wooded knoll which afforded good protection because not only was I covered but I could see in all different directions. As daybreak began, I would say about 5:15, I was hidden in the brush. Then suddenly I heard something. It was very strange sounding music; like a woman chanting. Later I was to learn this music was from a North Vietnamese radio station, being broadcast over loudspeakers. These speakers exist throughout the country at an interval of I'd say no more than a half-mile.

I later learned this was part of the incredible control system the government had over the people. They'd start off their mornings with an exercise recording. First there was this kind of Vietnamese sing-song music and then this woman came on and kept up a count for people to exercise by. And everyone in North Vietnam got up at 5:15 in the morning and was supposed to do their three or four minutes of exercises. Following the exercises, Vietnamese music came back on.

It sounded really weird to me, especially that first morning since I had no idea what it was. At first I didn't know whether I was hearing things, maybe hallucinating because of the drugs I'd taken. It would have been useful to know about that in advance from an intelligence briefing. I'm sure that somebody, somewhere in our intelligence network must have known that this kind of a thing existed in North Vietnam. This was just the sort of thing about the daily life of people that would have been nice to know. It would have removed a little of the unknown, making less to be fearful of as I went through my effort to escape.

As the music played I peered out from my hidden position in the brush. Much to my surprise, and chagrin, I could see that my little knoll was located right smack dab in the middle of two enormous communes. These are big farms that are communally farmed by many families. There were rice paddies some fifty feet below me, and lots of other crops being grown, too.

Right off the bat, about six in the morning, people began to come out and go about their work in the fields. I was pretty scared thinking that they'd be coming after me but much to my surprise, and delight, it seemed everyone was more or less going about their daily work without regard for any unusual incident in the area. I was about ten miles from the crash site and I figured they were not on my trail right at this moment. These people were just peaceful and matter-of-fact as they went about their work.

I watched them there for awhile, and then I slept. It was the sort of in and out sleeping, not the deep kind, but the superficial kind when you are excited or alert. About three in the afternoon I woke up from a doze and was incredibly thirsty. I realized that the only thing I was missing in my survival gear was water. Given my circumstances, I would say that there were a lot of things in my seat pack that could have been eliminated in favor of putting some water in. A couple of the right things in the pack were a headdress-type of mosquito net which I had put on, and a little ground poncho which I had laid out and was sleeping on. I took off my survival vest and used that for a pillow. I kept my gloves on tight and tucked into my sleeves.

I was wearing dungarees instead of a flight suit which turned out to be very handy. Another thought for my debriefing was that a flight suit is not the best clothing to try to run around the woods in. It's baggy and when you have to relieve yourself it requires some gymnastics. If you are in a hurry to do these things, it's really much easier to have on a pair of conventional pants and a shirt, both of tough material so they and you don't get all cut up climbing through brambles.

I also had some mosquito repellant in my kit. This was the government issue stuff; a dark brown liquid that actually seemed to attract more bugs, as far as I could tell. It was worthless. That said I don't know that you're going to find an anti-bug preparation that's going to do the job in the jungle. The only thing that's going to keep the bugs and mosquitoes off is protective clothing and the mosquito net.

Whether I woke up because I was so thirsty, or because I heard the roar of propeller driven aircraft overhead, I'm not sure, but airplanes overhead certainly got my attention. I looked up and my heart leapt into my throat as I saw two "Spads," propeller driven A1s, grinding along at about

6,000 feet. As soon as they came into view and hearing, the people in the fields made it into the brush at the edge of the fields. It looked like the planes were zigzagging, doing reconnaissance in the area. They would bend one way then turn back toward us. Then they'd bend the other way and again turn back straight for us.

They flew right overhead of me. Of course as soon as I heard the engines I had torn into my survival pack for my radio, pulled the antennae out, turned it on, and started talking my head off. I couldn't be sure, but it seemed from the way the radio was operating that my voice was transmitting okay. I kept calling to these aircraft as they flew right overhead, repeating my call sign, "Mayday, mayday, this is Beefeater Four, downed Navy pilot Phillip Butler." But I received nothing back in return.

Finally, as they were overhead and continuing on with no sign of recognition, I asked them to make turns if they heard me. But they made no turns. Maybe they didn't hear me because of my radio. And there's also the possibility that since the A1 has a very loud engine and as my radio call was probably weak they just couldn't hear me over the engine noise.

There is also the possibility that they weren't listening for me, given what happened to my plane. At any rate, I didn't get anything out of them. It was to be one of the first of many great disappointments in my life in North Vietnam. I sat there on the ground and watched them tool off into the blue. I pushed my things around there and made my bed a little more comfortable, lay back down again and tried to get some sleep.

As the day wore on, it got extremely hot. I unbuttoned my shirt, lay back in the shade and fanned myself. I was getting extremely thirsty. I learned that after a really scary or dangerous experience you are always very thirsty. I don't know exactly what the reason for this is, but it is a fact. Also during my trek the night before, I had used up a hell of a lot of my body water and I was perspiring a great deal because it was hot.

The day wore on until the late afternoon when the people began to leave the fields. I was alone again on my little knoll. Of course the only thing I had in my mind at that point was to find some water. It got dark around 7:00 and I noticed there were still people moving around. It wasn't until after nine that I saw there was no one around. The radio I'd heard going all day, the people talking in Vietnamese and the music, shut off about 9:30. When the radio shut off so did the people. It was real quiet.

I had my map out and I'd been making my plans for where to go that night. I decided that now I had to move west and south. I was going to try to follow the foothills until I got south of Vinh. As I started moving out

84

that night I went down that hill and stepped out onto the commune. I was careful to stay up on the banks of dikes and not get into the paddies or into the fields. There was soft dirt in the paddies and fields, and I thought if I stepped into a wrong spot I might sink right out of sight. Then there was the issue of leaving footprints. My size eleven boot prints just wouldn't match up to a size five, barefoot print that someone there made. So I tried to stay on hard ground and move on the dikes.

I traveled along for about an hour or so before I finally stumbled into a ditch. This ditch had some murky looking water in it. I looked at that water. I remembered all the lectures I'd had about amoebic dysentery, cholera, all that other bad stuff, and I then thought about how thirsty I was. I also recalled learning that a person could die from heat exhaustion if he doesn't get enough water to drink. So I figured I'd better get a drink.

At the edge of the stream, about half submerged in the water, I found a long piece of bamboo that someone had fashioned into something useful. It was about three feet tall and five inches in diameter with a handle carved on it. It was obviously designed to carry water and I had no idea why but it looked like somebody hadn't wanted it and had just pitched it into the water.

It looked like a pretty useful little apparatus. It certainly held a lot more water than the in-flight pee bags we were supposed to use for water in an emergency. I had a half-dozen of these bags. I took the big bamboo water carrying tube, filled it up with water, and dropped three or four of my water purification tablets in it. Then I capped it off with my hand and gave it a good shaking. According to the instructions on the bottle of pills, I was supposed to wait thirty minutes. I waited about fifteen; I was too thirsty. My thirst conquered my worry that I needed to wait the full half-hour.

I downed the whole tube right then and there. Then I filled up some of my little "relief" bags with more water, tied them up with the parachute cord, and then tied them to my survival vest. Then I refilled the tube, added some purification tablets, and strapped it to my back with more of the parachute cord.

With a full load of water, I was ready to move on again. I headed off toward the south-southwest. I traveled for about an hour or so and then came out of the brush into a clearing. In the moonlight, I saw what appeared to be a low shed, an unusual structure. It was maybe six feet wide and five feet high and it had no walls, just a roof. What was most unusual about it was that it stretched for what looked like a half a mile. There was a little barbed wire fence that surrounded this hut. I looked to my right and could see one end of the shed fifty feet away. When I looked down to my left, even with the moonlight, I couldn't see the other end.

Curiosity got the better of me and I stepped over the low barbed wire fence to check it out further. Of course I was looking around to make sure nobody was in the area watching, keeping myself low on my hands and knees. The place was deserted. When I got closer to the shed I could see that it was divided into stalls, probably three feet wide. Every single stall had a little wagon in it.

However long this shed was, divided by three feet, it had a huge number of wagons and that meant this was an enormous commune. I realized, too, that I was standing in the middle of it. The sheer size of the place was intimidating. There obviously were a lot of people living on that commune and I suddenly wanted to get as far away from there as I could in a hurry. I retraced my steps, got over the barbed wire, and hustled my ass away from there.

I traveled on for probably 30 minutes and stumbled onto a little road; actually, it was smaller, more the size of a footpath. I'd remembered from my survival training and from briefings on the ship that you want to stay away from roads and paths when you were trying to evade capture.

That was what they told us. But from my experience the opposite was true. The fact was I had to move on a path because the brush was too thick to penetrate. It would take an hour just to go 75 yards through the thick brush. The undergrowth was unbelievable and in this part of North Vietnam they had these thick vines running all around and up to about waist high. Worse, they had sharp inch-long thorns – more like spikes – that could puncture light clothing. Plus, these vines were so strong I couldn't pull away from them. The only thing I could do was try to cut myself loose. I was very glad that I had my survival knife, but I wish I had known not to waste my energy trying to cut my way through the jungle.

There was also the matter of cutting a path so if someone was trying to find me I was making it very easy for them. Even if they didn't find me, it would take me decades to get to Laos. So when I found this little road-type path, I was relieved. The fact that there was nobody around firmed up my conviction. I found that my perception was right, that between 10:30 at night and 4:30 in the morning I could just about go anywhere and do anything that I wanted to unnoticed.

I was so pleased to find this path. And I was so anxious to get to a safe haven that I started to dog trot. The path was going in the right direction for a while and then when it stopped heading where I wanted I would get off. Then I'd go a short distance through the brush until I came across another path. It made sense that people who had been living in the area for centuries couldn't have gotten through the brush either, so they made this network of paths and small roads.

That night, because I was able to dog trot along pathways, I made close to 20 miles. Though I had my compass, I was mainly navigating by the stars and moon. About 4:30 the sky was starting to lighten and it looked like daybreak was not far away.

I came upon a small footbridge over a stream, crossed over it and on the other side descended the bank to the stream and stepped in. It was shallow and I walked along in the stream bed. There was a solid sheet of jungle on either side of the stream. I walked about a hundred yards when I came to a place where I thought I might hide during the day.

I climbed through about 25 feet of brush there and found a spot to sleep. I made myself a bed on the ground with my poncho and got out my mosquito net headdress. I lay down and was really pooped. I immediately went to sleep.

This was something that should have been emphasized in the survival training, that you never travel during the day when you are going through enemy territory. Especially in such a high-density population area, you do not move anywhere during the day. Any movement will be detected by someone in North Vietnam during the day. My only chance of escape was to travel during the night.

Sometime that morning I woke up to a loud screeching, wailing, crying sound that just seemed to penetrate my eardrums. It was a startling way to wake up. I almost jumped up from where I was, thinking I must be surrounded. When my eyes focused I saw a wild, jungle parrot about 15 feet above me. This bird was a foot or so tall. He had a really bright plumage — reds, greens and iridescent colors.

I guess he was just giving me hell for breakfast. I had invaded his territory and he was standing up there calling me everything he knew how to call me. I was amazed as I watched and listened to his vocabulary and repertoire of noises. He obviously had picked up every sound he had ever heard in the jungle and every sound he had ever heard from a human being.

I continued to sit there and watch him with amazement for about five or ten minutes until I started getting sick of him. He was driving me out of my gourd. So I picked up a few pebbles and tossed them up at him. That didn't seem to do any good at all. He'd either ignore them or when they'd come close enough to him, he would just jump to another branch and continue his rebuke of me. This went on for about thirty minutes before he finally got tired of it all and whistled off into the day. As I lay there it began to get hot and I drank some water from the bags that I carried. I lay back down again and went to sleep.

This time I really went to sleep, not waking up until maybe noontime. I had been sleeping soundly and I woke up to sounds coming from upstream. I was able see through the brush to the stream about 30 or 40 feet away where there was some motion. From the sounds I thought it was children coming downstream, but as they came closer these "children" came into view through the foliage. They were two men.

They had on short pants, no shirts, were barefoot and they each had a bamboo pole about ten feet long. Slung over their backs they had what appeared to be potato sacks. And as they were walking along in this little shallow stream, they would occasionally beat the stream with their bamboo poles. I watched this in amazement. For a minute I couldn't figure out what they were doing until finally one of the guys yelled, jumped over to where he had just beat his pole down and picked up a little fish that he had hit.

I knew then that fish had to be very plentiful in that stream if they could just walk along with a bamboo pole and knock them in the head. I had fishing gear in my survival pack and if the fish were that plentiful, I was going to be able to feed myself. Fishing would wait a couple of days though. I was going to try to make as much time and distance as I could from my original down point. But it was nonetheless an encouraging sight.

I was lying on my side, my head propped up on my right hand, peering down towards my feet as these two men made their way some 20 or 25 feet away from me. I was well camouflaged and they couldn't see me. But as I lay there and watched these guys, I suddenly had that feeling somebody or something was watching me. If you've never had the experience, it's unique. It's something you often learn when hunting. You never forget it. You also learn that it's probably more than just a feeling.

At that moment, my focus was down the length of my body toward the stream and the men I could see fishing. For some reason I didn't move my body. I just shifted my eyes so that I was looking straight ahead of me. That's when I saw a huge king cobra. Its face was about eight inches away from my face. He was coiled right there in front of me and he had his hood spread. His tongue was darting in and out. He was smelling me and trying to figure out what I was.

I was scared stiff but that was probably a good thing. There was no way I could have moved and he wouldn't have struck me. At that distance he couldn't have missed. The chance of surviving a cobra bite was less than if I had stayed in my plane. Even if there had been room to move, the ruckus I would have made would have alerted the men in the stream and for sure I would have been captured. I didn't really have an option. I had been still and I remained that way, frozen right there in my position. I maintained an eye-to-eye stare with the king cobra until finally, after what seemed like an eternity and probably was no more than ten seconds, he folded his hood in, dropped his head to the ground and started to move away from me.

He rolled away down the length of my body and as his head got down to about where my feet were he made a turn away from the stream. When he made his turn, with his head down around my feet his tail was passing by my head. I would estimate that he was probably a typical cobra you'd find in Vietnam, some seven or eight feet in length and his body was probably an inch and a half in diameter.

The cobra and the two Gooks who were beating the stream left, and suddenly all the gas went out of me. The first thing I had to do again was take another big shit. I guess that's where the expression comes from. I literally had it scared out of me. When I was done I bedded back down again but it took another 30 minutes before I got my heart back to a normal beat and managed to go to sleep. I slept without further incident until about dark.

That day I was looking around for my big sheath survival knife when I discovered that I had lost it somewhere along the trail the night before. And that was truly a foolish thing to do. It stuck in my mind that it is very important for someone who falls into these circumstances to not make such a mistake. One thing you must remember to do in an evasion situation is to inventory all your equipment and make sure you don't lose what you may need. It can mean your life. For goodness sake, tie everything to you and be attentive. Don't lose it on the way.

As luck would have it, I had a survival pocket knife so I had some back-up. However it was not nearly as good as the big sheath knife for cutting vines and otherwise making a path when I needed to.

I slept there until nightfall and then worked my way down to the stream. I refilled my relief bags and my bamboo water tube. I returned to my "campground" where my poncho and my other gear was, sat down, got my map out and did my navigation work with my penlight flashlight based on where I'd been the night before. Then I found a tree branch with a fork and cut it down. Now by damn I had a snake stick like the ones we used to make in Oklahoma, only this one had a fork big enough to stop an elephant if need be.

About eleven o'clock or so I was really feeling grubby. Not only grubby, but low. My morale was low because I hadn't seen an airplane and it was beginning to look like there wasn't any chance of being picked up. I decided I had to do something to improve my morale just a little bit. So I got into my survival kit and took out my shaving gear, my toothpaste and toothbrush, my soap, and my little washcloth. I rolled up my sleeves, took out my little mirror, penlight and made myself comfortable on the bank of the stream. I brushed my teeth, washed my face and hands with soap, and shaved.

When I finished doing that I felt like a million dollars. It was a tremendous morale boost and very refreshing. I think this is basic psychology, just feeling good about yourself. Sometimes if you can't feel good about your circumstances, you can raise your spirits by fixing another part of you like your appearance, or how you feel. It's very important for people who are in stressful situation like I was, alone in enemy territory, hundreds of miles from any possibility of rescue. Pay attention to your physical well being and to your morale. It will help your performance.

After I'd shaved and shined I put my gear back together, found myself a pathway and got into the dog trot again. I started heading to the south-southwest and then to the south through most of that night. My progress was almost completely uninterrupted except when I would come to streams. When I'd come to a stream I'd make a diversion for dogs by going down or up the stream, then out for a few steps, then retracing my steps back into the stream and going the opposite direction down or upstream before coming out again. I did this in streams probably a half dozen times during my trek to throw off dogs.

On the third day I found a place to hide near the pathway I had been traveling on. I was really exhausted but was careful to cover myself with brush after putting my poncho down to sleep on. I hadn't slept more than an hour when I heard a noise coming towards me. I froze there in the brush and almost got stepped on by a water buffalo. A small kid was herding his family water buffalo along the path and in my exhausted state I hadn't realized that I was only a few feet from the path. Neither of them saw me so I got away with it.

The next night I made really good time and passed Vinh City. At times I could look from ridge lines to see the lights of the city as I passed by a couple of miles to the west. The moon had been a good friend of mine

90

during all of these nights of travel. It had come up on the first night, damn near full, and lasted the whole night. But with each new night it became less full and shone less of the night. I lost about an hour of moonlight each night at the beginning of my travel time.

Moonlight was really valuable because the batteries in my flashlight began to poop out in no time at all. I had a normal sized flashlight plus I had one little pen light. The pen light was great because it enabled me to use a minimal amount of light to check my compass, watch, or my map. The big light wasn't much good except to size up a bad obstacle of some kind that I had to get around. It might have been a big rock or bunch of brush that I couldn't make out in the darkness.

I moved on past Vinh City and came to a big river. It flows in from the hills northwest of Vinh, runs across to the south of Vinh and then out to the ocean. I knew I would come to that river and I had planned that I would come to it towards the end of this night.

But I didn't know how in the hell I was going get across it because I had always been told there are lots of people around rivers. You don't want to try to swim, because you might get in trouble and drown doing that. It is also a likely place to find guards looking for people to cross the river.

I came to a place on the pathway that led to a house located next to the river. I moved away from the house. I could see the river in the moonlight. It was probably 150 yards wide. I walked down and suddenly I saw a levee that went across the river. I climbed up on the levee and simply walked right across the river, like anybody else would, although they wouldn't be doing it as I was in the middle of the night.

Once across the river I walked no more than a couple of hundred yards where I found a stand of trees. This stand of trees was located between two large communes. It was approximately 150 yards in diameter and looked like it would be a good place to hide. I walked to it and checked it out briefly, then went back to the river and started to fill my, my relief bags and bamboo water tube which were now empty after a night of walking. Also I had not had a drink in quite a while.

When I looked up the river I noticed some activity was beginning probably half a mile away. I could see people moving around. I wasn't seen because the distance was too great but I didn't want to press my luck. I decided I didn't have time to stick around so I went on back to the stand of trees. I cut my way through the secondary brush and when I got inside I discovered a 50-foot clearing in the center.

A small overgrown path led out of the clearing. I followed the pathway to the outside edge. This stand of trees was shaped like a doughnut with the clearing being the doughnut hole. It looked like a pretty good place to hide out the coming day. So I went back inside where it appeared to be safe because it was completely hidden from view from the outside.

I built myself a bed there with the ground cloth. Then I lay down to take a nap. About three hours later I woke up. It was very, very hot. I was on my back and when I opened my eyes, and looked above me, the seemed to start spinning around. I was very dizzy, like being reeling drunk. I knew immediately that I was dangerously dehydrated. I felt sick to my stomach. I could feel the heat and the air was very still in there because there was no breeze. I got up and crawled towards the clearing area and lay down in the grass in the center.

It was a little cooler there and I immediately felt a little bit better. But I also noticed that I was very weak. I had made a big mistake. I had not procured enough water that night. I had pushed myself on until almost daybreak without any more water, thinking I would get some before I found a place to sleep. And that was a mistake. I should have maintained full water containers as I traveled rather than let them run out.

So now I was faced with going through this entire day without any water. That wouldn't normally have been too bad, just uncomfortable, except that it was the very beginning of the day with the heat yet to come. And I was already dehydrated, weak and dizzy. I managed to get back to sleep and it was probably early afternoon when I awoke again.

What woke me was the sound of screaming jet engines. As I looked up I was looking right down the snout of an F105 that had rolled in on me. Actually, it had not rolled in on me but on a target near the river, on my side of the river. It was a flight of four and what they were after was probably no more than 100-150 yards away from me. As I opened my eyes and saw this guy coming down the chute, I saw bright flashes start from the nose area and the next sound that greeted me was the ferocious "whoom" sound of Gatling guns going off. It was very scary until I realized they weren't shooting at me. But that realization didn't hit me until the shells began to explode some distance away. It was close enough that I could feel the ground shaking and rocking with the impact of all those 20mm, high-explosive bullets. By the time the next guy started to roll in I had my radio in my hand and, calmly and coolly, I started screaming my head off at these guys to stop shooting. I didn't think the radio would work because it hadn't before. Sometimes you do things you know won't have any effect just because you have to do something.

But it seems I was heard, because the number two man was coming down the chute just as I started screaming into the radio. He immediately went into the weirdest dive that one could imagine. I must have yelled so loud I could have broken his eardrums on guard (emergency) channel. His airplane practically went out of control. He pulled out of his attack dive and then the four planes went into a circular orbit above me.

I got hold of myself a little bit better and started telling them who I was, "This is Beefeater 4, downed Navy pilot off the USS Midway, name Phillip Butler." I asked them to roger my messages if they could hear me but I couldn't hear any response on my radio. Then I stumbled on the bright idea of asking them to light their afterburners if they read me. The first time I asked them was for one afterburner if they read me. But they probably gave me fifty burner lights. These guys were just banging afterburners on and off as fast as they could.

It was exhilarating. I finally had contacted friendly forces. I told these guys I had gone down four days previous and they "rogered" after every message with an afterburner. I told them my intention was to head for Laos from my present position. I gave them the track that I was going to take and the position where I planned to hole up the next night.

I told them my condition was still good and that I thought I would be able to make it in about three days. They kept rogering by giving me lots of burner lights but finally they had to go home. I made a final call to them, saying "Thanks a lot guys. I'll see you around." Then the flight leader got his wingmen joined up and they gave me the saddest, slowest wing wobble you can imagine as they tooled off into the distance. Boy I sure wished for some kind of magic skyhook that day, to pick me up and take me with them. But as fate would have it, I was never going to "see them around."

After that excitement, I guess adrenaline had caused me to perspire a lot more. Now I began to really get dehydrated. I felt sick, probably suffering from heat exhaustion. I even started to feel a little delirious. I noticed that my thoughts were disjointed. I would go from one subject to another, skipping around and things were starting to not make much sense. The trees seemed to sort of swim in front of my eyes. I knew I was in pretty bad trouble. So I went back to sleep, thinking I was better off that way until night when I could get some water.

I was in and out of sleep there for probably a couple of hours when I heard noises outside the stand of trees. It sounded like a whole lot of people running in a large group. Then I figured the Gooks had finally caught up with me and they were on my trail. I crawled up to the little pathway that led to the outside of the stand of trees. I crouched down behind this bush from where I could look up the pathway. My thinking wasn't very clear. I pulled out my personal sidearm 9mm German Luger pistol, cocked the first shell home, pointed it down the pathway and waited for them to come.

I knew for sure that it was a bunch of people after me. I could hear them coming around the bend and then I could hear them thundering down the pathway. I was determined in my muddled mind that I wasn't going to be captured, that I was going to shoot it out with them. As I sat there with my pistol pointed down the pathway, a black shape suddenly came over the top of the bush. I hadn't seen it coming down the path. I didn't know where it came from, maybe off from the side somehow. In any event, it was in mid-air before I saw it.

It was a German shepherd. It was small for the breed, probably a 50 pound bitch. She came over the top of the bush and in a flash she had my gun hand. The gun went flying out of my hand, off to one side, and she pulled me around and pinned me to the ground. She pinned my gun hand to the ground. I scrambled around with my left hand and just about had her by the scruff of her neck when another German shepherd came running down the pathway and grabbed that hand. Together they pinned me to the ground.

Now both these dogs, each one holding me by a wrist, had me literally spread-eagled to the ground. They were really well-trained. They didn't tear meat off my arms. All I got were some scratches and bruises where they held me. But they held me like a vise and I was pinned to the ground. Within a second or two, the lead guy in the group of my human captors came roaring down the pathway. From his uniform insignia I could see he was a North Vietnamese regular army lieutenant.

He had a Browning automatic rifle in his hand. He came running up the pathway and stopped about ten feet in front of me as I was spread eagled on the ground by those dogs. His eyes were as big as saucers. He stopped, looked at me with those saucer-like eyes, and I guess before he even knew what he was doing he pointed that automatic gun at me and started firing.

He sent a spray of bullets at me with an automatic weapon from a distance of ten feet away, and he missed. It was incredible, impossible to believe, but somehow he missed me. The bullets started hitting the ground just below my feet. They traveled up my right side, the bullets skipping over my arm as they passed up the side of my body. I don't know how he managed to miss me but he did. Evidently he was so panicked he lost it.

After he fired off that last bullet, I guess he got a little better control of himself. And the other people were now ganging up behind him. He tossed the weapon aside and with the other people there, they just leaped on me like a big "tackle the man with the ball" contest. They all jumped on me and pretty soon another guy showed up who was the dog handler and he got the dogs to let loose of my arms.

My captors immediately stripped everything off me. I felt like a walking dime store during a sale. They took my watch, survival equipment and all my clothes down to my shorts. They left my boots on me. I don't know why but that was a lucky thing. Normally, I learned later, they take your boots and socks as well and leave you barefoot.

And there I was. Surrounded by the one regular officer, several militia guys and about 40 peasants, I was a "had Dad." I was a captured American officer in enemy North Vietnam.

3. Beginning the Long Nightmare

The only regular army officer or army person in the bunch was the second lieutenant and he was leading the search. There were anywhere from four to six militia men and probably 40 or 50 peasant villagers. Most of them were without shoes, dressed in rags and had weapons that amounted to farm implements, machetes and things like that.

They stripped me down and had me sit right there while a couple of them held guns on me and so forth and they jabbered amongst themselves. I could see they were pretty proud of what they'd caught. I knew at that minute from the way they were acting they weren't going to bump me off. It was quite apparent to me that they had themselves a prize and they were going to keep me in good condition.

The officer tried to talk to me in French. Now at that time I didn't speak any French. Even if I had, I wouldn't have talked with him anyway. But he did say something in French that I recognized. And that was something I was interested in – water. And I told him yes, I damn sure did want some water to drink. So he nodded his head and said okay. And we just sat there and waited for awhile, with all the people sitting around watching and I guess they'd sent runners off to the local village to report they had caught me.

While we were waiting, the guy that had the dogs had them sitting off to one side and he had a big grin on his face; He came to me and handed me my hard hat. I had taken off my hard hat back where I was shot down. Then I went 100 yards east of where I shot down and then retraced my steps. That hat is what they'd used to track me down. The dogs had used it for my scent. They had been after me for four days and nights.

So I knew from that they had actually been tracking me and were probably having a little trouble tracking me because I was making pretty good time and also because I had created a few diversions on the way by walking in the streams.

At any rate, they had caught me. A little while later as we were sitting there in the center of this stand of trees, a guy came in with a camera and had me stand up. They put a couple of villagers beside me and then snapped some pictures. Then they had me sit back down again and they brought a few people in to look at me.

This was my first close up look at what Vietnamese people looked like.

96

I had never been in South Vietnam or anywhere in Southeast Asia except the Philippines. I guess it was interesting to see what they looked like, but not really at the moment. They were certainly very poor. They were in rags and didn't have anything. It was pretty understandable to me at that moment why they were so anxious to get my survival pack and all the goodies that were in it. They were carefully dividing up all my fishhooks, knives and other stuff that they could find in my gear.

Pretty soon a gal came in and she had a big water bottle with her. The officer told her to go over and hand it to me which she did. I guess this water bottle probably held a couple of quarts of water. I started drinking this stuff and the first thing that surprised me was that it was warm. But I didn't let that bother me too much. The other thing was that it was real sweet. They had not only given me water but this stuff had sugar in it. It damn near made me sick because at this point I was so thirsty and dehydrated. But I drank it anyway.

When I finished I nodded my head to the guy and he nodded his head back while we continued to sit there. He asked me again if I was thirsty and I said, "Yes, I was." And pretty soon he ran and brought another water bottle back in for me. I guess I had a couple of these.

It started to get dark and that is obviously what they were waiting for. Then they began to move me out. They let me put my pants, shirt and boots back on and they tied my hands behind me. A bunch of guys walked beside me carrying guns and whatnot. We went out of the stand of trees and started across the rice paddies to a little village.

As we were making our way along there were people all over the place. It looked like they had come from miles around to see what I looked like. These people just looked curious more than anything else. They didn't really seem to display a lot of hatred. As we came to the little village, I noticed a sort of meeting hall there and they took me into this room. It was a dirt floor place and there was a desk in the center of the room, a light bulb hanging down from the ceiling and a big picture of a guy I'll probably never forget for the rest of my life, old "Uncle Ho" (Ho Chi Minh.)

They had me sit down on a little stool while they ran around and gobbled and cackled and I guess made arrangements to do all sorts of things. I just sat there. Pretty soon they came in and got me again and took me out of the meeting hall, down through this little village and into somebody's home. It was a dirt floor home and had little wooden beds. They had me sit on one of these beds and the guy wanted me to take my shoes off so I took my boots off.

There were a bunch of people in the room watching me. They brought a meal in to me. I couldn't believe it when I saw this meal. It must have been enough for about sixteen men. Boy they were really putting on the dog. There were all different foods: rice fixed different ways and pieces of meat cooked up in little baked dishes. It was all weird looking to me.

I got quite a surprise because with the first bite of the stuff I tasted I noticed it was extremely highly seasoned. It was hot enough to knock your head off. And I really couldn't eat it. They gave me some tea and I drank the tea down. That tasted pretty good. But I was not hungry and ate little of the food.

Pretty soon they took away the food and I just sat for a little while. Then they all got up and told me to put my shoes back on and we moved outside into the village. For the record, it seems like I must have been captured about 5 o'clock in the afternoon. As for location, it was just south of the river that I had just crossed. This little village was probably six hundred yards east of the clearing where I'd hidden that day. I would place the village about ten miles southwest of Vinh.

I left the house and was taken out into the dirt road that led through the center of this village. And here my memory doesn't serve me too well because I was still in the state of extreme heat exhaustion and probably quite a bit of shock too from being captured. As best I can remember I probably went through four different villages or it might have been five. We went out into the street of the first village, where I was taken when I was captured, and walked some fifty yards or so to an outdoor meeting place. There was a table set up with an electric light bulb hung up on a wire above it out on a sort of green, lawn area.

As we approached this area I could see several hundred people in a ring, a very close ring around this table and light. I was led up to this area by the guards with guns. As I began to walk towards the crowd the people were standing there with a lifeless Asian Communist look. There was no emotion whatsoever. They were just watching me. Perhaps some of them were a little curious.

Then several men and several women in the crowd, with red arm bands around their arms, started shaking their fists in the air and yelling out a chant. Immediately the people picked it up and as soon as they did they became enraged. These leaders with the red arm bands are known in North Vietnam as cadres, from the French word, meaning the framework of the Communist party. They are the framework of the social life and existence of the people.

They are the members of the Vietnam Workers Party and they are spread throughout North Vietnam into all the little villages to try to bring the people around to Communist ideology. When they started their chant they got the people all whipped up into hate and anger. As I walked into the crowd a number of people tried to run up and hit me or throw rocks at me, etc. However the guards were ganged close around me and they mostly prevented the people from attacking me. I was hit a few times by people in the crowd but not anything serious, not anything that really caused much pain nor left any marks on my body.

One young guy, probably about 25 years old, somehow or other got by the guards. He ran up to me. He had a flashlight in his hand. He rapped me on the noggin with his flashlight. When this happened the guards stopped and while several of them kept control over me three others ran into the crowd after him. They caught him, threw him down on the ground, and beat the hell out of him right there on the spot.

The rest of the people just stood around and watched this action. And when it was over those guards came back with me and we proceeded on up to the little table. They stood me out in front of this table and led more chanting and yelling at me for about five minutes or so. Then one of the political cadres got up and made a speech. Then all the people started chanting and yelling again.

Then just as suddenly as it started, the cadres held their hands up and it was turned off; like you turn off a water faucet. Then we left that area and we walked down to the road again. But this time a truck was there. They put me in the back of this truck, all the time my hands were tied behind me. Several of the guards got into the truck with me and we traveled down the road for probably a thousand yards or so to the next little village.

Then this same thing happened in each village. I would be brought to the town meeting hall or to the town green area where they give their propaganda speeches. It's where they also probably showed their movies. They have little movie trucks that go about the country. I learned that later.

The show was the same in each village. I was a one-man side show. I call it my one-man circus act. I learned that almost every guy who was shot down experienced something similar. We were props in a nationwide propaganda campaign. As the war lengthened American captives were displayed on tours that might literally take weeks and months before they finally arrived in Hanoi. Of course they couldn't do it without cadres to whip up the hatred.

The people who had captured me didn't seem interested in finding out anything from me. I was never interrogated. There was also the issue of none of them speaking English. The program simply called for me to be brought into each village, be fed, given tea, maybe a cigarette, and then brought out for the citizenry to be exhorted to hate me and express their support for the government.

I was bound loosely with my arms behind my back at this time. I was not blindfolded nor were my feet tied. It was not unduly uncomfortable. However let me state again that later in the war, as the suffering increased for the people in Vietnam, the Americans who were captured were treated much more harshly. Some guys were bound up very tightly and blindfolded. And in a truck this can be torture in itself, having the circulation cut off while bouncing around in the back of a truck. There was no padding in their trucks and the roads are very rough. Guys were badly beaten up just from riding in the back of a truck while being tied up.

This all took place, traveling through the four or five villages, over just a matter of hours. And this was in the middle of the night, probably 10 o'clock at night until 3 o'clock in the morning is my guess. At this point they really weren't taking me anywhere. They were just showing me off in the local area. I'd been captured in that local area and they were just driving me around to all the little villages, showing me off to the people. It seems that they were trying to whip up the spirits amongst the people, resistance for fighting the war, by showing everybody what a bad guy I was.

To these Asians, you look like a bad guy. You're a hell of a lot bigger than they are. And I had a real short butch haircut that all the guys on the ship were wearing at that time because of perspiring in the heat while flying with a helmet. I looked pretty much like a mean old ogre, and they were showing me off to be that. It reminded me of the World War II posters and how they depicted Hitler, Mussolini and Tojo. I was the ugly enemy.

Finally, after going through this they put me on another truck and we headed toward Vinh. When they put me in this truck, I discovered I was sitting on a bunch of machinery of some kind. In the dark I felt around and discovered this machinery was two twenty millimeter cannons. One of the guards riding in the back with me smiled and pointed to me and then to the two 20 mm cannons. Evidently they were the two guns they had recovered from what was left of my airplane.

It was very common for them to do this. They used the 20 mm guns for their own antiaircraft weapons. They set them up on tripods and used them against our aircraft. They used every kind of gun that they could get their hands on, and effectively too I might say. The most effective defense against aircraft is to just put up a barrage of lead in the air. That's the way those people fought their air war. They would just fill the sky full of lead and you'd have to fly through it.

While we proceeded on to Vinh, my guess was that I was eventually going to be transported to Hanoi. I had not been told what I might expect since it was so early in the war. I was only the seventh American pilot to fall into enemy hands and none of my predecessors had gotten their stories out yet. So I had no idea what was to happen to me. The whole thing was just a complete mystery to me. I guess in my own daydreaming there I just figured they were taking me to Hanoi. I don't know why, but as it turned out that was what eventually happened. So we went traveling on up the road to Vinh.

4. Vinh Prison

We went on up the road for fifteen miles or so. That took us an hour and a half because of the way their roads were set up and because American planes were overhead attacking whatever targets they could find; what I was doing four days earlier. As the planes flew in, the trucks would have to pull off the road and let our boys roll in and drop their bombs or rockets.

Although that might sound a little nerve wracking, at that point I was so numb that the bombs going off around me didn't mean anything at all. I was not contemplating the irony of possibly being blown up by American bombs dropped by American pilots – my friends and colleagues. We went on up the road and drove into Vinh City. I could see the fluorescent street lights as we came up Highway One towards the city.

We drove through the outskirts for ten or fifteen minutes and finally pulled off just before reaching the main downtown area. This was what we later referred to as the Vinh way station or Vinh prison. A number of guys who were shot down later in the same area spent some time in this way station prison. We pulled into a military compound through a gate with a guard, and drove up to a long, low dark building. I was taken out of the truck and walked into this building.

This building was a temporary Vietnamese-type structure, made out of bamboo and not stone. We walked inside into the large room and I was met there by a half dozen or so North Vietnamese officers, the most senior of which was the camp commander of this particular complex. His insignia, a bar and four stars, showed that he was a senior captain, which is a damn high rank in North Vietnam.

I'd say he was close to fifty years old; an old, gray-headed guy. They dumped all the equipment I had with me on the table, among which were my knives, pistol, radio and other military gear that the peasants had not been allowed to take. The guards came over to me, led by a bar and three star sergeant who looked like he had been through all the wars that Vietnam had ever fought. He was an older, 40 something looking sergeant.

They stripped me down and gave a search of my clothes and my body. This was the one and only good body search that I ever had. I had many body searches later on as a prisoner but never anything like this. These guards checked my underarms, crotch, and inside my mouth and ears. I finally figured out the primary thing they were looking for was a cyanide pill or something I could bite down on and kill myself. They were convinced that I had one of these and at all costs they were going to keep me from bumping myself off.

As it became obvious to me that this was what they were looking for, I began to take a little heart. It actually boosted my morale because I figured if they were interested in me not killing myself then they were probably interested in keeping me alive. They conducted this search and then they had me put my clothes back on, but just my shirt, trousers, socks and underwear. Then they took me outside and walked me down a pathway. As I walked down this pathway, on my right I could see a radar antenna. I only recall that it was anti-aircraft type radar and there were six or seven gun mounts nearby.

We walked up to a long building, probably sixty feet long or so, that was a permanent stone structure with a tile roof. They walked me into the building and opened an iron door in one end of it. I walked through this iron door into a narrow walkway area that led around two corners. I had to make a sharp left and then a sharp right. This was the outer area of the cell block where I was to be held. It was a double-walled cell area. Then I walked through another door into my cell.

It was an incredibly depressing experience, not only to be in this first cell, but in particular because of what this cell was like. It was especially drab, approximately four feet wide and about six feet long. Three feet by six feet of it was taken up with a wooden bed. When I say bed, it really was nothing more than a board. It was as if you took a door off its hinges and dropped it on the ground. That's what you sleep on. I should note that a hard wooden bed of this sort is better any day than many concrete beds I later experienced.

They brought in a blanket, thank goodness, because though most people have the impression that Vietnam is just jungle and it's not. There are places where it gets very cold, and it was cold in this cell. The rest of the "furnishings" consisted of an old wooden bucket on the floor, and that was what I was to defecate and urinate in. They clanged the iron door shut and went away.

The cell had a very high ceiling, probably twelve feet, and up on the very top of the wall was a little window, maybe two feet tall by a foot wide with bars in it. Exhausted, I lay down on the wooden bed. I threw the blanket over me and with no pillow or anything, just my head on the wooden board, I fell asleep. But in just a few minutes I woke up. I was having wild, fantastic dreams about things grabbing hold of me and crawling on me. As I woke up I discovered that in fact I was covered with rats.

These North Vietnamese rats are pretty aggressive. Varying in size from about six inches to a foot and a half in length, they were literally swarming all over me. That's when I really woke up. I jumped off the bed and the rats all scurried away. I began to feel around and discovered the bed was covered with bugs and cockroaches, gigantic sized cockroaches. And I was covered with them.

I was in a pretty bad way and I needed to sleep so I figured I might as well try to forget about the rats and bugs and try to go to sleep. I was so tired that I fell back asleep. Later that night all hell broke loose when there was an air raid and all the guns around the camp opened up. My building shook from the shock waves of the muzzle blasts.

When morning came around and I looked around I noticed the roof of the cell had partially caved in. Probably the anti aircraft guns caused it to fall apart. But being that it was twelve feet up, there was no way I could get to it. It had all partially caved in and pieces kept falling down on me. I was to discover the next night why it had caved in. This is where the rats were coming in. I would watch them crawl through the hole in the ceiling and then actually crawl vertically down the wall. They are the most amazing creatures, so coordinated and agile they can literally run right straight up a wall with any surface whatsoever to it.

Shortly after daybreak the cell door opened and an old guard was standing out there with a Tommy gun. There was another younger guard who also had a gun and he was stationed outside the double wall complex room. The old guy beckoned to me to come out, though I didn't realize it at the time. He held his hand out, palm down, and wiggled his fingers.

In our society, if someone holds out their hand, palm up, and then gestures by curling the fingers toward themselves several times, we'd know immediately that we were being summoned. But with the palm down, I had no idea.

Not to put too significant a point on this, but the variations in cultures are enormous. For instance, in our society if somebody laughs that means they are happy or something funny has happened. In another social culture, it might mean that guy is embarrassed, angry, or insane. In some cultures, people stand right in your face when they talk, but we would find that uncomfortable. Touching people in certain ways is all right in our culture but taboo in others, and vice versa.

When the guard gestured at me in the way he did I thought he meant for me to stay in the cell. That got him pissed off at me, enough so that he came in and rapped me across the face once. That gave me the idea that I'd better follow him, and I did. We went outside and he led me around the corner of the building. Now we started walking outside, down the length of the building with my cell. As we were walking along I looked up ahead and could see another low building some 100 feet away.

As we walked along I could see through barred windows in the other building. Inside, behind the bars, was a huge open bay room that I would guess was 50 feet long by about 25 feet wide. And it looked like there were 80 or 90 people jammed into that one room cell.

They seemed to be living there and from what I could tell it was very crowded. I thought of how frat boys would try to cram ten guys in a telephone booth. But these weren't frat boys. These were all Vietnamese people. Some of them were old, some young and even some children. They were men and women of all ages and descriptions. What they had in common were blank, forlorn looks on their faces. Typical of their culture, they showed no emotion as I walked by less than 10 feet from them.

But then suddenly their faces lit up into great big grins, seemingly uncontrollable. I only saw this in my peripheral vision because the grins came once my guard had passed and wouldn't notice them. Some of them, sure they weren't seen by him, actually waved to me. I knew one word in Vietnamese and that was "chow," which in their language meant "howdy." So I looked around at them and smiled big and waved my hand and just said "chow."

Those people inside just went ape shit. They were climbing on the bars, tears streaming down their cheeks, waving to me. Of course it was an emotional experience for me too. It was my first indication that not everybody in North Vietnam was an asshole. Some of them were probably great people. These people certainly seemed to be on my side. I would suspect that they were political prisoners. They didn't appear to be soldiers. They had probably been picked up in the northern part of South Vietnam or maybe they had even been herded there from places in North Vietnam.

We were in fact headed toward the crapper, and when we arrived I saw that they were what we call "squatters." There is nothing to sit on. There is just a hole in the floor and foot positions where you stand and squat down. This was a new experience for me and one that I did not cotton to easily, but after a year of using this system it became quite normal for me.

When I came out of the crapper my two guards had been joined by an old man dressed in rags. He had a little Ho Chi Minh goatee-type beard, long gray hair, and a little bit of a moustache. He was a tiny fellow and he couldn't have weighed more than 75 pounds. With him was a young boy about the same size, probably around 14 years old. These two civilians stood there and looked at me.

The guard motioned me over to an area where there was a big tank full of water with a bamboo screen around it. He indicated for me to go behind the bamboo screen and take my clothes off. They were going to let me wash. I took off my clothes. There was no soap, no towels, no nothing, but the boy came over, picked up a bucket full of water and he started pouring water for me so I could scrub myself. It was as if I was standing by a faucet, filling my open hands and splashing the water on my body. There was a little chitchat between the guards, the old man and the boy, but he continued to pour water for me.

When I was through I put my clothes back on; my old dirty clothes that I had trekked through the jungle in for four days. Then I walked around from behind the screen and we started back towards the cell area. All the people were smiling and waving as I went by again. I came around to the cell area and opened the first door. The old man said something to the guard. The guard nodded his head, continuing to hold his gun on me, and the old man took me to my inner cell door. He opened the door and with his finger pointing into the cell – there was a sneering quality to it – he gave me one of those grunts that Vietnamese people give to their water buffalos and other animals when they want them to move.

I walked into the cell and turned around to face him. He just stood out there and glared at me. He put his hands on his hips. I sat on the floor. He took the cell door and slammed it closed with all of his might, locked it and walked back outside.

I sat just there, trying to figure out what I missed. I kind of laughed to myself, decided that I didn't really give a damn, and sat down on the bed. I had begun to think about my overall circumstances when a little while later I heard the outer door open again. It was the old man and the boy together this time. I could hear the old man outside cursing and swearing, probably making a big to-do about what a pig I was and so forth.

He opened the door and I could see that the boy had gone back around and was talking to the guard who had the Tommy gun. That left the old man alone at my cell door. He had a plate of food for me. This plate of food consisted of a little handful of rice with some pumpkin on top of it and an egg, a cooked egg, one of the few that I was to ever see again in North Vietnam.

106

The old man handed the plate to me with sort of a gruff gesture. I set it down over on my bed and just stood there and looked at it. The old man swore at me a few times and then he looked around behind him to see if the guard was watching. He was not. Then he old man turned around to me again and this time he had a grin as wide as a mile on his face. Tears started coming into his eyes. He reached into his pocket and pulled out a little piece of paper that was wrapped up in a packet. He gestured for me to come quickly, which I did.

He grabbed my hands and turned them palm up so that I could hold something. He put the little packet in my hands, closed my hands on it and then patted me on the shoulder. He stepped back so that the outside guard could see him if he were looking and then proceeded to swear at me and curse me again, shaking his fist at me. Then he slammed the door with all of his might.

Of course I was a dumbfounded at this whole scene. I sat down on my bed and my head was whirling. I couldn't figure out what the hell was going on here. It took me a moment to gather my thoughts and then I opened my hand. I opened up the little paper packet. It contained a little handful of salt.

Imagine my surprise, and delight, to receive this gift from an old rag-tag man who was all the while showing my captors how loyal and anti-American he was. And in this hidden moment he was showing me that he was my friend. I imagined that he was impoverished, that he had absolutely nothing in this world. And here he was giving me this little packet of salt that was probably worth a great deal in his life. That was my thought as I ate my meal this extraordinary first day in my first prison.

Later that evening they came in and got me again. Again they were the old man, the boy, and the two guards, one with a Tommy gun. It was the same routine. They took me down to the crapper area. But this time as I was coming back the young boy was beside me. Somehow the old man had managed to get into a conversation with the two guards and they were lagging behind us about 15 feet or so. The boy and I were leading the way. And as we rounded the corner, out of sight to the guards, the young boy threw himself upon me. He started crying and patting me on the head and on the shoulder, saying "American, American." It lasted only for a few seconds because he knew that was all the time he had. Just before the guards came around the corner the boy straightened up and we went on as normal. We went back around to my cell and they locked me in again.

An interesting sidelight to this story is a buddy of mine, J. B.

McKamey, who was shot down in June of '65 had the same experience. He was brought to the same way station. I was in Hanoi by then. When we met about a year later and were comparing notes, J. B. said just about the same thing had happened to him. But his story took an interesting turn. Late one night the old man and the boy came up to feed him and the old man got in the cell with him. Through sign language and drawing on the floor, the old man was able to indicate to J. B. there was going to be an escape that night. J. B. said he was excited at the thought that they were going to get him out of this hole; that they were going to break him out. They told him it was going to be at midnight. J. B. was all ready to go. Suddenly there was the damnedest yelling and screaming outside in the compound. Then he heard all of those Gooks running out of that padlocked area. Apparently they all ran out into the countryside, just going to the wind. But the old man, the boy and J.B. were still there in his cell. They left him high and dry. You can't blame them because a big white man is pretty hard to hide in that country.

Later that day I got my meal but I wasn't very hungry. It was a good thing because there wasn't much there. They took the dishes out and then about dark two guards came and got me again. This time they took me in the opposite direction from the crapper, back to the original big barracks and meeting room. There were several long tables and a main table was set up in front of me. There were people sitting on chairs all around the room. In the center of the big table was the camp commander. On either side of him were various Vietnamese officers. There was a 30-ish civilian fellow sitting about four chairs away from the camp commander.

When I walked in, recognizing him to be the camp commander, I stood at attention and saluted him. He stood up at attention and saluted me back. This was the first and last time that would ever happen to me in North Vietnam. I guess he didn't have his signals straight yet. He didn't know that I wasn't to be treated as a prisoner of war but as a criminal.

From that point on they made it real plain that I was a criminal, not a POW, and that was the line they maintained the whole time we were there in North Vietnam. He told me to sit down, which I did, and then the young civilian fellow came up and started talking to me in very broken English. Broken may be generous. I'd say his vocabulary was only about 100 or 200 words. He asked me if I could speak Russian. I said no. He asked if I could speak French. I said no. He asked me what my name was. I told him. He relayed it to his camp commander.

The camp commander started asking questions in Vietnamese and this guy started trying to interpret, though clearly he was having trouble. The camp commander wanted to know my rank, service number, and date of birth. I told him. He also wanted to know what "division" I was in. But division didn't mean anything to me, as a Navy fighter pilot off an aircraft carrier. He was asking, through the erstwhile interpreter, if I was division 7 or division 2.

I finally figured out what he was getting at. He wanted to know if I was in Seventh Fleet, which to him was the Seventh Division, or if I was in the Second Air Division. In other words he was trying to figure out if I was Navy, Air Force, Army, or just what the hell I was. I wouldn't tell them. He asked me what ship I was from. I wouldn't tell him that either. Then he asked me what airfield I was from and they went through several names like Than San Nut, Takli, Korat, Da Nang and others in South Vietnam. I wouldn't answer any of those questions.

This went on for four or five minutes; then the camp commander stood up, and everybody else stood up. I stood up too when everybody else did. He came around the table and he stood in front of me for 15 or 20 seconds, looking at me and me looking at him, both of us giving each other blank stares. Then he broke into a smile and he said something to his interpreter in Vietnamese. The interpreter said, "Camp commander wants to know if you have any requests." And I said, "Yes I do." And the camp commander nodded his head and said, "Go ahead, what's your request?" I said, "When will I go to Hanoi?" The guy interpreted that and the camp commander just smiled.

I got to know that smug Gook smile very well over the years. They believe in answering a question with a question, or answering with just that superior smile. The smile could mean anything, such as they knew and weren't going to tell me, or they didn't know.

So the camp commander smiled instead of answering my question and then he asked, "Is there anything else?" I said, "Yes." He said, "What?" I said, "I'd like to have some cigarettes."

He smiled again, but this time it was because that was something he could do something about. He reached in his pocket and pulled out a pack of cigarettes and handed them to me. Then he stepped back with a proud grin. Then he said "Anything else?" and I said yes. He said "What?" I said I would like to have some matches. He laughed like hell and so did everyone else in the room. He reached into his pocket and handed me some matches. Then he said "Anything else?" And I said "Nope."

He stood up beside me, patted me on my shoulder a few times, and then he indicated that I should leave the room. I was taken back to my cell. I will reiterate that I was probably lucky to have been captured so early — lucky in that they weren't as furious and hate-filled at Americans as they would became as the war continued and we were killing so many of them with our bombing. Just months later when J. B. arrived, the treatment at the Vinh way station had changed dramatically. J. B. got the holy hell beaten out of him by a one-armed interrogator who spoke fairly good English. Through the torturous treatment, they actually extracted a biography from J. B before he even got to Hanoi. I was pretty lucky that the one-armed interrogator wasn't there yet.

They took me back to my cell and I went to sleep. The same business with the rats and so forth took place that night. About 2 o'clock in the morning I was awakened by my cell door coming open and there was a whole bunch of flashlights shining into the cell. There was a bunch of screaming and yelling and cursing and I could hear somebody just raising hell with the guards out there. This guy had a white uniform and he had on green instead of red collar insignias. Later I found out the green collar devices meant he was a civil defense guy. Obviously he was of some importance. They flashed light on the rats in the room — the room was just full of rats — and apparently this incensed the official.

They told me to put my blanket under my arm and come outside the cell. I walked out and several guys bound me very tightly with my arms and hands behind my back, and they put a blindfold on me. They walked me down the pathway and then shoved me into the back seat of a jeep. I didn't know it at that moment, but I was on my way to Hanoi.

5. Hanoi Bound

My trip to Hanoi started around 2 o'clock in the morning on the 27th of April. I was tied up tight with my arms behind my back, blindfolded, sitting in the back seat of a small jeep. Someone poked the barrel of a rifle in my side and a voice said to me, in Gook-slang English, "Keep very still. Do not move." And that's what I did, not that I had a lot of choices. We sat there for probably twenty minutes. All I knew was that I heard considerable commotion, a lot of jabber I didn't understand, and people I couldn't see scurrying this way and that.

Finally, the engine was started, and the rifle was pulled out of my ribs. The guard who had been keeping me from escaping climbed into the front of the jeep and another guard climbed in beside me. A voice from the front seat said "Do you know where you are going?" And I said, "No." And he said, "Maybe New York City, huh?" And I said, "Really I don't think so." Then he laughed. Now at least I knew the guy had a little sense of humor. That was somewhat of a relief, even thought I truly didn't know where the hell I was going.

I ventured a question: "Are we going to Hanoi?" And he said, "Uh, maybe so. You will see." They started up the jeep and we began to roll out. When I said I was tightly bound, I meant painfully so. The ropes were biting into my arms and wrists to the point that I was gritting my teeth since I was bouncing around due to the road conditions. After about forty minutes of this, the guy in the front seat finally turned around and said, "What is wrong with you?" I said, "These goddamn ropes hurt." And he said, "Oh."

Immediately the guy beside me took them off. Just like that. The guy in the front said, "Anything else? Are you alright now?" I said, "Take the damn blindfold off." He said, "All right." They took off the blindfold. Suddenly I was sitting there just as comfortable as can be.

This would happen frequently for me throughout my captivity, and yet it kept surprising me. I would face a difficult situation straight on, and it would be resolved. Not always, but more often than I would have imagined. Sometimes things seemed so simple. I don't know whether it's that the people were sometimes so ignorant and or maybe just simple or straightforward. I would be in a situation where I had some kind of a problem, for Christ sake, and I'd tell them so and they would fix it.

My advice to everyone is don't just sit there like a dildo and suffer. Tell them what your problem is and they might do something about it. At least give it a try. If it's intentional they won't do anything about it. But if it's not intentional, they'll do something for you. For God's sake, look out for your own welfare wherever you are and whatever you're doing. Don't assume anything. Especially don't assume that whoever is causing you grief necessarily knows it, or wants to, so if you tell them, they'll stop. It's like someone standing on your toe and not knowing. Once they know they'll move their foot and apologize.

That was one of the biggest problems we all had during the interrogations and general treatment of prison life. We would make assumptions – basic assumptions that weren't necessarily true – about what our captors were doing. Most of the time the things that happened to us really had such a simple explanation, like the guard who was too lazy to bring water to you, or he dropped your food plate. That's why you didn't get all your food that day. They didn't usually have some devious scheme in mind. It was just a straight-forward simple thing that happened. Whereas the normal American mind conjures up what is their plan, what are they trying to get at, what are they trying to do, what psychological game are they playing with me now? More times than not, there wasn't any.

There we were, somewhere, heading to somewhere else. I didn't know either of the somewheres. It was pretty uncomfortable, actually quite bruising, but it was a lot better with the ropes and blindfold gone. At various times during the night, before daybreak, we would have to stop while my buddies bombed and strafed the road. We would pull off the road when the air raid warnings would sound. Between attacks the roads would be clogged with people and traffic. And as soon as there were aircraft in the area, the word would be passed up and down the road and all the vehicles would turn off their lights and pull off the road and wait for the planes to go by. It was a remarkably simple tactic against the high tech attacks from the Americans. It was a long miserable ride, riding around in a truck or jeep in North Vietnam.

We drove along that way until about daybreak and then the guys got out and camouflaged the jeep and we proceeded on. Again, their approach to camouflaging the jeep was simple. They just pulled the vegetation, trees and branches, off the side of the road and stuck them in the top of the truck or jeep. It was extremely effective and very easy to do. Those branches and leaves will last about a twenty-four hour period before they have to stick some new ones up there, before they start going brown. They

112

do that with everything. They even put the stuff in their helmets or their hats. People working in the field wear them in their sun hats.

I was absolutely amazed at all the teeming people and vehicles and all the crap that was down there that I had never seen from 8,000 feet and 250 knots. It was just fantastic what actually was down there. From the air it's just brush and trees. It's not a truck, person or bicycle or a water buffalo or anything else - just a bunch of bushes and trees.

We drove on through the morning, going from one clump of trees to another for cover from aerial attacks until about 11 o'clock. Then we pulled off the road in a little farm and the guys in the jeep got out. They put ground cloths out on the ground and two of them plopped down and proceeded to take a siesta. They left one guard posted to watch me. This guy watched me for about two hours and then one of the other guys woke up and the new guard posted on me for about two hours while the previous guard slept.

The guard just sat on a rock ten feet away or so and watched me. He put his gun across his knees. Besides, there were people and vehicles all over the road and all over the countryside. I wasn't going anywhere.

A note about siestas in Vietnam, it's very important to them. Actually it's more than important. It's almost imperative. They will religiously take their siestas even when you're being transported someplace or something is going on. Everything stops during siestas. Even if you have to be tortured for five days in a row, they will knock it off for siesta. They will take you through the night but when siesta time comes they will all take a break and have their siesta. You might even say it's a civilized practice.

After siesta time we started back up the road and as we did we got out of the bombing area. We were then free to scoot on down the road. From the maps I had studied, I decided this was Highway One and that we were on our way to Hanoi. We stopped several times along the way and there crowds of people would come down to look in the jeep at me. Some of the adults reached out a hand to touch me. The little kids just looked at me. Most had never seen an occidental person before. I was a curiosity to them. They weren't hurtful toward me.

We made our way to Than Hoa, where I saw the Than Hoa bridge in all its former glory. Now it was just a huge twisted mass of steel girders and concrete, but it was still standing. Maybe it was bad intelligence, but our guys kept flying missions against this bridge which was in no way usable and they kept getting shot down. The foundation of the bridge was solid steel-reinforced concrete. It was so solid there was nothing our guys could drop on it to reduce it to rubble. All around the bridge were bomb craters, one on top of another.

Because the bridge couldn't be driven on, they had a ferry boat to get us across the river. While we waited in line for the ferry boat I could look out on the river where I saw families bathing in the water and little boats coming and going, many little paddle boats. We finally got onto the ferry. It was really a barge that was big enough to hold two vehicles, run by an old man and a boy. The boy had a rifle. He looked like he was about 12 or 13 years old.

The old man started poling us across the river and two of my guards got out of the jeep, standing out on the barge to enjoy the breeze. That was when the young boy came up to me. He stared at me through the side window of the jeep from maybe ten feet away. Then very cautiously and quietly he pulled a shell out of his pocket, inserted it into the rifle and rammed the bolt home. Very quietly he looked around to see if anybody was watching and then he swung the rifle around and pointed it at my head.

I confess that at this point I was physically and emotionally exhausted. I think I didn't give a damn whether he shot me or not. I just sat there and stared at him. I didn't move. Suddenly, the guard sitting next to me saw the kid. He leapt out of his seat and grabbed the rifle from him. He threw the boy down on the barge and kicked him a couple of times. The rough activity drew the other guards back to the jeep where they talked excitedly about what happened, or almost happened. I can't imagine they would have been warmly greeted in Hanoi if I had been shot by a kid while they weren't looking. Anyway, they gave the kid back his rifle and sent him up to the front of the barge. I didn't see him again.

We got across the river and at that place we crossed the twentieth parallel so from that point on there wasn't any bombing going on at that time. Then we started up the road towards Hanoi. As we traveled along the guy in front would occasionally try to make conversation with me in English. I wouldn't pay him too much mind.

This guy was a young fellow, probably in his late twenties, a member of the Civil Defense force. What was most noticeable about him was that his ears stuck way out. We later referred to him as the "Rabbit." I say later because it turned out that Rabbit had been assigned as an interrogator at the Hanoi Hilton, probably because he could speak some English. And I was his first customer, so to speak, his first American prisoner. No wonder he was excited that I had almost been taken out of his hands by a 12 year old.

As soon as we got to the Hilton, Rabbit would switch from Civil

114

Defense to Regular Army. It turned out he was also an officer. This explained why he was asking all sorts of questions as we bumped along our way north. He would ask me questions like what aircraft I'd been flying, but I would just shake my head. He'd say, "Why don't you tell me? I know what you were flying." I'd just sit and look at him. He would say, "You were flying A4D 2N."

That was the old designation for the A4C that I had been flying. I guessed that they had recovered pieces of my wrecked plane, and some of those pieces were from the old A4D 2N. Since mine had been the only aircraft to crash in that area, they knew the wreckage had to be mine.

As we went on towards Hanoi, I saw a sight I'll never forget. We were driving along a river as dusk was falling. There was a whole bunch of junks that were moving up the river toward Hanoi. The sun was setting behind them. In spite of my circumstances and my fears about what was in store for me, I still remember remarking to myself at that time that this was one of the most beautiful scenes I have ever witnessed. It was literally breathtaking. The sails on these junks caught the final rays of the setting sun and turned all different colors. The reds and purples were just beautiful.

I also have to say that the countryside in that area of North Vietnam was astoundingly beautiful. You could see the big mountains and lush green forests and agricultural land. There are also these amazing rock karsts that come right up out of the floor of the countryside in amazing formations.

We continued up the road as darkness started and soon we pulled over to the side of the road. There were people walking up and down the road all the time and the Rabbit stopped an old lady who was plodding along with a shoulder pole. She balanced the pole on her shoulder and at each end of the pole was a big basket. The army can ask for whatever it wants from civilians and the civilians will almost always give what they are asked for. The alternative is probably less attractive than the confiscation, and most everyone probably knew it.

In response to Rabbit's talking to her, the old lady produced a teapot. He took out his canteen and she filled it up with tea. Then he told me to get out of the truck and he took me over to the side of the road. Standing there in the grass, he took my shaving gear out of his backpack and told me to take the hot tea and shave. Of course, as I was shaving there alongside the road, I collected a crowd of probably 150 people to watch. When I had finished, Rabbit took back the gear and I climbed into the truck.

When we were under way, the guard sitting next to me began to strike up a kind of conversation in sign language and so forth. And he wrote in sign language what he told me was his name. He wanted to know what my name was. So I told him what my name was. And he told me what his age was. I think he said 22 or 23, and that he had three children. He wanted to know how many children I had but I wouldn't tell him. I was either savvy enough to know that they were trying to get information out of me that they could use later, or I was paranoid. Either way, I didn't play the game.

After a while he gave up and obviously started to get sleepy. He leaned his head up aside the jeep and fell asleep. There wasn't anything else to do with his automatic weapon so he just put it over in my lap and bagged out there. It seemed amazing to me at the time that he would do this, but when I thought about it I realized there was nothing I could have done with his rifle since escape was impossible. Even if I grabbed the weapon, with the other men in the truck and with all the people clogging the road around us it was obvious I wasn't going anyplace. Why not rest the gun in my lap? That typified what I came to understand as the Vietnamese attitude. Quite often they were practical people.

Finally I saw signs by the road that told us we were getting closer to our destination – Hanoi, 50 kilometers, then 30 kilometers, and so on until we reached the edge of the city. As we drove into Hanoi the guards put up side screens on the side windows. It was not so much to prevent me from looking out as to keep the people from seeing me inside. We drove into downtown Hanoi and by the prison Hoa Lo, that we later named the "Hanoi Hilton." I remember seeing it as we went by.

We then drove a couple of blocks further up the road and stopped at a little restaurant. The Rabbit got out and went inside and in a few minutes came back with something to eat. Then the two other guards went in and came back with food. They gave me a bowl of noodle soup that really tasted outstanding. It wasn't just that I was hungry, it really was delicious. It had a lot of hot pepper sauce in it but I like hot Mexican food and so it wasn't a shock to my system. I wolfed it down and they gave me some tea.

Then came a huge surprise. Looking back, it was the last experience like this I was to have in North Vietnam. The Rabbit came back with a smile on his face and handed me a large glass, the size you'd get ice tea served in. It was full of an iced orange dessert. I couldn't believe my eyes. It was a frozen orange drink made from real oranges, and it had a wooden stick sticking down in it. Frozen around this stick was something popsicle-like made of the same frozen orange juice. God almighty, I couldn't believe it. I wolfed it down in about three seconds!

I can still remember how good it tasted. I also remember the next time

116

I tasted anything that good was eight years later, when I got off the Medical Evacuation flight to freedom from Hanoi at Clark Air Force Base in the Philippines. It's funny how small things matter. Later I told my buddies in prison about this wonderful orange treat and they just couldn't believe that there was any ice cream in gook-land. I guess I was just about the only POW in North Vietnam that ever had any ice cream.

Then they cranked up the jeep and we drove a couple of blocks to a big iron gate in a prison wall with a guard tower. Guards swung the gate open. We drove in and I fought back the tears.

6. Welcome to The Hanoi Hilton

Upon our arrival at Hoa Lo, my guard removed my blindfold. He wanted me to see the horrible place I was about to enter. In front of us was a 30 foot high stone wall, with barbed wire and glass imbedded along the top. We stopped before two huge iron doors, which were then opened by a pair of Vietnamese guards who then waved us inside. As we drove through those doors I fought to hold back the tears because for the first time in my life, I could feel the icy fingers of despair encircling my heart. It would not be the last time, but I didn't know that then. I didn't know that I would endure horrible treatment in that and ten other Vietnamese prisons for eight years.

The downtown Hanoi prison where American POWs were kept was originally known as Hoa Lo. The term in Vietnamese means the furnace and was so named because the main street outside the building was famous for street vendors who cooked meals for passers by. However, the furnace has another, less benign meaning. From the time the French built the prison not long after the turn of the century, through the Japanese using it during the Second World War, to the Vietnamese maintaining it for their own purposes afterward, it was known as a place where people went in and didn't come out. Like a furnace, the captives were fed into the figurative flames. In the early days of resident American POWs, we named it "The Hanoi Hilton," a reflection of our sarcastic, but sustaining sense of prison humor. Nevertheless, the Hilton was an evil and savage place.

The Hanoi Hilton is a big complex, entirely surrounded by high double walls. We drove through the first gate, through a little archway tunnel, then through a second gate and out into a courtyard area probably 100 feet long by 50 feet wide. This courtyard had ivy plants growing in the center and walkways down either side. On either side of the walkways there were buildings that climbed probably four stories.

These tall buildings had windows and doors, not like a prison but more like office spaces. This was apparently the administrative center of the complex. The jeep drove down one of these little narrow walkways to the end of the courtyard. That's where I saw some cells and a little cell block area and that's where we parked. The Rabbit got out along with the driver while the guard stayed in the car with me.

I sat there for a while, just looking around, when another prison guard came up to me and told me to scoot down in the seat so I couldn't see out. I thought this was kind of strange because it was night time and there wasn't really anything to see. This was my first introduction to an attitude or policy that was typical during the rest of my prison life. The North Vietnamese have a penchant for not letting people see anything. This was the case to some degree or other during my entire captivity. It was quite an annoyance since it was meaningless. There was nothing to see, and nothing to do about it even if there were.

I waited there in the jeep for perhaps 45 minutes while the Gooks were deciding what to do with me. Finally, another guard came by, an old guard, and he told me to get out of the jeep. He led me around into the cell block area and down a small narrow hallway with what appeared to be four cells on either side. I noticed that the lights were on in all the cells, despite the fact that it was about midnight. The cells had iron doors, with a peek hole with bars on it. There was a flap that could be opened so they could see in through the peek hole. The only window was up at the very top along the ceiling about a foot high by 2 feet wide with bars on it.

During the early time of American captivity we found it necessary to talk about what cell, cell block area, building, and other prisons we were in. This was so we could keep our communications about our location straight. First we realized that we would have to come up with a system for numbering the cells because the Vietnamese very often didn't have numbers on the cells themselves. And this was always the case in the new prisons.

This is the way our numbering system worked. When you walked into a cell block area, the first cell on your right was number one, and as you walked down to the end of that cell block area they'd be numbered in order; for instance one, two, three, four. Then on the left side of the hallway would be number 5 and then 6, 7, and 8. If we were talking about a cell located in another building, looking at the building from the outside, then the cell on the far left was number one and they'd go in order from left to right. If there are cells located on the back side of that building then the cells continue numbering as they did in the cell block area. This became our standard numbering system after awhile. We held this pretty much true, with only a couple exceptions where the Gooks already had large numbers printed on the cell doors. And sometimes we would use their numbering system anyway in that case. This might seem like minutiae but even the smallest details of our lives as POWs were important, both for our relationships then, and to have a record when we got out.

The first cell I was put in was part of a unit that we later called "Heartbreak Hotel," which was one cell block area within the Hanoi Hilton compound. Heartbreak Hotel was actually seven cells. Cell number 8 was a shower room. Actually all the shower room consisted of was a spigot that comes out of the wall and a drain on the floor.

I was led down to cell 4, the door was opened and I was told to go inside. I got my first real sense of being a prisoner in Hanoi when I heard the ominous sound of the big iron cell door clang behind me, the door bolt being rammed home and the snap of the big lock. The cell was painted with white wash. The floor was rough, loose, broken concrete. There were two bunks, just concrete pallets, one on either side of the cell.

The room was probably seven feet long by six feet wide, leaving only a narrow space between the "beds." Those beds were about hip high to me, which was rather high off the ground. Of serious concern was that on each of these concrete bunks, bolted in a very permanent way, was a set of stocks. That sent a chill up my spine and then a sick feeling in the pit of my stomach.

As it turned out the stocks were not really all that bad as the first look indicated. They were confining, of course, and uncomfortable, but it certainly was not anything you can't mentally adjust to. I know, since on one later occasion I spent two months in a set of stocks. The real problem was that you couldn't do anything about things like batting away at mosquitoes, when they didn't allow me to have a mosquito net. Also leg muscles atrophied from being confined in them for long periods. These stocks were designed so they could be opened by the guards from the hallway outside the cell by pulling out the long bolts that locked you in.

That night of my arrival I sat there in my cell, twiddling my fingers and walking back and forth in the confined space. The light was on and I was pretty irritated at my plight. I climbed up on one of the bunks and looked out through the little window at the top of the outside cell wall. The prison had been built to hold Vietnamese prisoners who were considerably shorter than my six-foot-two, so by standing on the leg irons on my tiptoes I could just manage a look out of the window.

As I was looking out I heard the sound of a tin cup clang from four cells down in cell number one. When I heard that my heart leaped in my throat and I thought their must be another prisoner around, maybe even American. So just a test I hollered out, "Is anyone else here?" There was no answer. I hollered it out again, "Is anyone else here?" No answer. And then for some reason, I don't know why, I yelled out, "How in the hell do you

120

turn the light off in this place? I want to go to sleep." This is the crazy stuff you think of and do in situations like this. Then an answer came from down the way, "You don't, that's the general idea."

I said, "Who are you?" and the voice came back, "I'm Captain Scotty Morgan." I told Scotty who I was and we said, "Howdy" and glad to met you. Scotty was shot down on April 4th just 16 days before my arrival in North Vietnam.

We didn't have a chance to get out any more conversation before I heard the cell block door open and my old friend, who had put me in the cell, came walking down the hallway. He was not wearing the red collar device that the regular army people wore, but one that was salmon-colored with a bar and three stars located on the bar, indicating he was a sergeant.

It took us a long time to figure out their ranks, but later on we did. Their enlisted ranks are fairly simple. They don't have as many enlisted ranks as we do, yet they have about twice as many officer ranks. Their enlisted ranks go one bar, which is a guy starting out (private first class), then a bar and a star (corporal), bar and two stars a sergeant, and a bar and three stars their top sergeant. The stars are located on the bar in each case.

The next step up the line is a rank that we don't have in our services but other foreign countries do. It's kind of a junior 2nd lieutenant; a 3rd lieutenant, if you will. They have a name for that, "alternate lieutenant." It is a single gold bar. This gold bar is smaller and it's a bar that is actually put on the collar device. It's about an inch and a quarter long and about a 16th of an inch wide, made out of a cheap gold material. From that point on they start adding stars and bars that go on into the top colonel ranks.

I didn't know it at the time but I later figured out that this guard was actually a policeman. It so happened that his duty was as a turnkey in the downtown Hanoi jail. He appeared to be pretty old, probably in his fifties, though I later found out from talking to him that he was only 46. He had a stony-looking face that was compounded by little round glasses that looked very old-fashioned. I decided to call him "Stone-Face."

Stone-Face came down the hall and stood in front of my cell. He looked in through the peek hole and saw me standing tippy-toe, looking out the window. I just looked back at him there outside the peek hole. He waggled his finger at me and motioned for me to get down. I told him to go to hell. He stood there and shook his finger at me some more. I told him, "Kiss my ass" and even gave him the finger.

This was not a smart thing to do. But I was understandably upset that night and not thinking very clearly. Finally I got down and then I heard

Scotty call for some water. He called several times for water. After a while I heard someone speaking English to him through his peek hole. It was muffled, so I put my ear to the door and listened. Scotty said, "I haven't had any water in eight hours. When am I going to get some water?" This guard said, "You will get some water," and pretty soon the guard came back and gave him some water.

Not much later, Stone-Face came into the cell along with The Rabbit. They had some clothes in their hands. They shut the door behind them and The Rabbit told me to take off my dungarees, my flight suit. I was standing there in my skivvies and he told me to take off my boots and socks.

He took these things from me and gave me a pair of blue and white striped pajamas. But these pajamas were made for Vietnamese prisoners, much smaller than I. I barely managed to squeeze the pants on and then to put the shirt on though I couldn't button it.

The Rabbit told me to give him my wedding ring. He said criminals were not allowed to have rings or jewelry. That he said "criminals" and not prisoners pissed me off, so I told him no, I wouldn't do it. Then he informed me that if I would not take my ring off and give it to him they would cut off my finger and take the ring from me that way.

I thought about that for a second and I thought I'd probably like to have the finger more than my wedding ring so I relented and took it off and gave it to him. I asked him when I would get it back and he said, "When you are released, if you ever go home. It will be kept for you in safe keeping."

As it turned out, they did this to every prisoner who came in. Out of the four hundred guys I knew there were probably 30 or 40 who got their rings back. I was one of them. It astounded me that I got the ring back the day before I left Vietnam

This ring thing, I have to put something in about this right now. Since the day my wife and I got married, in a double-ring ceremony, neither of us had ever had our rings off in the whole four years. So I was emotionally tied to having this ring on, and having to give it up caused a big drop in my morale. My suggestion to guys who fly combat, or anyone in combat who might become captured, is to take off your rings and any other important personal jewelry like a watch or religious medal so you don't get in a situation like mine. If it means that much to you, let your wife take it off you before you leave home. It will sooth your inner soul so you won't ever have to go through this thing of having the enemy take it away from you, because it can be a big hit on your morale, making your captivity even worse. It may just be a ring to them, but it might mean a lot more to you.

They left the cell. And I felt lower than whale shit on the bottom of the ocean because they had taken my wedding ring away from me. I sat down on my bunk. I walked around for a little while. Pretty soon I heard a call from Scotty. I jumped back up on the leg irons again and just started talking to him. Then Stone-Face came back down the hall, this time with another guy. He opened the cell door and they came in. The other guy was notable for the fact that his ears stuck out. Also, he looked pretty important, and sure enough it turned out that he was the camp commander. Pretty soon another couple of guards came.

The camp commander informed me that I had disobeyed the regulations of the camp and that if I did not stop disobeying the regulations of the camp I would be beaten and I would be put into the leg irons. By this time it was 12:30 or 1:00 in the morning. He told me to get on the bed and go to sleep and the next morning they would see me again. I said okay. The cell door clanged behind them when they left. They had put a pretty good threat on me so I climbed up on the bunk there. Scotty yelled down to me one more time and he said we should cool it for the night because they were putting the pressure on him too.

So I went to sleep which was no trouble at all because I was completely exhausted. I essentially hadn't had any sleep in a couple of days. I had been awakened in the middle of the night in Vinh to make the trip to Hanoi. I had lasted this long on adrenalin but at this point I was really bushed. I went to sleep on the concrete, no problem at all.

The next morning, about 5:30 or 6:00 the cell door opened and there stood Stone-Face. He said, "Get up and follow me." Actually, he didn't say that, but he indicated that I should follow him. I should mention that they had also given me a rattan mat to sleep on. These mats are very thin, and really the only purpose they served was to keep clean, or at least cleaner than the dirty concrete surface that I was sleeping on.

He indicated "Bring your mat with you and follow me." We went out of the Heartbreak Hotel cell block and around again into the main courtyard, then back towards the main gate. I followed Stone-Face through a little archway and then into another very small courtyard. This one was only about 40 feet long and about 40 feet wide, but with one corner cut off so that it was almost a triangle. As with the main courtyard, there were walls and doors that looked like office spaces.

He took me around a corner to the left and into another cell block area much like the one I was in before. Later on we named this area "New

Guy Village." This one had four cells and he opened the door to the first one and let me in it. This cell was slightly larger than the one in Heartbreak Hotel, about fourteen feet long by about eight feet wide. It also had two bunks, each bunk having leg irons. He closed the door behind me. I sat there and twiddled my fingers for a little while. I was pretty damn hungry because I hadn't had anything to eat and that got me thinking about eating.

Pretty soon he came back and gave me a little crockery water pot that held five or six cups of water. It had a little spigot and a top you pulled off to fill it. It was very crudely made but effective enough to hold water. He also gave me a tin cup. He left and came back with a spoon and a fork. They were not the same size and were of weird construction, very cheap and very old. Then he left but in a few minutes he came back and indicated for me to follow him.

I followed him through the little courtyard and he opened another door. He took me inside a room that had a kind of sunken hole in the floor about four feet wide and twelve feet in length. There was a spigot dripping water into the hole. He indicated that I should wash. The sunken hole had rancid, filthy water in it that had been standing for God knows how long. I had never seen anything like it in my life, even in visits to Tijuana or the back streets of Hong Kong and Olongapo that were as filthy as this room. It almost made me sick.

I went over to this spigot and washed my face and hands as best I could. He handed me a tiny dull drab yellowish towel. It had been used before, so often that it was almost worn out. I dried off with it and the guard indicated that I should leave the towel on a concrete bench. Then I followed him out through the courtyard again into the little archway that I had come in. We walked on only a couple of feet when he ordered me to stop and opened the door off the archway. He said something to someone on the other side of the doorway and gave a salute. Then he held the door open and gave me one of those famously-snotty Vietnamese motions that meant to hustle in. Yes, I know it was more as a show to the people inside than about me, but it still it irritated me.

I walked inside to what we would later refer to as "The Blue Room," and saw three Vietnamese sitting behind a table. There was an electric fan directed on them. A light bulb hung down from the ceiling over the center of the table just above their heads. In front of the table was a stool and this was to be my first interrogation. Very early in 1965 we began to use the whimsical term "quiz" for an interrogation.

I stood at attention in front of the desk and saluted. The three Gooks just sat there and looked back at me without making any motion or sign. So I dropped my salute and one of them told me to "Seet down." I sat down on the stool. Then this young Vietnamese, who was the interpreter, began to talk. He did not introduce himself nor did the other men sitting with him.

This was common. It always happened throughout my stay in Hanoi. They would never tell you their name. The only rare exceptions were a couple of occasions at the very first part of the war and on one occasion at the very end of the war. Otherwise they kept their names secret. Maybe it was a plan for their own protection. I don't know. Another penchant they exhibited was not allowing me to see anything. It's somehow beneath their dignity to allow you to know anything or see anything.

And finally there was this point about their attitude. The war had not got cranked up to its full extent yet. That would be three years later. But Hanoi had never been bombed and the way Asians are, their outlook on things varies depending on how directly they are affected by something. So for instance, since they weren't being bombed, it didn't mean much that some other part of their country was being bombed. They didn't seem to have much empathy for each other. In 1965, in Hanoi things were pretty calm and cool. They appeared convinced that they would win the war with ease and that the U.S. would simply quit. They didn't foresee a real problem with us or the South Vietnamese. They weren't sweating the whole situation too much. At least that's the way it seemed to us prisoners in those early days. That their country was being bombed below the 20th parallel and people were getting killed, didn't seem to be much of an issue for the North Vietnamese.

This young guy started to ramble on about the 1954 Geneva Conventions and he asked me what I knew about them. I said nothing. I just sat there. When he started talking about the Geneva Conventions, I thought he was talking about the 1949 Geneva Conventions, the ones that contained the articles on prisoners of war. But he wasn't. He was talking about the 1954 Geneva Conventions and how North Vietnam was to be temporarily separated from South Vietnam, et cetera. After about 30 minutes of this lecture he asked me what my name was. I told him Phillip Neal Butler. Then he asked me what my rank was. I told him Lieutenant, United States Navy.

Then he asked, "Are you a Lieutenant senior grade or Lieutenant junior grade?" I said Lieutenant senior grade. He said, "No, you are Lieutenant junior grade." This pissed me off and I said, "No, God damn it,

125

I'm Lieutenant senior grade." I had been a Lieutenant senior grade for three whole days before I went down and I wasn't going to let anyone call me a junior grade at this point.

He then produced my identification card which hadn't yet been updated, so I understood why he was pressing the point. He said, "Your Identification Card says you are Lieutenant junior grade.' I said, "No, I am now Lieutenant senior grade" and they talked and they nodded their heads and took my word for it. Then he said, "What is your serial number?" I gave it to him, 647398. Then, "What is your date of birth?" and I gave him that, August 11, 1938.

Then he said, "How old are you?" I just shook my head and I said, "I will not answer that question." He looked at the identification card again and said "You tell me your date of birth, but you will not tell me how old you are?" And I said, "If you want to know how old I am you can figure it out."

That was the first thing other than name, rank and service number I had said. So they talked about that for while. Then he said, "What Squadron were you in?" I clammed up. I wouldn't say anything more. "What airplane were you flying?" "What ship were you off of?" and so on and so on and I wouldn't say anything. Then he went back to, "What is your name?" and I told him my name. He asked what airplane I was flying, what weapons I was carrying, et cetera. I didn't say a word.

This went on for 20 or 30 minutes, the same old bullshit while these other two men just sat there and looked. Finally one of them got up. He was the guy whose ears stuck out – the camp commander, whom we would later refer to as "The Dog." He stood up, walked around the table and out of the room. I was now left with a guy who had on civilian clothes and the interrogator.

The other fellow looked like he was about 50 years old. He had graying hair and was a fairly distinguished looking older gentleman. This guy became known to us as "The Eagle." The Eagle at this time did not speak much English and he used this little interrogator, whom we named "The Owl," because he had a round owlish face. The Eagle used him for everything he wanted to say.

The Eagle at this time was a congenial guy who never really put any pressure on you. He was a soft-sell sort of fellow and so was the little interrogator who was working with him. The Eagle changed his approach later on and became a mean son of a bitch, as all the rest of them did. The Eagle learned English and turned out to be, to my knowledge, one of the few Vietnamese interrogators who later had his finger on military information. He really knew his stuff. In 1967, a couple of years later, when the guys were going to see him, The Eagle showed he knew a hell of a lot. He knew more than we did about our aircraft, weapons and delivery systems, our flight endurance and g-tolerance envelopes and even our newest electronic counter measures (ECM) equipment. He was sharp and on the ball.

The Eagle opened a brief case, pulled out a pack of cigarettes, asked me if I wanted one and then he gave one to me. He had a cigarette lighter that he flipped across the table and I used it. He was chain smoking as we went along. He pulled a book out of his brief case and handed it to the interpreter who opened it and began reading. He started reading this stuff about the 1954 Geneva Convention, which is what he had been talking about earlier. Now he read this propaganda book in English. He read and he read and he read.

I would guess he read for almost two hours while I sat there on that damn stool. My ass was killing me. There's another thing I've noticed about these Gooks. They have iron asses. I had gotten a sore ass from flying an A4 for four hours, so I knew that when you begin to go beyond that it's a real pain to just sit there. Especially listening to this silly crap being delivered in a painfully boring monotone voice, on and on as though it would never stop.

I would gaze around the room, deliberately not looking at them. I would sit there, pick my nose and play with my feet. I acted as unconcerned as I could. I crossed my legs, and they would tell me to uncross them. Crossing your legs in that culture was a display of rudeness. Then I'd focus my gaze on the left ear of the fellow talking to me and never look into his face. Or I would just focus my gaze on his hands.

I discovered these little tricks were successful in disconcerting some of the interrogators, especially the inexperienced ones, which most of them were in the early days of the war. They are a self-conscious people anyway, a condition that was magnified by their attempts to try to express themselves in a new language to a new person. The ploy of focusing on their hands had quick results. It didn't take long before they became so unnerved that instead of holding their hands steady on the table they began to shift them around. They would scratch their ear and then finally in utter desperation they'd put their hands down below the table. When this happened I would simply shift my gaze to maybe a point in the center of his neck, or on his collar lapel, or one of his ears. This became very disconcerting also. It's just a subtle way of inducing some static into the situation without actually being overt about it. Making them nervous probably helped to get the interrogations over a little faster.

I was able to understand The Owl about 95% of the time which was outstanding, especially for this time. He was by far the best English speaker in North Vietnam then. His vocabulary was limited and his pronunciation of words was often a little ragged. He was a young fellow in 1965, about 22 or 23 years old. I later found out that his real name was "Ha." That was his family name. Ha is also a Vietnamese word that means river.

This bullshit in my first interrogation went on for about two hours until finally he put the book down. The Eagle started talking to the interpreter in Vietnamese and The Owl interpreted it to me a sentence at a time. It was the same old shit about the 1954 Geneva Conventions and their position that somehow those agreements meant they didn't consider me a prisoner of war.

It was their view that I was in their hands and I must do what they told me to do. My government had no way of helping me here. I was completely within their power. I did not have any rank, on and on and on. Finally, after maybe another half-hour of this rant, the door opened up and Stone-Face came marching in and gave The Eagle a salute. They told me to stand up and leave the room. Stone-Face led me back to my cell and when I got back there I noticed a tin pot of food which Stone-Face told me to carry into the cell. He closed the door behind me. So there it was. "Het" for my first interrogation. "Het" in Vietnamese means "the end."

I should note that at this early stage in the war they didn't know enough to ask anything other than basic questions. Later in the week they started longer interrogations, sometimes going day and night. I was pissed off by all of this, of course, so I started telling them bullshit. That's called using the second line of defense; giving your interrogators something to make them think they're succeeding, even though the information is worthless. It actually became a game for me to give them the most outlandish horseshit that I could think of and they bought every bit of it.

In later interrogations they seemed more interested in my personal life than in military information. They were trying to get close to me, I guess, though that would never happen with these people and most Americans. The first "quiz" as we called these sessions started with a "Hi, How are you?" and more trying to get to know you by telling you how things stand. A lot of, "Here's the Geneva Conventions of 1954, and that's why you're a criminal and not a prisoner of war," et cetera, and how they didn't abide by the 1949 Geneva Conventions, and how the Geneva Conventions card I had in my wallet meant nothing to them.

I wasn't blindfolded or tied up during these early interrogations, nor did they use any physical force against me in the beginning. The rough stuff came later. Occasionally I got slapped. The interrogator would get so pissed off at me that he couldn't see straight. I would give him 18 reams of bullshit and call him an asshole to boot. I would have completely provoked him, and then he would come around the desk and slap me off the stool.

I learned that provoking him would get him to give up and get the quiz over with. Sometimes it was worthwhile getting socked three or four times so they would get irritated enough to get the damn thing over with and send me back to my cell.

After the first interrogation I walked back into my cell with my little chow plate set-up. I say set up because it was a series of enamel plates and bowls fitted on top of each and held in place by a strip of metal with a ring on top for carrying the whole thing. I walked into my cell and opened it up. I looked in the top little tray and there wasn't anything in it. There was a slice of bread, almost like you'd get off your table, in the next one. The next dish was a very small portion of some kind of a vegetable. As I remember it might have been something like green beans. And with the vegetable was a patty of some kind of crude hamburger meat. The main pot on the bottom had soup in it.

I was damned impressed. It looked good, almost like chow you'd get at home. There wasn't much of it and I wolfed it down in about three seconds. It didn't come close to filling me up. I drank as much water as I could hold, emptying my jug. Stone-Face opened the peek-hole and looked in on me. I showed him that my water jug was empty. He nodded his head, opened the cell door and told me to hand him my jug. He walked across the little hallway to an old wooden water pot with a wooden dipper and he dipped out some more water for me.

This water was hot. When you're in a hot country and you are drinking hot water, that doesn't set too well with an American. I really couldn't figure it out. When he handed me the water pot he held his hand on it as if the pot was hot, and he motioned to me to come near. He took my hand and put it on the water pot. He got a big smile on his face and a real proud look and pointed to the water pot.

Finally it dawned on me why it was hot and why he looked so proud. The Vietnamese boiled their water before they drank it. I learned later the government has battled for five or six years to get the people to boil their water before they drank it to help prevent diseases. It seemed like such a primitive accomplishment, but Stone-Face was clearly very proud of the fact that I was receiving boiled water and would not get a disease from it. That was why he wanted me to know why the water was hot.

He indicated I should go to sleep. He pointed to the two on his watch. It was getting close to noon, so I got the idea that something was going to happen at 2:00 and that I was supposed to bag it till then. I noticed there were no noise out on the street and no noise in the whole prison complex. There was just dead silence everywhere. I immediately got the idea that this was siesta time and everybody was bagged out. Since I was bushed, the idea of getting some sleep seemed most inviting.

I fell asleep on my concrete mattress, and after a while awoke when the radio speakers came back on. There were speakers placed all around the prison complex. They issued Vietnamese jargon I couldn't understand, and their twang-twang music. The speakers made it clear that the siesta was over. And it was about quarter to 2:00. Soon my cell door opened again and Stone-Face motioned for me to come out. I was on my way to my second quiz.

To put this into a chronological perspective, I was shot down on a Tuesday and captured on Saturday. Saturday night I was in Vinh, and left about 3:00 on Monday morning, arriving in Hanoi Monday night. So this was Tuesday morning, a week after I had gone down. My best days were behind me.

From this point on there were quizzes almost around the clock. They would go something like this: They'd pull me out of my cell about 6:30 in the morning and I sat in quiz until about 11:00. Then I'd go back to my cell for siesta but of course it was so the quizzers could take their siesta. Then I'd come back about 2:00 and I'd sit and get quizzed until about 5:30 or 6:00. I'd then go back to my cell and eat. Then it was go back to quiz again about 7:00 or 7:30 and sit in quiz until about 11:00 or 12:00 at night. In other words, I was getting four hours in the morning, about three hours in the afternoon, and then another 4½ hours at night. I was getting about 12 hours of quiz a day.

Then after a couple of days of this schedule, they started quizzing me in the middle of the night. They'd get me up about 2:00 or 2:30 in the morning and take me in and I'd sit in quiz till about 5:30 or 6:00 in the morning, go back to the cell, sleep for an hour and then go back out to quiz again. That meant 16 hours a day of this nonsense.

Yes, it got old in a hell of a hurry. It really wore me down. They would double up on me, with the quizzers switching off so they wouldn't wear themselves out. These quizzes did not involve The Dog, the camp commander. They involved The Eagle and The Owl, sometimes together, sometimes The Owl by himself and sometimes The Eagle with The Rabbit who spoke very poor English. The Rabbit was there to spell off The Owl to give him a rest break.

Regrettably I had no one to switch off with so I had to be there for all of it. There I sat, hour after hour, listening to this same damn bullshit as I described above, hearing the same stupid questions. This around-the-clock stuff went on for about 4 days until about Saturday or so. Finally, about Saturday morning, no this would be Sunday morning at about 2:00 in the morning, I was pulled out of my cell by Stone-Face and this time he had an automatic weapon with him. He pointed the weapon at me and motioned me towards the quiz room.

Up to this point I hadn't told them anything but my name, rank, service number and date of birth and maybe an occasional, "Go to Hell." I hadn't received rough or bad treatment. I'd been slapped a couple of times for being snotty. But I can't put too much blame on them for that. That was entirely my fault. It was what we were told would happen when we were in our survival school POW training phase. You'd get slapped if you were snotty. You knew you were going to get slapped, and hell, an American interrogator interrogating a Gook would have done the same thing. The only difference would have been a 180- or 200-pound man would have been slapping you instead of a little Gook who only weighed 110 pounds. Or so you'd think.

Despite the fact that these little guys only weighed 110 pounds or so they could slap like a mule can kick. They could just flat rattle your cage. They were strong little guys, amazingly strong for their size. Their muscle development didn't appear to be too great but they could really carry a lot of gear for their size. You could give them a shoulder pole and little 110 pound man or 90 pound woman could carry twice as much weight as most people twice their size. It's really quite astounding. Carrying things on their shoulders like that must be a matter of adaptation and developing strong legs. Plus there is a special coordination involved in the way they walk when they carry these shoulder poles. But they can really tote stuff for miles and miles on end. They proved that in the war coming down the Ho Chi Minh Trail. That's how they did it.

I walked into The Blue Room and The Owl was sitting there. Stone-Face followed me in and sat down on another chair with the automatic

131

weapon across his lap. The Owl pulled out a paper and read it to me in his own clumsy fashion. He said that by order of the camp commander, because I refused to cooperate, I had hereby been sentenced to death. Then he went into his familiar line of bullshit that I'd heard over and over, about how no one knew I was there, that I'd been declared dead, that everyone in the world thought I was dead, my wife thought I was dead. She was bemoaning your death. My mother thought I was dead; my mother, Mrs. Mae Butler, my wife, Mrs. Karen Butler, and my little daughter, Diane Butler. In fact all this revelation was interesting, meaning they had gotten information about my "demise" from our U.S. newspapers.

Then he went on with stuff about how they knew that I had graduated from United States Naval Academy. They knew I flew A-4Cs off the USS Midway and on and on. They had gotten all this from *Time* magazine and various other publications that had been kind enough to write of my demise. Apparently there was a full blow-out on me being lost on a heroic mission.

The Owl went on with this tripe and wound up saying that since the whole world thinks I am dead that I am of no use to them. Since I refuse to cooperate I am of no use to them, so now here at this prison and by order of the camp commander I've been sentenced to death.

At that point I really didn't give a shit. The threat of being killed just didn't matter at that point. Plus we had learned in survival school about this kind of treatment. They taught us how they would have me dig my own grave and then put me up in front of a firing squad. I had expected they might pull this kind of crude treatment on me, and that's just what they did. I was taken out of The Blue Room and into the courtyard.

They had me stand up against the wall. The Owl held a flashlight on my face and Stone-Face locked and loaded his automatic weapon. The Owl said, "Now, do you have anything to say?" I said something stupendous like, "God Bless America" or some horseshit like that. Stone-Face then pointed his rifle at me and pulled the trigger. "Click."

There was no bullet. The Owl just gave up in utter disgust and they marched me back into the quiz room again. By this time I was getting pretty damn sleepy. I hadn't given them anything at all. I was really tired and worn out and I looked at him and said, "How about letting me go back to my cell and go to sleep?"

That kind of brightened him up because I had finally said something to him. He said, "You like to sleep?" And I said, "Yeah, I'm tired and so are you." He looked just dead. He smiled and kind of laughed and he said,

"Yes, I am tired also." But he said, "You see now, you come to this room many, many times. You spend much time in this room. You must talk to us. You must. You must. We are very patient people. You must talk to us."

It began to soak in as I added two plus two that I needed to figure out a better plan than just stonewalling. The number one factor was my health. They had promised that if I would give them basic information, like what squadron I was in, which they already had, what airplane I flew, which they already had, and what my wife's and mother's names were, which they already had, that I would get some items in exchange.

What did I want? First and foremost was a mosquito net. I was just about wiped-out from the damn mosquitoes. They were incredible. Sheer torture. They were clouds of buzzing and attacking that could just about drive someone out of his mind. And they were after me from sunset to sunrise. During the day they were off digesting my blood, but during the night they were such a plague that if you haven't experienced it, you can't understand.

The second greatest need was for my feet which were causing me a lot of problems. The bottoms of my feet had cracked opened, I guessed from the dehydration, and everywhere I walked I left a trail of blood. My feet were infected and swollen from walking around in the dirt and they had told me that they would get me a pair of shoes, what they call shoes, if I cooperated.

The third item I was promised was a blanket to sleep under. It was April. It was hot as hell during the day, but cold at night.

I thought about these little niceties and this hero shit of going name, rank, and service number until the day you die. I thought about this round-the-clock interrogation stuff. The Owl said I would be going through this again on Monday, so when then sent me back to my cell I thought about this stuff all day long Sunday. I paced up and down the cell and there was no one that came to me other than the guard to give me my food and water. I cranked this stuff around and around and I decided I needed an alternative approach.

Here I was all on my own. I had received survival-school training where I had been told to give up nothing but my name, rank, service number, and date of birth. To go against that training required a momentous decision for me. But when I weighed going against my training and dying, I decided that I was here in Hanoi alone, on my own and I had to judge things according to the situation I was in. Simply put, my situation was not the same situation I had in survival school. It was different.

My Naval Academy training began to come back to me as well. One thing that stood out in my mind, and also began to occupy the time, was a little book we were given at the beginning of our first year as plebes. The book was "Reef Points." This little pocket-sized, 300 page book contained an enormous amount of wisdom, Navy lore and traditions, leadership and poems that we were required to memorize. In fact the upper classmen held us responsible for memorizing the entire book. It was just amazing how much I remembered seven years later. One of the 27 "Laws of the Navy" we memorized came back to me in a powerful way. "On the strength of one link in the cable...." Well here I was. And I was that cable to be tested.

From the way these people talked it was obvious to me by the end of that first week that they were dangerously stupid. They not only didn't know anything but they weren't asking for anything that would be harmful to my fellow fliers. There was one question they had been asking me over and over and over and over: "What airplane were you flying?" They knew I was flying an A4C from the wreckage. And I knew they knew because they had told me so

So when I marched in that Monday morning, sat on the stool, I was asked my name, rank, service number, and date of birth and I answered those questions. Then he went into about an hour of bull shit again and then he said, "What airplane were you flying?" And without even batting an eye I just looked at him and said, "An A4C."

He almost fell off his chair, literally. He got up, walked around to the door and called the guard. The guard came and took me back to my cell. I sat in my cell for the rest of the day and that night. I wasn't called out again until the next morning. As it turned out, that was the end of the round-the-clock quizzes. About an hour after I got back from the quiz, the guard came back with a blanket, mosquito net and a pair of rubber, go-ahead sandals.

Perhaps you wouldn't think so, but the fact was that I felt like the lowest cur on the face of the earth. I felt like I had betrayed my country. I felt that I had accepted special favors for revealing this information, even though I knew they already had it. I felt that I had disobeyed the code of conduct, that I had violated every military law that ever existed. All these things ran through my mind. I felt like I was a traitor to my country. This is what went through my mind. I had made the first step into hell.

I think this was felt by every guy who talked, and eventually all of them did. When I say talk, I mean that they rarely provided information the enemy didn't already have. And our guys knew they had it so what they were saying wasn't really treason. Still, to a varying degree depending on the guy, we all felt at some point the horror and shame that I felt.

I will say that I neither suffered this guilt the most nor the least. My feelings were probably on the milder side. A lot of guys ate their hearts out for months on end over what was a little thing. If American military people ever risk getting captured, the survival schools should teach them this second line of defense. That it's okay to talk, to tell the enemy more than name, rank, et cetera. That it was not only okay but smart.

Having decided to pursue this second line of defense, I encountered those doubts, those psychological problems. And I must reiterate that no one benefits from this self torture. For me at that time it was a question of what is right versus what is selfish. But what it really amounted to was survival. It seems silly to think that the blanket, the mosquito netting and the shower shoes were rewards for selling out my country. Those things were being held out as a bribe, for sure, but that didn't mean that any reasonable enemy wouldn't give them to a prisoner of war in the first place.

Anyone who might be in my situation should be aware of this whole ball of wax. There are always the doubts, the fears and the pain. They need to understand the psychology of the situation so they can defuse this self flagellation. They need to be told that these feelings might come up at any time and any place. Suddenly you would experience a deep sense of guilt and depression.

For the next week or so I had maybe a quiz a day. These would come at different times during the day. Sometimes morning, sometimes afternoons and even on one occasion I had a night quiz. It wasn't in the middle of the night, but after evening meal. I was allowed to bathe each day which was a big deal for a POW, especially later, and I was even given soap. No, it was not a moisturizing bar. This was like a block of laundry soap. It was heavy in lye and pretty tough on your skin, but it did the job.

I was also given a Vietnamese toothbrush and toothpaste, both of which were of extremely low quality. The toothbrush snapped off in my hand about the third time I used it, which was a something of a nuisance. The guard came in one day and happened to see it. He told me to hold the broken ends together while he stuck a cigarette lighter on it which welded it back together. This seemed to be a standard technique for them to fix their toothbrushes too. The plastic was so cheap you could weld it back together with a cigarette lighter or match flame. I got a kick out of the toothpaste named "Hoa Mai," after a Vietnamese flower. It also said in English "Much bubble, nice taste." Well, not quite.

I noticed that strangely, from this very earliest period on, the

Vietnamese seemed primarily interested in biographical data. Shortly after the beginning they showed a lack of interest in military information. In the beginning it seemed more out of curiosity when asked about military information. For instance, they wanted to know what it was like to live on an aircraft carrier, but it was obviously curiosity on the part of the interrogator. He wasn't really searching for anything strategic.

I remember that they did ask me a question one time about the radar the ship had but I couldn't have told them if I wanted to. It wasn't anything that I cared or knew about. It made sense, in a way, that they weren't asking military questions because they didn't know enough to make use of any information I might have. I mean, when I say they were really stupid, I don't think I'm giving the full picture. They simply didn't know. They didn't have a context for anything I might have told them.

There was one quiz when that became unassailably clear. One day they asked me a question that shocked me though I tried not to show it. They asked, "Where are the pigs, and chickens and cattle kept on board the ship?" It was such an odd question, I couldn't figure it out. What did they mean or why did they ask it? Then I realized that they didn't have any refrigeration. So if they had a big boat, well, they just put their pigs and whatever they needed on it.

What an opportunity that was for me. And I jumped on it. I could basically just tell them what they didn't know, making up whatever I wanted, and they'd be happy. So I explained in great detail where the pigs and chickens and cows were kept on the USS Midway. Another theme I discovered was that they thought there was a huge, dirty divide between the officers and enlisted men. They thought we officers were dirty bastards who treated enlisted men badly. So when they asked me about the swimming pools on the ship I assured them that yes, we had swimming pools. And yes. we had an officer's swimming pool and an enlisted swimming pool. This fit their political biases about us so my answers sounded perfectly square to them.

There was the occasional military question that I would refuse to answer. For instance, one question they kept pounding at me for about a week that was, "What is the range of the A-4C?" I couldn't answer that. That was important information. Though thinking back on it, I'm not sure they would know what to do with the information that I could have given them.

I had in mind fuel figures for different bomb loads, with in-flight refueling and non-refueling, profiles for different altitudes and so forth.

These situations and configurations define the range of the aircraft so it is complicated. It makes a vast difference, anywhere from a combat radius of 100 miles to 700 miles. I wondered if they knew the significance of the information I was refusing to divulge since they kept asking about it.

Their persistence worried me. The Owl kept going after me on this question and he wouldn't let up. Finally I was being quizzed on this one afternoon and he seemed bound and determined to get an answer out of me. Over and over again in this quiz he kept asking me about the range of the A-4. He kept me later and later until it became obvious to me that he was being required by his superiors to find out, regardless.

I finally equated the bureaucracy of his system with the question. I recognized it because we have bureaucracy in our system. It's probably the same everywhere. When a requirement comes down from headquarters for such and such, those who get the order have to somehow "fill the square," as we say. Well that was the square The Owl had to fill and he had to fill it that day. He'd been dicking around with me for about a week on this thing and gotten nothing.

Finally, in utter desperation, in tormented fury and screaming and yelling and gnashing his teeth and pulling his hair, he finally said, "Why will you not tell me the range? I must know what the range is. I know the range. I know what the goddamn range is, but you must tell me!"

I thought about that and realized I had been thinking on a sophisticated bent and had not been thinking on this man's or on their level. And as he continued to talk he said, "You must tell me, I know that the range of A-4C is 250 miles. I know that, but you must tell me!"

So I said, "You are right, I don't know how in the world you ever got that information, but that's exactly right. It is 250 miles."

That produced a smile that could have lighted the whole of North Vietnam. He even thanked me profusely and wrote it down in his book and told me I could go to my room. And that was the last I ever heard of that.

For the record, very briefly during this military question stuff, they seemed like they were going to question me about the performance capability of the aircraft but they were very crude in their manner. I inferred that they didn't understand enough to even ask me what they thought they wanted to know. During one session the interrogator picked up a pencil and swept it through the air in a motion of an airplane making a loop and he said, "Can you do this in your airplane?"

I said, "Sure, no problem at all." Then he took the pencil and swept it around in an outside loop and said, "Can you do this in your airplane?" I said, "Sure. No problem, no problem at all." I could just see an A-4C if you tried to do an outside loop. Neither you nor the airplane would live through the negative G forces. But that was the only time I was questioned about the capacity and characteristics of the airplane.

I remember that they did ask me what altitude we flew at, but again they didn't seem to know what they were talking about. The question itself shows they were just asking what they were told to ask without understanding anything about how planes fly. We flew at altitudes anywhere from fifty feet off the ground up to 40,000 feet.

I decided I had to give him an answer on this one, so I just picked a figure. I said "12,725 and ½ feet," and he wrote that down in his book. Another time I was asked about a dive angle we used when we released our bombs. Of course, I wouldn't tell them that. The truth is that the angles vary according to the kind of attack we were making. We used different dive angles and different release altitudes so it would have been tough to answer that one even if I wanted to. He stayed on that for a few minutes and then dropped it.

These were some of the military questions they put to me. And while they seem important, compared to the rest of the interrogation questions they were just a small piece of what they asked. And I wouldn't, and didn't, ever give them anything useful. Maybe their problem was the people they used for interrogators didn't understand the technical areas they were getting into.

One day about two months later, when I had not had an interrogation in a month and a half, I was called into a quiz room and The Owl sat there along with another guy that I had never seen before. They had some piece of metal wreckage in the room with them. The Owl told me to look at this stuff. He wanted to know what it was. I told him I didn't know. I was lying though. I knew it was a Shrike missile. This was a very new technology that we had just started to use, the first air-to-ground guided missiles.

Then he proceeded to explain to me, "This weapon was fired at a truck that had radar on it. It went off too far away from the truck and did not harm the truck." He just told me that point blank and said they had recovered this wreckage. He said, "What is the name of this wreckage?" I said, "I don't know." He said, "Have you ever used this weapon?" I said, "I cannot answer that question." And with that they sent me back to my cell. All in all, the interrogation process during those first few months was pretty low key. And the only time I got slapped was when I was acting up, being deliberately and obviously difficult, acting surly or swearing at them.

7. Communication, Humor and Optimism

While part of me was dealing with my hosts, most of my attention was focused on making and maintaining contact with my fellow POWs. Maybe it seems surprising, but the first thing that came into my mind the instant I was separated from my normal life was to make contact another American. From my experience, I think it is an instinctive thing for an American to do. I would add that I think this instinct that we have has played a great part in our being able to cope with problems. There was social glue, a bond that got us all through the roughest times.

We all shared this strong desire to communicate with each other and we would take considerable risks to stay in touch with each other. I started off on this communications jaunt probably more from this instinct than thought. One of my first actions took place in the shower around the second day I was in New Guy Village at the Hanoi Hilton. When I was left alone in the shower without the guard, using a rock, I scratched my name on the shower wall. The guard quickly noticed it and rubbed it out.

Our communication efforts were rudimentary at this early time. We'd pick up little pieces of paper here and there out in the yard when the guard wasn't looking. They would be just tiny scraps of paper. We would also always ask the guard for matches to light our cigarettes with. After we struck a match we had burnt carbon and if we wet it just the tiniest bit with the tip of our tongue we'd have a writing implement. If we wrote very lightly we could actually write out twenty or so characters with one match stick. That's how we wrote our first notes. Later on we developed more sophisticated means of communicating which I'll get to later.

Later in my cell, frustrated at my lack of communications equipment – like a pen, pencil, paper – I managed to pull a brick out of the window sill in the back of my cell. I broke a piece of it off and ground it down on the concrete floor until it was flat. Then with another piece of sharp brick I carved my name in it, along with "USN" and my rank. I hid this thing in the crotch of my trousers and the next time I went to the shower I left it in the back of the crapper stalls. I set it up on the stall and hoped some American would find it. No success really came from that.

But it turned out in a way I was successful with my next effort. They had taken out the Vietnamese woman who'd been in the cell next to mine and had put in an Asian man. As soon as the door closed on him, this guy started to bang on the walls. Then, maybe an hour later, he began to tap on the wall. He tapped three taps. Immediately I was at the wall. I didn't know who was there. But I thought it might be an American. I tapped three taps back to him. He tapped four and I tapped four. He tapped two and I tapped two.

Then he started laughing like hell. For some reason he seemed to think this was the funniest thing in the world. Knowing the guard wasn't around, I called out to the other prisoner through the back window. No response. So I tried a new language. I whistled a little tune, and lo and behold, he whistled back at me.

I don't know to this day whether this guy was Thai or Vietnamese or whatever. But for days we'd whistle back and forth to each other; just two cons sitting in their cells. It didn't seem to make much difference that I was an American POW and he was someone who had gotten on the wrong side of someone with the power to put him in prison.

One day it occurred to me that since the French had been in Indo-China for a long time, maybe I could communicate with him through French. I started whistling that French ditty, "Frere Jacques." He picked up on it immediately. He laughed and whistled the song back. Soon we were whistling back and forth to each other in rounds.

This guy would laugh and cackle all the time. So I decided to call him "Crazy Charlie." "Charlie" of course was from our nickname for the Vietnamese "Viet Cong." About the fourth day I was there, during siesta time, the guard had let Charlie out of his cell. They were keeping him in the stocks, but with only one leg locked in. They always gave special treatment to us Americans later on. When American prisoners were put in stocks it was with both legs. For the Vietnamese it was one leg. Americans didn't get any exercise outside while the Vietnamese got to exercise outside every day and so on. This preferential treatment lasted until the end of 1969. We were the receivers of the longest sentences and the worst treatment, befitting our being their worst criminals.

So one day Stone-Face came down and let this nutty guy out for a little exercise but he didn't take him into the courtyard. Instead he left him in the hallway onto which our four cell doors faced. I guess the guard had to go take a leak or something because he walked out and left Crazy Charlie locked up in the hallway outside our cells. As soon as the guard was gone Crazy Charlie was at my cell door. I didn't know it when he opened my peek. I thought it was the guard. He damn near scared the daylights out of me because I heard the peek go open and when I looked I saw an apparition looking back at me.

Crazy Charlie didn't have any teeth, which was quite evident in the huge maniacal grin he had on his face. The wild toothless smile was accented by his beady bright eyes. He was a perfect caricature of a crazy person. So there was this picture of insanity leering in at me through the peek-hole. As soon as he saw me looking at him, he started yelling, "Aah aah aah aah aah," laughing and giggling.

Back home I would have had nothing to do with someone like this, but there in the Hanoi Hilton my social life was a little thin so I put my elbow up on the door and said, "Hi, how ya doing?" Crazy Charlie giggled and laughed and smiled his crazy grin at me and then he stuck his fingers through the bars in the peep. He wanted to touch me so I let him touch me. Then he reached into his pocket and pulled out a crackle-bar.

A "crackle-bar" is something they gave the Gook prisoners. It was a piece cut from the top crust of the huge pots of rice they cooked up every day. It was a kind of a rice wafer cracker about 8"x 8" and as hard as a brick. You had to break it over your knee because it's almost impossible to break with your teeth. They gave these things to the Vietnamese prisoners with their rice and green soup.

He pulled this crackle-bar out of his pocket and thrust it through the bars at me. I said, "No, No, I can't take this thing." He said, "Uah uah uah uah uah." He wanted me to take it and he was pushing it through the bar. Finally a thought seemed to come to him, and he said, "Oooh" and pulled it back. Then "wham!" He busted it over his knee and offered me half of it, while holding the other half up to his mouth. He was acknowledging that I wouldn't be taking all of his food. He was saying, "Let me give you half."

Of course I couldn't refuse - Crazy or not, Vietnamese or not, in prison for what I couldn't even guess. I took it from him and we stood there grinning at each other through the peek hole, munching on our crackle-bars together.

This didn't last long because Stone-Face came back. Stone-Face opened the cellblock door and immediately saw what was going on. He was angry. He ran over and grabbed this old guy, threw him up against the wall, and began screaming at him in Vietnamese. He shook his fist in his face.

At first the little old guy acted scared. But then he looked over Stone-Face's shoulder and he saw me at the window watching the action. He looked back at Stone-Face and then suddenly he got angry. He reached up and grabbed Stone-Face by the front of his uniform. He whipped him around and slammed him up against the wall and started giving him the same business. What a reversal. It was just hilarious.

When he had gotten through chewing out Stone-Face he let him go. Then Crazy Charlie stood real tall and proud. With his shoulders thrown back he walked over to my peek hole and stuck the rest of his crackle-bar through to me. I took it from him and said, "Thank You." He smiled real big and nodded his head. Then he took my peek-hole door and slammed it shut. I heard him march back to his cell with Stone Face. That was my only encounter with Crazy Charlie.

French songs were not the limit of my back window repertoire. I also whistled American songs in a continuing effort to make contact with Americans. One day I got a whistle back. It was off-key, from someone who can't whistle too well, but it definitely came from an American. I placed it as coming from cell four which was three cells down from me.

I was so excited I almost wet my pants. Of course I whistled "Anchors Away" and this guy whistled back the Air Force song. I immediately knew I had myself an Air Force jock as a neighbor. The guard came around and told us to stop. Clearly it was his purpose to prevent contact among the prisoners.

When the guard finally left the area, I called out the back window, "This is Lieutenant Phil Butler. How do you read?" I have a loud voice anyway but I must have shouted it in my excitement. This guy called back to me, in a thick Boston accent that was the most beautiful sound I can remember: "Gee! Not so loud."

He was Air Force Captain Ron Storz as I quickly discovered from what little talk we could make out our back windows down the alley way. Later on we established a note drop area in the crapper and we would exchange notes to each other by hiding them under a brick there. I found out from him that there was another prisoner in our area. He was also in New Guy Village but he was in a room that was off the main court yard. This turned out to be Bob Shumaker. I'd known Shu was shot down and was happy to know that he was in our general area.

I asked Ron by note where Alvarez might be but he said he did not know. I asked him if he knew anything about Scotty Morgan and he said "Who is Scotty Morgan?" He apparently hadn't been in the Heartbreak area and hadn't run into Scotty yet. So I told him about Scotty and I also told him about Ray Vohden. Ray had been shot down on the 4th of April. I had known about that before I went down from a briefing on the ship. The Vietnamese interrogators had talked about Vohden, informing me that he was injured and was staying at another camp. That turned out to be a lie.

142

We were all staying in the Hilton compound.

I told Storz what I knew about Ray and about a day later he told me that he had contacted Shu by note drop. Shumaker was using the same shower we were, but they were always taking us separately, not letting us encounter each other. But soon we got Shu in on the hidden note process with us.

It turned out that Shu was in a room where he could watch us go in and out of the shower when it was our time. He had been watching us for days through a crack in his cell door. We learned this through hidden note communications. So from then on when we'd walk out of shower stall, we would aim a big smile in his direction, or give him the finger. It was a little morale boost for him. Shu later told me those little things made his whole day.

I can't overstate how much our communications, as limited as they were, meant to us. It really and truly meant our sanity. Our communications were so limited that on the surface they were almost meaningless. So there was a sense of humor about them. Part of it was that we were communicating with each other and the guards didn't know it. No wonder they wanted to keep us apart. It was that important to our morale. It literally meant survival to all of us.

In prison life you could never lose your sense of humor. Whether it is with the guard or with your buddies, you had to keep a grasp on humor. This was imperative especially during the worst times, those moments of such deep despair that death looked equally reasonable. We all knew that if we didn't somehow keep our sense of humor we would be in serious trouble.

Pretty soon Ron, Shu and I were in regular contact with each other through our crapper communications system. Bear in mind I had never seen Ron or Shu. I never got a look at them face to face. I tried to slide my peek-door open. I had made a little wire gizmo that I could snake outside the crack in the peek to work the latch to slide it open, but the first time I tried it there was the guard standing outside. I had been trying to slide it open just as Ron walked by my cell so I could get a look at him, but it didn't happen.

During our "conversations" it was revealed that Shu was the senior in rank, followed by Ron and then me. I asked Shu if he had any instructions for us. At first his instructions seemed vague, but as time passed I realized how sage he really was. He told us that he didn't have any specific advice for us at that time. We were beyond name, rank, service number and date of birth with the Vietnamese at that point, just as he was. He told us not to feel low for having gone to a second line of defense. He also told us it was vital that we keep our sense of humor. And, he said, we needed to keep faith. That wasn't so much religious as faith in ourselves and our country that we would get back home some day.

He also told us that he did not know of any torture or of any bad treatment at that time. This was early on, just a few months from the time they captured their first Americans and their practices would change all too soon. But at the time it was a relief for us because we didn't know what to expect. Another thing was Shumaker had bugged them enough that they finally gave him a pencil. He used the pencil in his room to work math problems to pass the time. Shu was good at math and engineering. But the Vietnamese didn't know that he was also writing lengthy notes to us with that pencil. He would write them in such a way that we had to only respond with yes, no or a very short answer.

Not long after that I was moved. It was the beginning of June; maybe a month and a half since my plane had blown up. Late one night they came to take me away.

8. Hanoi Hilton – The Stock Yard & "Showtime"

I moved to my new digs, just another of many different areas in the Hilton, in the first week of June. To my knowledge no other prisoners had lived there, or if they had it was very sporadic. But since I had this area all to myself I gave it my own name. I called it the "Stock Yard," so named because there was a pig and chicken pen just outside my cell.

I was surprised and briefly pleased to discover that it was actually a room, not a cell. And it was even a kind of double room with an archway separating the two rooms. A door with a lock had been installed in the archway. I was also delighted to see that instead of a concrete slab there was a bed, a regular bed with an iron rail. Less delightful was the fact that the bed had boards on the top of it with no padding.

Also in the room were a chair and a very small, crude desk. In the back of the cell was another doorway. It was through this door that I was taken out into a gravel court yard where I could wash myself with the water from a spigot.

This door at the back of the room had a lock on the inside of the room. The guard would come in through the front door and unlock the back door to let me out unto the courtyard to bathe. As soon as I saw that lock on my side of the door, I began to get ideas. I started working in my spare time, most of the 24 hours in every day, on a way to open the lock. I didn't know what I was going to do once I got it open because I was in downtown Hanoi, but I was going to try to get it open. That was the kind of one-step-at-a-time thinking that was common among prisoners.

I worked with nails and wood until I finally found the secret to this lock, and that was to make a little bend in the nail on the front end of the point and then a larger bend on the back of it so I could use it like a key. I worked on it one day during siesta and finally, much to my amazement, got the lock open. This was particularly exciting because I had no real idea what I was doing. It was just intuition and fiddling around.

But now that I had it open I thought about what that meant. What was I going to do? As I was sitting there considering my success and wondering what I was going to do about it, I heard the end-of-siesta bell go off outside. I knew I had better lock it back up fast because my guard would be around soon. That's when I discovered that this old lock was more amenable to being picked open than locked up again.

It was a Chinese lock, about as big as my hand. Try as I might, I couldn't get it to lock. Pushing it into place wouldn't do it. I had to figure out how to turn the "key" that I had made the other way before it would lock. I started worrying because I knew I had to get that thing locked again before the guard came to let me out into the courtyard and discovered it unlocked.

I started working frantically and as the minutes clicked away I knew the guard was on his way to my room to take me outside to wash my dishes. I knew I would get caught with that damn thing open. I knew what that would mean. I would be in leg irons or some kind of max security.

Luckily he was late that day. I swear just before he got to my front cell door, I could hear the jangle of those keys. And that was when I managed to get the bastard locked again. It couldn't have been a closer call.

About the first day I was in there I was called out to a quiz. I walked in to see The Owl again and sat down on the stool. The Owl said, "You know of course that Ray Vohden has been wounded."

I said, "Yes, I know that and I've asked you many times to be allowed to see him because he is a wounded officer."

He said, "Yes, I know you have requested many times to see Lieutenant Commander Vohden."

I said, "Yes, this is only right and not only that, it is the only humane thing to do. It is only humane that he should have someone to help and look after him, another roommate, if not myself some other prisoner. He should be allowed to see someone if he is wounded."

The Owl nodded his head and said, "Yes, yes and that is why I called you here today. You are going to be allowed to see Vohden."

I said, "Good, when will I be allowed to see him?"

He said, "You will be allowed to see him this afternoon," and he said, "The reason you will be able to see him is because Vohden is going to have an operation."

I said, "What kind of operation?" These people were in the dark ages with medical technology.

He said, "On his leg."

Vohden's leg was broken with a compound fracture and the bone was completely separated at the break just above his ankle.

The Owl said, "You will be allowed to see him because he is going to have an operation and right now Vohden's spirits are very low and he has a great fever and we fear for his life. We want you to go in and cheer him up. We will give you fifteen minutes."

146

I said, "All right, very well."

He said, "Go back to your cell now and this afternoon you will go see Vohden."

I thought this was just another one of their tricks. I went back to my cell and I began to conjure up all kinds of stuff again about psychological tricks and dealings they were trying to play with me.

But as usual, none of my wild speculations were true. They weren't that sophisticated.

That afternoon they brought me out. I went to the quiz room and then they took me to a room where Ray Vohden lay on his bed. His leg was all wrapped up, propped up on a couple of old bloody, dirty blankets. Despite his obvious discomfort he was glad to see me, as I was glad to see him. He was the first American I had seen since leaving the USS Midway.

I sat down by his bed and we talked for about 15 minutes. The whole time I sat there I could smell the rancid odor of rotting flesh and I knew Ray had gangrene in his leg. He was in a lot of pain, He said as much. The Vietnamese would very rarely do anything for his pain. Only on rare occasion would they give him any morphine.

As it turned out they took him out that night to have a so-called operation which consisted of going into his leg and cutting away some of the bone and flesh that was gangrenous. That's all they did for him. They took him out that evening about 8:00 to some sort of hospital. They gave him some sort of anesthesia, possibly ether. When they were done cutting on his leg they loaded him back on a jeep and sent him back to his cell.

Ray was coming out of the anesthesia when he was being wheeled back into his cell. They threw him back on that wooden board and let him scream. We could hear him scream in pain all over the Heartbreak Hotel area. We could hear him screaming for the next couple of days.

On the 6th of July I was called out to the Blue Room again for another quiz. This time The Dog was there along with The Owl and The Eagle. We called the camp commander The Dog. It was probably unfair to dogs, but the reason we called him that was because talking to him was just like talking to an animal and not a person. He was just as stupid and stubborn as could be imagined. He was a Communist Party hack; just a complete tool with no other thought processes whatsoever.

They told me to sit down. I knew that with all three of them there it had to be important, but I couldn't imagine what it could be. They told me I was very fortunate to be selected to meet a delegation.

"To meet a what?" I asked.

"Meet a delegation," they repeated. "We are going to take you downtown in Hanoi and you will meet a delegation."

This is the first time any of them even admitted that I was in Hanoi. I had asked them more than once where I was but they would never tell me, even though it was obvious.

I said, "I don't want to meet a delegation."

They said "go back to your room."

So I went back to my cell and I began to think about this thing.

A lot of things started to go through my mind. First, that in all of my training, there had never been anything mentioned about going out to see a delegation or being taken some place to meet foreign visitors. This had never been discussed in my training. We'd been told to try not to be used for propaganda purposes, like having our pictures taken eating a cookie or drinking a beer or smoking a cigarette. Even though I never understood what kind of propaganda they could make out of a picture of you in your cell smoking a cigarette. I mean, what in the hell difference could it that make?

And yet there was a big emphasis on this in survival school, as in, you're going to rot in hell for being a traitor if you let a Gook take a picture of you smoking a cigarette. That seemed pretty asinine to all of us prisoners after we'd been there for awhile. That was my frame of reference while I was waiting for whatever was to develop. Really, if they came in here and told me to go outside and get into the jeep what could I do about it? I mean, if you're in jail some place and your captors tell you to go to another cell or to get into a vehicle or put on a certain kind of prison uniform, there isn't one hell of a lot you can do about it. You have to go along and do what you are told.

The next day they came around and gave me a razor and told me to shave. So I shaved. Then they brought a pair of pants that looked like ivy-league style about 1922 with pleats down the front, and shirt that was a civilian shirt. The guard Stone-Face threw the stuff on the bed and he indicated that I should "Put it on." I said, "No." He indicated again "Put that stuff on," pointing to the gear. I shook my head no.

He went outside and he gave a call and a couple of other guards came into the cell. He pointed again to the clothes and indicated to put them on. At that point it became obvious to me that I was going to put on the clothes and I figured doing it without a busted nose was the best way. So I went ahead and put on the clothes. Then he took me outside to the central court yard area where a jeep was sitting and indicated for me to get in. I got into the jeep.

Stone-Face got into the back with me while the driver and the interrogator, The Rabbit, got in the front seat. We drove into downtown Hanoi a few blocks away. We stopped on a back street and walked up some steps into a building, climbing up to the third floor. This building was a ramshackle mess. The plaster was falling down, the floors were torn up, and the windows were knocked out. It seemed to me like typical Vietnamese maintenance, but I couldn't believe that they would dress me up for some delegation and then take me to a place that was in such disrepair.

They marched me into a room and there sitting at a large round table were maybe a dozen Occidental men. I couldn't believe my eyes because I hadn't seen anyone but Asians in all this time. There was a stool in front of this round table and they told me to sit down, which I did. There were also a number of Vietnamese in the room, including the camp commander.

The interpreter started off by giving my name to those assembled. Then he came back to me and told me these men were Russian journalists. These guys had cameras around their necks. He said they wanted to talk to me today. I told him I was not going to talk to them. With that the Russian who was in the middle of the group, a little older guy, started speaking English to me, and he spoke very good English. He said, "Lieutenant Butler, I've been in your country on four occasions in the past. I am a journalist and write articles in my home country in Russia. We would just like to talk to you for a few minutes."

I said, "I'm really not interested."

He said we would not talk about military matters and then he kind of introduced the other people sitting around the table to me. One of them handed me a cigarette and pretty soon a guy came up and sat a beer in front of me and beers in front of all these guys. He said, "You may drink, and also you may eat." There was a big plate of cookies and other foods on the table.

Now I should note here that this was on the 6th of June and I had been shot down on the 20th of April. During that time my weight had gone from 180 to about 145 pounds. I was getting damn little to eat, only two small meals a day. I looked at those cookies and I was some kind of hungry. I said, "Why do you have cameras?"

He said, "If you do not wish us to take your picture then we will not."

I said, "I do not wish you to take my picture."

He said, "All right."

I looked all around the room and couldn't see any cameras. I looked all around the table and couldn't see any cameras. So I started grabbing cookies and shoving them down as quickly as I could. Then he started up a conversation. He talked like he knew the people in my family and their names. He knew I was the son of a carpenter. This was all information that I had "revealed" during the interrogations, after I'd learned that they knew it already. They had wanted to know what my father's occupation had been and I told them he had been a carpenter. That seemed like a good lie to give them because my father had actually been a contractor, a home builder.

Obviously the camp commander had supplied these Russians with what I had given him in the interrogations. So it went on like that for a while. I wouldn't talk to them. I just ate cookies. After my release I found out that they were able to take a picture of me during this meeting with the delegation, although I never saw the camera. The picture I saw was of me holding a banana in my hand. Be that as it may, as I looked back on it, if I were in there again I'd do the same thing. I'd grab all the chow I could and wolf it down. This was less about feeling hungry and more of concern about my deteriorating physical condition from not having enough to eat. It wasn't about propaganda. It was about withstanding the conditions at the prison.

The Russian guy gave me a cigarette and the guy sitting next to me lit it for me and he looked at me, smiled and said, "Ah, you smoke the Vietnamese cigarette."

"Yes, I do," I said not missing a beat.

"What do you think of the Vietnamese cigarette?" he asked.

The other Russian guys are kind of sitting back and grinning, you know.

I said, "They are okay."

He said, "I know, the Vietnamese cigarette, the Russian cigarette not as good as the American cigarette. We know you Americans make the best cigarettes in the whole world. We know that. That is known all over the world. But I tell you one thing though, Lieutenant Butler, we Russians make the best Vodka."

None of them ever identified themselves or gave any names. I thought they were probably missile technicians, since we knew the Russians were helping the North Vietnamese and that would make sense. The guy who was speaking to me in English though, I really thought he must have been a journalist. He obviously had been in the United States before. He told me about things he'd seen in the United States that no Russian, or any foreigner, would know unless he had actually seen them in person.

The guy who was talking to me was a moose. He must have weighed 275 pounds, solid muscle. Their interpreter was a Russian. He was a young guy who interpreted Vietnamese to Russian. I thought he did a pretty good job.

An interesting note is after I got back to the camp and was called into quiz one of the interrogators asked me if I had noticed this Russian guy speaking Vietnamese and I said, "Yes." Then the interrogator kind of screwed his nose up and said, "Those Russians cannot speak our language properly. They only speak it very poorly. It's almost impossible for us to understand them." There I was, really impressed in this meeting thinking all the time that these Russians are really cool and that they really knew how to handle these Vietnamese with diplomacy. I was impressed that they had their own people speaking Vietnamese and they were smooth as glass. But when I was in the quiz room I found out the Gooks really thought the Russians were slobs.

I have to say this for the Russians. I must have impressed them with how hungry I was because as I left the room this guy who spoke all the English said to me, "Lieutenant Butler, I understand why you could not talk to us today. That is quite all right. I understand." Then he said, "You seem to be very hungry." I said, "Yes, I am." He said, "I understand."

I turned around and walked out of the room and then back down to the street where we waited for the jeep to pick us up. Then a Vietnamese man came up to me with a newspaper rolled up into a big package. I looked inside and discovered that it was a whole batch of cookies and bananas and other goodies. The Vietnamese man spoke English and he said, "The men who you have just seen have told me to give this to you to take back to your cell." That meant a lot to me. Obviously these Russians felt sorry for me. I guessed that because they were big men too, they understood hunger and they knew what it must be like for me, subsisting on a Vietnamese level diet.

We got back into the jeep, preceded back to The Hilton, and back to my room in The Stock Yard. There was no big to-do. I was just taken back to my cell. They had me change back into the prison garb. They shut the door and left like nothing had ever happened. I spent the rest of that day thinking back on everything that I had said or not said during the meeting with the delegation, which was really just a press conference with the Soviets. I couldn't think of anything I had said or done that was prejudicial or would give propaganda other than the fact that my face was there and that I was alive.

Though I felt pretty good about what had happened and my role in it, I was determined that somehow or another I would have to foil any future such events. My thinking was that it was inevitable if I continued to go to these things, some way or another, they were going to be able to extract some good propaganda out of it. Over the next several days I thought about how I might make things worthless for the Vietnamese in propaganda terms, how I could get them off my back, to stop asking me to do them. That is, if they should ever ask me to do another one. They had not hinted to me at this time that I would ever go out to meet another delegation, but having little else to think about, I exercised my mind considerably over the possibility.

The next opportunity came again a couple of days later. I was called out to a quiz and was told I would be taken to a press conference, a meeting. I told the camp commander that I did not want to go to this meeting. He informed me that the jeep was waiting outside and I was to put on the clothes the guard had for me and that I was to get into the jeep. He said I had no choice. I warned him that while I had no jurisdiction over what clothes they put me in or where they sent me, my conduct was something they had no control over and that I would act according to my feelings.

He warned me to be a "good boy" and to not do anything that was out-of-line. I told him flat out that if they were looking for propaganda they would not get good results from me. I got into the clothes and there were a number of guards there again to make sure I did, one way or another. They put me in the jeep and away we went.

I had Stone-Face the guard in the back of the jeep with me, and another young guard on the way out there. This young guard got sick to his stomach. He threw up all over the place, which I thought was just hilarious. Stone-Face and I were laughing at him. This meant the young guard lost a lot of face and he was really down in the dumps over it.

This time they took me out on the edge of the city limits to a place they call their "War Memorial Museum." It consisted of an arcade with pictures and a yard with pieces of plane wreckage, along with some pilot's personal equipment. It was a junk yard, but what could you expect when they were furnishing the place from crash sites. There are a lot of similar "War Memorial Museums" around the country, and they pretty much look alike.

As soon as I got out of the jeep l saw a whole bunch of people with cameras descending on me. When they did this I made grimacing facial features, a big frown and flung out my arms in a "Get the hell out of here" manner. I was looking so nasty that they shut their cameras off and walked away from me. I don't know who they were. I didn't see any Caucasian people, but I'm sure there were both foreigners and Vietnamese.

I was led by several guards to a place about 30 or 40 feet away where a large desk was set up. On either side of this desk were small tables with four tape recorders. I was told to sit down on a stool in front of the desk. As soon as I sat down dozens of photographers and one guy with a huge movie camera on rollers came zooming up. I just sat there with my nastiest look and glared at them. I told the interpreter who was standing there to tell those cameras to get the hell out. He spoke to them and the cameras backed off.

Then another guy sat down across the table from me. He was a Japanese reporter from a communist newspaper in Japan. He introduced himself in Japanese and a Vietnamese interpreter translated the Japanese into Vietnamese to my interpreter who translated the Vietnamese into English to me. I knew right then and there that this was a can of worms and I decided I was not going to say anything whatsoever.

The Japanese guy informed me through the two interpreters that he wanted to ask me some questions. I just sat there and didn't say anything. They started all the tape recorders and he started asking me questions which I completely ignored and said nothing. Now the Gooks around me started getting a little excited because the situation was not panning out the way they had thought. They spoke to my interpreter who asked me what was wrong. I didn't answer him.

The interpreter said, "There is one thing a prisoner must say and that is you must give your name, rank and service number and date of birth. Will you do that?" I nodded my head. They had turned off the tape recorders and now they turned them on again. These recorders were in reach of me and I had noticed they were all National brand tape recorders and I happened to remember how the on/off switches worked because some of the guys I knew on the ship had bought them.

So as soon as they started the tape going and the camera men started moving in, I stood up and punched the off buttons on the tape recorders one by one. Then I flailed my arms around as I had done before to get the cameras out of the way. This caused a lot of excitement among the guards and people came running up. Pretty soon they all settled down and a woman came up who was serving as a kind of waitress. She offered me a tray that had some cookies and cigarettes and a bunch of other goodies on it. I turned it down and just waved her off. The Rabbit said, "All we want you to do is to give your name, rank, service number and date of birth." He added, "The cameraman wants to have your picture while you give this." He asked, "How can this be propaganda?"

I thought about it for a little bit and I thought okay I'll just give them my name, rank and service number and date of birth. So they left the tape recorders off this time and the cameraman came up. And suddenly I got a bright little idea and I indicated just by hand motions to The Rabbit to turn the tape recorders back on. And he did. They got all four of them going and all the cameramen came up and the movie guy started his movie reel.

Everything was in motion, everybody was poised for action. I said, "My name is Phillip Neal Butler, I'm a lieutenant in the United States Navy, Service Number 647398, date of birth, 11 Aug. 1938 and I have a statement I'd like to make to the world. God Bless America."

I stopped at that point and they clearly didn't like that. People were all pissed off and they were running around and jabbering. Then The Rabbit told me to stand up. I did. A bunch of guards got around me and led me out to go through this little arcade area. The cameramen came as I walked over in this direction and this guy with the big movie camera on rollers came towards me with lights and they started this shooting again.

I realized that what they wanted was film of me with all the war memorial wreckage in the background. I suppose they thought it would show that I was going around viewing all this stuff. So I turned around, pushed the guards out of the way, and walked back to the table. Not really knowing where to go or what to do, I just stood there. All the guards and cameramen went ape-shit and came running back towards me.

Then the movie guy got around behind me and tried to get a picture of me with the background of those wrecked aircraft things. When he did that I turned around, looked squarely into the camera and stuck my tongue out at him. Then I turned on my heels, left all the guards and people and walked back to the jeep. I climbed in it and sat down in the back seat.

The next guy who climbed into the jeep was Stone-Face. He had an angry look on his face. He sat down with his automatic weapon on his lap and just glared at me. The other little guard who had been sick didn't get in. Pretty soon the driver came along and then The Rabbit. They got in the front and we started driving to Hanoi. Stone-Face and I just sat there and stared at each other for about a minute or two as we drove off. Then all of a sudden, much to my surprise, Stone-Face changed his glare into a smile. He sat there and smiled at me for a few seconds and then he reached across and patted my shoulder about three or four times and nodded his head. We went back to the camp.

I guess I hadn't been a bad enough boy that day because the very next day they came and got me again and away we went to another meeting. I suspect that while I'd embarrassed them sufficiently they had already scheduled three events. They had already told the world that I was going to appear and they couldn't cancel them.

I learned from the camp commander before I left that another prisoner would also be at this press conference and that when I got back this other prisoner and I would live together and be roommates. I asked the camp commander if I would be in this meeting with this other prisoner. He gave me a typical Gook answer, "I don't know."

Getting a roommate was certainly good news. But I was really pissed about going to another one of these things and when I left the camp commander's office he could tell. He told me I had a very bad attitude and had not shown myself in a military way to the world the day before. He warned me that today I had better not do the same. As we drove to the meeting, I found out from The Rabbit that the other officer would be Lieutenant Commander Shumaker.

As we drove I began to plot in my mind what I was going to do and say. I decided that the problem yesterday was I had been a stinker in my actions but I hadn't said things that were lousy enough. So I determined that when I went to this one I was going to be a real ass-hole in what I said. The day before I hadn't said too much; just that one statement. They really hadn't got information from me that made them mad enough.

This trip took us back downtown and to a large building. They took me upstairs into a very large conference room. I walked in and learned that Shumaker had been there ahead of me and had already gone back. There were approximately 60 people, all sitting at different desks and tables around the room. I occupied a spot in the front of the room in the limelight.

This turned out to be the meeting of the "World Federation of Trade Unions," a commie organization of national rebels that run around stirring up commie crap. They were all commies from all over the world. Most of them were Asians. There was one fellow there who introduced himself as being from Albania. There was a black fellow from the Congo. There were also three people sitting in the front row close to my desk who introduced themselves as Americans.

Calling these people American was not quite accurate. They actually were not American citizens. One guy I recognized as someone who had been expelled from the United States in the late 1940s or early 1950s, about the time of the McCarthy hearings. His name was Sidney Rittenberg. This ass-hole was from either South or North Carolina. He was expatriated from the United States. Another one I had seen in some commie propaganda magazine that they had given me. She was a woman named Anna Louise Strong. Strong was a hard-core Communist. She was born in the United States and raised in Oregon or Washington. During World War II and after, she was stirring up a lot of trouble in unions in the United States. She also was expatriated from the United States around the McCarthy era. Rittenberg had been making his latest domicile in Cuba. Strong had been tossed out of Russia sometime before and I heard since that she was living in Peking.

The third guy I didn't know but he was a similar type international rebel. They were all people with no country. There was another Caucasian guy who I found out during this conference was from Great Britain. He told me his name at the time, but I didn't remember it. I wish I had.

The event started off and this time they had brains enough to sit me down at an empty table so I wouldn't refuse any food or cigarettes they offered me. There was an interpreter who was one of the most amazing I have ever seen. He was Vietnamese, about fifty, smaller than most, and he spoke seven or eight languages. Most impressive was that he could switch from one to the other instantly. He spoke outstanding English. As a matter of fact he spoke the best English of any Vietnamese I heard in the entire eight years. And he was not only fluent but he appeared expert at handling this crowd.

He started off with a bunch of stuff on my background. But the Strong lady interrupted. She was an old lady, probably close to 80. She said, "Before we get on with all that, let's get his name." Then she said, "Lieutenant Butler, will you give me your name please, sir?"

I said "All right," and I gave her my name, rank and service number and date of birth.

Then she started a conversation with me and she said, "Lieutenant Butler I will be returning to the United States soon and when I go back to the United States I will be happy to deliver a letter to your wife and tell her about your health. Would you like me to do that? I said, "I think I recognize you. You are Anna Louise Strong are you not?" She said, "Well, yes I am."

She had not introduced herself, but I said, "Miss Strong, I don't see how you can go back to the United States. As a matter or fact I know you cannot go back to the United States. I know you cannot go back to the United States because you were thrown out of the United States in the early '50's, isn't that correct?"

She kind of swallowed and coughed and the color rose in her face and that ended my conversation with Anna Louise Strong.

Then this black fellow from the Congo stood up and he had some questions to ask. He spoke in French. I could understand only a little bit of what he said, but it was all being interpreted for me. The text of his conversation was why did I come to Vietnam to bomb innocent women and children, to destroy this country 10,000 miles away from my own home? Why do I come here to drop napalm on innocent people, to drop toxic poisons, and gas, and blah, blah, etc?

They asked for my answer and I told him that I was here to perform a mission for my country and that I was fighting a war for my country, and that Communists like him and all the rest of these people in the world are going to have to realize that they could not push their way of life on us or on our allies. That pissed him off a bunch and he started waving his arms and swearing at me. I'm glad they didn't let him get to me because he was about a 240 pounder and about 6' 5" tall.

The next guy who jumped up was the man from Albania and he had the same sort of questions. He was an acid little guy. I replied to him by saying that his comments were so twisted, distorted, out of line, unreasonable and wrong that I would refuse to answer him. I told him that it was below my dignity as an officer in the United States Navy. He sat down in a huff.

Then the guy from Great Britain said, "Lieutenant Butler, may I speak to you for just a moment?"

I said, "Sure, say all you want." I was obviously really pissed off, glaring at everybody in the crowd.

He said, "Lieutenant Butler, it's my understanding sir, that you do not wish any pictures to be taken. You do not wish any propaganda to be made of you in this visit, is that correct sir?"

I said, "That is correct."

He said, "Sir, I wish you to consider for just a moment, and then he lapsed into a very fast-clipped English jargon that I was able to understand and that those ex Americans were able to understand but no one else in the room could, not even the interpreter. I'm sure that most people who spoke English could probably have understood it because it was full of slang and clipped phrases.

What he said was this, "Lieutenant Butler I have some very quick questions to ask you sir. I do not think you will regret having answered these questions. Please sir, please reconsider. Look at me now. I think I have something at stake for you in this and I have a good mission."

The way he looked at me and leaned forward and looked so earnestly, something clicked in my brain. I don't know exactly what but I just had the feeling that this cat was a double agent; as a matter of fact I'm just sure that he was. So I said "All right, go ahead and ask your questions."

He said, "All right sir, are you living in solitary confinement?"

I said, "Yes, I am."

He said, "Are you subsisting on a diet that is below standards to maintain your good health?"

I said, "Yes sir, I am."

He said, "Are you sleeping under improper circumstances, let's say, a concrete bunk or a wooden bed with very little clothing or necessities of life?"

I said, "Yes sir, I am."

He said, "Thank you, sir." He then said, "Lieutenant Butler sir, if you don't mind I have a camera here and I would like to take two very fast pictures of you and I don't think you will regret that either."

I said, "Shoot away."

He stood up real fast and he looked around him like he was real worried. He aimed his camera, snapped a picture of me, rolled the film real fast, snapped another, shoved his camera into his pocket and sat down with a smile on his face. And he said, "Thank you very much, Lieutenant Butler. I assure you, you will not regret that."

With that the Gooks came running up to me and told me to stand up. I went out of the room and got into the jeep with out further ado and was taken back to my cell.

That was the last time I was ever invited to play a little role at press conferences.

I was taken back to my cell in The Stock Yard again and there was nothing more said or even heard from about these meetings I had been to. I didn't get an interrogation nor was any pressure put on me to go to another. That was the last one I was invited to go to for the rest of my seven plus years there. This treatment changed later for other prisoners. When others refused to go to these meeting they were tortured at great lengths until they agreed to go. As far as I know, practically all of the guys who went to these press conferences did so under the threat of torture.

It turned out that it didn't matter how we behaved at these things. Whoever the so-called reporters were, they just printed whatever they wanted to make their allies, the North Vietnamese or fellow commies, look good. Whatever we said or did, they could make it into propaganda and they did. We couldn't protect ourselves or our country no matter what we did. It didn't matter about complying.

When I returned here to the United States I saw a copy of an article from "Pravda" that had been written by the Russians. It was just a pack of lies, most of it based on a complete fabrication of my background. They got most of their information from the Gooks who had gotten what they knew from articles that were published in newspapers and "Time Magazine" when I went down. Together with the biographical lies I gave them, the whole mess actually sounded sort of credible, at least the way they put it all together. Especially when they added quotes I didn't say. You can see that they are going to get their ten cents worth of propaganda no matter what.

I wasn't asked, but I think the way our government handled the whole POW issue in connection with these propaganda campaigns was complete nonsense. Maybe it was only military thinking or screwed-up politics, but they just shouldn't have let us go through this absurdity. They could have saved us a lot of pain if they had been sensible. They could have taken the pressure off of us.

It was our job to go out and fight the God damn war and when we were captured it was our job to sit in the prison camp and conduct ourselves as military men. Prior to the new shoot downs coming in 1972 and 73, 95% of us in Hanoi had been tortured. Of the around 500 of us who were in during that time, 40% of us had lived in solitary confinement for more than six months. I was included in both of these categories. 20% of us had lived in solitary confinement for more than one year and 10% for more than two years. There were some men up there who had been in solitary confinement for five and six years. Of course that kind of treatment is utter bullshit as is the torture.

But I think the United States government and military handed the Communists an opportunity to treat us badly by ordering us not to cooperate with the bullshit propaganda. It was the inflexibility of our administration and our armed forces that forced our resistance that resulted in the inhumane treatment we got. I don't think they did it deliberately but I don't know whether they thought it out. Or if they thought our suffering was worth whatever they thought they gained from it.

I think what our government should have done was announce to the world that American POWs should say whatever they needed to in order to protect themselves from torture and other mistreatment. There should have been an announcement by our government to the world that we were going to participate in such and such an area in a war, and that the men of our armed forces who were captured were given full rein to say anything whatsoever that was necessary to prevent them from being harassed, tortured, and degraded.

If this sort of announcement had been made before we wound up as POWs, then everyone in the world who saw a picture of an American bowing in front of some Vietnamese or making statements at a press conference...it would have just completely invalidated anything we said or did. And that would make it ridiculous for our captors to continue with this nonsense. It would also remove a reason for them to torture us.

We were told that it was our job to fight the propaganda game and to do everything we could to avoid being a part of it. That's wrong. It was our job to act as military men within the prison and to be left alone.

There were other guys who were taken to these meetings. Hayden Lockhart had gone to the War Memorial Museum ahead of me. When I talked to him about it later, he told me he had done just about what I had done except that he hadn't said anything at all, and he also had stuck his tongue out at the camera. He was never invited back. Robert Shumaker had also gone to the same War Memorial Museum as Hayden and I had. Bob had been captured about a month earlier than I had and they had taken him earlier.

Bob said that there was an Australian journalist at his event. Though I'm not positive, I'm pretty sure from the way he described this Australian journalist that he was really a well-known Communist who traveled throughout Indochina by the name of Wilfred Burchett. We POWs affectionately referred to him as "Will Read Bull Shit."

Another guy who was trotted out to the press conferences was Air Force Captain Richard Keirn. It was probably because he was a friendly sort of guy. He probably chatted up the people at those events. All of us warned him not to say anything because it was harmful no matter what he said, but I don't know how much good it did. We called him "Pop" because he was an old solider compared to most of us in the camp. He had fought in World War II as a B-17 gunner. He'd been shot down over Germany and had served as a prisoner of war there for about nine months. Pop was our only two-time POW! He got out of the service after WW II but then came back

160

in, became a pilot, and spent some time in Korea, and right on up until this war.

Pop was flying an F-4 over North Vietnam when he was shot down again, the poor son-of-a-bitch, and wound up being a POW again. He was a nice guy. I couldn't say enough good about him. Maybe because he was gregarious or because he was older, the Gooks kept pulling him back into these meetings. They put a lot of pressure on him. They would scream at him, yell at him and slap him around until he finally got to the point where he would get awfully scared. More than the rest of us. Maybe it was because he was older and maybe because he'd been through it before. Although he said the Germans didn't torture him. Plus it was worse being with the Vietnamese because their culture was so different.

Of course there isn't a thing in the world wrong with being scared, especially in something like our situation. As a matter of fact, a man with real courage fights even while he's scared and that's what Pop was doing. He was fighting even while he was running scared.

9. Fun with Guards and Interrogators

From the beginning of my arrival at the Hanoi Hilton until September of 1965, about 5 months, I experienced the routines of prison under Hanoi policemen. We had few Army personnel around at that time. The Dog was regular Army, as was The Rabbit. The Owl appeared to be a civilian interpreter who was learning how to be an interrogator. The Eagle was still of an unknown origin at that time. But all of our guards were Hanoi prison jailors, each with unique personalities, but not bad guys on a mission to kick us around.

In addition to Stone-Face, there was another guard who watched over us. We called him Rudolf because he had a red nose and blood shot eyes. He was a little younger than Stone-Face and a real character. He was a practical joker who liked to laugh and joke and have a good time. He was a little screwy but a pretty good guy. On Sundays Rudolf would bring his kids around to our cells. He had a couple of toddlers and some older kids. Rudolf would open the cell, bring his kids in, and let them look at the American criminal.

None of these guards spoke any English but we all knew inherently that we had to somehow relate to them. It was essential to our well being to establish some kind of rapport with these guards, hopefully good relations, without sacrificing any of our ideals or dignity. They were our life blood. Whatever they thought of us determined what was going to happen to us.

The guard Stone-Face was a very efficient old cop. He was very exact and he did his job. He had a real sense of responsibility. We could tell this after he had been around for a few days. As an example of how a prisoner could screw up, I was snotty and surly toward him in the beginning before I realized how important my relations with the guards were going to be.

This is not the way to treat one of these guys who is a highly efficient and duty-bound person. The way to act around these guys is to act like a good soldier and stand tall. When he tells you to go some place, just go there and keep your mouth shut. That way you will quickly establish a rapport with this type of individual. I began to do this after the first couple of days and pretty soon I had a pretty good rapport with Stone-Face. After that he gave me no more trouble.

Another learning experience came when I didn't ask for toilet paper. I felt I shouldn't ask for anything and as a result I didn't get what I didn't ask

162

for. I soon realized that this was stupid. If I needed something that was vital to me, for God's sake I had to ask them for it. Making that realization even more clear was how quickly I got what I asked for, when it was within reason.

My experience until then, presuming you want to know the nitty-gritty details of imprisonment, is that I would take my daily dump in the shower if I could hold it till then. I would wash myself in the shower room since there was no paper available. One day, on the way back to the cell, I noticed that Stone-Face was carrying a newspaper. I indicated to him, asking him if I could have it. He gave me a kind of questioning look, wondering why I wanted a Vietnamese newspaper. As we walked back to the cell he kept questioning me by poking me and non-verbally asking why I wanted that newspaper. He couldn't figure this out.

Finally, I answered him with hand signs that I wanted to use it for toilet paper. He stood back and looked at me. Then he took off his glasses and looked at me like I was some kind of a lunatic or imbecile. He motioned to me to go into my cell. He shut the door and about five minutes later he came back and opened up the hatch and shoved a bunch of their rough kind of toilet paper through the window. He couldn't believe that I'd been so stupid not to ask for what I wanted. I should go ahead and ask for it, if it was not an unreasonable need.

As far as dealing with Rudolf, he was a joker and loved to have fun. So he liked a guy if he liked to laugh and have fun. Obviously it wouldn't work for a prisoner to be dead pan serious with him. So I acted differently around Rudolf than I did Stone-Face. Pretty soon I established good rapport with Rudolf too. Rudolf would bring cigarettes around to the cells and shove a couple of them in through the peek. Sometimes late at night he would pass by and shove a couple in as well.

I was a smoker and sitting in the cell aching for one was a downer. So getting one from Rudolf or the other guards could do more for my morale than someone might imagine. There wasn't going to be a steak dinner in Hanoi so the cigarettes meant a lot to us.

Rudolf used to do some crazy things. For instance, he came around one day, walked into my cell and pulled his wallet out. He set his wallet down on the other bunk. He had taken out his wallet so that he could fish around in his pockets, apparently looking for things. This was typical of Rudolf, who was kind of a clod; sort of clumsy. I grabbed his wallet and acted like I was going to put it into my own pocket. This was Rudolf's kind of humor; the kind of gag that really got him going. It was probably

Vietnamese style too, maybe their version of American slapstick.

Rudolf laughed like hell so I opened up his wallet and started pulling everything out of it and laying his stuff down on the bunk. He came over by me and just watched as I went through his wallet. In fact I got quite an education in that farcical moment. I saw pictures of him and his family. I saw that he had a wife and five kids. I saw what their money looked like. I saw his ration card. I saw what appeared to be a driver's license and similar items. I got a good idea of what everyday articles look like that these people have.

It couldn't have been more interesting if I had been a sociologist and not a prisoner of war. It wasn't like the information was going to be of any use to me, even if I could escape. I didn't have a printing press and I was six-two, blond, and round-eyed. So getting out into Hanoi wasn't a good idea. I just didn't fit in.

One day I decided to give Rudolf English lessons, after a fashion, and he really got a big kick out of this. One of the first things I taught Rudolf to say, and this took quite awhile, was "Vote for Goldwater!" I worked on that for about a week and finally he got it down pat. I could peer out of my cell and see him saying it to other guards. One day I noticed him out talking to the camp commander, repeating the phrase.

Rudolf came back to my cell the next day and he pointed his finger at me. He had a big frown on his face. He said, "Vote for Goldwater - humm humm?" Then he broke into hysterical laughter because he had found out what it meant. Apparently the camp commander had explained it to him and he wasn't amused.

Another English lesson I gave Rudolf was I'd point to my eye and I'd say, "I'm" and he'd mimic that and I'd point to my ear and say, "queer." Rudolf did that beautifully. He'd say, "I'm queer," to all the other guards. He also would go around and say this to other American prisoners. Of course the other American prisoners would obviously know that it had come from another American prisoner, and they would get a huge charge out of it when he'd try it on them.

This sums it up about my experience with the guards. A prisoner needs to try to establish a rapport with those people, and also keep a sense of humor consistent with what theirs is. If you're dealing with sophisticated people like Germans or Russians or somebody like us, then their sense of humor is going to be more like ours. If you're dealing with less sophisticated people, then your sense of humor is going to have to be tailored to their level in order for them to appreciate it.

That's advice for dealing with the guards. The interrogators were different. They were tougher. They were focused on getting information from me. They were also in my life for short periods of time, while the guards were around us most of the days and nights. It was possible to develop a sort of rapport with an interrogator on rare occasions, but it was more in the nature of a relationship in which he'd leave me alone.

I guess it really wasn't about a rapport. Either I irritated him enough or I was repulsive enough that he didn't want to talk to. Or that he thinks I'm stupid and can't give him anything. Sometimes we found that a particular interrogator might begin to like us and he laid off for that reason. But that was rare.

We had to be careful with the interrogators because they could make our lives miserable. Trying to manipulate them could lead to trouble if we weren't careful how we went about it. Some of us, in the very early days of our captivity, developed something of a positive rapport with interrogators like The Owl. Later on we certainly did our best to appear repulsive, or very stupid.

It wasn't so easy to convince them that we were stupid since they knew we were American airmen and college graduates. They probably understood that to mean we were ten times as smart as they were to begin with. A few guys were able to pull it off with some interrogators, but mostly it didn't work.

From my experience, I think the best thing I could do was to go in there and use my own personality, and not give them anything. I used the subtle techniques like looking at their ear, hands or something. You can be as difficult and obnoxious as you want, but if you go too far they're likely to bang your head against the wall. Then you want to back off a little until they calm down, and then go at it again. If there is one rule to follow, it is to just keep your damn mouth shut as much as possible.

That's relative of course. One route we tried with some success was to pretend we were having difficulty understanding them because their English was so bad. And then whenever we did answer, we'd make our responses impossible to understand. So it looked like we weren't resisting so much as having trouble communicating.

So, for instance, an interrogator might say to me, "Now you come to meet me for first time today and so now I ask you how are you? How are you today?" Then I would simply sit there like a bump on a log and give him a blank look. No expression is the best approach with these Asians.

Sometimes he would sit there and look at me for what seemed to be an eternity. Finally he would get nervous and want to keep this going. So he might start into a line of patter on his own and continue to do this. That way I put a huge burden on him because he has to do all the talking while I'm just sitting there. He doesn't want to talk. He wants me to talk. One of his primary motivations was for me to talk so he could learn English. He can't learn if I won't speak to him. So the best thing to do was to just sit there like a bump and only answer when I absolutely had to, and that's rare. If he didn't get upset but just frustrated, then I'm more likely to be left in my cell instead of wasting his time.

10. Warriors Begin to Organize

Some new POWs came in late 1965 and they had some disturbing news. We learned that President Johnson had made the statement to some high military officials in which he said, "Tell those guys in Hanoi to keep their mouths shut." It was very demoralizing for all of us. Our feeling was, Jesus Christ, if you can't even expect the faith and trust from your own President while you are a Prisoner of War, then what the hell can you expect?

That may have had some effect on Pop, too, because while he made a few more appearances at these press conferences during that year, he finally knocked it off and started fighting the Gooks. But by that time the Gooks thought they could pull his string and get him to dance for them. So when he clammed up on them, they were worse to him than they might have been. Pop suffered a tremendous amount of torture and abuse in 1966 and 1967.

To put his plight into perspective, while most of us were in our twenties Pop was in his mid-forties. When he arrived at the camp, he was a big, husky, strong 225 - 230 pound man. A year later if he weighed 135 pounds he was lucky. He also was constantly suffering from boils. He had them all over his body, maybe fifty or sixty of them at a time, huge things that caused him a tremendous amount of pain. When people were going through what Pop Kern especially was, then to have the President screw it up the way he did only made things worse for us.

Later in 1965 and beyond the Gooks stepped up the torture. They wanted us to confess. They would systemically torture an entire camp to get us to give them a stupid little four or five line confession of our being a criminal for having bombed innocent people. They went through an entire camp I was in, and it continued through 1967, '68, and into '69. But in 1965 we were still under the control of the Hanoi cops, though the camp commander was an Army officer.

That doesn't mean that guys who weren't tortured weren't suffering. The lack of nourishment was particularly punishing. This wasn't some sort of diet. It started when the first guy, Everett Alvarez, arrived in August of 64. Even then it was clear that they weren't prepared to handle Caucasians and especially big men. They started off giving Everett more or less what the Vietnamese ate, not only the same food but the same amount. They gave him rice and vegetable soup; a green soup made of turnips and other vegetables.

He was fed that stuff until December of 1964 when the Gooks realized that Everett's health was failing. They decided they had better do something so they started sending a guard out of the prison and down the street on a bicycle to a local restaurant that catered to foreigners who came to Hanoi. They started giving him this restaurant food, more than he could eat, bringing it to him in these little carrying-case lunch boxes.

Following Alvarez into the prison were Shumaker and Lockhart who also enjoyed the food that was brought in for Alvarez. They said they were getting food they couldn't believe. They were getting meat like hamburger patties, green beans, good desserts and just all kinds of good food no prisoner would ever expect, and lots of it. Sometimes it was even more than they could eat.

It couldn't last though. More Americans were captured and brought to the prison, and they were given this food too. But the amounts weren't increased. That meant that more men were sharing the same amount of rations. The only thing we could figure out was they had a certain amount of money allotted for the year 1965 for Yank prisoners, so they would go and pick up the same amount of stuff and distribute it to more guys. By the time I arrived there in late April of 1965, the food that they were originally serving to three men was being split up among seven.

There were more men so less food. By June we were getting about six tablespoons. So we were all losing weight and getting skinnier and skinnier by the day. In August they realized we were not getting enough food to survive. I think the guards knew it sooner but they probably had this bureaucracy and it just took a long time to change their system.

One bright day they brought around soup, the lousy prisoner soup made from various kinds of vegetables, plus a side dish of some sort of meat and a banana or two a day. We also got one of those small French loaves of bread. That was supposed to keep us going and for some guys it was enough, but not for me. So I used our communication system to tell the guys who didn't want all their food to drop it off in the shower.

At one time in early '65 I got so hungry that I ate food out of a garbage can. I was rice from the Vietnamese prisoners, in the shower stall. Evidently they were getting more than they needed to eat. This garbage can was rancid and the rats had run around the top of it all day long, so I was pretty cautious. I didn't want to make myself sick. I gave it the taste test I had learned in survival school. I dug down into the center of it where the rice wasn't rotten, took a little bit, and chewed it up and waited until the next day.

I gradually built up the amount I consumed and when I didn't get sick it got to where I was eating out of that garbage can pretty regularly. I had to ensure that it was pretty fresh garbage though and in order to do that I used to do the guards' work for them when they weren't looking. I would throw away the old stuff and leave a garbage can empty so the next day when I came in I'd know it was fresh stuff that had been thrown in.

The rats were quite something for most of the guys to get used to. There wasn't any trouble getting used them as far as seeing them. They ran all over the place. Once you got used to them, they were a source of amusement, or at least distraction, particularly when we were in solitary confinement. You could peek out your cell door and watch them running here and there and even see them screw. It wasn't titillating, just a relief from the boredom.

The rats, the sparrows and the geckos were really the only entertainment. But the rats were also a real annoyance when you were trying to sleep. They would come into the cell and if we had any food at all, anything that we might be saving like a little piece of bread, the rats would go after it. If we had it in bed with us they'd go in after us. They would chew a hole in our mosquito net and come after it.

They were so aggressive that once they got inside the mosquito net they would invariably bite. I was bitten by rats on a number of occasions throughout my stay in North Vietnam as were many other guys. None of us ever got anything from it. The Vietnamese seemed unconcerned when a guy was bitten by a rat. They used to say, "Our rats do not carry diseases." This sounded pretty farfetched, but in fact of all the guys I knew who were bitten by rats, none of them ever got sick from it.

The only guy I knew that was ever given any anti-rabies vaccine or anything like that was Commander Cole Black. But I believe he had been bitten by a dog and it was a rabid dog. They gave him the series of shots in the stomach. As badly as they treated us, the Gooks didn't seem to want us to die, at least not while under their control.

Except for such an emergency, medical treatment in '65 was just about zero. If you had something wrong with you it was just tough titty. If you had a bad headache and asked for an aspirin, they would just laugh at you. Once in awhile the guard or a medic-type-guy would come around, bring some Lysol disinfectant and let you squirt the stuff around your cell. It didn't disinfect anything but it made the place smell better for a few hours.

A little Vietnamese gal who was a nurse visited us in late '65. She didn't do much except just hang around. She had little pig tails on either side of her head that kind of stuck straight out. She was as cute as a button. When she would come around and peek into my cell, I would saunter on up to the door there and put on my best pigeon Vietnamese trying to woo her. Eventually she would laugh and then turn on her heels and bop off, wiggling her ass at me. She was really cute, and it wasn't just her age and the fact that there weren't any other women around.

I stayed in The Stock Yard until sometime in late July or early August 1965. Then one evening around eight, Stone-Face came into the room. This was pretty unusual. He gave me the roll-up signal which meant that I was to roll up my belongings in my mat and that I was going to be moved. I rolled up my meager property, happy to be getting out of the cell where I didn't have contact with anybody. In fact I had not had any contact with any Americans since I had been in The Stock Yard. Being out of touch had been both boring and unsettling.

A little while later Stone Face came back and he led me over towards New Guy Village. I was a little disappointed because I was hoping he would take me to Heartbreak where I knew there were guys. But instead of turning left to the four-cell block where I had been earlier, we made a right turn into a room we later called The Knobby Room.

So then I knew that's where Shumaker lived and I assumed I was going in there with him. They opened the cell door and when I looked in there was old Shu, standing there with a great big grin. I had a great big grin on my face too, as we shook hands. When the guard left we were just like two kids in a dime store the night before Christmas. We immediately sat down and started bull-shitting, both of us talking about a mile a minute.

In about an hour the door opened again and another guy walked in. It was Bob Peel, and we welcomed him into the group. A few minutes later the door opened again and it was Hayden Lockhart. It was old home week! We almost lost our voices from not having talked to anybody as we sat talking throughout the night. Nobody went to bed. All we did was talk. It was really a thrill to get those first roommates after being solo for so long.

This room, the "Knobby Walled Room," became a primary torture room in the camp later, but for the moment we called it home. An important aspect was we had a view of the shower entrance directly across from our front door. We could see who went into the shower through the cracks in the door. This was important because it helped us figure out who else had been captured. So we posted a watch for any new prisoners going into the showers throughout the day.

We did see two that came from the New Guy Village area. These new shoot downs were Larry Guarino and Jerry Denton. Denton at this time was a Navy Commander and Guarino was an Air Force Major. When we saw these men go to and from the shower we began to make plans for contacting them. It turned out that Commander Denton was a real hard-charger. The first time he walked into the shower he got a rock and carved into the wall in huge letters, "I am CDR Jeremiah Denton U.S.N. - roll call - everybody check in." Below that he wrote numbers "1. 2. 3. 4. 5. 6." Anybody who came into the shower after that was supposed to check in with the commander. We really got a charge out of that. It was funny but it was a big morale boost for us. We promptly dropped a note off in the shower and he got it in no time at all.

Another guy we contacted was J. B. McKamey, a Navy lieutenant when he was shot down. We left a note for J. B. in the shower. At this time we were a little worried about whether he would pick up the note or not. So in the note we told him where we were in relation to the shower. But we had to know whether the guard intercepted the note or if he had gotten it. We knew he went to the shower in the afternoon and so in the morning we left him a note that said if he got the note, when he came out of the shower stall and he got off the steps, to spit off to his left side. Then we watched, and as J. B. stepped out on the steps and he looked at the room, he gave big smile and scratched his nose, leaned over to the left, and spit about six times. He marched off with a big grin on his face. It didn't mean anything to the guards because they have the habit of spitting all the time.

We knew how important it was not to have the guards find our messages, so in our notes to each other we gave instructions about how we would hide messages and what signals we would provide to show that there was a message. We made a kind of little treasure hunt out of it. The first signal was a big rock placed in a conspicuous place. It meant to check such and such a place, and in that place there was another note, and then it said to check another place.

We used American slang so if the Gooks picked up a note they wouldn't understand it. Another way to assure the integrity of our communications was that we left identifiers in our notes. For instance, we would tell someone new that when they wrote their next note to us they should tell us something like the little gal's name on "The Mousketeers" show. Things like that. They were simple trivia things that Americans would normally know.

We got a little over-complicated for J. B. because one time he wrote back and said "Jesus Christ how am I supposed to know that kind of stuff, you guys? I can't remember any of that crap." But at any rate we knew he received the note and it hadn't been intercepted by some Gook, since they wouldn't have answered that way.

It wasn't too long before we got caught. That was because our first attempts were clumsy and the Gooks were able to find us out. Later as we became more sophisticated, they paid more attention and their attempts to find notes got better. But we always seemed to stay just ahead in the game. But we also paid severely for being caught later on.

We were living in this small group together for the moment but I ought to talk about solitary confinement. First of all, you don't lose your mind or go berserk if you're put into solitary confinement. But we are social creatures so being in solitary is like being socially starved. The worst that can be said about it is that it's boring, extremely boring, but there are different ways of adapting to it.

One of the first things you discover is that there is only one person in the world who counts and that is you. In American society you are almost never alone. Actually, the only time you are ever alone is when you sleep and not even then if you are married. As a result, I believe we don't know ourselves well enough. We never got to know ourselves because it wasn't part of our culture. As a result, we never learn who old number one is.

Some guys, I'll even say most people, when they get into solitary confinement the first thing they are confronted with is themselves. The next thing you discover is that your self is going to be one of two things when you first get into solitary confinement – either your best friend or your worst enemy. And it's going to be up to you to decide which. A lot of people in solitary confinement find out they don't like themselves. It's a new experience.

What you need to do is resolve to talk things out within yourself, and ultimately to find out that you really do like yourself and that you can enjoy being alone.

You can occupy your mind during waking hours with thousands of projects – everything from time-consuming amusements like playing number games to serious endeavors like making plans for the rest of your life. You can go through recollections of the past like trying to figure out when things happened to you from the very beginning of your life. You can try to figure out what you're going to do when you get home, like family activities, vacations, career plans or just any number of things.

You can get into great detail. I used to spend hours and days on end with such exercises and the time would go by without my even thinking about the time. It would just be the end of the day before I even knew what happened. For instance I would plan from start to finish a picnic with my family, with all the tiny little details of packing up that picnic lunch at home and then starting out. Just going through every detail, what I would say to my wife and daughter and so on.

The point is you can occupy your mind with just anything. Sometimes you might feel that you're not accomplishing anything, that you should be doing something productive, because all of your life you've always been doing something that there's a purpose to. You've never been idle because you've always been busy.

Another thing you can do is sit back and relax. Just relax and don't feel you have to do something. Just talk yourself out of it. Just realize that all you have to do is put the clutch in and let the engine idle. Anytime during the day if you should feel the slightest bit tired or bored just flop out on your bunk and go to sleep. Sleep is a damn good way to idle away solitary confinement. I went through periods where I'd stay up late, get up early in the morning and stay up all day long because of mental projects, because I had things to do. I was busy.

The next day I'd get up and not feel like doing a damn thing. I was tired of my projects. I might spend the next two or three weeks sleeping all the time. There were times in prison when I slept as much as 20 hours a day. This happened especially when my treatment was horrible and I might be depressed. You can do it. You can sleep 20 hours a day and sleep sound as a rock. It's all a matter of adaptation.

So solitary confinement is tough but it isn't a big bad ogre and it won't make a nut out of you. It's just a matter of learning to deal with it. Just like escape-and-evasion training, being alone should be taught as part of what happens if you become a prisoner of war. Guys need to learn what it's like to live with themselves and how to be independent, completely independent, and what it's like to make all your decisions on your own. It's especially important to have some training on how to come to rational conclusions while being in a solitary situation since it is so different from the world we are in today.

Letter writing was always a huge issue for us and the gooks restricted it to a ridiculous extent. They never even came close to honoring our right under the Geneva Conventions to communicate with our families. The Gooks told me after a few months in 1965 that I would be allowed to write home, which of course I was very eager to do. I had given the name of my wife and her address so that I could do this. It was obvious to me that it was going to be on the letter anyway and it would be better for them to have this information so I could write. On the sixth of June – I remember this date because it was two days before my wedding anniversary – they brought a normal envelope and stationery to my room in The Stock Yard. They said I could write a letter home. There wasn't any briefing on it. They gave me about three sheets of paper and they told me I could write whatever I wanted that would fill up the three sheets of paper.

I learned later that my wife got the letter, though I'm not sure how it got home. I believe it was probably transported home by some peace group that was in Hanoi at the time. Maybe it was even someone associated with the Anna Louise Strong group. Some days later when I moved in with Shumaker, Peel, and Harris, we were told that all of us would be allowed to write a letter home. Stationery and envelopes were brought into our room and we sat down and wrote our letters. I believe that these letters were also delivered to our homes.

At this time we did not know who was being allowed to write. We had not had good communications and we just assumed that other people were being allowed to write home too. The next time I was allowed to write was a year later. There was quite a dry spell and there were a lot of problems encountered in writing a letter. By that time we knew only a few of us were being allowed to write and that the vast majority were not.

Of course we searched our minds and talked to our friends throughout this time as to whether or not we should write since they were not being allowed to. We were perfectly willing to forgo this privilege in protest for the other guys. But it was decided by all concerned that it was necessary for us to write in order to try to get some information home that we could put in the text of the letter. We might get information out that would benefit those who weren't able to write, and their families, by association.

So we continued to write when given the opportunity, though they were very few. It seems that in the first group of us, the first 10 or so guys, they allowed maybe seven of us to write. Then after that it really petered off. It got to where they would allow maybe 10% of the guys to write. Their policy of who was allowed to write and how often didn't seem to follow any rhyme or reason. I guess the major thing to them in those days was whether or not they had released your name as one of their captives. Most of those guys were allowed to write, but then again some guys whose names were released were not allowed to write. It was a strange thing.

When I moved in with Shumaker, he showed us a letter he had received from his wife and this was amazing to us. We didn't think we would be receiving any mail. He had actually received this letter seven days after he was shot down in North Vietnam. It had been delivered by the American Red Cross. Shortly after it was delivered Shu was called into a quiz one day and told that the Red Cross would never again be allowed to deliver any mail or packages or anything for us because they were no longer allowed to come to the prison. They said it was because the Red Cross had tried to assert themselves and work their way into looking into the camp. They had, as the Gooks put it, "showed an improper attitude."

I don't know what this was all about, whether the Red Cross had pushed too hard or whether it was just a smoke screen on the part of the Vietnamese. I suspect they just didn't want the American Red Cross in the picture because that made it look as though we were prisoners of war instead of the way they wanted to show us to the world - as criminals.

I received my first letter Christmas of 1965. It was a very short letter from my wife. My next letter was in April of 1966. Then I went for two years without any mail or without being allowed to write home. It seems the situation was similar for most of the rest of the guys. Usually we seized the opportunity whenever it presented itself. But there were times when, speaking for myself and Hayden Lockhart when we were living together in 1966, the treatment was so bad that we refused to write, as a protest.

But for the most part we considered it normal that prisoners of war should be allowed to write home so we wrote. This was despite the fact that the Gooks were getting some propaganda value out of our letters. We attempted to keep our letters as bland as possible and not put anything in that would give them propaganda value. But just the fact that they were letting us write home put them in a good light. Of course we could never put anything in our letters that had anything to do with how we were being treated. That was definitely not allowed.

In the beginning we weren't told what we could write. Later they came up with a seven-line letter form they made us use. On these forms it said you could only write about family and health - nothing else. Later they began to sensor letters very heavily. They would just cut out big portions of our letters. When the letter form came along they instituted a policy of having us write a rough letter first, which would be reviewed by the people in the camp or big-wigs in the government. Then it would be sent back to the camp and we would copy our rough draft minus the things that had been crossed out. But this came about later. They obviously had a bureaucratic chain of command. In these first few letters there was no censoring whatsoever but later they decided they needed a systematic approach that would exploit us for propaganda.

My first three or four letters were some 350 to 400 words long. After they came out with the seven-line letter forms my first attempts were about 75 words long. It has always been my habit to write medium size to large. But I practiced to the point were I could squeeze the letters and words down in size and put them closer together. In the end result I was able to increase my seven-line letters to about 140 words. That was much better for saying what I wanted to say and to get as much out as I could.

As far as incoming mail, we received the early letters intact. Later on some of us did receive letters with portions that were blacked out but very often we could hold the letter up to a light and generally figure out what it said. The strange thing was they were always innocuous things the Gooks would black out. We never could figure out why. It was just their weird way of thinking.

Of course their best way of censoring was just not to give us our letters at all. As an example, in my first five years as a prisoner of war I received five letters. My grand total for the 7 years and 10 months was 16 letters. The last letters I received were in 1971 and they were all dated 1965 and 1966. I received 6 pictures from my family. It didn't seem to make any rhyme or reason about who got mail or wrote. It was just up to the whims of those immature little idiots.

We often compared our captors, and I think it was a very good comparison, to a bunch of junior-high school girls. This pretty well describes their temperament and their ability to switch emotions, determining the way we were treated. They were pretty irresponsible up to 1969 when Ho Chi Minh died. He died September 3rd and after that we noticed a dramatic change in treatment. For example, all of us were able to write and receive letters from then on. They stopped the little selection system and they released everybody's names that we were in contact with. And everybody for the most part was allowed to write and receive mail. Also packages were allowed to come in but that was very sporadic and they were heavily pilfered.

Communication was essential. They knew we would be a stronger force to reckon with if we had unity so they did everything they could to keep us isolated from each other. Therefore, out of necessity, we soon invented ways of communicating that the Gooks couldn't intercept. One of these means of communicating has a long history.

11. Shave and a Haircut

One day one of the guys in our room, Smitty Harris, said, "You know, I learned something from Air Force Survival School and I want to tell you guys about it. I don't know if we'll ever get to use to it but at least it's something worth knowing. In survival school a guy that I was talking to just mentioned this in class. It wasn't brought out as a matter of formal training or anything, but he told us how prisoners in jails in times past, and how guys in Korea, were able to talk to each other through walls. They did this with a little code by tapping on the wall."

As Smitty explained it, you arranged the alphabet in five groups of five starting with A, B, C, running horizontally on the first line. You continue this through Z, and you leave out the letter K. This gives you a five-by-five matrix. In order to tap the letter D for instance, you tap once to indicate the first horizontal row and then you tap four times to indicate the fourth letter in the row. He said that in order to tap a K you just tap out a C because that would do just as well. If you wanted to make sure it was understood as a K, what you did was tap a stuttered C. In other words instead of tapping something like dit - dit/dit/dit, you would tap a dit - dit/dit-dit. You stuttered it at the end so you knew it was a K. The prison tap code matrix looks like this:

Tap Code					
First	Second				
	1	2	3	4	5
1	A	B	C	D	E
2	F	G	H	I	J
3	L	M	N	O	P
4	Q	R	S	T	U
5	V	W	X	Y	Z

In order to tap numbers you would simply make one tap for a one, two taps for a two, et-cetera. You could tell it was not a letter because it's only one-half of a character.

As we developed this communications system, we discussed how we could get in contact with a new guy so that he knew we were American. We came up with a real easy way. Just get on the wall next to us and the new guy we wanted to contact. Then we would tap "shave and a haircut." That is something the Gooks never heard of or experienced. If a Yank heard that coming through the wall he'd know damn well there was a Yank on the other side. The reply to this was of course "two bits," or what we called a "Roger" - a dit/dit.

We all filed this code away in our memories. Later we became fluent in "speaking" through the tap code out of necessity. It saved our lives. It was our life line because it was paramount for survival that we were able to communicate with each other. Communication was essential to keep up our spirits because so many of us were in solitary confinement for such long periods of time. It was important that we knew what other people in the camp were doing and that other people in the camp were in the same situation, and were supporting you.

It was also an important morale booster because we could talk to your neighbor next door as much as we wanted to during the day. We became very sophisticated with this code. It got to the point where we would tap to each other on the wall and it would sound like a typewriter; it was that fast. It seemed to work out better than Morse code because everything was a dot and there weren't any dashes. We needed a rock or something hard to send a dash and then it made a mark on the wall. Then the Gooks knew immediately what you had been up to.

The tap code was also invaluable in working outdoors. For instance, if we had a hoe in our hands and wanted to talk to a guy in a certain room, we could send one-way communications to him in the way we worked with the hoe. We would stroke with the hoe in the tap code. The guards would be standing around and they had no idea what we were doing. If we had a broom in our hands and were sweeping up the court yard we could talk to a whole gang of guys in another building and tell them what our building was doing, make arrangements for note drops, or just pass any kind of information.

We did this constantly through the years and it was absolutely invaluable to us. We developed a sense of hearing and awareness that was quite extraordinary. Anytime we heard noise, anytime we heard somebody sweeping, hoeing, chopping wood, then everyone went silent so we could pick up the "radio broadcast" that was coming over to us. We would listen to this stuff all day long and hear our buddies call over and say "Hi Phil, how ya doing? How's your ankle today? Are those cuffs bothering you too much? Don't sweat that shit buddy, we're all with you." Such chit-chat was invaluable. Without it I don't think many of us could have pulled through.

Sometimes when new POWs came in who didn't know the tap code, we could explain it by talking out our different windows. In a well-organized camp, guys in another room would clear the area and give a "danger cough" if a guard was approaching. But sometimes when we couldn't talk to him to explain the code we had another approach. We'd start off by just tapping the number of digits to illustrate a letter in the alphabet. For instance the letter Z would be 26 taps and the letter A would be one tap. So after getting a "two bit" reply from the new guy, we would send 8 taps followed by 9 taps. Most guys would soon get it, that we had sent "H" and "I" or in other words – Hi! Then using this laborious method we could explain to him, through the wall, the shorter method we called "The Tap Code."

Also later on we developed something we referred to as "The Hand Jive" or "Mute Code." It was a visual method of sending the alphabet. We always used our right hand. For example the letter "a" is illustrated by holding your hand out in front of you with your index finger held up to look like a number one. The letter "b" was indicated by putting your thumb and forefingers to form an "o" while holding your other fingers together pointing straight up so that the person looking saw it as a small letter "b."

The letter "q" was indicated by giving the guy the finger; what we used to refer to then as the queer sign. The letter "d" was sent like a "damn you" sign, shaking your fist at a guy. "x" was indicated by crossed fingers held vertically to look like an x. "y" is signaled with the thumb and little finger held up to make your hand look like the letter "y." Some of the letter signals are difficult to explain but they almost all follow in what looks like the letter. Here is the complete alphabet as drawn by my old POW friend and cell mate, Mike McGrath.

Through considerable practice, guys learned how to speak rapidly with this visual code. We could literally transmit information by hand jive almost as fast as someone could talk. Some guys became as adept at this form of communication as deaf people are at talking to each other with their hands in sign language.

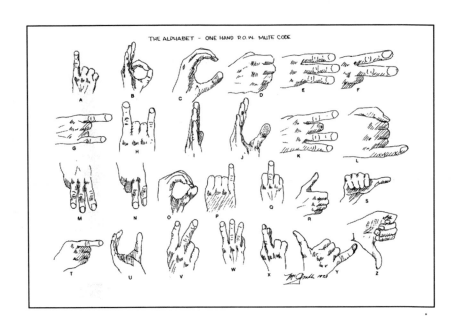

THE ALPHABET - ONE HAND P.O.W. MUTE CODE

12. Last Days with the Hanoi Cops

We stayed in the Knobby Wall Room until one day in August when we got caught passing a note. That night we were called out to a quiz. The four of us were lined up in the camp commander's office. He told us we were going to be punished because we had tried to communicate with another criminal. They separated us and put all of us back in solitary confinement. At this time we were getting three cigarettes a day so they took us off our cigs. Big deal. They didn't pound on any of us or beat us up so we didn't sweat the small stuff.

We were only apart for a couple of weeks. Then they were getting too many prisoners in and they were running out of rooms so they threw us all back together again. We stayed together until August 31st. Then that evening a fifth guy walked into our room. It was Hayden Lockhart. I was to live with this guy off and on for the next seven years. I lived with Hayden a total of five years, most of the time in a cell just the two of us shared together.

I tell you its unfathomable unless you've done it how well you can know a guy when you live with him 24 hours a day in a two-man cell. Hayden and I were very compatible, which was fortunate. We always told each other stories and then told them over again. We kept on listening and enjoying each other's company. We were lucky. A lot of guys were put together who were not compatible. That was a terrible thing. Sometimes guys got together who just absolutely hated each other yet they had to be in the same two-man room together 24 hours a day for literally years on end.

That was truly a prison within a prison. Cellmates had to agree on what they were going to do and how they were going to act with the guards because it was paramount that we were on the same frequency. Luckily, Hayden and I seemed to fit. We agreed on virtually everything. We both took the approach that we were going to be ass-holes with the guards and the interrogators. Sometimes we would challenge each on who was going to get knocked in the head the most that day. It sounds weird, but it was a way of supporting each other. Other guys took different approaches but cellmates needed to agree. The important thing wasn't so much the approach but that we were together on it and on common ground.

That night, August 31st when Hayden moved in, they took Harris and Shumaker out a few hours later. We didn't know where they were going.

181

We watched as they rolled up their bed rolls. We wished them good luck and God bless as they walked out of the room.

The next morning, September 1st, the guard came and told the three of us, Peel, Lockhart and myself, to roll up our gear. Then they moved us to cell 4, the area of the four cells, in New Guy Village. The cell only had two concrete bunks in it so they brought in a wooden bed board and put that on the floor. Since I was the senior man in the group being a Navy lieutenant – Bob Peel was an Air Force 1st lieutenant and Hayden was an Air Force 1st lieutenant – they mutually decided I was going to sleep on the floor. So I took the bed board on the floor. It didn't matter that I out-ranked them. I was out-numbered by two Air Force guys.

We always had fun with little stuff like that. We were in that cell for no time at all when Peel got up on the concrete bunk and started screaming out the back window down to the other cells to see if anybody was there. We knew that Jerry Denton was in cell number one. Pretty soon Jerry came back and said, "Not so loud you guys!" We started talking with Jerry.

As soon as we made contact with Commander Denton, we informed him we were not sure but we thought he was the senior man in the area. He took the lead right there on the spot. He immediately started issuing policies on how to act in an interrogation, how to hold the line, when to take the second line of defense, to say as little as possible, and to give them bullshit when you had to say something.

There was no doubt in our minds that he was the senior man. Commander Denton also told us, "Okay, guys, we will talk to each other by whistling tap code to each other." So for the most part our conversations out the back were whistling tap code. The way we did that was to whistle a tune, with the timing devised so that it sent the characters you wanted to communicate. The Gooks didn't know the difference. To them our music sounded pretty strange anyway, as theirs did to us. It didn't matter because they didn't suspect much. It was much later in our imprisonment that they finally caught on.

Denton informed us that Guarino had been moved and we told him that Shumaker and Harris had also been moved. We told him we had heard a jeep in the area and suspected that Shumaker and Harris had possibly been taken to another camp. He told us that I, being the next senior man, was his executive officer. He immediately started command operations with just the four of us. If anybody else came into the picture that we could get in contact with it would continue work in accordance with military rank.

As his exec, I took care of administrative things for Jerry by helping get him up to speed on our communication tricks. I also picked up things for him that we were able to drop off at his cell. I'd leave implements in the shower corner so he could write more efficiently and we began to formulate plans for contacting people in other places. We devised some clever methods, based on our incredibly limited resources.

For instance, it seemed that we were all being served our food in those chow tray buckets I described earlier. These buckets had handles on them that were made of steel, formed in a u-shape about a foot long. We discovered that they were being used interchangeably with other sections of the prison. Guys in the Heartbreak area might be getting ours on some meals and we might be getting theirs. So we started writing notes in pencil on the inside of the handles.

One of the advantages to being put in solitary confinement and then moved back with other guys was that we knew more about each other and the different places where prisoners were held. For example, we knew from Shu and Smitty that other guys were at Heartbreak. They had gotten contact with these guys because they had been put in solitary confinement in the Heartbreak area. It was very nice for us that the Gooks had moved us around. That allowed us to establish contact in other places in the camp.

It was ironic that Gooks were constantly moving us around, thinking it would disorient us and keep us from maintaining contact with each other. But it was typical of the Hanoi screwed up thinking. The fact was that moving us around enabled us to solidify our communications with new prisoners. Later on it even enabled us to contact other camps and to know the names of everyone who was a POW.

About a week after we tried using the chow bucket handles to communicate, we got a chow bucket back in the room that had another note on the handle. They gave us names of some new guys who had just come into Heartbreak. So we had very poor, yet some communication with the other side of the Hilton.

Jerry told us he was worried about Larry Guarino. Larry had gone into an interrogation and the Gooks had questioned him about his career. I guess they had seen something written in our newspapers, that Larry had been a 20-year-old P-51 pilot in WWII and had flown 20 missions over Hanoi bombing Japs. Larry confirmed this to the Gooks and they got pissed off because he had bombed Hanoi. It shows how stupid the little bastards could be. There he was, helping them in the previous war.

Larry got pissed off. He was Italian, with a typical Italian temperament, and he started cursing, swearing and waving his arms in the quiz room. So they whipped him out of the quiz room and put him back in his cell, locking one of his legs in stocks. This was the first case we knew of that this had happened. This put Larry pretty much down in the dumps. He was in stocks for two or three weeks. They also cut his food rations.

That was pretty extreme treatment from anything we had experienced so far. Jerry said he was pretty worried about Larry. He said that Larry had lapsed into a depression. So Jerry suggested that we all go on a hunger strike. While it was true that Jerry was an extremely aggressive officer, courageous and always willing to sacrifice himself for the benefit of one of his fellow prisoners, he would often do things that were a bit extreme. Sometimes it would be over issues that were probably not worth the effort, nor worth the recriminations we might bring upon ourselves.

I relayed back to Jerry as his second in command that I thought we should not go on a hunger strike. First because I felt it would not do Larry Guarino any good, and second because I felt Larry's personality was such that he was prone to, shall we say, little theatrics every now and then. And third, I told Jerry I thought if we did this the misery that we would heap on ourselves would not be worthwhile, not to mention we were all undernourished already. I was also concerned that such an organized effort might expose our method of communication, which was at this point very vital to us.

I sent this information back to Jerry in a note and that night he called out the back window and said, "Thank you for your note Phil. You have gotten my thinking straight and I agree with you that we will not take that line of action." I think this was typical of our senior officers. All of them were under stress too and there were many times when an SRO, Senior Ranking Officer, was not clear in thinking out a situation to take the best action. But almost always, with very few exceptions, SROs did consult with the other people below them before they came out with any decisions. Or if there were many people then they would consult their staff before putting out a policy or decision. In a POW situation you don't rule by autocratic leadership. You have to get consensus.

As it turned out Larry was just experiencing a little fright from being in solitary confinement and just had temporary claustrophobia in his cell. Within a few weeks he was all right.

This leadership style worked to our great advantage in avoiding irrational actions that would lead to bad consequences with the Gooks. We all knew what we were trying to accomplish and we all knew our goals. It's just that there were invariably different approaches to an individual problem. SROs were always well aware of this. So they always consulted people who were below them in rank.

Another point about making a decision or passing out an order in prison is it had to reflect people's morals and ideals. It also had to be a decision based on sound reasoning that was clear to the men below. That's because if it was not, there was an excellent chance that someone in a far corner of the camp who was living in solitary confinement would choose not to execute that order, knowing full well there were no disciplinary consequences.

On September 9th, 1965 Stone-Face opened our cell door and he had a North Vietnamese English newspaper called the "Vietnam Courier." This particular little piece of shit was passed out to us at various times. We understood later that it was also available in Hong Kong on the newsstands and in some places in the United States. It was all bullshit and propaganda. He gave us a bunch of cigarettes and I thought he'd made a mistake. He just looked at me and smiled and then he left. When chow came that day it was an extra good meal and we had some bananas to boot.

The newspaper said it was Independence Day of the Democratic Republic of Vietnam so we figured we were helping them celebrate their holiday. Of course we didn't give a rat's ass, but it was a good deal to get the extra food and cigarettes, so we were happy to celebrate their Independence Day with them in that manner. From that time on these things continued. It seemed the Gooks were wild about holidays – their holidays, our holidays, any holidays. They just loved to celebrate and when they did they would also give us a little extra to celebrate.

Throughout the years we would get an extra good meal and extra cigarettes, and maybe a little candy on New Year's Day, Easter, the 4th of July, on Sept 9th, the Vietnamese Tet (Lunar New Year,) on Christmas, and in later years even on our Thanksgiving. Anyway, they enjoyed it and we sure as hell did too. Even when the treatment was the worst, like when a guy would be all tied up in ropes and stocks and such torture, they would come in and untie us on the holiday. We'd get our good meal and the next day they'd bind us back up, continue the beatings and it would be right back to business again.

It was really screwy and it underscored how different the cultures were. It was enough to make a nut out of someone just experiencing that. It says that prisoners of war – as long as we have wars – should at least be treated somewhat from their own cultural perspective...so they don't get driven crazy.

185

This note about that "Vietnam Courier:" there was a little article that I thought at the time was so ludicrous I memorized it. It reflected for me what the Vietnamese were all about, at least in the North. The article gives you a picture of their communist thinking and their obsession with who they were and the war they were in. It read, "The people of such and such village in such and such province have recently completed work on a new cultural and art center for the children of the province. The children of the province are now allowed to come to this cultural and art center to learn every day and each week about art, culture and guerrilla warfare." Ain't Communism wonderful?

So life, such as it was, proceeded along during that week after the holiday. Jerry Denton and I played chess by whistling our moves out the back window. We all played with him and he cleaned our clocks. He was really good at chess. We made chess sets with little pieces of paper, grass, and stuff we'd picked up in the yard. There were times later when the guards were so strict on what we had in our rooms that we couldn't even do that, so we just kept chess boards in our minds. We learned how to play chess by memorizing where the pieces were as the game went along. Not being chess masters we couldn't get too complicated so we would take only two or three moves a day. This often led to interesting arguments, such as, "Your queen is not on B2 it's on B3, God damn it! If it was on B2, I'd be checkmated in three moves and that's not right." We had big arguments through the walls all the time. It added humor.

On September 15th I was called into a quiz where I met The Owl and Stone-Face. The Owl told me I was to go back and tell my roommates that we would be moving soon. God knows why they did this. They had never done it before and never since. Maybe it was just their way to say goodbye. They told me that I'd be moving to a new camp. Then The Owl told me something that really set me thinking. He said, "When you move to a new camp you will leave our control." That's all he said, and he said it with that kind of "aura of the unknown" that Gooks are fond of doing. He smiled and sent me back to my room.

I went back and told the guys about it. We couldn't figure out what the hell was going on. The next evening a guard came by who we called "Big Stupe." Big Stupe was a tall guy, by Vietnamese standards, probably around five-eight. He always wore a smile. He was a cop who was maybe 29 years old. He was a hell of a guy. He'd do all kinds of things for the prisoners. He'd bring water in the middle of the night if we needed it. He'd never give us any crap. Big Stupe came by and stuck his head in the window and waved us to come over to the peek hole. And through signs and so forth he told us we were going to be leaving that night. Then he sat back and grinned and waved to us like we were going bye-bye. Then he made signs like a driver with a steering wheel to show us that we would be going some place in a vehicle.

He looked up and down the passageway to be sure no one was coming and he looked in his pocket and pulled out a whole pack of cigarettes and gave it to us. That was Big Stupe's good-bye. We told Big Stupe good-bye and good luck and he wandered on down the hallway. That night the guards opened up our door and told us to roll up our gear. As we walked down the passage way we yelled out to Jerry Denton, "Good-bye, see you around."

Jerry yelled back, "Good luck, guys, and God bless you." We walked out of New Guy Village into the Hoa Lo center court yard where a jeep carry-all was waiting. The three of us got in and there were two other guys in the jeep. One was Larry Guarino and the other a guy I didn't know. I sat down next to him. We were blind-folded but I folded my blind-fold up so I could see and he folded his up. We shook hands and he said, "Everett Alvarez." It was the first time Everett Alvarez had ever been seen by another prisoner.

Before leaving we contacted Norland Daughtry and Ray Vohden who were living in the Knobby Room. Both of these men were badly injured. Norland had both of his arms broken and Ray still had his broken leg. They were not in good shape. They could not even empty their own shit buckets. Norland couldn't even perform certain cleanliness functions. So even though he had a broken leg, Ray had to wash him and wipe his ass for him. It was a pretty bad situation in that room.

Stone-Face had been having me empty their shit bucket, in part because I had established a pretty good rapport with him. This might not sound like a very good deal, but it was to us, and Stone-Face realized it too. When I would go up to their door, their shit bucket would be sitting outside where Stone-Face had put it. It meant that I was able to say a few words to them, while Stone-Face deliberately looked the other way. He was pretty good about that.

One day I came up to the door and the bucket was sitting outside. I picked it up, took it down and dumped it. When I brought it back, I stood in front of the door with the empty bucket and indicated to Stone-Face that he should open the door so I could put it inside. Stone-Face shook his head no. I said, "Yes." He said "No." I said "Yes, God damn it, Yes!" I glared at him, and finally he shrugged his shoulders in that Vietnamese way and got that sly little grin. He walked over, unlocked the door and threw it open.

There the two guys were sitting. I walked in and put the shit bucket down, went over and introduced myself; shaking hands with Ray and squeezing Norland's shoulder. I gave them a few words of comfort and a little briefing on who was located in the camp. Stone-Face, meanwhile, was whooping at me a little bit, telling me to get out of there. I went over and fixed Norland's and Ray's mosquito nets for them and did a couple of other little things that they asked for and then I left.

After that Hayden Lockhart, Bob Peel and I then began to raise hell with the Gooks to let one of us, or all of us go live there so we could take care of those guys. We were really being obnoxious about it with any Vietnamese we could find to talk to. It must have had some effect because when they moved Hayden and me to the new camp they moved Bob Peel in with Ray Vohden and Norland Daughtry. He moved in with them and became their nurse.

This was the first and last humane gesture that the Vietnamese ever did for the wounded guys. Bob told us later that he had stayed in that room for a number of months with those guys. Then another Air Force Captain who was also badly injured was moved in with them. He was Captain Quincy Collins. It was a good thing Bob was there to take care of those guys. He really did them a good service. All three of them later said he was the greatest nurse they ever had.

Then September 16th came, the last day of an era at the Hanoi Hilton.

13. First Briar Patch

9/16/65 - 9/23/65

We got in the jeep and started rolling out of the Hilton complex. We didn't know it at the time but this move was not to be a good one for us. This was where the control switched from the Hanoi cops to the North Vietnamese Army and it was a pretty poor trade. Of course we had no idea where we were going. We were closed up in this French carry-all with side curtains. There was room in back for four or five guys.

We were able to pull the curtains aside occasionally and peek out from under our blindfolds. Meanwhile we were all counting out seconds in our minds. We were mentally calculating how much time went by and trying to figure out what direction we were going, so maybe we could locate where the new camp was. As pilots, this kind of directional calculation is very familiar to us, called "dead reckoning."

When we got to a new camp everyone would submit his time and direction. We would then average out about where we were. In some cases when we'd get a hundred or so guys telling their time and distance we got a good location of the camp. Even with just three or four guys we could get a pretty accurate fix on our new camp location.

We headed west from Hanoi. The trip took about a couple of hours and the road was hell; one chuck-hole after another. Finally we arrived at the camp that became known as "The Briar Patch." The camp had nine buildings, laid out in a "tic-tac-toe" matrix with each building separated from the other by a wall. They took Hayden and me over to hut "alpha" at the southern corner of the camp. We assigned each building an alphabetical letter for our communications purposes.

Each hut had four rooms arranged in a square, just like the camp was laid out in a nine-hut square. Each cell was separated from the others by walls. Two walls inside each cell were solid; one had a window and the other a door. Each cell's door faced out in a different cardinal direction. So the windows also looked out in four different cardinal directions. The arrangement went something like this: If you were to walk clockwise around the building, you would see a door, then window, door, window, door, window, door, window and back to the first door. The solid walls extended outward about 5 feet from each cell to create more separation, presumably

189

to prevent communication. So for instance, we couldn't look out our window and talk to someone in the next room looking out their window.

Hayden was put into room 3 with Smitty Harris and I went into room 4 with Bob Shumaker. We hadn't known where Shu and Smitty were being taken when they'd been moved from the Hilton some days ahead of us and we were happy to see them again. We immediately established communications by tapping on the back walls of the cells and found out we had four other guys living in the building with us. They were Bill Tschudy and J. B. McKamey in room one and in room two was Paul Kari and Bob Purcell.

Then I sat down and Shu started telling me what was going on at this camp. It seems that our guys were bombing the hell out of a target that was no more than 300 yards away from our building, just east of camp. He said, "Just wait till 10 o'clock in the morning and we'll really get an air show." He said the F105's come at 10 o'clock every morning, and that they are getting the shit shot out of them because the Gooks start making preparation about a quarter to 10. They were arriving right on time every day and also ridiculous was that the reconnaissance flight came by about 15 minutes after that. So they were all sitting around waiting for that too. Shu said, "Phil, I swear to God it is just like clockwork...everyday."

He was right. It was like clock-work and twice as insane. The next morning the guards came and opened the door and this time it wasn't the older guards we were used to before, but really young guards. They were wearing army uniforms but they looked to be about 15 years old. They were new recruits and I found out from Shu that our camp commander was The Rabbit.

The next morning they opened the doors and we got our first meal. We got two meals a day. Our first meal came at 5:30 in the morning and our second at 6:30 in the evening. We also got water then. It wasn't a great chow schedule but it was typical of the Gooks. It was kind of an added harassment of the prisoners. Another form of harassment was that after feeding us that way for six months, they'd shift the times so we got our first meal around noon and the second at 3:30 in the afternoon

At 10 o'clock that first morning, Shu said, "Well it's about time. Come on over to the window and we'll watch the air show from here." In just a minute or two we heard the drone of airplanes and then we were watching F-105s, coming down the slide, their 30 degree dive, and then dropping bombs on a target just a few hundred yards away. It was truly a great show. Our whole building was shaking and rattling. The blasts were so powerful that we had to hang on to the bars to keep from flying through the air because of the over-pressure from the bomb detonations.

We enjoyed every second of it. We were cheering our heads off! And just as Shu had explained, as soon as the 105s left we saw the reconnaissance flight flying through. The Gooks were shooting like hell at them, too. A couple of days later when we were watching the show we saw a 105 pilot get his canopy shot away. That one turned out to be a very famous Air Force officer who no more than a few weeks later joined our ranks. He was Colonel Robinson Risner. And I had the pleasure of watching him in action, and getting his canopy shot off.

Life was pretty boring in The Briar Patch other than air raids. The Gooks were just getting started on things. The new guards were pretty confused as to what their orders were. They were supposed to keep us separated and not let us talk to other Americans. However, for the first couple of days they got their orders mixed up. They were not letting us see the Vietnamese who brought the chow around, but they were letting us see the other Americans.

They were just screwing up...doing the opposite of what they were supposed to do. It showed that there was no logic in their minds. They just blindly followed orders, as best they could understand them. So in those early days we got to talk with guys in the other rooms and the other buildings.

There was a latrine hole dug in the court yard of building bravo and we guys in alpha would go over there each morning to dump our shit buckets. When we did we'd go right over and talk to Larry Guarino and Everett Alvarez who were there in separate cells.

Also in bravo building was a Thai prisoner whose name was Tem. He too had just appeared on the scene. He had been captured in the summer of 1965. I believe he had been a T-28 pilot. He had inadvertently flown over North Vietnam and gotten himself shot down. The Gooks were using him to help prepare the chow.

Things were pretty bleak at The Briar Patch. The sanitation conditions were absolutely terrible. We weren't allowed to bathe the entire time we were there. We weren't even allowed to wash our hands and face. We had to do that with what little drinking water we were given. There were no supplies of clothing, soap, toothpaste or toilet paper. It was complete neglect.

We were given very little food, just small portions of rice and some fish. The fish was a trash fish, a variety of carp which actually tasted good but there wasn't nearly enough of it. We were getting soup made from greens that grew wild around the camp. We later affectionately referred to this stuff as "swamp grass soup."

We only stayed at Briar Patch for a short time and finally the Gooks got nervous about things. They decided with all the bombing going on we would get killed if they didn't move us out. So on the night of September 23rd 1965, they brought trucks into the camp. We loaded in and made the 45-mile trip over torturous mountain roads back to Hanoi again. The trucks had no springs whatsoever and we were jammed into the truck beds, blind-folded and handcuffed. It was sheer misery the whole way.

Usually we were able to get a look around on these rides by raising our blind-folds. Normally they'd have from eight to twenty of us in the back of the truck and only a couple of guards to watch us. So they just couldn't physically watch us all at the same time, which meant we had opportunities to peek around. Normally on a truck ride like that if we got caught talking to a buddy, the worst treatment we'd get was a slap. So it was well worth it to look around and find out who our buddies were on the truck. There wasn't much they could do to us while we were being transported. And when we arrived at the camp, or wherever, things were always too disorganized for them to bother punishing us. That left us more or less free to push the rules when we were in transit.

We were all happy to be leaving that damn camp out in the country and going back to Hanoi. I speculated to myself as we drove along that we'd be going back to Hoa Lo but as it turned out this was wrong. They had opened a new camp which we called "The Zoo." It was a relief to leave Briar Patch, but I didn't know then that I would be taken back there again for a year, and it would turn out to be one of the worst years of my life.

14. The Zoo — Part 1

9/23/65 – 12/25/65

We arrived at "The Zoo" which was located south-southwest of the center of Hanoi, in the high-population-density outskirts. This "new" camp was completely overgrown with chest-high weeds everywhere amidst a series of stone and tile buildings. The place looked completely run down, but we could tell that at one time or another it had some function. We speculated it probably had been a rest camp or something on that order. We peeked around our blindfolds and saw all this when the guards weren't paying attention.

I was led blindfolded off the truck by a guard. We walked up to a little building and I was shuffling along very slowly since we weren't wearing shoes, only open-toed shower clogs. The guards had a lot of hate and the one leading me didn't tell me that I was approaching a step. I stubbed my toe on the step hard, bending it back and mashing the toenail.

I wouldn't mention it or remember it clearly because it was a typical wound or even a scratch in Vietnam. But anything like that, with the poor diet and lack of medical treatment, could turn into something serious. This was an example, because for 1½ years after that I suffered with an infected and painful big toe on my left foot.

I was finally cured by a cellmate, Air Force Captain Bud Flesher. I moved in with Bud and had been with him for a couple of weeks when one day I was complaining about the damn thing. It was swollen up, puss was dripping out of it and I was having trouble walking around. Bud asked, "How long have you had that?" I said, "A year and a half." He said, "Hell, I can cure that thing!" I asked, "What can you do?" He answered, "We'll bug the guards to drive a medic around."

And that's what he did. He bugged the guards until finally a medic came around one afternoon, probably because they got tired of Bud's nagging. Bud asked the medic if he could have scissors and some cotton. The medic wanted to know what he wanted it for and Bud showed him my toe. Miraculously, the medic said okay and reached into his pocket. He stuck some cotton and a pair of scissors through the bars and walked off.

Bud got me up on my bunk and my other roommate held me down while he began to work on my toe. First he cut the nail back, just like a doctor would, to the center area and peeled it back. Then he began to squeeze all the pus and infection out of the toe. I was climbing the walls but I was also being held by my other roommate so there wasn't much I could do.

When Bud finished he washed it with soap and water. Then he used the scissors as a wedge and rammed cotton back up underneath the nail. I'll be damned if that thing didn't heal in about a week. Eventually the toe nail grew back out and my toe was completely normal. I really have him to thank for that because that was a lot of misery and pain for a long time. He did the job as well as any doctor I'm sure.

After stubbing my toe, the guard led me up to a building and opened the door. The door had no lock. It was just a flimsy wooden door with a window in it; the window glass was painted. I walked into the room and there were Hayden Lockhart, Bob Peel, Smitty Harris, and Bob Shumaker. We threw our gear down on the floor. The place was filthy, just piles of dirt all around and rat shit everywhere. There was no furniture or beds or anything. We talked for awhile and then began to look around. We found out there was a back and a front door to the place. Guards were posted outside each door because there were no locks. There were also two windows in the front and two windows in the back of the room, none of which had bars on them.

We were pretty tired so after we talked for awhile we went to sleep. The next morning I woke up first. Sunshine was streaming into the room. We had hooked up our mosquito nets to some nails we found in the walls. I crawled out of my mosquito net and walked around a little bit. Then I saw a big toad hopping along through the room. I picked it up and on a whim I threw it in Shu's net with him. He woke up with a scream and came roaring out of his mosquito net. He was really pissed off at me.

Bob and Smitty got up and they were pissed at me too. They told me there were toads in this country and in Thailand that were poisonous. They said some of these things were actually deadly poisonous and I shouldn't be screwing around with toads. I still thought it was funny. Shu might still be pissed off about that today.

We sat around most of the morning and nothing happened. Finally, about noon, we were getting hungry and thirsty. We peered out the front and noticed that the guards had started to build a wood fire out in the yard. They had a big pot and were throwing some rice and water in it. They also had a pan with some of the carp trash fish that they were cooking over the fire. That was our meal, delivered about one o'clock that afternoon.

194

The whole situation looked like an after thought. Everything was disorganized. We had just been thrown into this place. They had not anticipated our needs. Apparently they had never anticipated putting prisoners in this place. I guessed they thought Hoa Lo was full so they had to open a new camp.

The next couple of days we made contact with the other men in our building by yelling out the window. Then we began to communicate by tap code. We discovered there were five other rooms in our building and they each held two to four prisoners. Some of the guys had come from Hoa Lo and some from The Briar Patch. A couple of days later we found out there was another building in the compound that had prisoners from Hoa Lo. They were new shoot downs. Among these men were Wes Schierman, Ed Davis, Robbie Risner, and Ray Merritt.

We managed to get contact with these guys by dropping notes off in their rooms. We were able to do that because our room had shit-bucket detail. At nighttime we would go out and empty the shit buckets for the guys in the various other rooms. We'd go to their rooms to pick up their buckets and we'd either leave a note in the bucket or drop one off in their room. Later on guys were dumping their own buckets and they would walk by our building. When they did we would talk quietly to them as they went by so the guard following behind wouldn't hear.

The new guys began to pick it up right away. They would write notes of their own and drop them in our room. Everybody participated and the communications were strong. We even got contact with Everett Alvarez, who was still being kept solo. He was segregated from the rest of us in a building that was off by itself. At the time we thought they might have intentions of releasing him because the war hadn't gotten fully cranked up yet and he would have been a prime choice for one of the first guys to be released.

We speculated that they wanted to keep him from knowing anything about the other prisoners so they could release him. If he'd never known anyone else he wouldn't be able to spill the beans about who else was being held. It was clear from the outset that one of the primary concerns of the Vietnamese was keeping knowledge of other prisoners a secret. They did not want us to have a list of guys who were shot down and they went to great efforts to keep us from communicating with each other. That's why they kept us with people who were already known to each other. So for the first four or five years they had this routine of keeping more or less the same roommates together. As I noted before, that could work with some people. But if roommates didn't like each other, as was often the case, to live together for years and years on end was its own form of torture.

We discovered there was a wood panel on the side wall of our room that seemed to have been added. It was held by nails driven into the concrete but we managed to work it loose. We found a large, window-like hole behind it so we could look into the room next door where Pop Keirn and Red Berg were. That kind of added to the community, with more guys to talk to all day long. We always had one of our guys keeping watch so when a guard would come we'd slide this panel back up and it looked like it had never been off.

On the other side of our other wall was Larry Guarino. There was a window leading out the front of our room right next to the dividing wall. So we could actually just whisper to each other and the guards couldn't hear unless they were standing right there. Larry was living solo at this time and seemed to be undergoing quite a bit of trauma from it. As I said, he was Italian and it seemed to be part of his culture to build things up in his mind bigger than they really were.

Even though we were talking to him all the time, Larry still would periodically go into periods of deep depression and great sadness. Particularly that first week in our new prison, when he had no roommate. We took turns so there was somebody talking to him practically all day long. Within a week or so we had him talked out of his depression and he got his spunk back.

Larry's mental state wasn't just because he was Italian though. Depression seemed to hit everyone when they first arrived, which was hardly a surprise. It's typical for any guy who just fell into the enemy's hands. Maybe he felt bad if he'd been a little too easy with the Gooks in his original interrogations. Maybe he began to get mixed up and wonder why in the hell he was there and why in the hell we were fighting. Was the war a legitimate war? Sometimes guys would buy into some of the stuff the Gooks were putting out and maybe begin to agree with them.

Many guys developed periods of depression from solitary confinement. At first by feeling sorry for themselves, but with just a little contact from some of the other guys, in every instance I knew about, guys snapped out of it.

One thing we agreed upon from the start was this was a different war from any the U.S. had fought before. The objectives could often be construed to be nebulous. There were many varied opinions among us on the war, just as among Americans on the outside. But we all agreed that no

196

matter what our opinion of the war was, we had to protect ourselves here. So we had to use the self-defense mechanism of taking an extremely conservative, hard-line, pro-U.S., pro-war approach with the Gooks.

It was all right if you thought we didn't have any business in a war with Vietnam, fighting over there. There was nothing wrong with that opinion. But when we went into interrogation we didn't tell the Gooks that. We told them we were there carrying out orders; orders we believed in very much. We told them we believed the President of the United States was the greatest man that had ever existed on the face of the earth. We told them everyone in our country was behind the war. We gave them the most radical viewpoint which really turned them off and helped get them off our backs.

They asked us about bombing women and children, old people, hospitals and all that sort of thing. We just took the doctrinaire approach and told them that our military mission had been to bomb military targets. We realized full well that bombs killed civilians as well as people in uniform, but well, that was just the breaks of war. That was what war was and if that happened that was too bad but that's what happened.

Of course later on they tried to get us to admit we had targeted hospitals and that kind of crap so we had to deny that stuff vehemently, over and over again. Starting in 1966 they were torturing us, demanding that we sign statements admitting that we targeted hospitals and such. Eventually, with torture, they got the results they wanted. Under duress we signed their confessions. But we made them subject us to extreme physical pain before we gave them what they wanted. We made them work for it.

If we didn't face them down for a while, we were in even worse trouble. We were picked out as soft and they worked on us even harder and made life even more miserable with repeated attacks. Also, if we didn't resist like that we were going to be fighting our own conscience for the rest of our lives. That was the idea we had at the time.

We stayed in this building for a couple of weeks and then the camp began to fill up. More guys were coming in, as we could see out the cracks in our windows. We had louvered windows so the only thing we could see was the sidewalk or the porch right below. Therefore we went to work on this and improved the view. We called this our TV screen. We discovered you could twist a nail, like a little hand drill, and make a hole in a pine or hardwood board a couple of inches thick. Given enough time, and we had plenty of that, we could drill a hole through anything.

Later when we got a little more sophisticated we found there were very tiny worm holes that had been eaten into almost all of the wood in

Vietnam. A worm hole that is smaller than a pin will give a beautiful view of the whole outside world. All we had to do was to put our eye directly against the pin hole. It's amazing what a large field of view we could have outside through a very tiny hole. A guard would never know this because he had never been in a situation to need it. That meant we were almost always able to have a view from doors that faced to the outside of the camp.

We would drill holes in concrete or brick walls in the same manner. We used pieces of metal, nails or wire. Then we carved out a larger area at the opening of the hole. Next we would manufacture a plug of the same material that we'd drilled out. The plug was inserted into the hole after we had gotten it drilled out. With a little water and rice we could construct a plug that fit like a filling in a tooth. No one could tell where it was. In fact sometimes we would have trouble finding our own plug.

Watching what went on in the camp served two purposes. First it gave us the routine of the camp so we knew what was going on. We learned the habits of the guards and of our fellow prisoners as they were scheduled to go to the showers and to pick up their chow. New people who were brought into the camp never escaped our attention because we'd hear a vehicle and everybody would man their TV screens. That was the first purpose but not necessarily the most important. Another purpose which was just as important was the morale factor. It gave us something to do, something outside of that room that we could experience while being locked in all day long.

I was in situations where only one room had a TV screen because it was the only room that led to the outside. In one instance Air Force Captain Bob Lilly was in such a room. I was next door in a two-man room with Hayden Lockhart. There were three other guys who were in solitary confinement and there were two other two-man rooms. Lilly was our news broadcaster. He would man his TV screen all day long from about 6:00 in the morning till dark at night. He kept us informed on what was going on by tapping on the wall right next to where he had his eye. All day long he would give us a running commentary on everything that was going on outside the camp. He reported everything from two fornicating butterflies that were on the front porch to a guard bringing in a new prisoner.

Bob would even give the noon and evening meal menu when he saw it arrive. The guards would set the food down on the porch and he would describe the portions each of us was getting that evening. He would also provide us with a blown-up description of the menu. He would report how many pieces of cabbage were floating in the soup, how many worms someone was going to get, how big our loaf of bread was, and so on.

He kept us in hysterics most of the day. This news broadcast sounded something like a typewriter going on the wall but to us it was the same as somebody talking. It was just a light tap that ran all day long and if we didn't feel like listening to it we could tune it out. It was really great.

After a couple of weeks the Gooks moved Hayden, Smitty, Shu, Bob and me to another building which also had a good view to the outside camp. In fact it had a particularly good view and we started broadcasting to the new guys whom we had taught the tap code.

With the war heating up and more of our guys getting shot down, there were a lot of new arrivals. We wanted to know who they were and to get them connected with the rest of us. We also wanted news from the outside world.

On one occasion we were taken outside and allowed to exercise, so to speak. While we moved around we talked to the guys in the other rooms by pretending to be talking to each other there outside. Since the guards only spoke Vietnamese and we weren't looking in the direction of the people we were really talking to, they assumed we were talking to each other.

We told the guys inside we would ask questions that only required simple answers. They were to respond yes by coughing two times, which would be just like the tap code "roger" on the wall: tap, tap. A single cough meant no and three meant "I don't know." In this manner we debriefed these guys without the guards realizing they were talking to us.

We were anxious for news of the war and life outside to keep up our morale. We had a lot of information for the new guys concerning the layout of the camp, the treatment they could expect from the guards, what to expect from the quizzers and so forth. We passed information back and forth this way for almost a year, until 1967, when the Vietnamese finally got the picture on what was going on. They realized we were passing information by coughing and sneezing and clearing our throats, etc. After that all we had to do was cough in our room and they would come in and beat the hell out of us. They were never really quite sure we were answering a question or had a legitimate cough so lots of times we could get away with it, even under the bad treatment.

One afternoon in our room Shu was talking to us while he was leaning against the door that led to the outside. By this time they had put a rudimentary lock with a weak little bracket on the outside of the door. It was typical of the half-ass arrangements the Gooks would make. As Shu was leaning on the door the hasp broke and the door fell open and he literally fell out on the porch. A guard was standing out there and he saw what had happened. Shu picked himself up, dusted himself off, smiled to the guard, said "Sorry," and stepped back into the room.

The guard came over and pushed the door shut. Then within a few minutes The Rabbit and a couple of other guards stalked into the room. The Rabbit said, "You have tried to escape." Shu said, "You must be out of your mind!" Rabbit 'said, "No, the guard has reported you have tried to escape and you will be punished."

This was typical of the kind of shit the Gooks would pull on us. They welcomed an excuse to get a couple of licks in. That evening they moved Shu and Smitty, putting them both in solitary confinement. That's all they did. They didn't beat them this time. So now I was living with only Hayden Lockhart.

Hayden and I kept on tapping on the wall of course. The guards would come around if they heard anything and badger us about it but we were careful. We would always clear the area to make sure no guards were nearby. The way it developed with Hayden and me was that we made a pretty good communications team. I was fast with the tap code and he had extremely good hearing. My hearing was lousy so Hayden was the one to make sure we were clear.

Hayden developed an ability to listen like a blind person does. He could tell me almost everything that was going on in the camp. He knew by the footsteps which of the various guards were outside, which one was walking and where he was going. He could tell from listening if this guard had picked up the chow, or whatever, to bring to us or if he was coming to take us to the shower. His listening was so acute and his attention to detail so focused he always knew what the guard's mission was.

Hayden could pick up any truck or vehicle in the area with his bird-dog ears, and know where it had parked. He could tell how many people had stepped off the truck. He could tell the foot steps of a Yank from the footsteps of the Vietnamese. It was utterly fantastic what that guy could do with his ears. It was seldom that anybody ever got by Hayden's ears. This kept us both out of a lot of punishment for communicating.

One day Ron Storz in the cell next door suggested that we bore a hole in the wall so we could just talk to each other. This sounded like a good idea. Hayden and I had been collecting stuff for tools and so far we had never had a room inspection of any sort.

As I said the Gooks were completely disorganized at this time. You could ask for shit paper for three weeks and maybe never get it and then one day a guard would come along just out of the clear blue and stick a wad of it in your room. We went without soap or such things for long periods. We went without shaving for a couple of months. We never got haircuts. Sometimes we would go many days or weeks without being allowed to wash or bathe. I had only one set of clothing, a pair of shorts and a shirt, and no underwear. These were given to me originally and they were getting pretty grungy six months later, as one might imagine.

Hayden and I had a copper alloy reinforcing bar that had come out of the wall. I had been able to straighten it by using a saw horse as a battering ram. We had saw horses to hold up our bed boards. The rod was about four feet long and I kept it hidden under my bed board. We also collected things like pieces of razor blades and we had nails galore. We had many burnt match sticks stashed away to write with. Hayden and I had even made a knife out of a piece of metal.

We started to work on our wall by using the reinforcing rod as a drill. There was an old blackboard on the wall that we pulled down and we drilled behind it. We would remove the nails that held it to the wall and lay it aside when we worked. Hayden always cleared and when the guards were coming we would put it all together again. I worked on this project about four or five hours a day for several days.

I finally got it almost all the way through to the other side, except I couldn't seem to get it through that last inch. I tapped over to Ron and asked him what the surface on his wall was like. We had to work together on this because our rooms were on different levels. He was on a higher level than I was. We also had to construct this hole in such a way that he could hide it when it came through. He said he didn't know what was wrong. It appeared to him that the wall was just normal concrete. But I told him that it felt like I had reached a piece of slate or marble covering on the other side of the wall.

Ron said, "Hell, I don't know what it is, Phil, but keep working on it." I did keep working on it for about another two weeks but I couldn't make an inch of headway. Finally I tapped over to Ron and said, "Sorry buddy, but it looks like we aren't going to get any oral conversation going here so we will have to use tap code." He said, "Okay, I agree with you that it does look hopeless." I sat down on my bed at siesta time with the reinforcing rod still sticking out of the hole there. And I looked at that thing, and I looked at that thing, and I paced around the room, and I thought and I thought about it. The more I thought about it the madder I got. I paced around the room for a half-hour. Hayden was sound asleep taking his siesta.

Finally I got so mad that I just walked over to the corner of the room and picked up a saw horse. Then I took a good position, planted my feet firmly, and hauled off with my best home-run baseball swing. I nailed that reinforcing rod with the sawhorse as hard I could. Hayden came about six feet off the bunk with the crash. Meanwhile, the rod went shooting through the wall like a Zuni rocket.

It went shooting right by Ron who was sitting on his shit bucket on the other side of his room. It went shooting by him at about nose level, just missing his face by about six inches, and imbedded itself in the wall on the other side of his room.

I got down to the hole and peeked through where I could see Ron sitting there on his shit bucket, with a terror-stricken look on his face. Ron could see my eyeball looking at him. He grinned at me. He got up, wiped his ass, pulled his pants up and walked over to the hole. Ron was from New England. He stuck his mouth up to the hole and I stuck my ear up to the hole on my side and in New Englandese he said, "Geez, that was close!" I guess I damn near killed him. But we had our hole drilled through.

Not only did we have the hole drilled through but the reinforcing rod was now in Ron's room. Ron said, "I'll go to work on my wall and get a hole through to Robbie," which he did. In a day or two he was finished because he didn't have that slate on the other side and his wall was thinner. In another day or two Robbie had his drilled through to Ed and in a day or two more Ed had his drilled through to Wes. We all had great voice communications with each other, room by room by room, through these holes. One guy would stick his mouth up to the hole and the other guy would listen and vice versa and we could carry on conversations. This meant a great deal to those guys in solitary confinement. It was really a big morale boost to them.

About this same time Robbie Risner, being the natural leader and commanding personality that he is, established himself as our senior ranking officer. He began to pass out policies, which were written down and then passed over to Hayden and myself to drop off to the other fellows in the camp when we were out on shit-bucket detail. Every evening we would pass out Robbie's policies and we would bring back any questions guys had, acting as couriers for Robbie.

In a few days Hayden and I received two new roommates. They were Navy Lieutenant J. B. McKamey and Air Force Captain Paul Kari. So we had four of us in the room again and our courier service even got better with the addition of these guys. At night we would go out in pairs and make rounds of the camp. Together the four of us were able to get a full spectrum of the camp layout.

Robbie's policies were about how vital it was to conduct ourselves in a military manner. Among his directives were "Walk tall and look proud." "Don't show any signs of weakness in front of the enemy." "Don't say anything more than you absolutely have to." "Don't go to meetings with journalists." "Don't give the enemy any propaganda." These were just general behavior guidelines and how to keep our morale up. He also advocated exercising in our cell to keep up our physical fitness.

This is when I really got started in high gear with my own physical fitness in prison. I had been doing a certain amount each day but when Robbie's words of wisdom started coming through I really heard him. This guy could put out messages that made us stand tall and feel proud to be an American fighting man. He was just a leader and a half! He got us really enthused and cranked up.

He also immediately began to bug the Gooks about the fact that he was the senior ranking officer. In doing so he was disregarding his own safety. He demanded to be able to see the sick and wounded and this upset the Gooks terribly. He was putting in our bitches to the camp to ask for more food, better sanitation conditions, and better medical treatment for his men. He demanded the right to observe religious services on Sunday and the right to have a Bible, to have written materials, to have educational materials, to correspond with our families and so on. He bitched constantly at the Gooks for us and never asked anything for himself.

Besides Robbie Risner, there were other senior heroes in our midst, special guys who stood out by standing up for the men. Among them, a name well known to the American public, especially after he was selected by Ross Perot to be his vice presidential running mate in the 1992 elections, was Admiral James Stockdale. Another was Colonel Robert Flynn. We had some marvelous leaders who were extremely courageous.

One day Robbie passed a request to Ron Storz to give him a layout of the camp. Ron said he would pass it through to us, since we had been outside the camp quite a bit. So J. B., who was the senior man in our room, said, "Phil, I'll give you that job. You lay out the camp for Col. Risner." I agreed and went to work on it.

I drew up a scale map by pacing off footsteps from one building to another and from one area to another when we went out at night. I finally got it all drawn up, with the rooms in each building, and the windows and doors as they existed. I showed where the Gooks lived, the interrogation rooms and where the food was prepared. I also showed where we thought the camp was with respect to town.

When I had this all drawn to scale, I said, "J. B., it looks like it would be helpful to give these buildings a number or name. That way in our communications with each other we could always refer to it by that and guys could tell where they are located." J. B. said, "Great idea, Phil. Name all the buildings in the camp."

I thought about it and decided we were all being treated like animals so I named the camp "The Zoo." I named the buildings "The Pigsty," "The Stables," "The Barn" and so forth. We were located in "The Barn" at that time. We also standardized a way of numbering the rooms. Standing in front of a building, rooms were numbered from left to right. If there were rooms in back, they began from the far right and went back to the left. So a building with five front rooms numbered left to right, one through five, and behind room five would be room six, then right to left.

The Gooks later messed up my great numbering system when they came in and partitioned off some back rooms into smaller ones, so they could put more people in solitary confinement in the smaller cells.

I called the area where the Gooks lived the "Gook House." This was to become significant few days later. I passed this map to Ron Storz and Ron passed it over to Col. Risner. I told Ron to be sure and warn him that this map was extremely sensitive. It was hot and if the Gooks got it they would fear an escape plot. We hadn't had a room inspection yet but we knew we had to be ready for one. Col. Risner passed the message back: "Never fear gang. I'll memorize this thing and get rid of it as soon as possible."

We were satisfied with that. A couple of days later I sent the query over through Ron again to Col. Risner to remind him that if he hadn't gotten rid of that map he should because we had noticed some activity in the camp that looked like they were getting ready to work on some of the rooms. If the carpenters came over and started working on our rooms, there was likelihood that he would be caught with that damn map.

I had used a large piece of Vietnamese shit paper, about two feet long by about a foot and a half wide, to construct the map of The Zoo. I used a piece of bamboo that I had filed down on the floor as a measuring stick and I used a nail to carve off measurements so I could detail the map to scale. I had also found another thing to use as a writing implement that worked like a lead pencil. I had discovered an old truck battery on one of my shit bucket runs. The contact rods that go down into the battery were made of lead and

I brought this plate of lead back to the room, broke it up into pieces and sharpened them down on the tile floor. They made outstanding pencils.

Another thing that worked as a pencil was their toothpaste tubes which were made out of a lead-zinc material. It didn't write too well but you could tear up a toothpaste tube and roll it on concrete so it had a smooth edge that you could write with in a pinch. If you were in solitary and had no other way of writing sometimes you could use a rock. In an emergency you could prick your finger with a bamboo stick and write with your own blood.

We tried all kinds of concoctions for ink. Later on the Gooks came up with a Vietnamese cure-all medicine that was good for rheumatism, lumbago, cancer, heart palpitations, ringworm and you name it. It was purple sheep-dip, literally. They used it on sheep and dogs for mange. The stuff just made amazing ink. We took a piece of bamboo, a sliver about 6 inches long, and filed down the point very sharp. Then we took a stolen razor blade and a nail. You go back up from the point and drill a hole with your nail. This was a hole to prevent splitting. Then we'd start at the point with the razor blade and cut a slit up to the stop hole. Then we had a point that looked like a pen point on a normal fountain pen. And the little stop hole acted as a reservoir for the ink. We could do beautiful, extremely fine writing with these bamboo pens. We could write very small, and we wound up making voluminous notes on academic subjects with these pens and this ink.

A couple of days went by and I wanted to warn Robbie again. When I went through Ron, he told me, "Gee, Phil, you think we ought to warn him? After all he is a Colonel." I turned to Hayden, my outspoken friend, and said, "Hayden, what do you think about that?" Hayden said, "Tell Storz I don't give a God damn if he is a damn colonel. You tell that colonel to get rid of that God damn map!" Ron said, "Okay guys, I'll tell him, but not that way." So Ron warned Col. Risner again. Colonel Risner responded, "Right guys, I'll get rid of it this evening."

But evening didn't come for Col. Risner because that afternoon during siesta the carpenter working crew slipped in on us. The guards opened our doors. There were about four of them that came into the room and the guards told us to move out of the room. Before we could even move a muscle the work crew guys and the guards spotted the blackboard that had been jimmied with. They could tell that it had been pulled down several times. They went right over to it and saw the hole we had drilled through to the next room.

When the guards saw this they went running out of the room and high-tailed it over to the Gook's shack to get the camp officers and camp commander. In the few minutes we had I got on the wall and tapped over to Ron to warn him what was coming. Hayden grabbed all the contraband of ours and J. B. McKamey and Paul Kari grabbed all the gear they could and we started stuffing it down through a crack between two walls. That was so at least they wouldn't be found on our persons.

The guards came running back immediately and Ron did not get an opportunity to warn Colonel Risner. Before we knew it they were in Ron's room and in Risner's room. They got all of Ron's, Risner's, Ed Davis', and Wes Schierman's contraband gear. They got the map from Robbie, and they were some kind of pissed. We had managed in the confusion with the Gooks, since we had four guys in the room, to do the old soft shoe act by double-shuffling and passing things behind our backs to each other while the Gooks searched us and flailed around in our room.

There was so much confusion that we were able to throw the remainder of our stuff out in the yard into the weeds so we didn't get caught with very much on us. We picked up our bed boards and were moved over to another building so they could work on that room. They were putting in solid doors with real locks and bars in the windows. They were finally making the place secure for our detention.

As we moved across the yard carrying our bed boards we shouted warnings to the other guys in the camp that contraband gear had been picked up over in the barn. We warned that there was a big search and shake-down going on over there now and for all the other guys to get rid of their contraband and any messages they might have, et cetera. We were able to get the word out as we were crossing the yard because the guards were busy with the action going on at Ron Storz's and Robbie Risner's cells.

Of course, the three guys who really ate it big were Storz, Risner and Davis because they were the ones that were caught red-handed with the gear. It turned out, later on, that the thing that pissed the Gooks off the most about the map they found in Risner's cell was not the fear of escape. It was the name "Gook House" I had given to their quarters. With their monstrous egos and small brains they really took it out on those guys for that, and also because they had all this contraband gear.

I might throw something in here about the ego thing. I described before how we had compared our stay there with being captive of some junior high school girls. Well not only that, but the Vietnamese had tremendous inferiority complexes around us Americans. They felt inferior in intelligence and also physically because they were so much smaller. We used to say, as prisoners, that they had a tremendous inferiority complex but it wasn't really a complex. It was true!

The Rabbit had been our sole officer and camp commander at The Briar Patch. When we moved to The Zoo he became the same there. The Gooks were operating with an absolute minimum guard force. In fact the entire shebang was being run by one turnkey (the guard with keys to our cells.) He was just a young guy who was completely disorganized with no one to help him. They had to deal with every room individually. They had no schedule for giving out toilet paper, cigarettes, bathing or bringing our chow.

As I said before I had just the single set of clothes that I had been wearing since my arrival in Vietnam. I had been asking incessantly for another set of clothes, like the other guys had, but with no results. Finally one day when I was in the shower room with my cell mates, I washed the only clothes I had. When the guard opened the door for us to go back to our rooms I marched back across the camp naked.

This drove the Vietnamese up the wall. They really got excited about it and in a matter of minutes I had a couple of officers in my room. The Vietnamese have different social customs. One is that not only is it bad for a member of the opposite sex to see you in the nude, but they feel the same way about members of the same sex. Men do not bathe in the nude nor do they present themselves in the nude to each other as we Americans do. They are very reticent and bashful about it. It creates the same sort of feeling as it does for us with a member of the opposite sex. Men will walk around with their arms around each other, or even with their hands in each other's pockets. But no nudity allowed.

My walking back across the yard nude was a calculated venture on my part. I decided to see if I could stir them up to get some action because I really needed another set of clothes. When the officers came around and asked me why I had done this terrible thing, I explained that I had been asking ever since I had been shot down for another set of clothes. I said, "I cannot wear the same pair of clothes year in and year out, I must have another set of clothes to wear like all my fellow prisoners here do."

Well, they saw some sense in that. One of the officers jabbered to the guard in Vietnamese and they all left. Five or ten minutes later the guard came back with another pair of pants and a shirt for me. It just goes to show you no matter what the treatment is like, if there is something that is reasonable then it's worth fighting for. You might as well give it a try anyway. Sometimes during the worst treatment, when the Vietnamese would punish guys for something that from our perspective seemed completely within reason, the punishment would be a token thing. They would just give you a rap on the knuckles, figuratively speaking, to save face. Then immediately afterwards they would give the guy what he wanted. It was kind of amazing how this worked.

So this one turnkey was just running around putting out little fires all over the place with all of these rooms. There was no schedule for bathing. Sometimes we got to and sometimes we didn't. In addition to this one turnkey there were maybe eight guards who were all teenage boys and The Rabbit as the camp commander. It was a hectic and disorganized mess. There was great opportunity to escape from the camp but if someone did he would be in the middle of wall-to-wall, Hanoi Vietnamese humanity. There was no way any Americans were going to get anywhere.

So escape was not a problem for them. There was built in security all around. As things began to develop in this time period, we started seeing The Dog on the scene more frequently. He was apparently traveling back and forth from the Heartbreak area to this camp, trying to divide his time between the two prisons.

The Owl had disappeared sometime in September of 1965 when the Vietnamese Army took over and he was never seen again. I'd assumed he probably went down south some place to be an interrogator for the NVN or Vietcong. I'm sure they used his talents some place because he was good.

We called this turnkey "Qui Hoi" because we noticed that when anybody wanted him they yelled out "Qui Hoi, Qui Hoi." We thought that was his name. When we called him that to his face he always got a big kick out of it. As time went by and our Vietnamese improved a little bit, we found out that it was Vietnamese for "Hey turnkey!" All our Vietnamese was learned phonetically so I haven't any idea how it might have been properly spelled.

The Zoo was laid out roughly in a square. Essentially there are eight buildings used for prisoners. In addition, there were a couple of small buildings used for punishment and torture. The prison buildings were arranged around the outer edge with a center area where a road led in from the main gate and then formed an inner circle.

This road circled a fish pond or "swimming pool" as we used to call it. As I said before, we thought this might have been an old rest camp from previous days. The "swimming pool," which I keep in quotes, appeared to have been a swimming hole at one time. However it was now filled with stagnant water, lily pads and other stuff growing in it. The Gooks used to throw trash and garbage into it. They would also raise the little trash fish out there that they fed to us. The guards would clown around and throw each other in it once in awhile. But it was never really used as a swimming pool.

The perimeter of the camp was a wall. We were physically confined to our cells and were not ever allowed out in the yard in numbers of any more than one or two guys at a time. This was when we would be escorted to the shower room. There was one shower room in the camp at this time over in The Pigsty.

We moved into a fairly large room, number five, in The Stables. A couple of us still had contraband material but at this time the guards weren't watching us as they were still busy on the other side of the camp. So a couple of us just walked out of the cell and threw some of our contraband materials into the weeds that were growing up in front of the building. No one saw us do this and now we were pretty clean. Pretty soon a guard came around and locked us in.

There was nothing in the cell at all. There were three large windows, one on the front, one on the side, and one on the back that was the end of the building. These windows had the standard louvered slats so when you looked out it was only down at the sidewalk. We immediately went to work trying to find peek-holes to see what was going on. This wasn't too difficult and soon we had a view of what was happening in the camp. There was frenzied activity with the guards in and out of Storz', Risner's and Davis' cells. Nothing much more happened that day.

That evening we received our meal as usual and later went to bed. We discovered before we went to bed that Alvarez was in room one of The Pigsty and some of the other guys were located in the front rooms there. At this time The Pigsty had five rooms and the shower. The rooms had not been divided up yet.

Alvarez seemed to be getting along quite well after having been in solitary for almost two years. He was in good spirits and he was a hard charger. The next morning the turnkey Qui Hoi came, along with some other guards, and they searched our rooms. Of course it was too late and all they got were some little scraps of paper, pieces of pencils and miscellaneous materials. We had nothing really big or dangerous since we had gotten rid of all the bad stuff. The guards picked up all these things.

One particular item they had gotten from Paul Kari was the 23rd Psalm. I copied it down for him because he wanted to learn it. I knew all that stuff from my childhood Southern Baptist training. A little while later

Paul was called out to a quiz and asked about the 23rd Psalm, which Paul hadn't yet had time to learn. The Rabbit asked him, "Where did you get it because obviously you didn't write it yourself?"

I told Paul before he left the room that if they asked him where he got it to just tell them I wrote it. I didn't care. So he told Rabbit that I wrote it. He came back from the quiz in a little while. The guard then indicated for me to go down to the quiz room. I went into the quiz room where they had a desk and a chair with the Rabbit and another Vietnamese who was in civilian clothes. This other guy was about 45 years old. He was rather tall and very well built. He looked tough and I could tell from my first look at him and by the way he handled himself that he was some higher-up in the government.

We named him "The SS Officer." This officer only showed himself for a couple of days in the camp and then he left and I never saw him again. The Rabbit started the quiz off by asking me for some biographical data which I refused to give. Then he asked about this 23rd Psalm and he asked me to repeat it for him. I repeated it for him and as I went along he asked me what each part of it meant and I explained it to him. I think it was more for the curiosity of the other fellow. The Rabbit was interpreting all this in Vietnamese.

He confessed to me that he did not understand what was written in our Bible because of the old English language in it. I spoke with him some because it seemed like there was a lot of pressure right now. And it seemed like this new officer was putting a lot of pressure on The Rabbit. So I tried to answer innocuous questions with bull shit, without giving them any information on my family or my biography.

After a little while the Rabbit worked around to who this guy was. He explained that this man was a high official from the government, from their security force. In other words, he said he was the same as the North Vietnamese CIA. This made my ears perk up a little bit. All the time this guy sat there with a stony look on his face, with an icy stare. He showed no emotions whatsoever during the whole quiz. The way he handled himself, I believed what The Rabbit said.

The Rabbit then informed me that many bad things had taken place in the camp the previous day. He said many prisoners had shown themselves as having an unruly attitude. He said he knew that I was the springboard in the center of the operation that had gone on. And he said I wasn't fooling anybody. He alluded to the fact, but didn't come right out and say it, that I had lucked out by not being caught with the goodies. He said that some of my friends had been "caught red-handed" with various things and they would pay for that. Later on in the quiz he said, "All of you will pay for what you have done."

Finally, he told me to go back to my room. I went back to my room and told J. B., Hayden, and Paul what had taken place. That day our meal came around and it was quite a surprise. There were four of us and they delivered a soup bowl that was about one fourth full of soup. It was about enough soup for two or three spoonfuls each. There was a half a loaf of bread for the four of us. This was to be part of our punishment; diminished rations.

Now the Gooks never came right out and said we were all being punished. They were very often that way. They were subversive in the way they went about things. They left it for us to figure it out on our own. They never said that we were being punished but this meal routine went on for a couple of weeks or so. We were literally starving to death.

Then McKamey became very ill. He started running a fever and he had tremendous headaches, day and night. They were so bad he was vomiting from the pain. We had no idea what disease he had but we had a strong feeling it might have been hepatitis. We had been trying to get medical treatment but to no avail. Then one day the guards came in along with The Rabbit and the SS officer, still in civilian clothes.

They had us stand with our hands against the wall, except for J. B. who was still in bed and couldn't get up. They searched us and our cell with a fine-toothed comb. They found a few small items again that we had collected in the interim period, pieces of paper and little nails and things like that. This was a completely thorough inspection and the SS guy was directing the guards how to go about it. He was telling them every move to make.

This inspection went on for about an hour and a half. The guards were learning how to do the job right. When they left and locked the cell they took the saw horses that had been under our bed boards. So we were back on the floor. Later on that afternoon they came in and took out our bed boards so now we were completely on the floor. We spread our mats on the floor and our blanket on top of that.

Some of the guys still had a few of their American clothes and they took those away also. Paul had a couple of pictures of his family that the Gooks had let him keep out of his wallet when he was shot down. They took those away from him too. He had been the only guy in the whole camp who had any pictures. No more. The SS officer left along with the guards and our turnkey.

We noticed our turnkey had been able to collect several items during the inspection. We had been watching him do this without the SS officer's knowledge. There were some pieces of paper and other items he was able to pick up on his own when he was sure the SS officer was not watching. When they all left our cell, we saw him stuff these items in his pocket. It was obvious that he was trying to cover his own "six," pilot slang for his back. The more he found, the less they found and the better he would look.

Let me explain that when we were back in The Barn, I had in my possession, in the belt hole of my pants, some top secret material. These items were written down in very small notes. I had written them down in an effort to memorize them. I kept them on my person day and night and I had in mind that when danger presented itself I would eat them. When the Gooks came storming in on us the first thing I did was reach in my belt and pop them in my mouth; no problem at all. There was no way they could get to me fast enough that I couldn't accomplish this. They were, like I said, very small and it was no more than swallowing a pill. This information would have been extremely dangerous if the Vietnamese had gotten it. To this day, I cannot explain what it was, but it was extremely sensitive.

The SS officer and the guards stood around and talked a while in the yard after they searched us and our room, and then they left. Then the turnkey went over to another cell where Shumaker and Harris were living. He was going to go down the line and check everybody out before the SS officer came back. We saw him come out of Shu and Smitty's cell a little while later with a bunch of written materials. Then we saw him go out into the yard, put these written materials down on the ground and look carefully all around. Then he took out his cigarette lighter and burnt them all up. It was a big pile of materials.

I later found out from Shu that he had not been quite as cautious as I had in keeping his top secret materials. The turnkey had picked this information up from him before The SS Officer came for inspection. I guess luck was with us that day because this guy didn't read any English and he didn't understand what it was. All he knew was that it was something that would get him in trouble if the SS officer found it, so he burnt it all.

It was a lesson we would never forget throughout the rest of our prison stay. Never again did we ever keep any written top secret material. We kept secret and confidential notes sometimes but whenever we did it was always coded. The rest of the stuff that was at higher classification we kept strictly by memory.

A couple of days later our front louvered window opened up and there were four or five Vietnamese officers, along with a great many guards, standing outside looking in the window. Among the officers was an old man with grey hair. He was very tall for a Vietnamese, about 5 feet, 11 inches. He stood very straight and he appeared be in his early 60s. He wore a white uniform with a closed top like our service dress whites. He wore no rank. His uniform was very white, starched, and he looked very important. We used to call these higher-up Vietnamese who would sometimes come through the camp "VIGs." That stood for Very Important Gooks.

This VIG stood outside and looked in while all the other officers and guards were jumping through their asses around him. The way they were catering to him we figured he was a very high state department type or a general. We took the clue and we stood up in the room at attention as others looked in. Then they closed the window and left.

A few days later the cell door opened up and some medical people came in. They were a couple of younger Vietnamese who looked like medics with white gowns and white masks on. There was also an older guy who had on a NVN Army uniform under his white smock. He also wore a white silk hat. This guy turned out to be a doctor; a genuine Vietnamese doctor. He came in and asked if anybody spoke French. We told him no. I told him I spoke Spanish and he said a few things in very broken Spanish. Between the Spanish and French we could communicate directly with him a little bit.

He wanted me to tell him what was wrong with J. B. I couldn't explain it to him very well because he couldn't understand what I was saying, so he started examining J. B. I was able to get across to him that we were closed up in this cell day and night, that it was very dark, that we were not allowed to bathe, and that we thought J. B. needed fresh air. I asked if they could just keep the louvered window open because the window had bars. The doctor nodded his head and he spoke to The Rabbit in Vietnamese.

The Rabbit then explained to me that he would allow the window louvers to be left open if we would not look or talk out of the window. He wanted us to walk around the room and not look out the damn window, as ridiculous as that sounds. So the doctor had the window opened up to let sunshine and fresh air into the room. He gave J. B. a couple of shots and gave him an intravenous injection of glucose. J. B. explained to him that he had very painful headaches and very painful joints and muscles.

Cobbling together various phrases in our pigeon French and Spanish we were able to get some basics across to each other. The doctor apparently did not want to use The Rabbit as an interpreter, though the reason wasn't clear. I was glad he didn't because we were able to communicate with each other better than using The Rabbit with English. After he left the cell our food situation improved. We were given more though it was still not much more than half of what we had been getting before. But it was an improvement.

We gave J. B. most of our food even though we were at starvation level. This was a tough task because it was almost impossible to get J. B. to eat more than his share. However, we just told him that if he didn't do it we were going to bodily hold him down and stuff it down his throat. On the first occasion, we got on his bed and held him down. I had the food ready and I asked him, "J. B., are you going to eat it or do we have to shove it down your throat?" He relented, saying, "All right, you guys, I'll eat it."

We continued this way for several days. We also still continued to talk out the windows when we could clear.

We got contact with a new guy down at the end of The Stables. He turned out to be Air Force Lieutenant Tom Barrett. We learned that he was in leg irons and hand cuffs. The reason was they wanted a biography from him and he was refusing to give it to them. He was holding out on diminished rations, getting almost nothing to eat. They kept it up for about three weeks or so and then they cut his water off.

Of course at that point he had to give them the biography. After that they moved him out of his cell, down to The Pigsty and in with Alvarez. We passed this news around the camp and I'll tell you there was not a happier group of guys that night in the whole camp. We were all thrilled, both because Tom was no longer being denied food and water, but because Alvy had finally gotten a roommate. It was probably as good for our morale as it was for his.

J. B. began to improve, though he didn't put on any weight, and finally he got over his illness. On December 5th the Rabbit came down to our cell and told J. B. and Paul that they were to roll up gear and they moved down to the cell in The Stables where Tom Barrett had been, which was cell number one. Hayden and I wished them well as they walked out. That same day I got sick; very sick. I started running a high fever. I felt very dizzy and sick to my stomach. By that night I was in bed with a high fever. When I say in bed, I mean on the floor. The weather had started to get very cold and we had basically nothing to keep warm with. We had two very thin cotton blankets which provided about as much warmth as four or five sheets. I got the chills and began to vomit.

My physical condition continued to deteriorate so Hayden began to bug the guards for medical treatment but we got nothing. He would badger them day and night. He yelled "Bau Cau" which were two Vietnamese words we were told we should use if we wanted a guard. In Vietnamese it means "report."

My condition continued to get worse. I turned very yellow with jaundice and the whites of my eyes were also very yellow. The inside of my mouth was raw and dry. I was nauseous, vomiting all the time. I could not eat anything. I could only sip some water occasionally and I was urinating blood. Around December 9th I went into a delirious state, according to Hayden. I don't remember much except the hallucinations I was having.

I don't remember how long it lasted. Hayden tells me the delirium ran several days. We figured my temperature was running around 105 degrees. From December 5th until December 25th I was unable to eat anything. Hayden tried to get me to eat a banana one day but after I got a couple of bites down I started vomiting again. My weight went down to around 100 pounds. I am 6' 2" and in shape I weigh about 180 pounds. I could carry 190 pounds without any trouble. I was proof that someone can lose a tremendous amount of weight and survive. Staying at this extremely low level for a long time can be very damaging physically. But at least from my experience, for a short period of time a person can bounce back without permanent damage.

Finally I started to improve slightly. The fever went away but I maintained the jaundice condition. Then toward the end of December the Gooks came in and gave us a sweater. This was a god-send because it was really cold. The temperatures at night would drop down to 40 degrees with the wind blowing through the open room. Without anything to keep us warm, and in our starvation state, it was like being in sub-zero weather. It was not anything like the guys in Korea had experienced but it was an extreme factor. It was also very wearing on us mentally, to be cold day and night.

During the several days I was in my worst condition, Hayden gave me one of his blankets. He did this without my asking because I was going in and out of a delirious state. It was an unbelievable sacrifice for him. It is something I will never forget as long as I live.

15. The Zoo - Part 2

12/25/65 - 4/21/66

On Christmas Eve of 1965 the guard came down to the room and told me to get up and come to a quiz. I managed to stagger to my feet with Hayden helping me. Hayden took a blanket and wrapped it around me. The guard said, "No, you've got to come in just your long clothes. You're going to see an officer and you can't come with a blanket wrapped around you." Hayden told him to "Kiss his ass," that I was going down in a blanket. The guard finally said all right.

Hayden helped me to the door and started out the cell with me. He was helping to carry me along and the guard told Hayden to go back to the cell. When Hayden went back to the cell I fell down on the porch and couldn't walk by myself. So the guard helped me up, put one of my arms over his shoulder, and he helped carry me to the quiz room. He was actually very kind about it

I walked in the quiz room and there was a sign on the wall that said "Merry Christmas." I sat down on a stool. I was shivering because I still had a fever and was having chills. I looked like the wrath of God; yellow all over from the jaundice and I was still very sick.

I looked through my foggy vision at The Dog across the table. He just sat there and looked at me for a long time. Then he said, "What is wrong with you?" I said, "I'm very sick." He said, "Why did you not report it to the guard?" I spit on the floor and said, "Fuck you, you bastard!" He said, "What?" And I repeated it for him. He said, "What do you mean?" I said, "I've been telling the guard everyday for twenty days now that I've been like this." I added, "You intend to leave me like this so I can die." Then, "Maybe I will die, I could care less."

He said, "All right, you will have medical treatment. I did not know. You cannot blame me. It is not my fault." I said, "Don't you call yourself the Camp Commander?" He said, "Yes, of course I'm the Camp Commander." I said, "Then why do you not know what is wrong with your prisoners?" He said, "You are not a prisoner you are a criminal." I said, "All right, then why don't you know what is wrong with your criminals?" He said, "It is not my fault, you cannot blame me, the guard did not tell me."

I said, "All right, I don't care if you can't keep control of your guards.

That's your problem. But I need some medical treatment." He said, "You will receive medical treatment." He said, "This evening I have for you a letter from your wife." He handed a letter to me across the table. It was the first letter I had received from my wife. She had written it in on October 3rd, and I was receiving it on Christmas Eve.

He said, "Are you going to open it and read it?" I said, "I'll read it later in my room." He said, "All right, now here is pen and paper you may write a letter to your wife." I said, "I am too weak to write and besides that, what I have to write right now you would not allow to be sent out." I added, "You Vietnamese are barbaric."

He sat back. He knew that word because that's one they used on us for bombing their women and children. I said, "You are very barbaric people to treat your prisoners like this." He just sat there and took it as I chewed him out. It was an amazing thing that he just sat there with his blank face, just listening to me, and occasionally he'd nod.

At the end of this he said, "You cannot blame me for this. The guard will help you back to your room." You might wonder why I referred to The Dog as the camp commander instead of The Rabbit. The truth is they changed personnel all the time. We called it Musical Camp Commander. The Vietnamese never told us a damn thing about who was in charge. They either didn't know themselves or didn't think it was necessary for us to know. On a rare occasion they might tell us what was going on, but usually some guy would just announce himself as the Camp Commander.

In a lot of camps a couple of officers would call themselves the Camp Commander. It was really screwy. The Rabbit had announced himself as the Camp Commander back in September when we moved into the camp. The Dog was transient, coming from Hoa Lo to Coo Loc, The Zoo. After a while The Dog came to stay more and more at our "state of the art" facility until he was there all the time. He was in fact the Camp Commander. He was a bar and four stars officer, the most senior captain around.

The guard came in and helped me back to the cell. This guard was a new turnkey. Qui Hoi had left the camp a couple of weeks earlier. We called this guy "Gold Tooth" because, as you might expect, he had a big gold tooth in the front of his mouth. He was a bar and three star sergeant, about 30 years old or so, and he was fairly competent. The only trouble with Gold Tooth was he was lazy. He was the guy we had been bugging all along for medical treatment and he had been too lazy to tell anybody or get any help. He was also bad about stealing stuff. We were supposed to get three cigarettes a day, which was our normal ration. Gold Tooth would often steal them from us. He did this to all the guys he took care of.

Gold Tooth helped me back to my cell and as we went inside he turned me around and he put a half dozen or so cigarettes in my hand and gave me a cigarette light. I went in and fell down on my bed roll exhausted.

I gave Hayden my wife's letter and asked him to read it to me. After he did I told him what had taken place with The Dog. Hayden patted me on the shoulder and said, "Good work buddy. We are going to get some medical treatment for you now, there's no doubt in my mind." I was doubtful so I responded, "Oh yeah, in a pig's eye."

About that time the door opened up and a couple of medics walked in. They looked me over, took my temperature and pulse and then they left.

The next morning when we woke up it was Christmas Day; our first in captivity. Maybe it was because it was Christmas but probably it was because my illness had run its course that I woke up that morning and, miraculously, for the first time in twenty days didn't have any fever. I also felt hungry for the first time in nearly three weeks. I felt as though I could eat something and keep it down.

Somehow it really felt like it was Christmas Day. Hayden and I of course wished each other a Merry Christmas. Then Hayden went over to the window and called out "Merry Christmas" to each one of the other guys. The other guys all began yelling "Merry Christmas" out their cell doors to other guys who were in earshot. Everybody seemed to be in very fine spirits.

Amazingly enough, always on holidays, whatever holiday it was, the guys had real high morale. Christmas was Christmas no matter where the hell you are. We weren't expecting anything, or at least I wasn't. Hayden kept telling me that we were going to get something extra that day. We were jokingly speculating that we were going to get a roast turkey dinner and let's see, there's going to be cranberries and yams and, and.... Hayden was walking around the room giving me this big blow out of the feast we were going to be served and all the presents we were going to get. He was very entertaining.

Just then the cell door opened and a couple of guards were standing out there with a big pot with a lid on it. The way they were holding it looked like there was something hot inside. Hayden said, "Here we go buddy, Merry Christmas!" The damn guards marched in and they had big smiles on their faces. They told Hayden and me to get our cups. I sort of propped myself up against the wall and Hayden put a bunch of blankets behind me. He got our cups and they filled them up with hot coffee.

Jesus Christ, that was the best cup of coffee I had ever had in my whole life. Now the Gooks really made good coffee. They made this strong espresso-type coffee, straight from the coffee beans and it's Vietnamese grown. Then they loaded it full of sugar. It was very sweet and it really tasted good. I swear to this day it's better coffee than we ever had in the Navy, and a lot better than any of the commercial stuff we have on the market.

So we had a hot cup of coffee and they even gave us a couple of "Dien Binh" brand cigarettes. These were their top-of-the-line cigarettes. Dien Binhs were so good they would even stay lit if you didn't keep puffing on them, like ordinary American cigarettes. They were really nothing but trash but compared to the other things we were smoking they were outstanding.

The guards were really in a holiday mood. As I said before the Vietnamese have a cultural thing about wanting to celebrate everybody's holiday. On Christmas Day they were Christians, on Hanukkah they were Jews, and on Buddha's Birthday they were Buddhists. Meanwhile they are Communists all the time. It's really a screwy philosophy they had. I had to think they were probably Communists because they had to be to survive.

Hayden and I enjoyed our coffee and cigarettes and we sat around speculating what the rest of the day would bring. When lunchtime came Hayden went out to pick up our chow, and boy, it was really something. There was a shriveled up little drumstick from a turkey, a real turkey probably, or some related fowl. It was cooked as hard as shoe leather but man it tasted great. There was some kind of salad. It was lettuce and cut up carrots with some weird tasting salad dressing, some kind of a hot sauce. They also gave us some green beans that had been cooked up with pig fat which tasted real good too. I recall there were some cookies too.

All in all it was an outstanding meal for us at that time. Considering what we were used to it was a feast. I should also note that our stomachs were attuned to the way food was prepared over there by then but if someone in the U.S. ate one of these meals they'd be sick for three weeks. They'd probably be a hospital case.

So we ate our big holiday meal and there was just a general fanfare around the camp all day. That evening they brought us a more or less normal meal but there was more of it than usual. They brought some of the leftovers from the feast we'd had earlier that day too. So it was a pretty good meal that night too and we were both surprised and delighted.

They also gave us some candy with our evening meal. This was extraordinary because we hadn't had anything sweet the whole time we had been there. I'd never been a big candy eater but the sweets that night were delicious. Maybe because I had gone so long without anything like it that my body had begun to crave something sweet. Anyway these were just little hard candies wrapped up in North Vietnamese paper with Vietnamese printing on them. It was actually low-grade, lousy candy but it sure tasted good at that time. I think they may also have given us an orange that day which was amazing.

It may seem as though I'm making a big deal about the food but since we were nearly starved to death we ate almost anything edible. And what they served us Christmas Day was definitely more than edible to our near-forgotten palates and shriveled stomachs.

The medics also came by and looked me over again. They didn't give me any medicine. I guess it looked to them as it did to me that the disease had run its course. Throughout that day and the next day I was able to eat all the food that was given to me for that holiday. Later on I was able to eat my regular food again. We went back to normal rations which were extremely small portions but not the starvation level that we had been on for punishment.

A strange thing happened on New Year's Eve. About seven o'clock, the turnkey unlocked our door and a strange Gook walked in. He was a young guy, about 21 years old, and he was a new officer. He had one bar and one star insignia, indicating he was a second lieutenant. He was short and pudgy and he came in with a big smile on his face. Hayden and I stood there with blank stares and looked at him as he began to talk to us in English. He told us that we were, of course, now in North Vietnam and that we were criminals. But because we were in Vietnam we must do as the Vietnamese do. Then he quoted the trite old saying of, "When in Rome do as the Romans do."

Finally, what he got around to was, "The guards that open your doors do not speak English and you must learn to speak Vietnamese." He said, "Now tonight I will come to your cell and you will be seeing more of me in the future and I will give you your first lesson in Vietnamese." He tore a loaf of bread in half. He gave half of it to Hayden and half to me and he said, "Bi me." He said "Now repeat this word after me," and he looked at Hayden. Hayden said, "bread." Then he looked at me and I said, "bread."

He said "No, no, no. You do not understand," and he repeated, "Bi me, Bi me. Now repeat after me." I said "bread" and Hayden said "bread." He repeated: "Bi me, now repeat after me." I said "bread" and Hayden said, "bread." He looked frustrated and pointed to our cups that had water in them. He said, "Now, you must learn the word for water; nuok." Of course Hayden said, "water," and I said, "water."

He and Gold Tooth finally got frustrated and maybe a little embarrassed so they turned on their heels and walked out. Hayden and I had a few big laughs at that. This turned out to be our first, last, and only Vietnamese language lesson. We don't know where this little character came from or where he went because we never saw him again after that. It was kind of funny. He had gone into our cell and then into one other cell where he got the same routine. I guess they sent him on his way to some other place. We know not where.

That was the only time they tried to indoctrinate prisoners in their language. From that point on the Vietnamese were always reluctant and in fact very careful not to teach us Vietnamese words. They did not want us to understand what they were saying about us. So the Gold Tooth incident just shows how disorganized they were. As the years went by we picked up some pigeon Vietnamese. They were mostly words we needed to tell the guards. Later on the guards were taught English words for objects we had like mat, net, shirt, pants, water, rice, food, etc.

All the guards, though they didn't know English, knew these words. You could ask a guard for something and he knew what you were talking about just by saying the word as long as there was not a lot of complicated stuff along with it. It was funny in a way because a lot of us continued to stick with Vietnamese words for certain objects and American words for others and the guards did the same. For example, water was never water it was always "nuok," which is the abbreviated way of saying water. Actually, "nuok" by itself means liquid and you have to double that word to indicate water. So water is actually "nuok nuok." If you want to say tea you say "nuok te" and so on. It's funny, looking back, how we and the guards came to agree on which language to use for which word.

About ten o'clock on New Year's Eve we were in bed asleep when the door opened up. The turnkey told us to roll up our gear. He took us out of our cell and over to The Pool Hall. The workers had been working on it, changing the interior construction by dividing the original four cells into ten smaller cells. The new cells were about ten feet by eight feet. There were no windows, only small air holes up at the top of the ceiling on the front of each cell. These were about twelve feet up and impossible to get to unless you stood on the other guy's shoulders. The doors were constructed out of some very hard wood, something similar to iron wood. They have very heavy hardwoods in Vietnam. They often used these in construction of their doors, bolts and other security pieces. The door had a peek hatch in it which was locked from the outside by a rotating hasp.

The first thing we noticed about our new cell was that it was very damp and clammy. Just our breath would raise the humidity in the cell to 100 percent. It would almost rain in there it was so humid. The weather this time of year was cold with the temperatures going down into the 40's or lower at night so the humidity made it bone-chilling cold.

The next day was New Year's Day and we got some coffee and another good meal and some extra cigarettes. It wasn't as good as Christmas Day but it was certainly better than the normal fare. We also got a new turnkey. He was a 2nd Lt., an officer and about 50 years old. We never figured this guy out though he served as turnkey in the camp for about a year. He spoke no English, only Vietnamese. What was noteworthy about him was that he had a sense of humor and personality that was really outstanding. He was a good turnkey and a good guard. We think he was much higher caliber because he was an officer, but whatever the reason he was a great old guy. We called him "Old Man Mose."

Old Man Mose would come around promptly about 5:30 o'clock in the morning. He had a punctual schedule that he followed and he was regular in his habits. He was more like you would expect an American guard to be. He was very careful and conscientious about his work. When he arrived in the morning he would tap a couple of times on the outside peek-hole and then he'd throw it open. We'd stagger out of bed and he'd be standing outside looking through the peek with a grin on his face. Then he would stick a pack of cigarettes through the door to us. He also had a lit punk and he'd give our cigarette a light.

The routine was that we were supposed to take six cigarettes out of the pack – three for each of us which were the normal ration – and hand him the pack back. Since there was just this small peek there I learned how to fumble with the pack and drop a couple out of the bottom of it down on the floor. The first time I attempted this little slight of hand maneuver I was pretty clumsy and the cigarette made a little bit of a spat as it hit the floor. When I handed the pack back to him he just stood outside the window and gave me sort of a wry, piercing look. Then he pursed his lips and shook his head from side to side. Then he pointed his finger at me and smiled.

Then he turned around and walked off. In other words, "You didn't quite get caught this time buster but don't try it again!" After that I learned how to handle the pack a little better and how to drop them so they didn't make any noise. I learned how to palm them in my hand so it would appear that I was pulling three but with my little finger and my fourth finger I would pull out a couple of extras. Hayden would be down at my feet to catch them as they tumbled down so there were no more incriminating spats.

This was my first training in stealing which stood me in good stead later. I used to practice in our cell after this. I'd practice on Hayden. I'd be carrying on a conversation with him and steal his tooth brush, toothpaste or soap and I wouldn't tell him until he discovered them missing. I began trying to develop my skills at stealing things.

One of the things I discovered is the only necessity for stealing something from somebody is diverting their attention. But diverting their attention is a subtle thing. You can't be too obvious about it. In other words you have to maintain your normal bearing, tone of voice if you're talking to them, and normal gestures. It helps if you're the kind of person who uses a lot of gestures because then hand motion does not seem unusual to that person.

Another thing I discovered was immediately after stealing something you should try to do some diversionary thing to attract attention away from yourself. You might point to something on the other side of the camp, or look down and kick a rock, or pick up a rock and throw it a couple of feet away. Just something to focus his attention so if he did have any beginning suspicion he'd probably forget about it.

Later in some of the larger camps I worked with other guys to steal things we needed or wanted. We called it a "procurement" team. It was fun and somewhat addictive. I swore off all stealing and lock-picking when I came home.

We stayed in this Pigsty cell until one day in late February. During this time my weight began to come back and I was beginning to look more like a human being. I'd say that by late January or early February I was back up to 125 or 130 pounds and feeling a lot better. I'd gone through the month of January mostly resting all day and walking very little. Then I began my exercise program again. At first I was just walking for short intervals in the cell then doing simple exercises like toe touches and finally building up to where I could do five or six push-ups and a couple of sit-ups. This process of working myself back into shape lasted six months or so until I was able to do 25 pushups and as many toe-touches and sit-ups. I felt much better by that time.

The first peace proposals were made towards the end of January, 1966.

They were accompanied by sensational bombing. A month or so earlier the Gooks had installed a radio speaker in each of our cells, up in the rafter area where we couldn't get to it. It was located so it could be adjusted from the outside by a step ladder. The first thing we heard over the speaker was a Vietnamese radio program. It was a bunch of gobble-goop and twangy Vietnamese music. Hayden and I decided they were attempting brainwashing by playing this crazy music and sounds all day. Either that or they were just going to drive us nuts with it.

The Gook who installed the speakers made a volume adjustment so it was at maximum volume. Then he left but shortly thereafter the speaker went silent. The next night a radio program came through about eight o'clock. It was "The Voice of Vietnam." We referred to The Voice of Vietnam as "Hanoi Hanna." This program lasted for thirty minutes and it was sheer, unadulterated propaganda garbage interspersed with music. Some of the music was Vietnamese and some American.

At first we thought we just wouldn't listen to this crap but then we decided that we would. What in the hell is wrong with listening to it? We could keep our marbles. We knew where the hell we were and this program wasn't going to do anything to us. It was pretty stupid to censor ourselves. So we started listening and it turned out to be quite entertaining. We'd laugh like hell at their battle reports of "8,000 American aggressors killed the day before with 70 thousand wounded, 50 tanks and trucks blown up, and so many units decimated, put out of action and on and on."

She would tell how many thousands of airplanes they'd shot down, always these ridiculous figures. What was really good entertainment was once in awhile they would play some American music. Boy that was really great. They were old records and some of her favorites were songs like Ella Fitzgerald's "Let's Fall in Love," which I'm sure she cut in 1946. Once in awhile we'd get an old Frank Sinatra record or sometimes there would be a more contemporary record like Country Joe and the "Vietnam Rag." That was a favorite. The radio added a little entertainment, or at least some diversion to our lives. Later on they started playing it in the morning and in the evening. We got the same program both times.

Then there was a cease-fire. But it was only a cease-fire on our part, the cessation of bombing on North Vietnam. We knew about it through Hanoi Hanna. We knew it was a bunch of bologna, because they were saying they would never yield to American bombs nor would they ever deal with the Americans at a negotiation table. They would never settle for anything less than complete victory. In other words they were telling us the whole time on the radio to just take it and cram it! It didn't do much for our morale.

The Vietnamese had a line that they had been pushing in quizzes and on Hanoi Hanna called their "Four Point Stand." This was their declared war policy the entire time we were there. This Four Point Stand basically said the Vietnamese people would never surrender to the American aggressors. They would never under any circumstances negotiate with the American aggressors. The only way to end the war was for the Americans to leave Vietnam completely. They had to withdraw all their forces from all bases and leave them to the Vietnamese. In other words the only way for us to get out of Vietnam was for them to have total victory.

"Tet," the Vietnamese Lunar New Year celebration, came at the end of January in 1966. According to Vietnamese customs, like other Asian countries, the Lunar New Year starts off their spring and the New Year. We didn't know what Tet was that first year but we heard firecrackers going off around the city. We began to understand how important it was to them when the guards threw open the doors and gave us another special holiday meal.

One of the things that we got this first, and succeeding Tets was a traditional Vietnamese dish called a "Banh Chung." It was really a lot of garbage but we enjoyed it at that time because it filled our stomachs. Banh Chungs are made out of boiled, glutinous rice. It was about six by six inches square and about 1½ inches high. Inside the rice were both some pork fat or little pieces of meat and some crushed-up peanuts. Sometimes it was deep fried and it made a real gut-bomb.

The damn thing is just a big soggy glob of rice with little goodies inside. But to us it was a damn good deal to get one. Hayden and I each got one along with another cup of coffee. We also got some indeterminate meat along with some salad and soup that was good. The soup was spiced up with meat and other stuff in it. At this time our normal diet was one small loaf of bread per meal and some very thin soup made of weeds, pumpkin or sometimes kohlrabi. Whatever it was, you'd get the same kind of soup for as long as six months before they changed to a new kind of soup. It got a little old.

After Tet we saw a lot of activity in the camp. We saw VIGs running around with a lot of guys in white smocks who appeared to be doctors or medics. There was a higher level of hustle and bustle. About 7 o'clock one morning Old Man Mose opened our cell door and told us we would be going to a medical inspection. Though he didn't speak English, he had been taught this for the occasion. He had a big smile on his face like, "Yank, we are going to give you a damn good deal, a medical inspection." Then he shut our door. I immediately got on the back wall and tapped to Bob Lilly and told him what was going on. I also relayed it next door to Alvarez and Barrett. They passed it on down the line to Guarino and Burns and then on through the building to the other guys.

My VA-22 squadron mate, Skip Brunhaver had been living right across from us in room one of The Stables at this time. He had been undergoing a working-over for his biography. They didn't know anything about Skip and they wanted to get a biography on him. So they put him in leg irons and hand cuffs and cut his food down to nothing, then finally cut his water off. That got him to write a bullshit biography; all of it lies. He told us later that he also inserted some hilarious things in his story.

They came down and got Alvarez first and then they took Shumaker from the other side of the camp. Then they got Hayden and me. They seemed to be going through us in order of shoot downs. We walked over to The Auditorium and then into one of the back rooms in The Gook House that had previously been an interrogation room. I looked like walking death because I was still just beginning to recover from the disease that had ravaged me the month before. I was maybe 125 pounds, a vast improvement from what I had been but still just skin and bones.

There were some medics in the room, and one of them asked in English, very good English, what my name was. He pulled out what looked like a medical form that had my name, rank, service number and date of birth. It had a bunch of blank spaces and Gook writing. He wrote some things then he asked me what my condition of health was and I told him. He asked me what had been wrong with me and what illness had occurred.

I started to explain this to him when an officer stepped in. We later called this guy "Marian the Librarian." Everybody called him Marian because the Gooks had just opened up what they called a "camp reading room," which was a cell where they had a bunch of their "shit books" (as we referred to them) or their "propaganda garbage." "Dum-Dum," aka "Marian," ran the thing. Naturally because he ran the Library we called him Marian. What else? Apparently that was his job while he was trying to learn to speak English. It was a skill he never accomplished. He was too incredibly stupid to ever learn English. He could say what he wanted to say in English but he could never understand what we were saying back to him.

Now Marian or Dum-Dum was probably the stupidest and most vindictive of all the Gook officers we ran into at The Zoo. He stepped in

226

and told me that it would not be necessary for me to explain what had been wrong with me. The medic said something to him in Vietnamese, then looked at me and said, "Continue please."

I explained the illness I had experienced and told him that I had received no medical treatment whatsoever. He nodded his head and wrote everything down in Vietnamese. Then he had me sit down at a table and he looked down my throat. He examined my eyes and took my temperature. He took my blood pressure, pulse and checked my heart by listening with a stethoscope. He tried to look into my ears but they were so packed with dirt and filth because we hadn't had a bath in weeks that he kind of let out a little Vietnamese "Ummh" which was their version of "Good Grief."

He got a pair of tweezers and cotton. Then he scraped out the inside of my ears and pulled out two huge wax plugs. I discovered that I could almost hear normally again. He had to do the same thing with Hayden when he checked his ears. Then they took us out into the next room where there was a doctor and more medics. They had me take off my clothes, lie down on a bunk, and they gave me a pretty thorough medical check. They were amazed at how much my ribs stuck out when I lay on my back. Then I went into the next cell where they had a doctor sitting in the center of the table. He had a bar and four stars, a senior captain, and he spoke fairly good English. Dum-Dum had followed me into the room.

The doctor began to talk and he told me to take off my clothes and stand in front of the desk. I did so and he spoke in Vietnamese to Dum-Dum and the other medics that were around. He was obviously chewing ass. I was standing there real bony and my rib cage was sticking out. My waist measurement according to our little tape measure that we'd made in the room at this time was 27 inches. My chest measurement was 34 inches. Today my waist is 34 and my chest is 41.

The doctor told me to put my clothes back on and then he asked me to explain again in detail about my illness, which I did. Then he asked me to explain again in detail about my treatment. Dum-Dum tried to interfere but the doctor stood up and screamed at him with a bunch of swear words that I recognized. He pointed his finger at the door and Dum-Dum hauled-ass out. Then the doctor sat down and told me to continue my explanation, which I did.

The doctor raised hell and then he gave me a vital lung capacity check. It was a round can-like thing with a tube that I blew into which pushes up a plunger that had markings on it. Then he gave me a strength test with a hand squeeze apparatus that showed how many kilograms of pressure I was able to squeeze. I squeezed it as hard as I could with both hands and ran it up to 55 kilograms. Then he had me do it again with the same results.

He was just a little Vietnamese guy, but he shook his head, came around the table, and said, "Now look," and he ran it up to 75. Then he had me try again. I still could only run it up to about 55. He nodded his head then had me sit down in a chair with calibrations on it. It was to measure my torso height and the length of my upper legs. Naval aviation did the same thing to find out if I could fit into an A4 such that my knees would not hit the canopy bow on ejection. They took those measurements and then had me stand up and measured my height but they did not weigh me.

Then they sent me over to an eye chart. I didn't do very well on the eye chart. My vision had been 20/20, great when I was shot down. But that day when I read the eye chart it was really miserable. My vision had deteriorated quite seriously during this illness. It was so bad I don't think they believed the results because they wrote down a whole bunch of stuff.

When it was all over I asked him what he thought my disease had been. He asked, "What inoculations did you have before you were shot down?" I told him all of the inoculations I had. And when I got to yellow fever he said, "Yellow fever? Are you sure that you had yellow fever inoculation?" I said, "Yes, I'm sure." He said, "I do not think so. If you did it must not have been done correctly. The serum must not have been good." I said, "Why?" He said, "Because I think you had yellow fever." I said, "Okay."

I thought I'd had hepatitis though and I still think so today but this Vietnamese doctor honestly thought I had yellow fever. We left the examining rooms and Hayden and I went back to our cell. The medical inspection continued throughout the camp with the exception of a few guys. The guys who did not get medical inspections were those who were under duress at that time for their biographies, including Skip Brunhaver.

A couple of days later a pair of medics came into our cell. They dilated our eyes and took a look to see for sure if anything was wrong with our eyes. Hayden had been wearing glasses at the time he was shot down so his vision was bad anyway. They discovered, for real, that both of us were damn near blind. I guess they couldn't believe that for American pilots! We figured out this medical exam was really to see what American pilots were like. They wanted facts and figures to compare with their own. Why, I don't know but that seemed to be the real reason for the whole exam. Maybe another reason was to find out what condition we were in and how the camp was taking care of us.

A day or two later Old Man Mose took us out of our cell and we went over to a shower in room two of The Stable, the room right next to Skip. As soon as we got into the shower, the first time we had showered in three weeks, I got on the wall and tapped a "Shave and a Haircut" over to Skip.

I heard some shuffling against the floor and I could hear Skip dragging himself over to the wall. He got his back against the wall and started tapping to me behind his back. I told him who I was and he tapped back, "God, Phil, it sure is great to talk with you! Sorry I didn't get over to you sooner, but I've been all tied up with other things."

Very cool! I thought. Skip was a squadron mate and he was shot down in August. This was my first real contact with him except for one short occasion in September where I'd had the opportunity to actually speak to him for just a couple of minutes. So we got to shoot the bull for a few minutes and Skip told me his spirits were up about 10,000 percent as a result of being able to talk to me. He told me he thought he was going to have to write his biography pretty soon.

I told him, "That's okay, just do the best you can buddy, and fight them as long as you can." I told him that this was just a biography of family information and he was going to give them bullshit anyway. I told him "Don't run yourself into the ground too far. Give them enough of a battle so they won't be on your back for being soft." He tapped back and said, "Okay, I'll do that." Skip, being the tough little knot-head that he was though, I thought he hung on too long and ran himself down too much.

I really didn't feel it was worth it. Later when I had to do my own biography I found out what it was like when these guys wanted something from you and they were putting you under duress. I also had a tendency to run myself down farther than I expected I would before. In most cases it was just because I got so damn mad at them that I wanted to fight them for all I was worth.

Actually I did myself a worse disservice than Skip for the same thing later on. It was just a matter of my personal pride. I might mention here that one of the guidelines that Colonel Risner had given us when he was our SRO back in The Stable was to be sure you maintain your pride and personal integrity. So for instance if we wanted to fight things like guards trying to make us bow to them, then by all means fight them tooth and nail to satisfy our own pride. Go to any length we think is necessary.

The same for the biographies and the other cheap shit they wanted from us. We had to satisfy our own needs because the most important thing was that all of us leave this country with our personal pride intact. That was sage advice and a guideline all of us tried to follow from that time on. I am one happy man today that I did that throughout my time in North Vietnam. I don't feel guilty about things they forced me to do because I know now in my own mind that I fought it all as hard as I could and I gave it everything I had. That is important to me now because I can look at myself in the mirror every morning when I shave. And when I put my head down on that pillow every night it's nice to be able to go to sleep.

Hayden and I were peeking through a couple of worm holes in our door the day after the medical inspections were over. We used to watch them set up the chow on the porch railing in the building across from us, The Stable. We watched to see what the menu was that day, and lo and behold when they put the soup down we could tell the bowls were full. The side dish what we called dog food, a small slice of rotten tasting meat that was mostly fat with some liverwurst in it was also bigger.

But really caught our attention was the bread. Instead of just a loaf it was a loaf and a third. We thought the guard had made a mistake. But then he went over to George's cell and opened the door. We watched George hop out as he always did to pick up his chow. We saw him look at the bread as though there was some mistake. Then George walked down the railing to look at Skip's and sure enough there was Skip's loaf and a third. George picked up his extra third loaf and was about to set it down on Skip's plate because he thought the guard was trying to give him some of Skip's food. But when he saw that Skip had the same thing he shook his head and with a big smile on his face nodded to the guard.

The guard, Old Man Mose, had a smile from ear to ear. He was just as happy as George. The same routine took place with Skip. You could see utter amazement on his face as he walked out. Hayden and I were laughing ourselves sick. Then Hayden and I went out and picked up our food and it was the same thing. The doctors had pressured the camp officers and given the order that we were to be given more food because of the medical inspection. This was the first food increase we experienced. Thank goodness for the doctors. They were about people, not politics.

Sometime in mid-March the weather started to warm up and we were very happy about that. We'd been freezing our asses off all winter. Our feet were numb 24 hours a day and at night they were so numb as to be painful. There was absolutely no way to get warm in our cell with it being dark all day long. There was just enough light to barely see each other. When we would go out to take a bath the sunlight was so blinding we had to hold our hands over our eyes and stumble along to make our way to the shower stall.

Old Man Mose continued to be our turnkey and he didn't give us any crap at all. He had been the guard that watched over Skip while he was in handcuffs and leg irons. On a couple of occasions we had seen him come up to Skip's window, look around both ways, and slip him an extra cup of water. It was a real humanitarian gesture considering his position since it was his duty to keep Skip's rations down. As it turned out, by being kind when no one was looking he did Skip a disservice because it made Skip endure the misery longer. I'm sure Old Man Mose was trying to be kind, at great personal risk to himself. He would have been in serious trouble if the camp commander or any other guards had seen him do this.

We used to set up a time during the day for group communications while we were in The Pool Hall. Hayden would put his ear down to the half inch crack between the door and the floor and I would put my mouth down there to it. Hayden would listen and I would talk. All the guys on the back of The Pool Hall would do the same thing. The guys on the front of The Pigsty and the guys in The Stable would do this on a prearranged signal of three coughs in the afternoon. Everybody would be clearing with the guys in the front side clearing out their doors. Everybody in all the buildings would be set up to give out a warning which was a single cough.

Larry Guarino, the SRO on our side of the camp, would conduct a conversation. We would also pass out little words of encouragement to each other. We would ask if anybody had any news about the guards, or the way they were being treated, or did anybody see anything unusual going on in the camp.

We were cut off from the other side of the camp which was The Garage, The Stable and The Office. We didn't have any "comm." (communication) with them because there just wasn't any way to do it. We were never taken out of our cells or over to that area and those guys never came over to us. We didn't know where Colonel Risner was at this time. We assumed he was still over there, but as it turned out he was not. In October he had been moved out of the camp back to Hoa Lo and had undergone 36 days and nights of torture for the first confession that was extracted from a POW. He was an amazingly tough and courageous man.

For our purposes the senior man in whatever group we had communications with was our SRO. There were occasions when we had very poor communications with another group in the camp or with another section of the camp. In that case the overall SRO might be in another group. Then he would delegate his authority to the senior man on our side of the camp to act as SRO until we could be advised by the overall SRO. In

231

any given instance the SRO might be the senior Lt. JG or he might be a full Colonel. It didn't matter. The Geneva Conventions specified these rules and there were even delineations for a case where two senior officers had the same date of rank. Then the senior person would be determined by which one had been promoted to the previous rank first, and so on. If every promotion was exactly the same, the oldest person was the designated senior ranking officer.

One afternoon about 5 o'clock we were having one of these jam-sessions when Old Man Mose came sneaking up on us. The Vietnamese were trying to stop communications at all cost and the guards would sneak around. They wore tennis shoes so they wouldn't make any noise because they knew we were listening for them.

Mose came tip-toeing up our way and I caught sight of him at the same time as one of the guys in The Pigsty. He knew we were talking because he overheard some of it but he was trying to catch whoever was doing it. He was coming up the walk-way with one of those really funny-looking, comedic tip-toeing. The guy in The Pigsty let out a single cough and everyone heard it immediately and everything immediately went dead silent.

Old Man Mose stopped tip-toeing along and he threw his hand up in the air and gave one of those finger snaps, throwing his hand down like "Drat!" Then he got a big grin on his face as he walked into our area. He came around smiling at all the doors, just like he had been foiled again.

At the end of 1965 and early in 1966 the Vietnamese started pressuring us harder about bowing to them. At first they tried to ease into it by telling us we had to show recognition to the guard whenever he opened our door. Recognition was to be shown by standing at attention and giving a head nod. Later on this evolved into a full bow to the guard or any Vietnamese we saw at anytime we were out in the yard or when going into the quiz room, no matter where we were. Later in 1967 they even forced us to make a full bow to the girls who filled up the water pots in the hallways and brought chow around.

They were doing everything possible to degrade us. They were trying to make us feel subservient. They wanted us to give in to anything they wanted. They wanted us to forget that we were officers in the United States Armed Forces. In fact it was a very degrading and demoralizing thing for most of the guys there. Most of us fought it as hard as we could. But the Vietnamese inevitably got their pound of flesh. And we were forced to do it for a period of time when bowing pressure was a constant thing.

Hayden and I made up our minds that we were not going to bow. Most of the more junior officers felt the same way. The older officers and some of the more senior ranking felt like it actually meant nothing, probably because of their greater maturity. They saw it as just childishness on the part of the Gooks and that we should fight it to a certain extent, but not to the point of running ourselves into the ground. They felt it was better to save our health and apply our efforts to something worthwhile, like attempts to gain propaganda.

A new officer in the camp dropped by our room one day, sometime in December. He was a bar and three stars officer and he spoke English. He told us we would have to show recognition to the guards by bowing our heads. We told him we would not do it. He told us we must do it. He gave us a Vietnamese, low pressure-type sales pitch, with a big smile. Our turnkey at the time, Gold Tooth, was always trying to get us to bow but Hayden and I refused to cooperate. This new officer was with us to the very end and almost everyone in Hanoi referred to him as "Frenchy."

Frenchy wound up being our camp commander at The Briar Patch camp later on. He was a particularly sadistic and wild-tempered guy. He was prone to schizophrenic shifts in personality between smiles and fits of anger. He also was a hands-off manager in the camp. He'd let the guards do just about anything they wanted and never checked on what they were doing. This was the cause of a lot of our grief at The Briar Patch.

Hayden and I started fighting this bowing nonsense. Skip and George Hall agreed with us. Larry Guarino and Ron Byrne called a general discussion out the door one day. We talked it over and everybody said they wanted to fight it because it was bullshit and we weren't going to comply. Larry said, "Okay, if that's the way you want to play it then that's the way we'll play it." Everybody said, "Roger" and we were all quite relieved to be on the same frequency.

But it turned out there were a couple of rooms that could see Larry and Ron's door when it was opened. And these guys could see that Larry and Ron were not fighting this as they said they were going to do. Instead they were head nodding to the guards when they opened the door. This affected our morale because we felt that if everybody didn't get behind this full bore then the Vietnamese would single out individuals who did not cooperate. Their compliance would make it tougher on those individuals. Plus our SRO wasn't playing it straight with us.

A lot of us younger guys took our licks, head knocks and a few missed dinners because of it. By the end of 1966 it became impossible to keep from bowing because the treatment got so tough and brutal that if we didn't we got rifle butt beatings on the spot by the guards. It was pointless not to comply when their retaliation became that vicious. In the end Hayden and I, with lots of other guys, felt like we could have beaten the bowing thing if everybody had resisted it. It probably would not have been worth it to the Gooks to beat the hell out of everybody all the time. It caused a lot of us grief and injuries because we fought it as individuals and not as a unified group.

One of the first things they did was open our cell door and have our chow sitting outside on a ledge. Previous to this we'd walk outside and pick up our chow. Now they'd open the door and the guard would just stand there and glare at us. Then we'd just stand there and glare back at him. Then he'd slam the door and walk off. Our food would be left outside from five o'clock in the afternoon till about nine o'clock at night. We could see all the ants in the world feasting on it. It also got cold and not really worth eating. Then he'd come around about nine o'clock and throw open the door and let us go out to get it. Later they started coming into the room and they would grab us by the hair and yank our head down. They would slap us and always be screaming "Bow, Bow!"

Sometimes we'd be walking along in the yard and some Gook would just stand there with his hands on his hips with a real surly, snotty look on his face. And when we didn't stop and bow the guard who was walking us would stop and smack us around. Then he would point us at the guard we didn't bow to and jerk our head down by the hair. Then they just started beating the hell out of us right there on the spot with rifle butts and fists when we didn't bow to somebody. If we didn't bow when we went into a quiz room there would be guards with the officer and they'd slap and beat us for not bowing to the quizzer.

This bowing thing accomplished absolutely nothing for the North Vietnamese. It just hardened our attitude. I still don't know why they ever instituted the policy other than as a response to their own inferior feelings. Maybe it was their monstrous egos that needed feeding by trying to degrade us and thus somehow to upgrade themselves in this ugly manner. It was really their childishness more than anything else.

But as far as attitude on our part it completely backfired on them. It just made every prisoner in Hanoi hate Gooks so bad it was unreal. We developed an incredible bitterness toward every Vietnamese during all this treatment. The two things – communicating among ourselves and not bowing to them – seemed to give them the right to whale on us anytime they wanted. They would punish us constantly. They would make us stand in our cell with our arms up in the air for days on end. They would make us kneel down for long periods of time. The bowing thing got it all started. It always stuck with Hayden and me that we were taking our licks for fighting it, while some of the senior guys were not.

It was curious but some days after the meeting when everybody agreed not to give in on the bowing thing, Guarino assured everybody that he and Byrne were not bowing. But they were seen bowing. We knew to expect some giving in under the tremendous pressure that was on us. Guys would weaken for one thing or another and we couldn't attack them for it. We had to use a soft sell approach with them. We had to appeal to another POW's sense of reason because an attack might drive them out of the mainstream and into the wrong direction.

This appeal to a sense of reason required a great deal of patience on our part to try to bring someone back into the fold. I think we accomplished this with great results during all those years in Hanoi. I don't think anyone ever assailed anyone else or attacked them personally for things they were doing that we thought were wrong. Everyone always exhibited a lot of patience and understanding. All of us had the experience of giving in and weakening from one pressure or another. We all realized how certain pressure tactics that would affect one man might not affect another man and vice versa.

One evening in the first part of March the Gooks came to our building in The Pool Hall and took all the guys on the back side of the building out. We were the first of the shoot-downs and all of us who had our names released to the public as confirmed prisoners. They took us out by two's, put us in a jeep and took us downtown.

Hayden and I went together and we were taken into a large conference room where big cameras were set up. There were no foreigners there, just Vietnamese. We were taken one at a time and sat down on a stool. A camera with flood lights was located above and in front of us. This camera looked down on us and they took our pictures a couple of times this way. The Gooks were really big on this for their propaganda pictures. They always took pictures of Ho Chi Minh or Madame Vinh or any of their respected people at an angle looking upwards at the face. It gave an allusion of a proud, stately appearance.

So when they took pictures of their enemy for propaganda they'd shoot the camera at a downward angle to make it look like we were bowing our heads in shame. They were big on all this cheap little Mickey Mouse stuff for their propaganda. It would be perfectly obvious how this picture was taken to an American who saw this junk in a newspaper or magazine. But I guess it didn't dawn on them what had been done. Hayden and I had our pictures taken and then they took us back to the camp. They did the same with Alvarez, Barrett, Guarino, Byrne, Berg and several other guys.

Hayden and I were moved to room seven of The Office about mid March. It had also undergone some construction changes so now there were two very small solitary rooms in each wing and two larger rooms where two guys could sleep. Hayden and I were in the back corner in one of the larger rooms. We had an air vent that looked out towards The Barn. I could get to this air vent by standing on Hayden's shoulders. By doing this we managed to establish contact with The Barn and got a link up with the rest of the camp. I would simply talk through this air vent to the guys in The Barn and they would yell back over to me. My voice contact guy there was a new shoot-down named Jerry Coffee. I was able to teach Jerry the Tap Code.

We had our usual clearing system with cough signals if guards were coming to our corner of the camp. Our warning system had to go through so many people here that it was complicated so we had to get a good lead on the guard in order for Hayden and me to be warned in time. Needless to say we got caught communicating several times.

Commander Howie Rutledge was in a solo room next to us. George Hall was in another one and Bob Lilly and Art Cormier were in the other room next to us. We had good tap code communications with these guys. As I mentioned earlier, this was where Bob Lilly maintained the TV watch all day long which provided us with something to do and think about. It was a big morale booster during this time.

On March 19th, 1966 the camp went into a stir. George and Bob who were looking out cracks in their doors announced to us that it looked like some camera equipment had been brought into the camp. Of course this set up wild speculations as to what in the hell was going on. The camera people went into The Auditorium and set up their equipment. That night we were taken out in two different shifts to The Auditorium with our roommate. Those in solitary confinement went by themselves.

They had constructed little stalls with blanket dividers between the stalls. We looked out straight ahead from the stalls and could see a movie screen where they showed us propaganda movies. One particular movie was called "Our Sons and Daughters." It had been taken at the University of California. It was pure propaganda and they showed one of the peacenik

236

marches where they blocked the street and marched to Oakland. When they got there the Oakland Police stopped them. And this was the best part of the whole movie, the part we really enjoyed. The Oakland Police would not let them in so they were standing there raising hell, making all this noise and they were walking along with a Vietcong flag.

Then the Hell's Angels appeared on the scene. The Hell's Angels were a pro-establishment group and they climbed into this group of marchers, started cleaning clocks and it was really comical. We enjoyed the movie and of course we started clapping and cheering when the Hell's Angels came in. You could hear what the Hell's Angles were saying to these peace marchers as they were beating the hell out of them.

We enjoyed the movie but not in the way the Vietnamese wanted us to. We were supposed to repent for our crimes by seeing what the "American people" thought about the war. All it did was impress us even more that the protesters back home were actually a minority.

Spring came and the weather started to get warm. Then it got very hot in our back corner room because there was no ventilation. At the same time we picked up a new guard who was a sergeant, about 30 years old and a real mean SOB. He was also a big Vietnamese and he really packed a wallop when he slapped you with his fist.

There was racism among the guards in North Vietnam. The guards who had dark skin were from the minority hill tribes and they were harassed and tormented by the other guards from the majority group. They had class issues and racism in Vietnamese society as well, even in the so-called classless communism they adhered to.

We POWs had two in our number who were black, both Air Force pilots and wonderful guys. One of these brave men was Fred Cherry. Fred was badly wounded when his F-105 was shot down and he was in a lot of pain and terrible shape. As it happened, Lt (jg) Porter Halyburton, a genteel southerner from North Carolina became his cell mate. Porter nursed Fred back to health, with practically no medical care from the Vietnamese. There certainly wasn't any racism in their room.

These guys were together in the Zoo when I believe they had been prisoners for just a few months or so and I had been a POW for nearly a year. No matter that Fred was in such bad shape, they still wanted their stupid biography from him which he resisted. We were all communicating with each other around the camp with our tap code and people were talking back and forth from room to room. One day, by tap code to all of us out in the camp, Fred sent, "You know what guys? They're treating us all like

237

niggers here." He no doubt appreciated the fact that unlike back home, they were treating us all equally badly. What irony! I know I was sad to hear they were hammering him but at the same time it made me proud that we made them treat us the same, black, white or whatever.

At this time we would go over to the shower and relay information from our side of the camp to the guys on the other side of the camp. The Vietnamese caught on to this and they took the American out of the cell that was passing along the information, and they put a Thai in there. We called him "Kim." Now Kim had been quite mixed up several months earlier.

One day I was out in the yard washing dishes in a large wash tub for the guys in my building. Kim had been detailed to carry a water bucket around. He walked up to me with the guards standing there and this is the first time I had ever met him face to face. I said, "Hello, how are you?" and smiled to him. He didn't show any recognition and I said, "Are you Thai?" He nodded his head. I said "Do you speak English?" He kind of smiled and looked at the guards nervously and nodded his head again. I said, "Why won't you talk to me? I'm your friend. We are friends."

Kim looked around nervously then knelt down beside me and made like he was helping me wash the dishes. He said, "You must look after yourself here. You must realize you are a prisoner here and no one can help you. Your government cannot help you here so you must look after yourself." Then he nervously got up and walked off across the yard. That was the first contact, but after a while we got to talking to him. He had been badly mistreated when he was first captive, but we were able to buck him up a little bit. Eventually he came around to being a good guy for us.

When they put Kim in this key room that we used for communication, they put a guard outside so we couldn't talk out the window. We taught him the Tap Code and for awhile Kim would relay information for us. Then one day the Vietnamese took him out and beat him until he gave them what we were talking about. He had to tell what kind of information he was tapping and what our comm. system was all about. They put Kim in another building and he was pretty hard to get to after that. He was real gun shy. But in spite of the fact that he was under a lot of pressure and not our nationality, he was our ally and I think the guy did a good job.

I have to give credit to him and a few other Thais who came along later. They were real good guys. We were proud of them and they did good work for us in the camp.

Sometimes when we were absolutely desperate for an immediate communication link to the other side of the camp, maybe a couple of times a year or so, these guys would drop a note for us.

On April 20th, 1966 I celebrated my first anniversary in Vietnam. That day we walked to the shower in The Pigsty. I remember that we knew there was a new guy in the room next to the shower. So Hayden cleared for me and I immediately started tapping, trying to contact him. We knew through the comm. system that this new guy had been taught tap code but no one had been able to get any information out of him. So I worked and worked, and we spent our whole shower period in there trying to get an answer from him. It was very difficult because I had to go very slow because he was having a lot of trouble picking up the code.

Finally, I got my name across to him and he got his name across to me. It was John Pitchford. He had a broken arm and I guess he was tapping with the heel of his foot. I tried to find out if he had any new information on the war. I also told him things about the camp, the comm. system, our organization, and other vital information. I gave him a big blurb of information even though I didn't know if he understood it.

I remember he tapped back to me and asked, "How long have you been here?" I tapped back to him "One year. This is my anniversary." He tapped back again and asked, "How long have you been here?" And I tapped back again, "One year." Then I heard this "clunk, clunk" for "Roger" and he stopped tapping. I guess I scared the poor guy to death.

On April 21st, 1966 in the evening, our turnkey opened our door and told us to roll up our gear. He made us give him our cups, all of our soap and toothpaste. We figured he wanted these items for himself. In other words he was stealing our gear from us. We were led out of the building and put on a bus with six other men. We left the Zoo that night on a trip back to The Briar Patch which was to be our home for most of the next year, a very bad year.

16. Second Briar Patch— Part I

4/21/66 - 7/6/66

Hayden and I got aboard the buses that night on April 21st 1966. We could peek under our blind-folds and see that there were six other POWs on the bus with us. We didn't have any idea where we were going. There were quite a few guards who loaded on with us and probably an officer though I couldn't really tell in the dark. We started out from The Zoo and went to the north for probably a half a mile. Then we made a left turn and started heading out west of Hanoi. Soon we hit the foothills and the real rough roads as we began climbing. Hayden and I then knew we were heading back out to The Briar Patch.

We always thought the location of The Briar Patch was west/south west of Hanoi but we discovered after we got out of prison it was west/northwest. We went out about 45 miles west of Hanoi but because of the poor quality of the roads and the climb up into the hills, the ride took a couple of hours. It was a real bad because they were less like roads than rough trails cut through the jungle.

We arrived and drove through the gate of The Briar Patch where we unloaded out of the bus. Hayden and I were taken to hut Foxtrot, room four. The next morning we woke up in this little cell. We noticed all the shutters on the window were closed, and it was to remain this way for a long time. The Gooks did not want us to see out. When chow came it was the grimmest we had ever seen. It was a small amount of rice and some watery green soup. There was no side dish; nothing else at all.

We existed this way for a few days, while bitching and raising hell with the guards that we needed a lot of things. We didn't have cups, spoons, toothbrushes or soap. We really didn't have anything except the clothes on our backs. We were not allowed to go wash or anything.

Finally, one day a guy in civilian clothes walked down to our cell, a small Gook with a big smile on his face. He had the guard open up the shutter on our cell and he talked to us through the window. He was too smiley; sickeningly sweet.

This guy, a civilian at this time, got a uniform maybe six months later. He turned out to be an interrogator we called "The Bug." This guy was probably public enemy number one for the whole eight years in Vietnam.

He was the most hated interrogator of them all.

We told him what we needed but got no response. We asked if he would leave the shutters open so we could get some light in the room. He just smiled about that, shut the shutters and walked off.

We got tap code contact with a guy in room one who turned out to be Air Force Captain Tom Collins. Tom had come with us on the bus. In a day or two we got contact with another guy, an Air Force Airman named Bill Robinson who was in room two of the hut. These guys didn't know what was going on either. Our attempts to communicate were fairly clumsy at this stage of the game. We tried to talk around the corner of these buildings but it was difficult because of the way they were designed. At that time we were not very sophisticated with our tapping because we were tapping real loud and not clearing the area too well. The building was designed such that Hayden and I couldn't clear at all. The clearing had to come from the guys in room one and two who had a view of the entry into the courtyard. The guy in room one had to watch one entry and the guy in room two had to watch the other entry, so it made for a coordination problem.

The guards caught Tom Collins communicating a couple of times and he was called out to a quiz and warned that if he was caught again he would be punished. This went on for a few days and finally one night the guard came down and took us out of our cell to room one from which they'd moved Tom Collins out. They had moved Bill Robinson from room two to room four and they brought a couple of other guys in. One was Ray Alcorn but I don't remember the other guy. It seemed like they were just shuffling us around.

After a couple of days they finally took us out and let us go down to the bath area. It was just a well. We washed without any soap and then returned to our rooms. The sanitary conditions were unbelievable at this place. They wouldn't even let us out of our cell long enough to wash our dishes. They'd come around with our chow and our plates would be sitting out on a little concrete platform that was right outside the door. This platform had a brick box-like affair built into it so it held water, primarily rain water that came off the roof. When we came back from the bath, which happened once a week or sometimes every two weeks, we'd bring a couple of buckets of water with us and dump them into this little brick box.

The guards would come around with the chow on shoulder poles. They'd take a banana leaf and scrape the crud out of our dishes from the previous meal and then fill it up with the new stuff. This would go on day after day and the plates and the bowls were absolutely rancid. Ants were crawling all over them and the hot sun would bake it all day.

We continued our efforts to communicate with the other guys in the building. We didn't know how many or who was there. We knew there were eight of us. When we would go to the bathroom we passed by huts Delta and Echo. It looked like there were people living there because each of them had a small square of paper on the front door with some Vietnamese writing on it. The shutters were always completely closed up so nobody could look in or look out and there was no noise from these buildings. As we'd go to the bath we'd say something to each other and the guard would yell at us to knock it off but we never could get any acknowledging coughs from these buildings.

One day when walking back we saw a set of handcuffs hanging up on one of the doors. Hayden and I talked about this and came to realize why the guys had not coughed. The security measures on communications at this camp were really tough.

We stayed in this room for a couple of weeks or so and nothing eventful happened. Then one day the guard came down, told me to put on my long sleeve shirt and I went to an interrogation. I met The Bug. He was all peaches and cream again and he gave me two letters from my wife, which I was allowed to keep and take back to the cell.

I went back and showed them to Hayden. Of course we were both very happy about that. Then that afternoon we were both taken out to the quiz room. We were told to sit down and that we could write letters home.

One day shortly after that we were moved to room one in hut Bravo. We passed through the courtyards of a couple of other huts. As we did we noticed there was a set of handcuffs hanging on a nail by every door. As soon as we got in our new cell, Hayden went over to the window and I got on the wall tapping. I immediately heard a "Shave and a Haircut" from the next room.

But Hayden said, "Cool it, Phil, I think there is a guard somewhere in the courtyard area." I said, "Okay." The "Shave and a Haircut" came again from the next room and then it came a third time and it sounded kind of urgent. Hayden said, "Go ahead and give it a try. I don't have his position right now, but go ahead and give it a try." I acknowledged a "Shave and a Haircut" and started tapping with Ralph Gaither, a Navy Ensign. This was the first contact with Ralph, but we knew each other from previous information back at The Zoo.

Just as I started my conversation with Ralph a guard popped out from right around a corner of the building. He had been standing quietly outside our door. After he put us in the cell he had not left. All the guards there wore tennis shoes. We were kind of amazed at that but we found out in rapid order that the reason they wore tennis shoes was so they could sneak around without being heard and catch us communicating.

The guard screamed and yelled, having heard the taps, at seeing me there next to the wall. In an instant the turnkey, a guy who had been a guard and turnkey back at the Zoo, opened our door. Back at The Zoo this guy was known as "Johnny Cool" because he was a real easy-going type guy. However here at The Briar Patch they had retrained him and he had been turned into a real asshole. So everybody changed his named from "Johnny Cool" to "Johnny Fuck Head."

Johnny Fuck-Head told me to come outside. The Bug was standing out there and said, "Now we will show you. You will be punished for having communicated. It's against the camp regulations and you are a criminal and you are not allowed to communicate with other criminals in nearby buildings or in adjoining rooms." They turned me around and took the handcuffs off the door. Now we knew what the handcuffs were for.

They put my arms behind my back and clamped the handcuffs down just as tight as they could. It was really painful. They put the handcuffs on so my hands were placed back-to-back rather than normally placed behind you. This twisted the shoulder muscles around and made it extra painful. There was a short chain link, about four inches long, between the two cuffs, which they twisted.

Then they put me back into the cell. As soon as they left Gaither got back on the wall again and started tapping to Hayden. He said, "Sorry, guys. I didn't know that damn guard was standing out there." Then he told us what the regimen was. You went into cuffs when you got caught communicating. Hayden asked him how long he thought I would be in cuffs and Gaither said, "Well for the first offense, the first time you're in the camp, it will probably be between 3 days and a week.

Hayden tapped back, "Jesus Christ, they got them bound down on him as tight as they can and he's going through Hell already. Besides that his wrists are turned around backwards. Gaither began to explain how I could rotate my arms in such a fashion, either by using the wall or your roommate and get my hands rotated around behind me in the normal position. It involved a 360 degree rotation of my arms behind my back. So I tried it and sure enough I got them back around the right way and it helped. They were still real tight though the rotation took the pressure off considerably.

243

Gaither tapped back and said, "Okay, you got them rotated now?" Hayden tapped back, "Yes, we do." Gaither said, "Okay, do you have a cuff key?" Hayden said, "A which-what?" Gaither said, "A cuff key. Get yourself a piece of wire you can find lying around the yard. Or you might look around the cell and find some there. Ron Storz was in that cell before. He might have left one under a bed post. We have cuff keys that guys have made stashed in just about every room in this camp. It's a piece of wire about an inch and a half to two inches long of strong enough gauge so it doesn't bend. A nail will work fine too."

He explained, "These handcuffs are like the old Dick Tracy handcuffs that you used to play around with when you were a kid. You can pick the lock. All you have to do is turn the tumbler around so the ratchet will fall and then you can loosen them up. What we do is we loosen them up after the guard clamps them down tight. Then we listen and when the guard comes back we just tighten them down tight again before he opens the cell door. The best time to tighten them back down is just as the guard is opening the door because he is making noise with the key, the lock and the door. Then the click-click as you snap them down won't be heard."

Hayden started looking around and sure enough he found a cuff key which was a nail that had been filed down. Then he went to work behind me. He worked for a couple of hours while continuing to get instructions from Gaither until finally he figured out the mechanism and got them picked opened. We were the two happiest guys in the world.

We loosened them up and I was pretty stupid. I loosened them up really far so my arms could wiggle around completely. We were sitting there on the bunk when all of a sudden J. Fuck Head came walking around and he looked into the room. We'd heard him coming but not soon enough. We had not learned how to be completely alert, but we were to learn in the next few days.

Johnny came around and he wanted to look at my cuffs. I was standing with my arms behind my back. I had gotten rotated back around but they were still loose. I didn't have any choice but to lean back against the wall and snap them back down tight. When I did that and when he heard those clicks from behind my back his eyes got big. He came running around and threw open the door again. He yanked me outside and threw me up against the wall of the building and looked at my cuffs. Everything was as he had left them before only he knew I had snapped them down.

We found out later that Johnny was suspicious of people opening cuffs. This business had been going on all winter with the original twelve guys who left The Zoo. They all had learned how to open their cuffs because, hell, they were all in them about three-fourths of the time. So Johnny was pretty suspicious. But it was kind of funny because it was a facet of Gook personality to let well enough alone, even though Johnny knew the guys were getting themselves out. But he and they all figured that as long as they didn't catch somebody at it then that was good enough. Gooks kind of have a philosophy that if you don't see it, it didn't happen. This was to pay off quite handily for us in many instances.

He kicked me back into the cell with Hayden and me cussing at him. He slammed the door shut and stormed off but he didn't come back with anybody. So I reversed them around again and Hayden got the cuff key and went to work on them again. This time he found out there was a little interlock mechanism, a button that you push down that locks the cuffs in place so they cannot be closed down or opened up. This took Hayden a little extra work to find out how to get that interlock popped back out so he could loosen the cuffs again.

I asked Hayden to explain to me what he had been doing back there. He began to verbally explain to me and showed me through drawings on the dirt floor how the damn things worked. I started practicing doing it behind my back. At first I was slow and it would take me a couple of minutes to get them open. But as I practiced and continued to work at it I found out I could open up those cuffs behind my back faster than a guard could with the key. In a couple of days I got it down where I could open them in a couple of seconds.

We needed a good place to hide the key. There was a scam that ran down the crotch of the underwear I was wearing all the time. So I lodged this little piece of wire in the lining of the cloth right down in the area of my scrotum and anus. This turned out to be an absolutely perfect hiding place because of the Vietnamese mores about seeing other men naked. It was many years before they ever even searched our private areas, so it was safe.

They'd search us everywhere else quite thoroughly. They'd go through all our clothing and our room. They'd come into the cell, tear the place apart, throwing everything all over the floor. This was the primary purpose of their weekly inspections, to harass us and throw everything down in the dirt and kick everything around. They'd search our blankets and mosquito nets quite thoroughly but they'd never get to the crotch of our skivvies. So I carried this cuff key with me, this original one I picked up there, for the next four years. We picked up more wire whenever we could and Hayden

245

made himself a cuff key, and we were both all set.

I stayed in the cuffs for three days when The Bug came around to the room and told me my punishment was over. He told us that if we'd be good boys and go along with the party line and not to try to do any more communicating we wouldn't get into any more trouble.

Ralph began to explain to us more sophisticated things about the tap code. He began to teach me all the abbreviations so I could improve my speed. Within the next few days I was tapping much faster. He told us guys were being forced to do work out in the yard. We did hoeing and occasionally dug latrines. The Gooks would take us out in the sun all day. We would communicate with other buildings by using the hoe or shovel whenever we went out for yard work. The most important information that we shared was who was there in camp and in which buildings. We shared with everyone as we were working near the various buildings by sending tap code with our hoes and shovels.

We stayed in that room until about the middle of May. Guys were being forced to write biographies. These were idiotic personal information-type questionnaires. They were about 30 pages of absolute garbage they wanted us to fill out. The questions were incredibly stupid. They asked us to name all the schools we went to, the courses we took in first grade, second grade, third grade and so on. We had to fill out all this shit.

They wanted to know what political party our cousins, aunts, uncles, parents, grandparents and great grandparents belonged to and what their names were. They wanted us to name everything we owned. Did we own an automobile, a TV set, a toaster, an iron and other things they had heard about? Each one of these little things had to be filled in. It was reams and reams of garbage. Of course all of us in the camp were fighting this.

The original twelve guys who had gone to The Briar Patch had been forced to write their biographies that winter while they were there. The guys that had gone in that first group suffered extremely gross treatment as they were the only twelve guys there. Their food had been absolutely nothing. They had not been allowed to bathe that entire time. None of them had a bath in three months. None of them had hair cuts or shaves or anything. They were completely shut up and in solitary confinement there.

I was the first of the new arrivals called out and taken down to the quiz room. They had built a concrete block in the middle of the floor. They had encased bricks in concrete so that it was physically stuck to the floor. In front of the concrete block was a desk with a chair for the interrogator. I sat down on the block and Frenchy came walking in. I hadn't seen him since back before Christmas. As it turned out he had left The Zoo with that first group and now he was the The Briar Patch camp commander.

Frenchy sat down and began to ask me questions about my family, which I wouldn't answer. Then he handed me this big pile of papers and said, "You must write and fill out all these papers." I said, "No, I won't." He said, "I will allow you to stay here and think about it for awhile." He left the pen and paper on the desk and walked out. He allowed me to think about it all that day and all through the night. The next morning he came back in again. There was a guard posted right outside the quiz room. They had the window open so he could stand there and watch me.

The guards would rotate every four hours. As soon as I'd start to fall asleep they would come in and rap me with the cleaning rods to their rifles. These cleaning rods slide down below the barrel like an old musket. So right away I found out that I was not to get up off the block, nor was I to fall asleep, but to sit just there on it.

The idea of the whippings with the cleaning rods was not so much to make us write as it was to force us to stay awake and stay seated on the block. They'd come in and rap us on the head and whip us on the legs, back and arms where there was cloth covering. That way they wouldn't make any marks. They'd just make bruises but they wouldn't open up any wounds. The rods stung when they'd hit us with them. It was like a little lash. It wasn't in itself painful enough torture to make you write. But it was very painful. And it would definitely get our attention to make us sit there and stay awake for a little while.

At this time I had dysentery. I was having to relieve myself about 10 or 12 times a day. They would let me go over to a bucket that was in the corner of the room. There was no toilet paper or anything to wipe with so I was really a filthy mess.

The next morning Frenchy came back in and said, "You must write. You must write. You will sit here until you do write. It is useless for you to evade. You must give us what we want. You must yield to us. You must surrender completely." They always used this "surrender completely" line. This went on every day for the next five days and nights, and he would come back in each day.

I began reeling around until I couldn't stay on the block any more. So they tied me to it with ropes and handcuffed me behind my back. They'd bring my food, taunt me with it and tell me I wasn't going to eat. When I'd eat a little bit of it they would take it away from me and throw it out, just playing games like that with the food and water.

But always the main thing was just sitting there. About the second day my legs and ankles began to swell up and then my whole lower body. Finally towards the end my ankles were about the same size as my waist and my feet were like balloons with little things sticking out of the end that were my toes. It became very painful and the dysentery was tremendous now, even though I didn't have much in me. I was unloading a lot of water all the time and I just lost control of my bowels.

About the fourth day I began to hallucinate. I remember looking at the walls and seeing color patterns that began to form and flow on the walls. Then the walls, floor and the ceiling of the room began to sort of flow like putty. This went on for several hours and then it would stop. Then it would come back on again and I remember thinking very disjointed thoughts about my family and my previous life back home. But everything seemed to be mixed up and out of place in time. Then I began to hear voices. I'd hear conversations going between two people.

About the fifth day I knew something serious was wrong with my bowels because everything just felt like it had broken open down there. In fact I now had what they call a prolapsed rectum, which is a rupture of your descending colon. (I had to have an operation at Navy Balboa Hospital, San Diego, to repair the damage when I came home.)

Then I knew I had completely had it. They were coming in and pounding on me with those cleaning rods and there was nothing left in me. I had nothing more to resist with so when Frenchy came back in I told him I would fill out the biography. He said all right, handed me the pencil and paper and I fell over on the table. The guards came in and yanked my head up. I took the pencil in my hand and the first question was something like fill in your name and I couldn't even see to write. I just did something with the pencil that closely approximated writing, making some scribble lines. That's all they wanted.

They took me out of that cell and down a couple of doors where they threw me into another cell. I collapsed on the bed board and fell asleep. This was probably about six in the morning. I slept there till a guard came in about six that evening and kicked and pushed me to wake up. He gave me my chow and brought a lantern into the room. He brought me the pencil and paper and told me to start filling it out. I worked on the first page of the damn thing until I couldn't stay awake any longer. Then I fell back on the bed and slept until morning. The next morning The Bug came around and said, "When you finish each page you will tell the guard and I will come down and check your work."

I started filling this piece of crap out and for every answer I just invented something. I invented something for every relative's name or everything in my background. I made all the answers relate some way to the truth so I could remember them later on. For instance my father had been a home builder so I put down he was a carpenter. I put down old high school friends' names as relatives. For squadron mates I put down baseball players names I knew.

They wanted a complete military history and I put down that I joined the military in 1961. I had gone to a year of college and worked as an oil driller and came into the military service as an officer and learned how to fly. I made a completely phony flight program up. I made it out that this was my first tour of duty so they wouldn't know that I had been on a previous cruise. The whole thing was fabricated.

The Bug came back in and saw what I had done. The answers were ridiculous and he knew it but he bought it. The only thing they wanted was to fill their squares. They didn't really care if the damn answers were truthful or not. They just wanted it all filled out. So at this point I began to realize my complete stupidity in taking this so seriously. I had given all this resistance for complete bull shit. Today I think it might have been foolish to resist this dumb biography form as much as I did. But that's what I did, and they had to work for it.

I finished the biography in a few days and was put in hut India. I was by myself in this building with no contacts with anyone except on occasion, when there weren't any guards in the courtyard, I'd try whistling. I got an answering whistle from hut Foxtrot which was the adjoining hut in the next courtyard. This turned out to be Ed Davis and it was his first use of the tap code. The guys in Foxtrot passed encouraging words by whistling the tap code. It was the only way they could contact me.

One day one of the guys got out into the courtyard and started working with a hoe. He passed reams of stuff to me. He told me Hayden was now undergoing the biography bit. Just as soon as I had gotten off the block Hayden had taken my spot. We found that they only had one block to sit on and as it turned out they kept it occupied all the time.

Later on more POWs joined us until we had 56 people there in The Briar Patch. At that time they expanded to two quiz rooms with concrete blocks. In the meantime they kept the block occupied all the time with somebody, to go after something. The object of the game for us at The Briar Patch became for everybody to sit on that block as long as we could. That way we were keeping it occupied and keeping somebody else from sitting on it. This compounded the problem for the Gooks. By stringing things out over a long period of time they got less information than they would have if everyone had yielded right away. This made their problems bigger for them.

After a few days, a new guard came to my cell and took me out. He was a tall, thin Gook sergeant who later became known as "The Goose" or "Shitty Slim." He was probably one of the nastiest guards who ever turned up there or in any other camp. He later developed into being one of their biggest torture experts. Slim took me back to my old cell and that night Hayden came back. He had done the same thing I had. He sat on the damn block for seven days before he, too, had written his biography. We sat there and talked over what we had written in our biographies, laughing about the answers we had given.

Things slowed down about this time. On occasion we were forced out into the yard to dig a latrine in the hot sun. We had nothing to protect our heads, faces or arms when we were out there digging. The sun was really brutal. Hayden and I went out one day and got severe sunburns but the Gooks didn't care about that.

One day we were sitting there when things were pretty quiet. Our room was locked up tight and the shutters were all closed. I had a way of standing up on my bunk and looking out sideways through the shutters so I could watch the camp entry gate by the Gooks' barracks. I'd always watch this spot and whenever I'd see someone come through the gate I'd jump down off the bunk and run over to tap to Ralph Gaither and tell him who'd come in. Ralph would pass it on and eventually it went to all the other guys.

This day I was standing up there on my toes talking to Hayden when suddenly the gate opened and about fifteen Gook officers came roaring through. The guards had all been acting real nasty the previous couple of days before this. They seemed really pissed off, irritable, and they were slapping us a lot. They were also coming around to the windows a lot to provoke us with trying to make us bow. The turnkey had been coming in and yanking our heads down. Treatment had gotten worse and we couldn't figure out what had happened.

All these officers looked pretty high ranking and they were all carrying these little briefcases along with them. I could see some high rank on the collar devices as they came through the gate.

None of us could figure it out. That afternoon they all went back out the gate again. Then the next morning Larry Guarino was called out to an interrogation and he did not come back for a couple of days. When he did

250

come back he told us that he had been placed on the block and had gotten the holy living hell beaten out of him. They wanted him to write a confession.

This is the first time we had seen requirements for confessions. Larry explained to us that what the Gooks wanted essentially was one or two paragraphs, saying we had bombed innocent women, children, hospitals, churches and schools on purpose. We were to confess that now we realized that we were criminals and that we wanted to be forgiven by President Ho Chi Minh for our crimes. This thing was to be done on a special form that looked official and had our signature at the bottom of it.

We all discussed this and realized that we had to go max out against it. We knew that there wouldn't be any giving in on this just from sitting on a stool. They had let Larry come back to the building and had not forced him to write this confession, though they had beaten him a lot.

Then we found out by comm. with other buildings that they were going to start guys out for confessions. Larry told us they had put him in tight cuffs and tight ropes down there. He explained to us how that worked, where they not only put the tight cuffs on us the way I had them on me. But they put them on us in such a fashion, with our arms pushed up towards our head, that it was incredibly painful. Then they used nylon straps to tie us up, extremely tight, so the combined effect of cutting off the circulation was really wild. He said they left him in this position for he guessed 30 minutes to an hour just to show him what it was like. Then they'd taken him out of it, kicked him around and let him sit on the block for awhile. Then they sent him back to his room.

This was starting in the summer of 1966. Towards the end of June we had bombed Hanoi for the first time. The Gooks had just gone mad about that! Up to this point, as far as they were concerned, there wasn't much of a war going on, at least not in this part of North Vietnam. All we were doing was clobbering the hell out of their country below the 20th parallel and this didn't really mean so much to them. We could blow up that sandbox down there all we wanted to. We were killing people down there but it didn't mean that much. What really got their knickers in a bunch was when we got started bombing Hanoi because they have a fanatical love for Hanoi. Then one day it all really hit the fan in Briar Patch.

17. Second Briar Patch — Part II

The Hanoi March

7/6/66

Hayden and I were sitting, minding our own business, on July 6th 1966 when the guards came around. They were all animated and excited. When they opened our door to give us our chow they were smiling, laughing and pointing to one another. One of the guards came around to our window and using his fingers he made the sign of a guy walking and he pointed to us. We didn't know what was going on. We figured we were going to walk somewhere, maybe to another camp or something.

That night they came down and got Hayden and me out of the cell. They told us to bring our mat, mosquito net, and toothbrush. They took us to a truck. We got into the truck with our little bundles of stuff. We couldn't figure what in the hell was going on. We were blindfolded and handcuffed together. We found that there were about a dozen of us on the truck.

We began to roll out and leave the camp. There were two other trucks in the procession; three trucks all together. We went down the bumpy road again towards Hanoi. We got into the city about seven in the evening. They drove into a large concrete structured area and pulled into a concrete building. They opened up the back of the truck and told us to get out.

From what we could see it looked like we were in the bottom part of a stadium. They walked us down a concrete hallway to an area where there were a lot of crappers and told us we could relieve ourselves in there, which we did. It was like being in a baseball park. Then they walked us back and got us into the truck. We had our blindfolds and handcuffs off and then they brought us some food. This consisted of a glutinous rice ball. It was a ball that had been rolled up about the size of a softball or larger and was stuffed with pieces of pork fat. They gave each of us one of those and a banana and told us to eat.

We still had no idea what in the hell was going on. When we finished eating they put the handcuffs back on us, closed up the truck and drove us out of the stadium. We drove down a street for a mile or two and stopped in front of the Hoa Lo prison, The Hanoi Hilton. They took us out of the truck again, and told Hayden and me to sit down in the street.

We could see a big crowd of people and as we looked up the street ahead of us we could see another pair of prisoners handcuffed together about fifteen feet in front of us. They were also sitting on the concrete in the middle of the street. Hayden and I turned around and looked behind us. We could other pairs of prisoners, two by two, back down the street just about as far as we could see.

Bill Tschudy and Al Brudno were in front of us. Directly behind us were Robinson Risner and Everett Alvarez, then Larry Guarino and Ron Byrne, then Robert Shumaker and Smitty Harris, and a then maybe a dozen more pairs of guys down the line. We all were handcuffed together, two by two, about fifteen feet apart.

It was hotter than hell that night and the air was extremely oppressive. The temperature must have been 115 to 120 degrees and that was at eight o'clock at night. We could hear jets flying low overhead. We looked up and saw MIG 17s and 21s go by. They were circling low over the city.

Finally word was passed down the line and the Gooks told us to stand up. When we did, a truck pulled up in front of us loaded with movie camera equipment and high-intensity lights. They flashed these lights on and we could see other trucks along side of the other guys with more movie equipment and high-intensity lights. There were also people walking along side of us with lights and cameras. The whole place was lit up like a Christmas tree.

We started to walk. We walked to the end of the street and took a bend to the left, then up the main street of Hanoi. As soon as we turned the corner we were met by a tremendous crowd. Guards, stationed about three feet apart, were walking beside us all the way down the line of prisoners. They had rifles with fixed bayonets pulled down and aimed ahead of them so the bayonets made a complete fence on either side of us. Beside each pair of prisoners were two Vietnamese Army people. One was an English speaker and one was a guard. As we stepped out into the street and began to march we heard a tremendous roar from the massive crowds of people, thousands of them packed on either side of the street.

We could see political cadres with red arm bands moving up and down the street whipping the people into frenzy. It seemed like these people had just completely gone insane. They were rabid in their fury. Then, in addition to screaming and yelling, they began to throw things at us. And then, more ominously, they moved in towards the guards.

The guards and the Gooks who were walking beside us were obviousl scared, really scared. It seemed like the crowd had gone completely out of control. Then rocks began to fly threw the air as thick as hail, hitting Hayden and me many times; the same with the other prisoners. The people were throwing gravel and then hurling beer bottles at us.

In addition to the missiles, the air was full of spit. Everybody was spitting down on us. It was as if it was raining spit. As the crowd got more intense and wild, the guards began to close our ranks up so we were marching only six feet or so apart from each other. This gave the guards less territory to cover. The guards were making a serious attempt to protect us and they were clearly as scared as we were of the potential of the crowds.

Despite the best efforts of the guards, people broke through the ranks. They ran up to guys and hit them in the heads with their fists, sticks, whatever they happened to have in their hands. I saw a couple of people with machetes. We weren't hit by machetes but I got narrow misses. I don't think we would have survived if they had gotten to us.

Then suddenly the lights went out. Not the movie lights; my own. Someone had hit me on the back of the head with a beer bottle. Hayden struggled to hold me up because we were handcuffed together, his left arm to my right arm. One of the photographers got the picture at that moment. There I am half out of it, with Hayden holding me up. It became a nation-wide, famous photo here in the U.S.

Hayden supported me along for a little while until I got my senses back about me again. No sooner did I wake up than I looked in front of us and saw this little Vietnamese gal who was about 4 foot 10 and probably weighed about 85-90 pounds. She was coming towards Hayden on a dead run. These little Vietnamese women were small but they were as strong as a little ox! They'd been carrying loads on shoulder poles all their lives and many were stronger than the men.

This little gal was coming at Hayden at a dead run and I said, "Hayden! Look out!" But just as I said it she connected on him right in the eye with a fist. He was walking towards her and she was coming towards him at top speed, so that it was a real haymaker. I've seen a lot of guys hit in bars and so forth but this was one that took them all. Hayden was knocked on his ass. I picked him up. He was reeling, as I had been moments before, and I had to support him for awhile until he woke up.

Now all through this thing the English speaker and guard who were walking along side of us were grabbing us by our hair and yanking our heads down. They were trying to make us walk with our heads bowed. The same thing was happening to the other guys. The crowds were going ape shit because we were all walking very erect, with pride, and that further inflamed them. They wanted us to bow and show that we were criminals as we went along, but we wouldn't.

This "Valley of the Shadow of Death," as we later referred to it, stretched on for about two miles. It was probably the worst experience of my lifetime. We look back on it now and still can't understand how we lived through the damn thing. Miraculously we were not killed. We were beaten up real bad. Our eyes were all swollen shut and we were bloody from head to foot from all the objects that were thrown.

We got off the street when we arrived back at the stadium and the guards ran us inside. I remember the gate of the stadium opening up. It looked like safety, but there were some guys running along beside us yelling out "Yankee Son of a Bitch, Yankee Son of a Bitch." I looked at these guys and it appeared that they were Cubans. There were all kinds of foreign Communist correspondents throughout, and Vietnamese also. The crowd tried to rush into the stadium with us but there were about 50 army guys there to keep them back while we managed to squeeze through the gate. They'd slam the gate shut after each pair of prisoners got inside to prevent the crowd from following and then they'd open it up for the next pair of men.

They took us into the stadium and sat us down on the ground. We looked up into the bleachers and there was no one there. It was empty. We sat there for awhile, just kind of in a stupor and then we were loaded onto the trucks again. We had left our toothbrush, mosquito nets, and other stuff on the trucks when we arrived, but now we were loaded into the trucks that weren't the ones we arrived in so we wound up with somebody else's gear. We all had also lost our sandals during the march so we were all bare-footed. And of course we never used any of the stuff they had us bring along anyway.

Then we started back to The Briar Patch. I will never understand the complete confusion of the Gooks in taking us to this thing. The entire march was just irresponsible and as screwed up as could be. It seemed as though the whole thing had been orchestrated, if not by our interrogators then with their knowledge and participation. We later found out that The Rabbit, The Fox, all the big cheeses in the camp and other interrogators who turned up later were at the march.

We all escaped being killed by a thin thread. And it tells you something about their incredible stupidity, or their cruelty, or both.

255

Tulsa Tribune

TULSA, OKLAHOMA, WEDNESDAY, APRIL 21, 1965

96 PAGES—4 SECTIONS

Tulsa Pilot Is Killed By Reds in Viet Nam

Lt. Phillip Butler, 26, Tulsa Navy pilot, was killed this morning when his plane was struck by fire from North Vietnamese ground forces and exploded.

He was the son of Mrs. Mae Butler of 442 S. Pittsburg Ave. Relatives said they were informed Lt. Butler's plane was on a reconnaissance flight when it was shot down.

Lt. Butler was a graduate of Will Rogers High School and attended the University of Oklahoma before entering the U.S. Naval Academy at Annapolis, where he was graduated four years ago. His wife and 6-month-old daughter, Diane Karen, live in LeMoore, Calif.

A sister, Linda, resides here with her mother.

His father, the late E. D. Butler Jr., was a prominent Tulsa builder and real estate agent who died in 1961.

His grandmother, Mrs. Maude M. Butler, resides at 2242 S. Delaware Ave.

He was an honor student during his term at the naval academy.

Butler

• • •

Phil's helmet, used by tracking dogs to find him

256

a Tribune

MA, THURSDAY, MAY 27, 1965   16 PAGES—3 SECTIONS   5¢

Radio Hanoi Reveals Capture

'Dead' Tulsa Pilot Is Alive!

LT. PHILIP N. BUTLER
. . . alive, but captive

A Tulsa Navy pilot whose plane was shot down by the North Vietnamese April 20 is a prisoner of the Communists, Radio Hanoi reported today.

Lt. Philip Neil Butler, 26, the son of Mrs. Mae Butler, of 645 S. Pittsburg Ave., had been presumed dead after the downing of his plane, which reportedly exploded in mid-air after it was struck.

The incident occurred while Lt. Butler was making a reconnaissance flight.

"You don't know how much this means," Lt. Butler's mother said today after she was told by a newsman that her son was reported a prisoner.

"I HAVEN'T KNOWN FOR months what had happened. This is the most marvelous news," she said.

Mrs. Butler, a widow, said she received a letter from her son April 19 (the day before his plane was downed) in which he said: "Don't worry, I think I'll certainly be back because I know my job well. I am doing what I am trained for, to protect you."

The broadcast from North Viet-Nam's capital reported Butler was shot down over Nghe An Province the night of April 20. It said Butler was born Aug. 1, 1938 at Blackwell, has a wife, Karen, and a young daughter, Karen Olsen Butler.

THE BROADCAST REPORT-ED Butler is being treated well. Radio Hanoi gave this account of Butler's capture:

"Hardly had he released the bombs when his plane was hit by ground fire. Its wings began

shaking like leaves and the plane began trailing smoke.

"Frightened, he bailed out and landed by parachute, while his craft went down he knew not where. After landing, he hid in a forest for four days and nights and in the hopes of being able to find his way to Laos and eventually to Thailand.

"A search party was sent after him but did not find him out. On April 24, however, an old man who was dashing past in the forest caught sight of him, seeing that he was a tall and burly white man, the old man decided he was an American, and went and informed the authorities.

"A party composed of security armed police, militia and self-defense men, accompanied by two Shepherd dogs, immediately

See PILOT, page 4

Pilot . . .

Continued From Page One

ately went out in search of the pilot. Upon seeing him, the two Shepherd dogs sprang up, each seizing Butler by one arm pulling him backward.

THE NORTH VIETNAMESE also reported the capture of three other U.S. pilots. They are Lt. Everett Alvarez Jr., San Jose, Calif.; Lt. Cmdr. Robert H. Shumaker, New Wilmington, Pa., and Lt. Hayden J. Lockhart, Springfield, Ohio, and Alexandria, La.

Lt. Butler's sister, Miss Linda Butler, lives with her mother. His grandmother, Mrs. Maude M. Butler, lives at 1561 S. Delaware Ave., and an aunt, Mrs. John M. Simms, lives at 1404 E. 11th St.

Lt. Butler's wife and daughter live in Lemoore, Calif.

He is a Will Rogers High School graduate, former University of Oklahoma student, and an honor graduate of the U.S. Naval Academy at Annapolis.

Tulsa Tribune

257

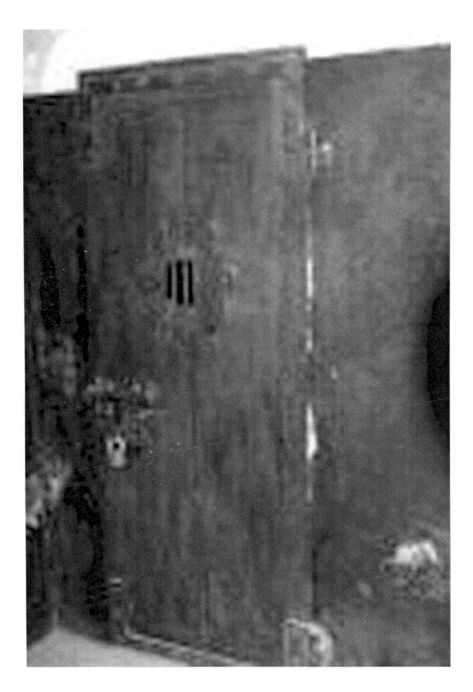

Doorway to "Heartbreak Hotel" at "Hanoi HIlton"

Phil at NVN press conference (1965)

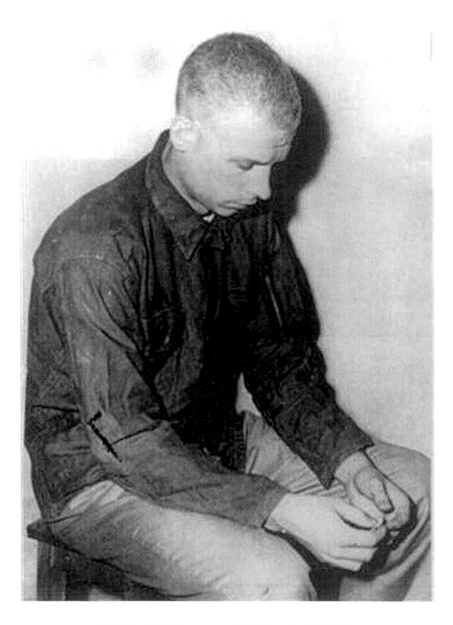

Phil in his first year in Hanoi (1965)

Hayden Lockhart helping Phil just after a bottle hit him in the head during the "Hanoi March of American POWs" on July 6, 1966.
Photo appeared in many American newspapers and magazines.

The Rabbit - The Evil Interrogator and Torturer

McGrath drawing - Torture with Rope Trick
(Courtesy of the U.S. Naval Institute Press)

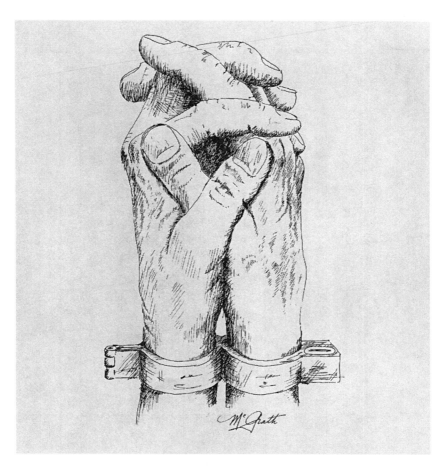

McGrath drawing - Torture with Manacles

McGrath drawing - Torture by Whipping

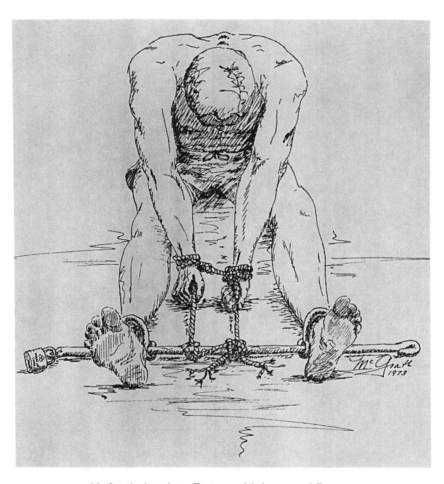

McGrath drawing - Torture with Irons and Ropes

Leaving Hanoi February 12th 1973

POW Bracelet

18. Second Briar Patch — Part III

Torture and Confessions

7/6/66 – 2/2/67

They drove us back to The Briar Patch and took us back to our cells. Hayden and I collapsed on our bunks. We were too amazed and beaten up to discuss anything so we just bagged out and went to sleep.

The next morning Hayden and I were called out to an interrogation. We went up to the quiz room and Frenchy was there. He told us to sit down, and he sat there with a big grin. He said the usual opening for a quiz, "How are you?" Hayden and I just both gave a couple of sneers. Frenchy continued on, asking us about our impressions of the march. He asked if we now believed that we'd be tried for being criminals.

He was clearly feeling us out about what we thought of the whole thing. We both got the impression from him that he felt like us and everybody else; that the thing had gotten completely out of hand and that it wasn't at all what they had expected it to be. We expected that now they were sweating the international implications of what they had done.

What they had apparently hoped to show the world was that we were being marched from our place of confinement at Hoa Lo prison to the stadium where they would conduct our trials on charges of being criminals. Frenchy appeared very worried, as did The Bug, about how it came off. (Later President Johnson put out the word to the Gooks that if they tried an American prisoner the United States would end a policy of restraint. That threat was apparently enough to get the Gooks to knock it off.)

By this time in The Briar Patch we had gotten a couple more installments of guys bought in from The Zoo and other facilities in Hanoi. That put us up to a total camp strength of 56 POWs. Also about this time we had two guys who were moved out. They were Navy Lieutenant Commander Jim Bell and Air Force First Lieutenant John Heilig, which dropped our strength to 54. Jim was moved out because he was extremely sick. He was down to 100 pounds or so. They didn't have the medical facilities or know-how to take care of him and they thought he was going to die on them so they moved him back to The Zoo.

After our little talk with Frenchy we went back to our cells. Now the harassment picked up at The Briar Patch. The guards started an intensive harassment program. They started coming around and they would open the shutters. They had long sticks or poles they'd cut with the ends sharpened. They'd ram these sticks into the cells and jab holes in us with them. They started doing this all the time during the day. Then they even started doing it at night when we were asleep.

Next the Gooks came around and they said for security measures we would have to be tied up. They said this was because American airplanes were flying in the nearby area and it was for our own security. So they tied our hands behind us. Hayden and I spent 60 days living with our hands tied behind us that summer.

They'd come around, open the cell door for us to go out, and the first guy out got clobbered. The minute we stepped out the door with the shit bucket in our hand we got a rifle butt in the head. It happened every morning, just like clockwork. Then we'd be kicked around out there. Whoever walked out the door first would be the guy that got it. So Hayden and I just traded off. He'd take it one morning and I'd take it the next.

The same thing would happen when we'd go out and get chow. We'd go out together to get chow and take the licks together. The same thing happened when we'd go out and work in the yard. It would be a day-long harassment campaign while we were working. They'd be kicking and beating us. We couldn't do anything right out there.

That was the general atmosphere in the camp. The guards were all doing it. Whenever we'd go down to the quiz room they'd have all the guards assembled around, along with The Bug. They'd all stand there and glare at us and shake their fists at us. They would get up right in our face and scream and swear things like "Mat su me!" which meant "American mother fucker" while we were walking down. This went on through July.

Soon after the Hanoi March they started torturing guys for confessions. First they took out Guarino and Byrne, then Shumaker and Harris. And we could just see them coming down through the buildings, room by room, one at a time. Finally at seven o'clock on August 11th of 1966, my 28th birthday, they came and got me.

They had me roll up my bed gear and drop it outside the quiz room. I walked into the quiz where they had a coal oil lantern sitting on the table. There was Frenchy and he said, "You must confess your crimes. Here is what you must write." I told him to get fucked and he said, "I will allow you to think about it tonight. Tomorrow morning I will come back, and then you must write." And he left the cell.

I sat there on the stool that night and he came back the next morning and stood outside. Another quizzer we called "Chester," newly arrived in the camp, came in and said, "You must write as ordered by the camp commander." Again I told him I declined that offer.

He stood up and said something in Vietnamese. Then three guards came in. The King Pin of the guards was Shitty Slim or The Goose, as I said before. They yanked me off the stool and shoved me up against the wall with my face to the wall. Then the three of them got behind me and brought my arms around behind my back. They pushed them both up into a hammerlock and held them up as high as they could. They were actually lifting me off the floor.

Then they took the hand cuffs with a chain link between them and put one hand cuff on my right arm about mid way between the wrist and the elbow. Then they took a little pry bar and inserted it into the ratchets of the hand cuff and they pried the hand cuff down as tight as they could get it. It was tight enough to actually break the skin on my arm. It smashed down into the flesh, against bone. It entirely cut off all circulation, instantly. Then they took the other hand cuff and twisted it about 180 degrees. When you take a chain link and you twist it, you know how it resists the twisting. They twisted it as far as they could and then they hooked that hand cuff in that position up to my left arm and pried it down with the bar as they did the other one.

Now I had my arms forced up behind my back so that my hands were clear up above my head and these hand-cuffs were on my mid arms. Then they let go of me so gravity and my shoulder muscles pulled my arms down against the cuffs. At the same time that created a twisting moment because this chain link had been twisted on my arms. Then they wound straps around my upper body and pulled them tight.

We called this torture "Hell Cuffs." The pain went into the unreal. It's the worst one I ever had to endure. Then they simply walked out of the room and locked the cell. They told me to "Bao Cao" when I was ready to write.

There were a couple of guys next door to that cell and the first thing I heard was a tap on the wall. I walked over and kicked it twice. Then these guys started tapping to me. They said, "Phil, we know you're there and you are the seventh guy so far that has come through. We know what you're going through." They just started talking to me, saying, "You've got those hell cuffs on you back there and we are going to be with you. If you start

270

yelling, you just listen to this wall."

They kept up that kind of chatter. They said, "Give it a fight, Phil. Give it all you have. Go ahead and give it the full works." I told them I would, that I would go all the way on this one. They said, "You know Phil, all you have to do is please yourself. And I said, "Right and I have to be proud of myself when it's over."

In about fifteen minutes my hands were completely dead with no feeling whatsoever. Then in about 30 minutes I experienced a sensation like somebody was holding cigarette lighters on my hands. This is when the nerves start being affected, actually killed, from the lack of circulation. This increases up to a peak in about an hour, and from that point on the pain was exactly like somebody burning me. It just gets worse and worse, and our hands and arms swell up huge.

After awhile I started screaming, kicking and crying. Then I was vomiting, urinating and defecating in my pants. I was just running around the room like a wild man! This went on for about six hours. In this kind of torture you will not pass out. You will not pass out from this kind of pain. It would have been a blessing if I could have. But it didn't happen. It's the most excruciating pain I ever experienced in my life.

After about three or four hours of this I decided I was going to try to commit suicide. I got in one corner of the room and lowered my head. The only way I could kill myself was to bash my brains against the wall. I ran across the room and smashed my head into the other concrete wall. All I did was knock the shit out of myself and I wound up in more misery and pain than before. I guess I have a hard head.

I tried calling up witches, demons, God, Buddha and everybody else I could think of but nothing worked. Finally after six hours I'd had it. I could not go another second. I felt like I was losing my mind. I had thrown up all over myself and all over the cell. It was just a hell of a mess. I was on the floor kicking and screaming, and I finally yelled "Bao Cao." The guard came to the window and said, "Hum, Bao Cao, Hum?" I said, "Bao Cao all right!"

Then he just turned around and walked away. It was just the most terrifying, desperate feeling I ever had in my entire life. They left me there for another two hours, just for a general "I'll show you" type thing. Finally, after two more hours they came back in. I was a complete blithering idiot. They yanked me up and set me down on the stool. Chester said, "Now will you write?" I said, "Yes, yes, God get them off!" He said, "You will write the confession?" I said, "Yes, yes," I was crying and pleading with him,

"Please get them off!" Finally, he told Slim to take them off.

When they took those things off and the circulation started again the pain started again! The pain of sensation coming back into my hands and arms was almost as bad as what I had experienced for the past eight hours. The human body is not supposed to be treated that way. The pain was so extreme I went out of my mind, falling to the floor, screaming for about ten minutes.

They just sat and watched me. When I got over my fit I got back up on the stool again. They handed me a pencil and paper. My arms and hands were absolutely blue, enormous from swelling and they were completely dead. I couldn't move them. I had no sensation in them whatsoever. I took the pencil and just by pushing my hand down against the table locked it between the fingers and started scrawling something he told me to write. Chester could see that I couldn't write and said, "All right, you will write tomorrow morning."

They put me in solitary in hut India and locked me in for the night. The next morning I woke up and two guards and a quizzer came to the cell. They walked in and handed me the paper and pencil and told me to start writing. My hands and arms were still dead. The nerves were all killed. I had no sensation so they were just completely paralyzed. I started writing by using my hands as a holder and my arms to write.

I wrote a confession. It was a ridiculous thing. I put in completely absurd sentence structure. None of the words were spelled correctly and nothing was punctuated. It said that this wasn't a confession at all. It didn't confess anything. So I wrote this and gave it to The Bug and he took it out. About two hours later he came back with the guards again and said, "Now this is not correct. You have tried to deceive us. This is garbage. You have not written what we told you to write."

The camp commander, Frenchy, had taken my "confession" and there were red ink marks all over the place. It was just like the way I got a paper back from my first grade teacher. He said, "You must do better." So I wrote another version and then the same deal. He took it out and so on. This went on through five different edits until they got one they would accept. All the time they were threatening me to do it again with the cuffs. I knew I couldn't possibly hack it even for an instant with those things on again. I thought I'd already lost control of my hands for the rest of my life. But I continued the poker game until the last version. The final one I wrote stated "that I was an Imperialist Aggressor criminal and had 'crimed' against the Vietnamese people and that the Vietnamese people had 'blowed up' my airplane when I was 'shooted down'."

I got some more bull shit like that in it, and I also said that I had "strafed women and children and old folks and bombed school yards and hospitals." The only thing I could think of as I had written it was how furious I was. I guarantee that right then if I had been the pilot of an A4C loaded with bombs and rockets, with a school yard in sight, I would have creamed it!

Then I was taken back to my cell with Hayden. He had gone through the same thing and had written a similar "confession."

So that was my confession. As I walked back to my cell a strange feeling came over me. I was so God damn proud of myself. I look back at it all now, even as I looked at it back then after having written it. I don't think I was ever prouder of myself in my whole life and I still feel that way today. If anybody asks me if I wrote anything in North Vietnam I'll be proud to tell them that I wrote a confession - absolutely proud to tell them!

As far as I'm concerned it was a highpoint of my life insofar as ever doing anything that I felt a real man could do. That's the important thing if you're ever placed in this situation. Make sure you do a job such that you will be able to look in that mirror for the rest of your life.

They were going to get their nickel's worth of propaganda. We were helpless and they were going to get it if they wanted it. But we could do something for ourselves by making them fight for it. We certainly made them work for it.

We had 54 men at The Briar Patch and I want to spell that with capital letters. All 54 men were tortured until they just blew their gourds for these silly-ass confessions. Every last man was tortured, and tortured as much as he could take. The Gooks went through the entire camp that way. I'm certain every last man who walked out of The Briar Patch is proud of himself today for the confession he wrote there.

Since we all knew what kind of torture was coming, we had each other to compete with. It was like, "I lasted three hours," and another guy would tap over and say, "I lasted three and a half hours," and another guy would tap over and laugh, "I only hacked it for two hours. Jesus, you guys must not have any feeling at all." It was a macabre competition but at the same time a big morale boost.

I actually went six hours and then was forced to go another two. But I gave in after six, which was a pretty good performance. This thing depends on your own individual pain tolerance and determination. It's a physiological thing. It's a matter of courage and determination but also just your own physiology.

We had a guy there named Jerry Driscoll. Jerry is a real quiet guy. I lived with him off and on in later years. He was an Air Force First Lieutenant at that time. He'd go into a quiz room and if a Gook would scream at him he'd get unnerved as hell. It would really shatter him. But they stuck Jerry in those damn hell cuffs and that son of a bitch stayed in them for a week.

We just couldn't believe the guy was real! He couldn't have any nerve endings in his body! There wasn't anybody else in the camp that stayed in them longer than did Jerry Driscoll. After a couple of days they sent him back, in cuffs, to his cell with his cellmate. His cellmate tried to get him to give in because we were all worried that Jerry would lose his arms. So that just shows you the difference. Some guys were in them for 30 minutes or so and had to quit. But no matter how long they were in the hell cuffs, if they were in as long as they could hack it – that was what mattered!

They took this first round of confessions to a war crimes tribunal in Stockholm Sweden. It was called the "Bertrand Russell War Crimes Tribunal." They displayed our confessions there. But when people read them it was obvious they were trumped up because of the way they were written. The Gooks were so stupid!

Some of the English-speaking peaceniks or communists from the United States were so offended at the obvious fraud that they walked out of that War Crimes Tribunal. When this got out to the world it sorely embarrassed the Vietnamese.

Once again they were embarrassed by their obvious mistreatment of POWs. And that made them all the more vindictive. LCDR Nels Tanner and his back-seat pilot, Lt. Ross Terry wrote confessions in which they listed people in their squadron, who had also "crimed" against the Vietnamese people. These "squadron mates" were all fictitious names, like their commanding officer "Clark Kent." That one had to be the laughing stock of the Tribunal. As punishment, Nels and Ross got six months of solitary confinement in stocks and irons for humiliating the North Vietnamese.

But that was a fine, fine performance Nels and Ross did! Absolutely beautiful! After we found out what they'd done, they were our heroes. Whenever we talked about confessions guys would always bring up those two guys and the service they had done for us by putting those cleverly screwy names in so people around the world would recognize that we were being tortured.

Marine Major Howie Dunn was the second senior man at The Briar Patch, below Larry Guarino. Howie showed fantastic leadership. When he was taken out to bathe, Howie would never take time to bathe. He would take off his clothing in the bath area and wash his clothes as fast as he could because we had a limited time there. Then he'd take his clothing and snap them, like you're snapping water out. He'd snap tap code and everybody in the camp could hear him. He'd say, "Hang on guys, the end is coming soon, just hang on. Good job to 'so and so' for max resistance. I'm proud of you, and you guys over in hut India are doing a grand job."

Every time he'd go out to the shower he'd do this. He'd even snap out jokes, hilarious little short ones. I don't know where he ever dreamed them up. He'd tell us to "resist all the way! Don't give them anything for nothing, Give it all you have!" And so it went.

Howie was doing this while Larry Guarino and Ron Byrne had gone into seclusion. Even though these guys had been living right next door to us, after the Hanoi March they refused to communicate. Larry refused to serve as Senior Ranking Officer in the camp. He would not pick up notes in the bath area. Hayden and I would go down and pick up the notes for him and come back and tap them over to him.

Larry would just give us some weak thing, like "put another note out there and tell them whatever you think." Then Hayden and I would write another note to so and so to resist this or that or the other, to go all the way, and sign it Larry Guarino. We'd take it back in there for him and we'd use his name on it. Larry would not pass out any encouragement to any of the other guys in the camp. He just went dead on us. He resisted himself but he would not assume leadership.

We tried to bring him out of it. We'd harass him. Hayden and I would tap next door to him and say, "You're the Senior Ranking Officer and there is a note waiting for you in the crapper. Go get it!" He'd tap back and say, "I want you guys to pick it up for me." We'd tap back to him, "It's your God damn job not ours. Get off your ass over there!" Of course when we'd tap something like that he'd just get off the wall and sit over there with Ron and refuse to answer. Then we'd call him back the next day and he wouldn't answer on the wall. So we'd say, "Okay you guys here's a funny story Hayden was telling me. You want to hear it?" No answer. Then I'd start tapping this stupid story that I'd invented, a stupid joke or something like that over to them, knowing they were of course reading me. They were just gun shy. They were scared.

During this time, Major Dunn was doing the work for Larry Guarino.

He was the toughest guy in the camp. When the Gooks got him for his confession, Jesus Christ they got themselves a whirling dervish! He was a Marine in the truest meaning of the word! They worked on him for a full damn month. They damn near killed him and he still wouldn't give in. Until ultimately he did of course give in.

Throughout September, October, November and December of 1966, they continued to go through the guys in the camp. It took that long because we were beginning to intentionally prolong it. The Gooks began making it a two- or three-week ordeal for a guy before they'd get a confession. They got us original guys with hell cuffs and it was a rush affair for displays at the Tribunal.

After the press on confessions for the War Crimes Tribunal, they started torturing guys in a more prolonged fashion. They'd put the hell cuffs on but they wouldn't put them on tight enough to make it do the trick in just a few hours. They would put them on so a guy would last for days and days. They'd take him out and throw him into a hole in the ground outside and make him live in that hole for a couple of days and nights. Then they would have the guards come down and play with him.

I'll never forget this; it's burned in my memory. One day I was peeking out the crack of my door and I saw a dirty little Gook guard, one that I particularly despised, with an American officer who had his arms up behind him in cuffs. He was skinny, down to 125 pounds and he had boils all over his body. He had a gag shoved in his mouth and a blind fold on. This little Gook bastard had a rope around his neck and he was dragging him so he had to run through the yard. He was running him into brick walls and over logs. I sat there and watched that for about fifteen minutes and just cried and cried. I couldn't believe it! In succeeding days I saw others having the same thing done to them. It was just incredible that a man could be treated like that.

This was a little guard we called "Pox," or also "Sniffles." He was not only evil but also a crazy little bastard. His face was so pock-marked that we all figured he'd probably had smallpox. So naturally most of us called him "Pox." He was big on stabbing guys with sharpened sticks or his bayonet, but apparently wasn't satisfied with that. So he would also torture the puppies of stray dogs that were always running around camp. He would sit in the courtyard, hold a puppy in his lap on its back, and pull its legs apart. Sometimes he would sit there and torture a puppy for nearly an hour. We could all hear the poor little creature screaming, on and on. It was just one more thing to intensify our hatred for them, as if we needed anything else.

The Gooks knew that we had a pretty effective communication system going and they knew it involved tapping on the wall. Of course they wanted to know how it worked. So they started trumping up charges of communicating against guys. Then they took them out and tortured them to explain how we communicated and also to tell them everyone we knew. A guard came by our window one day, looked in and then he pointed to me and made a motion like tapping on the wall. Then he pointed to Hayden, did the same thing and then he buzzed off.

Hayden said, "Well, it looks like we're going to go out and be tortured again, buddy." I said, "Yeah, it looks like it, doesn't it?" Pretty soon the turnkey came back, opened the door and took us down to the quiz room together. The quizzer said, "You have been caught red-handed communicating."

This was a weird quirk the Gooks had. They seemed to always have to trump up some kind of charge to take you down and kick your ass. They always had to have some excuse. God knows why. It might have been for their conscience, or because they thought they were fooling us. Maybe it was a little of both.

He said, "You have been communicating and now you will write down everyone you know and how you communicate." Of course Hayden and I sat there and told him to "get fucked!" So they took us back to our cell, got hand cuffs, put them on us and mashed them down tight. They used the crow-bar again so they were real tight hell cuffs and then they threw us in the room together.

This was kind of a novelty for North Vietnam. I think it was one of the only times that two guys were ever tortured together. Hayden and I sat in there together on our racks. I guess I was the first one to start crying and Hayden would come over and bump against me and say, "That's all right buddy, just go ahead and cry it out. It's really hell, I know it hurts!"

Hayden is really tough. So he was kind of being a mother to me there. Finally after crying it out a little bit I got control of myself, got myself over against the wall and just started gritting my teeth and hanging on. As soon as I did, Hayden started crying. So I tried telling him the same thing. We went through the day that way. That night they came in and took them off us.

The next morning they came in and put them on us the same way again. By about afternoon that day we'd both had it! We had to write. Then they took us out to question us separately. They thought we couldn't coordinate our stories and they knew we'd have to know the same people.

But while we were being tortured there together, Hayden and I made our stories up. We made up a list of about fifteen or twenty guys we had lived with or lived next to. And we put down our means of communicating as tapping Morse Code on the wall, not the tap code.

As it turned out they already knew what the tap code was. And it didn't make a shit bit of difference because no Gook could duplicate our tap code anyway. They didn't speak English well enough. For that matter no one would ever be able to duplicate the tap code until they'd been a con for awhile and had used it everyday. Plus we used many abbreviations, and our proficiency was so tremendous that I could recognize anyone on the other side of the wall. If they moved a new guy into the next room and he tapped to me I would know who it was because I knew his particular code signature; just like a Morse Code operator can recognize transmitters. Or the way a Navy signal man can recognize who another person signaling with a light gun is by the way he sends. That meant it was impossible for the Gooks to use the tap code to try to intercept communications by pretending they were Americans on the other side of the wall.

They originally picked up our tap code because back in earlier days at The Zoo somebody had put a 5 X 5 alphabet box in huge letters on the shower wall and written "Tap Code." So when new guys walked in they'd see it and get the big picture. Notes were also always passed and dropped off to guys on little pieces of paper with how to do the Tap Code and the Gooks would pick these things up. Also earlier purges on communications had gotten guys to tell them how it worked.

What was funny as hell was that in 1967 the Gooks tried to duplicate the Tap Code. They got guards to come around on the other wall from us in the shower or the next cell and try to tap to us. Those stupid bastards did not even know how to properly send a "Shave and a Haircut." That was something that is American. We have lived with "dum, dum-dum dum dum" for our whole damn lives. It comes from American jazz music. So they just didn't have the rhythm for it. That was pretty funny. We would always know when there was some clown guard trying to tap to us. We would just go on about our business and ignore it.

The guards would catch guys dropping notes or would find notes and then they'd torture it out of them where the drops were. But when they'd torture one drop spot out of us we'd switch to another spot. No problem there. As soon as the heat was on one place we'd find another route because we didn't have anything else to do but dream up other ways to get the job done. So we always stayed ahead of them.

They'd usually beat us up in the quiz room, send us back to our cell and put us in hand cuffs behind the back for maybe two, three or even four weeks. It just depended on their mood at the time. We never knew how long we were going to be in cuffs. God, a guy would come back from a quiz, maybe our next door neighbor. He'd been caught tapping or something like that. They'd take him down and beat the hell out of him, put the hand cuffs on, bring him back and throw him in the cell. Then just as soon as the guard would walk away the first thing that son of a bitch would do was get on the wall and give us a "Shave and a Haircut" to tell us what had happened. Then they also started putting guys in the bomb shelters.

After Hayden and I wrote our synchronized names lists, we were sent back to our cell. Then we were told that we would be punished because we had communicated. This time we were put in loose hand cuffs behind our backs. Every cell had a little bomb shelter that was dug underneath the bed platform. It was about six feet deep, and one foot long by two feet wide.

They put me down in the bomb shelter first, handcuffed behind my back, and I lived down there for about a week. Hayden lived up on the bed so he would go out and get the chow and hand it down to me. Then the next week he lived in the bomb shelter and I lived up on the bed. Hayden and I both thought that was the greatest thing in the world to get down in that bomb shelter for a week. When we were down there the guards didn't come in and harass us.

Except one day when I was down in the bomb shelter we had some real excitement. A snake crawled into our room under the crack of the door. Now I was standing there with my face looking at about floor eye-level and only two feet away from the door. Suddenly this guy was staring right at my face. Well I started screaming and yelling and then Hayden, on the bunk above me, saw it. This damn thing was a Krait, in the pit viper family. They are incredibly poisonous snakes. So Hayden started yelling and screaming and jumping up and down on the bed above me, trying to shoo this thing back out under the door. Finally, instead of coming over and nailing me in the face it turned around and went back out the door. After that, along with my first experience with the cobra when I was evading capture, I was sick and tired of looking poisonous snakes in the face!

We finally got out of cuffs and a couple of months later the sensitivity in our hands and arms was starting to come back. We were at the point where we could actually move our fingers and squeeze our hands shut, though with not much strength. It was a gradual healing process though even six months after the hell cuffs, the backs of our hands and thumbs were still dead. We could stick pins or pinch the back of our hands and thumbs and not feel anything. Then after about eight or nine months our hands and arms were back to normal. We both had heinous scars on our arms where the cuffs had cut in. Almost everybody had those scars after a number of years. Some guys' scars stayed permanently while for most of us they eventually went away. We proudly wore our "Vietnamese bracelets."

The food during this time after the war tribunal had been absolutely horrible. Hayden and I were down to skin and bones. Hayden was five-ten and normally about 175 pounds, though he told me at one time he weighed over 200 and was fat as a grape. But at this time I would guess he was weighing 125 dripping wet. I was probably tipping the scales at about 130.

We had god damn boils all over us. Hayden, that bastard, used to open boils for me on my back. I've got a scar or two back there today from his surgery. Actually he did a pretty good job. We used a sharpened nail and a lit cigarette to sterilize the tip. We sharpened the nail to a needle-sharp point by rubbing it on the concrete. We would open the boil with the nail and then squeeze the core out of it. Then we would wash it with some soap and drinking water. It worked.

Hayden and I started to notice that our feet hurt like hell, especially during the night. Others in camp had the same symptoms. It turned out that we were suffering from beriberi, a vitamin B1 deficiency disease. We also experienced diarrhea and dysentery. Our food rations were not only insufficient in quantity but also in quality. The malnutrition we were experiencing was such that we were even more exposed to various diseases and infections.

One other incident was how the Gooks attempted to blackmail some of us. Frenchy called out two of my friends and told them that the Gooks knew these American guys had slept with whores in Thailand. He said their intelligence gave them the names of the whorehouse and the whores, and the guys who visited them.

These guys told us the information the Gooks had was bona-fide. It appeared that the Gooks did get the information sent from Thailand all the way back to Hanoi from some communist Thai whores, with specifics about who had done what. The bosses in Hanoi sent it out to the Briar Patch and the camp officers tried to use it on these guys, to force them to comply with whatever they wanted.

Our guys just said, "Fuck you, go ahead and print it. I don't give a shit!" Of course when those guys were sitting in a prison like they were, not knowing whether they were ever going to get out, the fact that they screwed a whore didn't mean much. So the blackmail didn't work. But it was attempted.

Around Christmas time one night we were taken to a flat lawn area near where the Gooks lived. A movie truck drove into the camp. They set up a movie screen and then showed us one of their shit movies. They propped blankets up on bamboo poles in such a fashion that each prisoner was separated from the others, to keep us from communicating with our buddies while we were watching the movie. We were in individual stalls, looking out at the movie, which was crazy in itself. It showed the demented minds these characters have.

All this time their big concern was who we knew because they were trying to keep our identities a secret from each other. Only a few names had been released to the world, the guys who were writing letters. All the other guys' names were not released. They were keeping it a big secret. I'm sure they had intended to keep guys as long as they felt like. Or that they could kill anyone they wanted and no one outside would know. It was part of their basic program.

Christmas came and the Gooks rolled out a big meal for us. We had turkey, fruit, candy and all this bull shit. We even got a beer at Christmas. New Year's was the same thing. Then something happened and they decided to increase the food. They started putting manioc root in the soup. They also started putting it in the rice and they began giving us more rice to eat. Then we started putting on a little weight. This went on for about a month or so, until we moved out of The Briar Patch.

The treatment also improved in late December and January. But they did call out Shumaker and one or two other guys in January to torture them for little special deals they wanted. A couple of other guys got mashed for communicating. But overall they had finished their eight-month rampage through the camp and the guards stopped the intensive harassment.

That winter they built trenches throughout the camp. These trenches ran through each section of the camp and into the courtyard. They ran to a central point at the gate and then from the gate they went on outside. These trenches were about five or six feet deep. One night they came down and got us, put us in hand cuffs and told us to be barefoot. They took us out and started walking us down these trenches, then outside the camp with guards on either side of us.

Then they made us dog trot in the trenches for a distance of a mile or better. They had dug them as a security measure, in case of the need to evacuate the camp in an attempted American rescue. It was incredible to see what those little bastards could do with a shovel! They could just dig a damn ditch all the way around the world! It meant nothing to them whatsoever. They just got a million Gooks out there and started digging. It might take them forever but they could build a Great Wall of China or whatever they needed to do. No project was too big for them when it came to manual labor because labor was nothing to those people. If they had made us dig those trenches we all would have died due to our poor physical conditions. Plus there would then have been a constant danger of escape.

About a mile away from the camp, at the end of the trenches, they had dug holes in the sides of the walls and put in wooden doors. They had dug individual little cages into the sides of the walls and they ran us down there several different nights as a practice drill. They put us in these little cages during their general quarters drill.

On February 2nd 1967, trucks came into the camp and evacuated half of us to a new camp we called "Little Vegas." Hayden and I were in that group. The other half of the camp went to The Zoo.

Apparently the Gooks decided to abandon The Briar Patch. I think it was for security, and because it was too miserable a place to keep Americans alive. I think they realized we were all going to die if they kept us there in those conditions. They thought it would be better to move us back to Hanoi.

Looking back at the Briar Patch now, I think the Gooks made a big mistake. And in later years they realized it. They even told us so and they were embarrassed about it. It was a Hell on earth for the men who lived out there at Briar Patch, a needless Hell on earth. The primary reason was because of outside events in the war and how Ho Chi Minh reacted to them. Apparently Uncle Ho was unhappy about the way the war was going and he had his underlings take it out on the easiest targets he had, POWs.

The second reason for the hell was our camp commander. The camp commander always had a lot to do with the way we were being treated. This camp commander, Frenchy, chose to ignore the treatment we were getting. He'd never walk down into the camp to see what was going on. He'd just look the other way when the guards did things. So the young guards had free rein to pester us as much as they wanted and the interrogators could do anything they wanted.

I want to emphasize again that the most important thing for us, and the biggest reason for our outstanding performance at The Briar Patch, was our communications with each other.

They learned at The Briar Patch that the only way to get anything from us was to pound us and that's what they did. They pounded us and got what they wanted until they were satisfied with their efforts. But it didn't do them any good. It was worthless to them because we all stuck together in what I think was a pretty terrific performance. I can't think of a group of 54 men I have ever known, or ever will know, whom I feel more strongly tied to and more proud of.

19. Little Vegas

2/2/67 – 10/25/67

On the evening of February 2nd 1967 trucks drove into The Briar Patch and we loaded aboard. As usual we were blind-folded and as usual Hayden and I were handcuffed together. I think Hayden and I spent half our lives being handcuffed together one way or another. Then we took that ass-busting trip back to Hanoi again. We had no idea what camp we'd be going to. We kind of thought we'd be going back to The Zoo. Then we rolled into the downtown area and pulled up at a wall.

We were let out of the truck and walked through a gateway entrance down a short corridor. We were seeing this under our blindfolds by peeking around them with the guards leading us. We were led into a cell block complex that had divided rooms and we were put into one of them. It was a four man room with two double bunks. Hayden and I were put in with Bob Shumaker and Bob Peel.

I had seen Bob Peel a few days before we left The Briar Patch. Hayden, Bob, Shu and I were called out to a quiz together. They had four stools and we sat down in front of Frenchy. He said, "Now because of the lenience of the Vietnamese people and the humane treatment we are going to let you live together. But you will have to write that you will obey the camp regulations." Shu, being the senior man there, was of course the first one to speak. He said, "Smack it up your ass!" The rest of us did likewise. So Frenchy said, "Very well, go back to your cells." Hayden and I went back to ours, Bob went back to his and Shu went back to his with Smitty Harris.

We knew that a move was coming and we figured we might be going to another camp and that we were going to live together. About an hour later we were called back to quiz again.

This time he said, "What camp regulations would you obey?" The camp regulations said stuff like you will not communicate and you must realize you are a criminal and all this other stuff. There were some innocuous regulations that said you must keep your room clean and when you have a health problem you must tell the guard. So we told them we'd obey those two regulations and he said, "That's not good enough."

We went back to our cells again and in another hour we were called out again. Obviously this move was coming fast and they were having pressure on them to have us four live together, whether we kicked Frenchy in the head or not. It was obvious that it was going to happen. This time he said, "You don't have to write a statement. All you have to do is tell me you will obey the camp regulations." We wouldn't do that.

So Frenchy sat there for a long time and finally he said, "Shumaker, all I want you to say is a word, just say yes." Shu said, "Why do you want me to say yes?" Then Frenchy sat back in his chair and beamed! He said, "All of you go back to your cells, you will be allowed to live together in the future." Gooks! It's unbelievable what went on in their little brains!

So we teamed up together there and it turned out this was a brand new camp we named "Little Vegas" It was actually the Northeast complex of Hoa Lo. We did not recognize where we were at first. We were in this cell block and it seemed like we were underground. All the walls were very wet and damp. It was the rainy season and it was also very cold. The outside temperature was low and we were freezing our balls off. That night when we came in we were taken out of our cells to a shower room. We were allowed to wash our hands and faces there and clean up a little bit. Then we were put back in our cell.

We didn't go outside during the day for the next few days. Were we able to go out and shower, at night, in these little shower rooms only every couple of days. We still hadn't figured out where we were. But as we began to talk to the guys in the cell block we got our computations of the way we'd come together and we began to study the structure itself including the way the walls were made. We climbed around in the cell and peeked out the upper windows. In a couple of days we figured out we were in a section of the Hanoi Hilton.

This section had been unknown to us, as we'd never known what existed over on this side. These cell blocks had been open bays, capable of holding forty or so prisoners. Gooks had prepared it for us by dividing it off into inside rooms with brick and concrete walls. Each cell block had a wall down the center with rooms on either side. The rooms were very small and crowded.

We started getting contact with the guys around us. John Heilig was one of the first. He had been in Heartbreak and was moved over to Little Vegas about the same time we came in. We also made contact with some newly-downed guys. This was really thrilling for us because we had not had any opportunity so far to get contact with new people.

As it turned out, we were a little disappointed when we did make contact with the new guys because they were not particularly optimistic about the war. Almost all of them told us that nobody in the outside world knew anything about POWs or was even thinking about POWs. We were kind of forgotten people. This was February of 1967, so it was particularly disappointing for the four of us to find out that nobody knew we existed. Each of us had spent in the neighborhood of two years there already.

There was another big "peace scare," our term for the phony U.S. cessation of bombings. Communications were supposedly going on between President Ho Chi Minh and President Johnson. Actually President Johnson had written a letter through diplomatic channels. I believe it was sent through Poland and China to North Vietnam. It was a secret message and Ho Chi Minh had responded to it through an open letter.

The Gooks told us this and we were hearing on Hanoi Hannah that Ho Chi Minh had told LBJ in so many words to jam it up his ass. Ho Chi Minh had also done a pretty foolish thing by responding to President Johnson's letter in the open. That ruined any opportunity for the diplomatic secrecy that should have been taking place. He could have responded in kind and respected diplomatic channels but he did not. This was another cessation in the bombing of Vietnam so things were at a standstill as far as we were concerned. We were just sitting around there while our government was playing around with peace proposals.

The food was better at Little Vegas than what we had at The Briar Patch. We were still eating rice and there was no bread available. But we were getting more of it and the soup they were serving was better. The pumpkin soup would sometimes have a few onions in it and a few pieces of meat so it tasted pretty good. The side dishes we were getting would often be green beans with pork fat. The medical treatment also improved. There were a couple of medics running around the camp and they even had a doctor who periodically came in and out.

The doctor was around because a lot of the new shoot downs had come in badly injured. Air Force Captain Hiteshew was one. His legs were all smashed up and he was in a full body cast. He was in terrible condition. There were other guys like him who were badly injured, so the doctor was running around providing some semblance of medical treatment.

Through our communication system with other cell blocks, we put up a camp-wide "Name the Camp" contest. Some guy came up with the idea of "Little Vegas." I don't know who it was. We all liked it so we adopted it. The cell blocks were named accordingly. When we first moved into Little Vegas we were living in the Thunderbird. Other cell blocks were named

Desert Inn, Stardust, Golden Nugget and so on.

Treatment of the new shoot-downs was particularly brutal. They were being brought in and immediately placed in "The Straps." The Straps is a torture with long nylon straps. They tied our hands behind us very tightly, usually with ropes. Then they tied up our arms. Sometimes they used a piece of wire or string to bind our thumbs together. Then they would tie the strap to our ankles, roll us up backwards into a ball, and then pull our feet up to the back of our head. Then they'd run this strap down across the front of us and around on either side.

A couple of Gooks would stand above the POW, who was stomach to the ground. They would put their feet on us and yank up on the straps. This would cinch our legs up clear back over our head so far that we could look up and see our toes out in front of our head. Then they'd just tie us very tightly in this ball position, kick us around the room and then just leave us for a couple of hours. The pain was unbelievable!

They also put us in a sitting position with our arms and hands strapped together behind us and they would pull our arms up toward our head. The bad thing about The Straps is that many guys got their shoulders dislocated. There were also guys with broken arms who were placed in The Straps. Some had nerves cut from broken bones being crunched around. Some lost the use of arms or hands from The Straps.

Sometimes they would hang guys who were tied up like this from a hook that was on the wall or overhead beam. This was terrible torture and no one could resist it. And this was how they began to interrogate new shoot-downs.

The mastermind of torture in Heartbreak Hotel turned out to be The Bug. He was the senior officer in the Heartbreak area and all the new shoot-downs came to him first. He had left The Briar Patch a couple of months before we did and had gone back to Heartbreak to run the torture program. He had four or five henchmen there who were particularly brutal guards. They were picked for their meanness and their love for this particular duty. They were all trained in torture and they ran quite a show there.

The ostensible goal of torturing the new shoot-downs was to get military information and biographical information. But in reality the Gooks didn't want much military information. They only asked simple things like, "What was your squadron?" And they would always ask guys the question, "What are the next targets?" But they knew that we didn't know what the next targets were. No pilots knew what the next targets were going to be, for obvious reasons.

The Gooks found out very early in the war that we really didn't have any idea what the coming targets would be. However they used that as an excuse to torture. Essentially it was more about their insane desire to kick our asses off. They hated us. We were "criminals." We were taller then they were, our eyes were different, our skin color was different. We were Americans. We were more intelligent than they were and they knew it. We had been bombing their country and killing their people. And they had a perfect opportunity to kick the hell out of us. Ho Chi Minh had allowed them to do it so that's what they were doing. It was just mostly about vindictiveness and getting even.

Tet came in February and the Gooks put on a big blow out for it. They decorated a room between the Desert Inn and Stardust with lights, crepe paper and all kinds of bullshit. They gave us a big meal that day. Then the four of us got called out for a quiz with Frenchy. He gave us some wine to drink and some cookies to eat while he talked to us. They did this with everybody in the camp. Frenchy was now the camp commander of Little Vegas and he had been promoted from a bar and three stars to a bar and four stars. I guess he had done such a wonderful job for them out there at The Briar Patch that they figured he needed a promotion.

New guys continued to arrive and we continued to make contact with them. The Gooks began to put up severe pressure to stop our communications. They would catch guys communicating and react violently. They would take guys out of the quiz rooms, beat them around and put them in hand cuffs. Then they sent them back to their rooms and put them in stocks. Stocks had been installed in all the rooms when the place was rebuilt.

These new stocks had a little bit of a twist. Each bed had stocks at the bottom of it, but they were not designed like the ones in Heartbreak that had been built by the French. These stocks were made with extremely small leg holes so when we were clamped into them we could not rotate or twist our legs. They were just big enough to fit tightly against our ankles. This not being able to move around compounded our misery about a thousand percent. Everything here was tailored for Americans. The whole set up of the camp was designed for us. The guard's duties were to run around and harass people with bowing and to try to prevent us from communicating with each other. They were really not there to guard us but to abuse us.

In addition to trying to get propaganda they were pushing in other directions. For instance, they were pressuring some guys to read news on the camp radio. They would come up with little news bulletins. They were translations of their own crap and they wanted Americans to read them instead of having an interrogator do it. When the interrogators read it no one could understand them so they wanted someone we could understand to do it.

Back at The Briar Patch they had gotten a couple of guys to read over the radio by pressuring them. These guys had done a beautiful job. They'd read the stuff and screw it up. They used ridiculous accents, like hillbilly accents. The Gooks hadn't really been able to catch on to what was going on. So it actually turned out be outstanding entertainment at The Briar Patch. Hayden and I would look forward to it everyday when these particular guys came on and read this shit. It was hilarious!

They were trying to do the same thing at Little Vegas. Only the word was out from the senior ranking officers to strongly resist this. Reading bulletins singled you out and always led to other things. Our SROs said, "Don't give them anything. Fight every attempt for propaganda. Maintain your military bearing and military discipline." There were quite a few high ranking officers in Little Vegas. We had some Lt. Colonels and several Commanders, including Commander Stockdale who was the senior ranking officer in the camp. They passed out reams of other policy guidelines to us. They did this courageously with little regard for their own personal safety.

That spring the treatment began to get worse and worse. In April the Gooks came out with what they called a new policy. This policy stated, "There were two ways." Frenchy would get on the radio and read this stuff over and over, for hours on end. He'd say, "There are TWO WAYS! TWO WAYS!" and on and on with that shit! In other words one was to live by going along with all the camp regulations and whatever else the Vietnamese people wanted us to do. We had to surrender to the Vietnamese people. The other way was the way of death, and that was what we all were doing.

They were dead serious about this. They called people out to quizzes and beat them around. When they saw that wasn't doing any good they intensified their orneriness. Then they started saying on the speakers that, "Some of the criminals in the camp had refused to listen to the fact that there were two ways." They went on with, "Some of the criminals in the camp, not many, some, not many, have a bad attitude. Most of the criminals in the camp are going along with the new policy and have realized their crimes but some, some…"

We knew this was all nonsense since we had pretty good communications with everyone. That meant that now we could see the

Gooks didn't know the extent of our communications. We could see the importance of our communication. It was especially necessary when a guy was in solitary confinement for a long time. It was vital for everyone to know that everything the Gooks said was pure bullshit.

They said, "Some of you criminals have not understood the new policy and some of you have even refused to understand the new policy. Those of you who fit into this category are doomed to big trouble, big trouble!" So we were.

They started kicking everybody's ass around the camp. They went in heavy with this bowing thing. We'd go out of our room and the turnkey would have a couple of guards grab us by the hair. When they would open our door to go out to get chow, for instance, they'd slap us around, kick us, yank our heads down and make us bow all the way down. This went on every time the door opened. They'd come around to our window and flip the peek hole open, then just stand there and look in on us. This would happen 20 or 30 times a day and everybody would have to get off their beds, stand in the middle of the room and bow to the little bastards! This went on constantly, day and night. We developed a hatred that was unbelievable.

Then they intensified their harassment and torture even more. They had two Vietnamese women who filled up the water pots. Before they had us put them outside our door so they wouldn't look into our cell. But now they'd come around, flip the peek open and scream and spit in at us. The guards would be out there and they'd open our cell door because we hadn't bowed to the little bitch. They'd make us sit down on our bunks and then let the little Vietnamese gals go in and slap us for not having bowed to them. Then the guards would come in and beat us up for not bowing to the women. Then to add to our punishment the little gals would only fill up our water jugs about a third of the way full, so we were always hurting for water.

They gave us dried fish from Korea. This stuff was a paste of mostly bones and scales, and it was very heavily salted. It was terrible tasting stuff. Of course we ate it because otherwise we'd starve but it created a big need for water. So we were thirsty all the time because they'd never give us enough water to drink. We were not just thirsty but dehydrated. Being thirsty 24 hours a day for months on end was in itself enough to drive us over the brink.

One day we went out to the shower with the guard kicking and harassing us and making us bow to various people as we went through the yard. Bob Peel and I went into the shower room together. Bob had a good temper on him like I did. Neither one of us felt like taking any shit off the guards at any time so we harassed them as they were harassing us. We came out of the shower and wouldn't bow so the guard came over and started beating us. Bob walked over to the clothes line where he had a shirt hanging up and he was so pissed off that he just yanked his shirt off the clothes line. When he did the clothes line broke and this really tore the guard up.

As we walked back to our cell the guard was beating on Bob all the way, hitting him in the back and in the head. Bob, Hayden and I got pissed off so we all stopped, turned around and glared at this guy. That scared him. Then we went on back into our cell. That night they came in and put Shu and Hayden in stocks on their bunks.

They put Bob and me in a small shower room, out in the open with no ceiling, with hand cuffs behind our backs and our feet in leg irons on the floor of the shower. It was wet and miserable. The guards made it much worse at night by coming around and turning the spigots on to let the water flow out onto the floor. This attracted mosquitoes in such great numbers they would just be a black cloud and they would chew on us all night long. I almost lost my mind from those mosquitoes, it was so intense.

Finally, after a week of this they took Peel and me out of the showers and put us in a cell together in the Golden Nugget. We stayed there for a few days and got in contact with a new guy who was living next door. We taught him the Tap Code. He was Air Force Captain John Clark. We had a good peek from this cell and could see guys going to and from the showers. We also got contact with some new guys around the corner that were badly injured.

After a few days in this cell they moved us into the Stardust, in the smallest cell I've ever been in. This cell was about four and half feet wide by about six feet long. You had to turn sideways to access a six inch wide aisle. There was one bunk about waist level and another at about eye level. This was where Bob and I lived 24 hours a day. We were never allowed to exercise or go outside or to do anything. We just stayed in this dingy room all day long. We sat on Bob's bunk and whispered to each other. If we talked in anything above a whisper the guards would come in, pound the hell out of us and accuse us of communicating.

They instituted strict regulations on getting up and going to bed. When the gong rang in the morning we had to fly out of the sack, roll up our mosquito net, fix our blanket just so, and it was never right. They went nutty on how we had to roll up our blanket and mosquito net. They did a lot of harassing on just how our bunk looked. If we weren't out of the sack, of course they'd come in and kick the hell out of us. We were not allowed to sleep until siesta. When siesta came we had to sleep whether we wanted to or not. We had to be in our bunk lying down and looking like we were asleep. When the siesta bell rang we had to get up with the same deal. Then when the gong went off at nine o'clock at night we had to be in our bunk the instant the gong went off. Despite all the mosquitoes at night we were not allowed to put up our mosquito nets till nine o'clock.

But at nine o'clock our mosquito net had to be instantly up and we had to be in our bed. They had us coming and going. Guards would slam our window open either two seconds before the gong went off or two seconds after. Obviously we were wrong either way. Either it was up or it wasn't or we were in or we weren't. So we caught a big load of crap no matter what. These were just some of the things they did to harass us. The mental pressure became extreme for all of us. I think this was the point in prison life when some guys started cracking.

We noticed the affects of the mental strain in many of our buddies. Some of them came to quite a dangerous level. For myself, I went completely into a shell. I just felt enormous bitterness and hate around the clock, 24 hours a day. I hated anything and everything that had to do with the Gooks. It was an all-consuming hatred. I couldn't think about anything else except how much I hated Gooks. They were on us all the time. The pressure was always there. We all lapsed into one form or another of mental disorder at this point.

In May there was another peace scare. This one lasted about five days. The Gooks started increasing the food a little bit again and they eased off the pressure some. Previously they had given us our cigarettes through the hatch. Then they'd come around to give you a light three times a day. A guard would stick a lit punk in the window and we'd get a light. Here at Little Vegas they wanted us to bow when the hatch came open. So Bob and I, living together, decided we wouldn't smoke. We quit because we were not going to bow for cigarettes, and we told the Gooks so.

After a few weeks they came around and tried to get us to start smoking again. They said, "When the guard comes to give you your cigarettes you do not have to bow." Peel and I said, "Fuck you. You can take them and jam them. We could care less about them!" This irritated them quite a bit.

During the peace scare they had a big room shuffle in the camp. Peel and I were moved in with two other guys who were new shoot-downs. They were Air Force Captain Bud Flesher and Air Force Captain John Fer. We were back in a four man room again. It was absolutely wonderful to get in room with these new guys and for the first time in two years to be able to talk with somebody about the outside world. There was so much to find out. We knew absolutely nothing that had been going on outside of our prison existence.

Bud told us about movies, cars, and just all the new things that had happened. John knew a lot about the political affairs that had been playing out in our country. They were a tremendous boost for Bob's and my morale.

At the same time, the Gooks put a top security clamp-down on communications. It was I believe the biggest effort on their part that ever existed at any prison I was in. They brought more guards into the camp. They had them posted 24 hours a day in the hall way of our cell block, listening for any noise. If we even sneezed or coughed they'd be in our cell.

As soon as the short peace scare was over the U.S. started bombing Vietnam again. We hit the big bridge outside Hanoi and there were some really good air raids going on. The air raid sirens were going all the time and we could hear the bombing.

The Gooks got really schizophrenic about the whole thing. They were having pep rallies every night right outside our cell block. All the guards and officers would go to these pep rallies and they'd sit out there and chant and sing songs. The government was producing a lot of beer to give them at these pep rallies too. So they would drink a lot of beer and get done about 9 o'clock at night. Then they would come back to our cell block in full force for some nighttime harassment. They would walk in with the interrogators leading the pack. They'd randomly go around, open cell doors and pound on guys. Sometimes they'd come in and put everybody in stocks. It was just wild. They were absolutely insane!

During all this lunacy, my morale got two boosts. One was because, as I mentioned before, I finally got my infected toe cured by Bud Flesher. The other was hearing from Bud and John about what was going on in the outside world. Both guys were very optimistic about the war ending soon. In a situation like we were in we tended to believe what we wanted to believe. I made it this far, more or less keeping myself psyched up by always being on what I called "my six month program."

This consisted of planning for my release to be within a six months to one year period. No matter how bad things looked I tried to keep this outlook for the whole eight years. I think this helped keep me on a relatively even mental keel. There were times it was difficult to believe that I was going to be released in six months to a year. There were other times, when there was some really big peace scare, that it was difficult to convince myself it was going to be as long as six months.

With that outlook I'd spend lots of time planning vacations with my family. I'd plan them for the season of the year that I was going to get out. I would plan vacations to all different parts of the world. Then months would go by and it would be a different season and I'd start my planning all over again. At first these vacations were fairly small, just normal things. Then they became more elaborate and that helped a lot. I would make plans for day by day, minute by minute. Of course every one of them turned out completely different when I came home. But that didn't matter because I maintained sanity over the years by keeping my mind active with vacation planning.

When I was in solitary confinement I had made a list of all the popular songs I knew the words to. It took considerable effort over several months to come up with the words to the ones I knew. I had to think back to places I'd been when I had heard the songs; associating the songs with places and times in my life. I had them alphabetically listed in my mind. Then I created a mental juke box. I discovered, as I paced around my cell, that I could plug in any singer or orchestra that I wanted into my mental juke box. I'd just start by saying a number to myself, like 23. Then I would picture this record flopping down in my juke box and it would begin to play. With practice this thing became so real it seemed to blot out the whole world around me. It was an escape mechanism.

Bud knew a lot of movies, songs, poetry and stuff like that. So I started learning them from him. John knew a lot too. So I added songs to the ones I already knew by getting a song a day from Bud and John. They both knew lots of lyrics and between the two of them I could usually construct an entire song. As time went on, I'd get them from guys who lived next door and they'd tap the words over to me. I also got them from other roommates. For a couple of years I played this silly game until I had over two hundred songs in my mental juke box. And then at some point I got tired and stopped adding to it. But I still have that juke box in my head. Even today it's fun to plug a song into my personal juke box.

One day around the first part of June, Bud was up on the top bunk looking out the window into the alley way. He was trying to contact a new guy who had just moved in a cell down the way. There was a Gook posted in the alleyway, sitting out there on a chair. But we didn't know he was there because he was out of sight to us. He'd been sitting there quietly all day long. So when Bud called out to the new guy all hell broke loose out there. In a matter of minutes the Gooks were in our cell in force. They yanked Bud out, took him to interrogation and he didn't return. They started to work him over down there like they always did when they caught us communicating. It was something they always used as an excuse to try to extract propaganda from us.

We found out they were trying to get a tape recording from Bud. They wanted him to say he apologized for having broken camp regulations. They thought this would lead to some worthwhile propaganda for them. They had him on his knees 24 hours a day, kicking him around. Then they moved him out into a shower.

One day the Gooks came in to our cell with an interrogator who was a real bad actor. We called this guy "Little General," or "Greasy." Greasy spoke excellent English and he was a particularly egotistical Gook; a real nasty bastard. Greasy opened our cell door and started talking to Fer, Peel, and me. He was all smiles but he was being very evil as always. He mentioned something about delegations arriving in Hanoi and asked if any of us would like to go see a delegation.

Of course, we said, "No." Then he said, "I think maybe one of you will be allowed to see the delegation." We said, "Delegation, hell, we want nothing to do with it!" He just smiled, shut our cell door and left. A day or so later Bob was called out to an interrogation. He was gone for several hours and when he came back to our cell he was really dejected. He walked into the cell, sat down on the bunk and said, "Phil, they've appointed me to see the delegation."

I was the senior ranking officer in the room at that moment so I started encouraging Bob about what he should do. I explained what he already knew. I was just trying to bolster his morale and will to resist a little bit. I told Bob he had to resist with everything he had. But if he was broken and had to go see this delegation it wouldn't make any difference when he got there. I told him he should just go ahead and forget the crap they had pounded into him about saying their scripted answers. I told him to always show the Gooks we have faith in our country, in our cause, that we know we are here to support our allies and all that good stuff. I told him to fight it with everything he had.

He said, "All right, of course that's what I'll do." That afternoon Bob went out and he didn't come back. They moved his gear out later that night and he was gone from us. We later found out they worked him over. Then they put him in irons and continued the torture. He gave them a good fight. He fought such a good fight for about a month or so that they finally gave up on him. I don't know if they got somebody else but Bob didn't have to go meet this delegation. They just considered him too unreliable. They didn't want to put him in front of a delegation and have him say the wrong things. Bob really had put great courage on the line.

While I was encouraging Bob in our cell, unbeknownst to us, a guard and Greasy were standing outside our room listening to what I was saying. So that afternoon when they took Bob out they also took John Fer out to a quiz. They tied him up in The Straps, rolled him into a ball and tortured him for an hour. Then they untied him and sent him back to our room. He was just stumbling when he returned. The guards kicked him into the room.

I caught him and kind of half picked him up, but he was really torn up. He was tortured so badly that his lower arms, hands and feet were dead. He began to explain what had happened. He had gone into this quiz and Greasy had told him, "Fer, you are a very, very foolish man. You listen to the wrong people. You listen to people who have bad attitude. Now I will teach you that you should not listen to people who have bad attitude. You and those people will be severely punished."

Then they put him into the ropes for an hour and sent him back to me. Greasy was big on this stuff. He was trying to freak us out. They allowed me to sit there long enough to talk to John; I guess a half hour or so. Then the door opened and they told me to put my long pants and shirt on and they took me to an interrogation. I knew what was coming. I knew I was going to get pounded. But I had no idea how bad it was going to be.

I walked into the quiz room and sat down on a stool in front of Greasy. He folded his hands and put them out on the table. He got a big, nasty smile on his face and said, "Who are you?" I said, "Lieutenant Phillip Neal Butler, United States Navy." He said, "What are you?" I said, "I'm a Prisoner of War." He said, "Who will win the war?" I said, "The Republic of Vietnam, and we will help them. They are our allies."

Then he sat back with a huge grin, put one arm across the back of his chair and said, "That is what I expected you to say, Butler. You are a very, very foolish man." Then a couple of guards came into the room and stood behind me. He said, "Now you must learn to obey the camp regulations. You must learn to be careful what you tell your friends. I will teach you. You must admit to me these three things. You must admit these things to me orally as I sit here at this table. There is no tape recorder, but you must admit to me now that you have no rank, that you are a criminal and not a prisoner of war, and that we will win the war. Also you will write the names of all the criminals you communicate with."

He said, "Now, I ask you again. Who are you?" I swallowed a couple of times, could feel my asshole start to pucker and felt the butterflies in my stomach. I said, "Lieutenant Phillip Neal Butler." I no sooner got that out of my mouth than a fist came from behind me and I was on the floor. I was kicked a couple of times, then picked up and put back on the stool. My ears were really ringing.

The worst beatings were when they had people standing behind me who were doing the whacking, or when I was blindfolded and they were beating me, because I never knew when it was coming. The fear of the unknown was just incredible, all-consuming. I was just so petrified it was indescribable. I could never find the words to describe that fear. I felt so helpless. I knew what was coming but I didn't know when it was coming or where it was coming from. When it did come it was a terrible shock.

Then they put me back on the stool and Greasy said, "What are you?" I said, "Prisoner of War." The same thing happened again and I was kicked off the stool onto and around the floor. They put me up on the stool again. He was sitting there smiling and he said, "Now, who will win the war?" I said, "The Republic of Vietnam would win with us as their allies," and then I got knocked off again. This time they picked me up off the floor, dragged me over to a wall, set me on my knees, shoved my face against the wall and twisted my hands behind me. They put on a set of hand cuffs, strapped ropes tightly around me, and then they put a heavy iron bar across my legs. They shackled this bar to my legs so it was resting on my Achilles tendons as I knelt there. The bar was about six feet long, an inch or so in diameter, and it was very heavy and extremely uncomfortable. Then he said, "You will stay in this position until you are ready to admit to me what I said." Then he walked out of the room.

They had a guard standing at the door. The weather was really hot. It was probably 120 degrees in that room. Within a matter of minutes all my clothes were soaking wet with perspiration from the effort of staying on my knees. This kneeling, sitting on the stool, holding our hands up in the air, or standing against the wall was something the Gooks used a lot. They forced us to punish ourselves. But what we were trying to do was buy time. It was important to buy time when they wanted something from us because you never knew when a new peace scare would come and then they'd drop us. They'd put us in those straps and torture us if we went in there and refused to do those things. That way they would get what they wanted within a matter of hours. That was our thinking at the time. So we would stay on our knees, hold our hand in the air or sit on the stool as much as we could, to buy time.

Looking back I think it was probably a mistake, and after 1970 or 1971 most guys began to change their philosophy, feeling it was an error. But by then the wholesale brutality had stopped anyway. Later on the senior ranking officers in the bigger camps where we were all together decided that it had been a mistake. So the policy was changed and we were no longer to subject ourselves to self-induced punishment.

Sometimes we were able to buy time with it and get off. This is one case where I did buy time, but it was expensive. I bought a little over two months of time but it was oh so expensive.

I stayed on my knees and in no time at all I was completely dehydrated. Greasy kept coming back into the room, asking me these questions every couple of hours or so. The guards came in with him and they'd knock me over and set me back up on my knees again. That evening he started going at it intensely. They stood me up in the center of the room. About every half hour they would come in and ask me these questions, knock me down onto the floor and kick me in the head and body. Then they'd yank me up again, grabbing me by the ears, stand me up and kick me over again. They had keys and cigarette lighters rolled up in their fists when they beat me with their fists. They kicked me in the stomach, the kidneys, and the back of my head, neck and face. They would stand on my head while I was down on the floor. One of them stood on the side of my head and bounced up and down. They even kicked me in the balls. They just generally pounded the hell out of me.

This went on through the night. The next day it was a lot of kneeling again. My knees started swelling up the size of basketballs and all the skin was torn off them. They began bleeding and got infected. I had cuts all over my body from one end to the other. They all got infected and I had little puss sacks all over my body from the bruises and wounds. They started kicking me around and holding me on my knees during the day and then at night they would go back to around the clock beatings. This went on for four days and nights.

It was a strange thing. Each time they would come in they wanted me to say these things. But I think more than anything else what kept me from doing it in the beginning was my anger and hatred. Later I wouldn't do anything because I didn't have my marbles anymore. They just beat me to a point where I didn't know my ass from my elbow. I was completely in a fog. I had concussions. Sometimes I didn't know who or where I was.

I remember it like a foggy nightmare. For two or three days I could see Gooks coming into the room, screaming. And then I could see the ceiling spinning around and this light bulb that hung over the interrogator's desk. It was whirling around my head like a merry-go-round. After a while I just more or less ceased to have any feelings for it. I can remember talking to people – my wife, my sister, father, my mother - with long conversations. They were very real to me. I remember strange music. I was completely out of my mind from all these beatings.

The guys in the other cell blocks knew I was out there and later they told me they could hear me, and the beatings going on, day and night. That's really tough, when you sit in your cell and listen to one of your buddies having that happen to him. They said they could hear me scream out names of people and just wild nonsense stuff.

At the end of the four days and nights I was just a bag of Jell-O. Then they dragged me by the leg irons out into the yard and over to a shower stall where they stuck me in. They tried to put me on my knees but I kept falling over. The guard kept coming in to set me back up on my knees but it didn't work.

I guess it was about the fifth day that I woke up. They had me stuffed over in the corner of the shower where it was shady and the Gooks were pouring cold water on me. I looked up with foggy vision. I had very little water to drink this whole time and now they were giving me some water to drink. I felt very cold and clammy. I knew then, even in my state of mind, that I had heat prostration. My tongue felt like it was five times normal size. All I could do was gurgle and mumble. One of my eyes was swollen shut and I could just barely peek out of the other one. I had blood all over me and my clothes were all torn up.

They kept on trying to make me kneel for a couple of days out in the shower. Finally one day, just out of the clear blue, they came in, took the cuffs and irons off and dragged me to a cell in the Thunderbird. They threw me in the cell onto a bunk board and put me in leg irons and hand cuffs behind the back. The bunk was next to a wall. And as soon as the guard left the room I heard a tap on the wall and I answered it.

It was Commander Bill Franke, and he said, "Are you all right, Phil?" I tapped back "I'm okay." He tapped back "My God, what have they done to you?" So I briefly explained what they wanted from me and what I'd done. He said, "God Bless you," and "You're fantastic!" and he tapped out a lot of other praise. I just sat there and leaned against the wall. Then finally the tears broke through. I just sat there and sobbed. I guess I was really feeling sorry for myself.

Bill tapped over a lot of encouragement and he said, "Jim Stockdale is in the next cell and he has some things he wants to tell you, some words for you." I said, "Okay, go ahead." So Jim got on the wall, and my hearing is bad and this was another cell down. I tapped over to Bill and said, "Bill, I can't hear him will you relay?" He said, "Okay." Commander Stockdale passed over the finest words of encouragement and praise I have ever had in my life. He said I had exhibited courage "above and beyond the call of duty," and that I was an example for everyone. He told me he would not forget what I had done after we were released. That brought me out of my stupor and made me realize who I was and where I was again.

Now I felt strong and I had my jaw set all over again. Those guys pumped me up so much I was ready to take more punishment. I was just waiting for those cock suckers to come into that cell so I could get back in that quiz room. I was ready to tell that bastard Greasy the same thing and go through it all over again.

I stayed there that night and then they came down and took me over to another cell block, the Desert Inn. They put me in an end room by myself. The guards had me sitting flat with my legs straight out and they fastened me into the stocks at the end of the wooden bunk. Then they took my right wrist and hand cuffed it to my left ankle so I was in a completely bent-over position. As I look back now this was one of my worst nightmares. In a short period of time I felt like every muscle in my back, shoulder, hips and right arm were being ripped apart. They left me in that incredible position for seven days and nights. It was something beyond horrible.

Somewhere during those seven days and nights a transformation came over me. My mind did something that never happened to me before nor has it since. I essentially became a wild animal. When a guard would come into the room to try to give me something to eat I'd spit on him. Of course he'd hit me. I'd scream and spit at anyone who walked in. All I could think about was how I could bite or tear at them like an animal would, if only they would get close enough to me.

Finally, on the seventh day, the camp doctor came to my cell and he looked in through the peek hole in the door. By that time I was ready when that little peek hole opened up; I would spit at it. He closed the peek hole and when the door opened I saw that he was a doctor. He was standing there in his white uniform. I knew who this doctor was, having seen him around the camp. He spoke French fluently and he also understood English very well. He could read it and write it. He came in with the turnkey and then dismissed him, sent him out. He told him to go away and lock the cell door.

The doctor locked himself in there with me. He sat down on the opposite bunk and I just snarled at him like an animal would. I tried to reach him to bite him but all I could do was spit at him. He just sat there and shook his head and said, "No, No, No." Then he showed me his little black bag and pointed to the wounds on my body and he motioned that he wanted to help me.

Well I guess that got through because even an animal wants to be doctored. He came over and unlocked the hand cuff that was hooked to my ankle. I just fell back on the bunk and lay there in complete exhaustion. He tore my trousers back and took my shirt off and started working on me. He cleaned my wounds and put iodine on all the cuts. As he worked on me I remember saying, "Pig, Vietnamese Pig, Lut!" Lut is the Vietnamese word for Pig. All the time the doctor kept working and he'd just shake his head and say, "No, No, No." I kept saying it to him, "You Vietnamese, You Pig, Swine!" Finally I gave up and let him finish working on me. I look back at it all now and I really admire him.

When he was finished he yelled out the cell door and the turnkey came back. The turnkey came over and took my right arm and tried to lock my wrist again. The doctor said a bunch of stuff to him in Vietnamese so the turnkey just cuffed my hands behind me and then they left. I suspect this doctor was responsible for my not going back and being tortured again to give the interrogator what he wanted. I'm almost sure he made them stop. It was one of the few cases I know about.

I think he was able to make them stop the torture because of the mental condition they'd reduced me to, a state of temporary insanity. Also I think they quit because they didn't really want propaganda or anything useful. It wasn't really anything the party or the command wanted. It was just this interrogator, Greasy, who was trying to salve his own ego. It was just a personal thing on the part of the interrogator.

As soon as they left the cell, with my hands behind me, I was able to get into the seam of my shorts and get my cuff key out. I unlocked one of them and fell back onto the bunk asleep. Sometime in the middle of the night, maybe two or three o'clock, I remember suddenly waking up. When I did I looked up at the door and the peek hatch was open. There was a

301

guard looking in at me. Now I was uncuffed. So I just very slowly slid my hands around behind me again and then I sat there and looked at him. Pretty soon he shut the window, walked away and I very quietly snapped my hand cuffs back on again.

I was really scared because I knew being caught out of cuffs like that would really be the living end. Up to this point I don't think anyone had ever been caught out of their cuffs. Guys had always been worried enough to keep the Gooks from finding out how we did this. We knew that they knew we could do it. But they had never caught anybody doing it because we were always too cagey. But here I'd been caught. I sat there waiting for the worst while the night went on and on. But that guard never came back and nobody ever came. I know that guard saw me out of those cuffs. I don't know if it was some humanity on his part. Or maybe it was just fear that if it had happened on his watch he'd get in trouble. Or maybe it was a combination of both. I guess I'm willing to give him a little credit and say there might have been a little human feeling on his part.

The next day they took me out of that cell and moved me back into my old cell block in the Stardust. I was put in a cell right across from Bud Flesher and John Fer. It was on the side of the building where the sun hits in the afternoon and they put me on the bunk next to the wall so I would suffer from the heat. They put me in stocks and hands cuffed behind me. I was just sitting there in my long clothes with no toothbrush, no soap, no bath, and no nothing. They came in to feed me twice a day. They let me out of irons once a day to take a shit and that was it. I sat that way for two months. I could tap on the side wall down to the next cell. It was a common wall that ran between the two rooms as opposed to joining the two rooms. We could tap effectively on it. There were four guys whom I was in good communication with and they could guard the entryway to the cell block. These guys talked to me as much as they could about everything in the world. They were a life saver.

They were Navy Lieutenant (jg) Coker, Air Force First Lieutenants Fred Flom, Leroy Stutz, and Hugh Buchanan. These guys kept me busy every day with jokes, bullshit stories and stuff we had done in the past. We talked about cars, motorcycles, fishing and just everything guys ever talk about; including girls and the times we got laid.

Our guys bombed heavily at various times. One of the heaviest bombings happened to be on my birthday, August 11th 1967. On August 10, 11, 12 they hit the big Hanoi bridge and we could see the sky full of flack. We could look up and watch the tracers going off in the sky. Jesus

Christ, it was the damnedest fireworks display I ever watched. The whole camp literally rocked and the noises were just deafening.

The Gooks were running all around and they made everybody get under their bunks. Not me of course because I was in stocks and cuffs so they just let me sit up there rather than take me out of the irons. I could still see the fireworks display. I was sitting there, scared shitless, though not for my own safety. I really didn't give a shit about myself at that point. Plus I guess I should say I just kind of had that blind faith that they wouldn't hit the camp.

What I was really scared about was for the guys up there flying. I couldn't believe anything could fly through that sky because every square inch of it was filled with lead. It was just incredible. That took courage! To fly a mission through that kind of shit at night where they could see the shells climbing up at them took a lot of guts. I never had to fly through flack like that myself, since we were bombing the southern part of North Vietnam. But just the little bit of flack that was thrown up at me during the early part of the war was enough to scare the piss out of me.

Something happened while I was in cuffs and irons that I will never forget. There was a family of sparrows up above my bunk in a hole in the wall. They had built a nest there. With sparrows, both parents take care of the young and it was really interesting to sit there and watch them all through those days. They hatched out their young and fed them and then finally the chicks tried to solo.

The day the babies soloed was a riot! I sat there in amazement and watched as the parents screeched and scolded and beat their wings to encourage them. It was really funny! Finally the parents were pushing the babies out of the nest. One of the little rascals couldn't hack it too well. He went into a half tail spin dive and landed right in my lap. Of course I was hand cuffed behind my back with both legs in stocks so I just sat there and laughed. There was this little fellow panting for all he was worth in my lap.

The parents didn't mind me because I had been pretty stationary there for all those weeks. They just considered me part of the scenery and they knew I wouldn't hurt them, or couldn't. They came down and landed in my lap too and went about their business to get him to launch off again. Finally he did. They succeeded with all their chicks. And I was really sad when they got all those little rascals soloed and they buzzed off out the window to make a life for themselves - in freedom. I was sad to see my cellmates leave me like that.

Finally, on September 1st the Gooks came into my cell and

unceremoniously unlocked me. Then they took me back to my old cell with Bud Flesher and John Fer. They had to help me because I could barely walk after being in stocks so long. And I was really a sight. Bob Peel was not back but there were Bud and John, sitting on their bunks with their legs in stocks. They said, "Welcome aboard, Buddy, good to have you back!" The guard motioned me to the top bunk above Bud and told me to get up there and get in stocks. He then took my handcuffs off. It was heaven to be back in the room with those guys, just to be in stocks and not to be handcuffed behind my back. We sat there and we bullshitted and bullshitted.

Then that night about nine o'clock the Gooks came around again and took us all out of stocks. They told us to stand in the middle of the room, but Bud couldn't stand because he'd been in stocks many weeks without ever being let out. He'd been in that same position and lost strength in his legs too. I couldn't stand either. So John stood while Bud and I sat on the bunks. The Gook interrogator came in. He read to us that we had been punished and we had paid for our errors. This would give us an idea of what we would go through if we were ever caught communicating again, and blah, blah, blah.

John and Bud had been put in these stocks, apparently due to the over-exuberance after one of the pep rallies. The Gooks came in one night and evidently picked their cell at random. Now we were let out of restraints. Most amazingly, it turned out that the reason they let us all out was the next day was September the 2nd, which is their National Day. Of course! We always celebrated their National Day.

It was another of those holidays when they'd let us have a halfway decent meal and give us some extra cigarettes and candy and shit like that. We celebrated their holidays and our holidays. I still can't believe it. They always gave us something extra on Christmas, New Year's, Easter, Tet, Thanksgiving, their National Day - September 2nd and even July 4th. I guess it was just part of their psychology. They thought they were showing us "the humane and lenient treatment" their government operated under. Ain't Communism wonderful!

The next day life went back to the way it was before, with the normal amount of harassment, the night time pep rallies and all that shit.

One night in early October all hell broke loose in another cellblock. The Gooks had come back one night from one of their pep rallies and then they started rampaging through the cell block. They got down to the room where Ron Storz, Marine Captain Orson Swindle, and two other guys were living. Those two were a couple of real hard-headed, tough-nut type guys.

Storz was probably one of the biggest knot-heads of all times. He had a nose of granite! He just wouldn't give a Gook the time of day and he'd go out of his way to provoke them. Sadly, Ron did not survive our POW experience.

The Gooks went charging into his cell and started to put him in leg irons. When they did his roommate started raising hell. While one of the roommates was protesting, the guards grabbed him. Then they started beating him up and throwing him into stocks. Then Storz got up and tried to intercede. Then they grabbed him and Storz started screaming "Torture, Torture!"

You could hear it all over the camp and the Gooks just went out of their minds! We could hear Gooks storming in from all over the camp! They ran into that cell and just beat the hell out of those four guys! They beat the living crap out of them! They threw them all in stocks, gagged them, blindfolded them, and tied them up. They really creamed them. One by one they took them out and put them in the shower stalls outside, put them in The Straps for several hours and just beat the shit out of them! They beat Ron up so bad they broke some of his ribs!

They kept this up for three days and then let three of the guys go back to their cell. They put Ron in a room located between two cell blocks, which we called The Tet Room. They put him in there on a stretcher because he was out of his mind! They cuffed him, hands and feet, to this stretcher on the floor. They just left him that way with his broken ribs and what have you.

Then they spread the other three guys around in different cell blocks. They brought Orson Swindle down to our cell block and put him in our room with us. This was about eight o'clock at night. He could barely walk he was so torn up. He couldn't move his arms at all because they were completely dead.

We put him up in the empty bunk. We got his mosquito net rigged up for him. We got some drinking water and some soap and started cleaning him up a little bit. Then he started telling us what happened. Meanwhile the Gooks were playing their little game again because Orson said, "You guys stop talking to me right now!" We said, "Why Oz, what the hell is wrong?" He said, "I've been sent here to be a stool pigeon." He said, "I'm supposed to find out from you guys how you communicate and who all you know. They want all the ways you do it. Then I'm supposed to report back to Greasy tomorrow." He said, "For God's sake don't tell me anything because I don't know if I have the courage to resist tomorrow at quiz. Just don't tell me anything!"

This was the first time this had happened and it scared us pretty bad. So we encouraged Oz and told him bullshit and told him to tell them whatever he had to tell them. We knew he was one of the toughest guys around. We told him not to worry about it. We said we didn't think they'd call him back anyway.

However he was with us for only one hour when they came and took him away. One of the other guys, George McKnight, had been put into a cell with Nels Tanner. Nels Tanner had been solo ever since 1966 when he was shot down. Nels was the guy who had used the phony name Clark Kent and all the stuff that had embarrassed the Hanoi government so badly.

They put George McKnight in with Nels as his first roommate. Nels was so excited he almost went nuts, finally talking face to face with the first American since he was captured. What a good deal for Nels, even though it turned out the Gooks were just parking these three guys briefly. In fact they were about to ship them off to another camp. But Nels got another roommate a little later on.

This other camp was the one we called "The Dirty Bird." I heard it was an old factory in the middle of town. It was located next to a big plant and a factory. They used these guys by parading them around in this area during the day so people on the streets would see them. The other purpose for parading the prisoners was so our intelligence would find out they had prisoners at this camp. The Vietnamese didn't think our guys would bomb the factory so close to where they were keeping our POWs.

I guess they were trying to find out if the Americans would bomb that damn factory with Yanks there. And they found out. Our guys went in and plastered the shit out of that place in the next few days. There was no doubt that they knew POWs were there at that time. But a war was a war and they jolly ass found out we were going to bomb targets that needed to be bombed.

This barrage on the target they thought was "protected" by POWs gave the Gooks shaky knees. So they brought these POWs back to Little Vegas and closed down The Dirty Bird. I understand it was never used after that.

None of our guys got hurt in the bombing. But they said it was the greatest air show they'd ever seen! Walls were falling in, plaster was falling and the Gooks were running and screaming. It was really terrific! You know as a POW, when your guys bring in-coming mail, what we called our bombs, you don't even think of it hitting you. At least I didn't and I don't think I was alone in that. I just thought about all those Gooks out there eating it big! We could hear them running through the rain and jumping into their wet foxholes in the middle of the night. Man, it's really great!

When Oz Swindle left us we were back to a threesome again. We had been in contact with a couple of guys in the next cell, Scotty Morgan and Tom Sima and we'd gotten pretty close to them. Then on October 25th, during siesta, the three of us were taken out of our cell and the two guys next door were taken out of their cell. They took us out into the court yard, stood us up against the wall and searched us. They also went through all of our gear. Then they loaded our asses and bags on a jeep carry-all and we drove out of the camp. We didn't know it at the time, but we were headed for a place where I was to spend another two and half years – The Zoo Annex.

The Little Vegas prison, from February 2nd of 1967 to October 25th 1967, was a strange place. The food was better than we had ever experienced before. There was more medical treatment available than ever before. But the mental pressure from constant harassment and the physical abuse were some of the most brutal we had ever experienced. I rate it along with The Briar Patch on a scale of pure misery. These two camps came right in a row and thank God I was never to experience a place that bad again. I had some rough times and treatment again in the summer of '68 and also in the summer of '69. But it was never to be quite so brutal for me again. I wish I could say the same for all the other guys. Some of them had it worse. The awful truth is there was no telling when any of us would catch it, anytime from 1965 to the end of 1969.

20. Zoo Annex — Part I

10/25/67 – 9/2/69

On October 25th 1967, John Fer, Bud Flesher and I were in our room just before siesta when the door opened. There was a guard who told us to roll up our gear and get ready for a move. There had been some moves going on in the last couple of days along with quite a few changes in the camp so we were anticipating this. We had hidden away our contraband, what little we had at this time, because the Gooks had been conducting inspections about once a week.

While we were inspected again in the yard, we noticed two other guys standing against the wall. They were Air Force Captains Tom Sima and Scotty Morgan. We were blindfolded and they gave us our bed rolls back, which we tucked under our arms. Then they led us blindfolded back through the kitchen area of Little Vegas, down to the alleyway and loaded us in a carry-all jeep.

This was perhaps one of the strangest moves I ever made because it was my only day time move other than the one when I was repatriated. There was heavy bombing in the Hanoi area but for some reason they decided they wanted to move us during siesta that day. We had driven only a short distance when we pulled into the back side of a brand new camp. This was another section of The Zoo we called "The Annex." It was a section none of us had ever seen, been in or knew anything about.

We drove in through a small gate, got out and were walked around a little pond into a room. There was plaster and cow shit all over the floor of the room. The floor itself was made of tile but the plaster and cow shit was about four inches deep. There were no beds or any place to lie down. There were Gooks working on the room as we were moving in. There was also work going on in the attic. They sat us down on the floor, left our hand cuffs on, left us blindfolded, and walked out of the room.

There were four vent holes in the ceiling that were covered over by wire mesh. These vent holes were round, about a foot and a half in diameter. There was a swiveling arrangement up in the attic that had four paddles on it. This thing swung around so the paddles, iron plates, could cover the vent holes. The workers had swung these iron plates aside from the holes so they could cover them with wire mesh. It was to prevent us escaping through the roof.

The ceiling was about 12 feet high. The back side of the room was a wall about three feet thick with a large window in it. The Gooks had constructed bars in this window from the inside of the room and on the outside they had constructed swinging flap doors that locked shut. The front side of the room also had very thick walls. There were doors on the inside of the front wall and also on the outside, both of which locked. There were also four ventilation holes in the floor that led to the outside. They had bars in them and also barbed wire mesh. These vent holes were about 2 feet wide and 8 inches high.

We discovered we were in a building that had two of these rooms. The adjoining room was identical to ours but opposite in configuration. Ordinarily we would have shared the same court yard but the Gooks had divided it by building a wall that was about 10 feet high with barbed wire on top of it. Our little court yard was about ten feet deep and 18 feet long. There was a well and an outdoor crapper in our courtyard. Next to the well was a small concrete stand and tank for washing clothes. Relatively speaking, it looked like a pretty nice arrangement. Our new room was big, probably 18 feet wide by 20 feet in depth and we were pretty tickled because it was the first time five people had been together.

The Gooks finally took the blindfolds and hand cuffs off and there we were. We immediately began asking the Gooks if we could clean the place up because we were absolutely filthy. It was impossible to stay clean because beside all the cow shit that was all over the floor, there was powdery plaster that floated around every time you moved.

That afternoon the "Goose," or "Shitty Slim" of The Briar Patch and Little Vegas fame, came around. He was to be our turnkey. He opened our door and told us we could draw buckets of water. He gave us a shovel to clean the cow shit out of the room and to try to clean the place up.

We worked at cleaning the room all afternoon. As we shoveled stuff out of the room we occasionally noticed pieces of film, like 16mm film, nails, pieces of wire and all kinds of stuff. Shitty Slim kept his eye on us so I was only able to steal four or five nails and a couple of pieces of wire. We got the room half-way cleaned up that day. It was a damn near impossible job because the stuff was so encrusted on the floor. They brought us bed boards to sleep on.

As succeeding days went by we discovered that there was a routine with the adjoining room. We would get to go out everyday in the morning for about 45 minutes to an hour to wash ourselves and our clothes. We had a little clothes line the Gooks constructed in the courtyard where we could hang out our clothes to dry.

We soon discovered we didn't go in the afternoon because our neighbors went out then. We tried tapping to these guys but discovered it was almost impossible to do so because the wall was so thick. But we finally found a spot that reverberated enough to carry the message across.

We discovered there was a double wall between us and the next room so it was strictly air pressure that was carrying the noise of our taps. We tried talking through the wall with cups but that was impossible. It came out too mumbled on the other side to understand. Then we tried tapping on the floor. We found a place where a floor joist crossed over and carried sound to the next room quite well.

These double walls were part of the original construction. The only thing the Gooks had done to modify was put bars and outer doors on the back window, wire off the vents and construct the wall between the court yards for segregation.

We decided that our buildings had been used for film storage. They had been constructed with ventilation and double-walls to stay cool. We found many pieces of filmstrips. While this had likely been the original purpose of the buildings, more recently the Gooks had obviously been using them for keeping livestock, which explained the cow shit on the floor.

We did not go outside of our little courtyard into the camp for almost a month. The Gooks were always paranoid about letting us see anything when they got us into a new camp. They usually loosened up and start taking us out after a month or so. I don't know why it made any difference when we were first in the camp as opposed to a month later. But that's the way they always operated.

Soon we noticed there were no quizzes and we were being left alone. The guy who was running The Annex, the camp commander, continued to do so for the two and half years I was there. I saw his name, Nguyen Chuc, on his dictionary one day. We named him "Chester." This was the same guy who had first showed up at The Briar Patch in late October of 1966. Chester was a fairly easy-going Gook. As far as interrogators went he was not a very dangerous type. He was also apparently well-liked by all the guards and the other interrogators. He did his job when orders were passed down from above. But he was usually pretty good about going at it fast and not dicking around with us. He didn't seem to get any sadistic pleasure out of messing with us. We were pretty fortunate to have him, really. We found him to be friendly and affable under ordinary circumstances when there was no pressure on.

The guys next door were Hayden Lockhart, Dave Wheat, Barry Bridger and Bill Shankel. They were all officers, grade 02, Navy Lt (jg) or Air Force 1st Lts. when they were shot down. All the guys in my room were 03s. We could already see the segregation by rank that was taking place. We tried to make contact with other guys in the camp when we'd go out in the courtyard. We bored holes in the concrete separating the bricks in our courtyard wall so we could peek out and see around the camp. Sometimes they had other POWs doing work in small groups but always only one group was out at a time. Sometimes we'd spot a guy going to a quiz. We didn't recognize any of these people. We tried whistles and even talking loud but could not make contact.

In the next month or two Goose, our turnkey, was his typical nasty self. But for the most part he would leave Sima, Morgan and me alone. But he was his typical nasty self with Fer and Flesher. If they did anything he didn't like he'd just haul off and knock the crap out of them right there on the spot. He especially had it in for Flesher who was pretty antagonistic toward the guards and the Gooks in general.

We discovered from the guys next door that it was the same with them. There were some guys whom he messed with and some he didn't. It turned out Goose left guys that had been at The Briar Patch alone. He had done all that torture there so I guess he figured he had us trained. But he was mean to new guys who hadn't had their initiation at The Briar Patch. It was kind of funny. It was like, "Well, you've had your ration of shit, buddy, so you're okay now and I'll leave you alone."

The Goose would typically come in our room and call me up front even though I wasn't the senior man. He'd always pick me out if he had something to explain or get across to the people in the room. He was one of the few Gooks smart enough to know that if he could make one person understand then that person could explain it to his buddies. He seemed to believe I would understand him better than the others.

The guards began to get obnoxious. There were two in particular who were out for kicks, raising hell and having a good time with the harassment. They'd come around to the back window, throw open the doors and want us to bow. They began to do this 15 or 20 times a day. They'd hang around and if they heard anything like a loud noise, anything above a whisper, they'd throw the doors open and want us to kneel down and put our hands up in the air. They'd keep us that way for the rest of the day if they could.

There was one that would walk into our courtyard with his bayonet fixed when we were out bathing. Invariably he would crack us in the head with it if we were standing there in the nude. We got some pretty nasty cuts from that character. We called him "Crazy Charlie" and he was just that. He was nuttier than a fruit cake! But he was nothing like my old New Guy Village pal Crazy Charlie with the crackle bar.

The diet at The Annex started to get real grim. We got soup and rice and that was all. There was no side dish. The quantity was small. One problem was we were in the far back corner of The Annex so we were at the very end of the chow line. Generally we got what was left over, which was damn little. The Gooks were also experiencing food shortages. Maybe they had a bad summer crop and they'd been bombed pretty heavily so their transportation was hurting. The guards and the chow girls who worked in the camp seemed to be hungry too. We watched them through cracks in the door as they brought our food into our courtyard. The chow girls would come in with the guards and take about half of our rice in their rice bowls. Then they would exit back over to the area where they lived.

This is pretty tough to take when you're starving to death. But when I looked back at it I realized they were hungry too so we really couldn't blame them too much. On a couple of occasions they got some extra food in the camp. When this happened Goose would always bring it to us personally. He really piled it on and he had a big smile on his face when we'd go out to get it. He seemed just as proud as could be.

About this time John Fer and I noticed that Scotty Morgan was having problems. Tom Sima had lived with Scotty at The Briar Patch and Little Vegas. He'd been living with Scotty in a two-man room for a year and a half. Tom said it was the worst thing that ever happened to him in his life. Living with Scotty was just Hell. He said he would have given any amount of money to be in solitary confinement rather than live with him. Scotty was very antagonistic and paranoid. His all consuming thoughts were how much he hated Gooks and that's all he could think or talk about.

Scotty slipped back into this at The Annex. He and Bud Flesher spent a great deal of time acting out when the guards would come around. They'd yell and scream profanity at the guards and of course then the guards would come into our room and go after Scotty and Bud. Things started building up into a pretty good crescendo and we were beginning to have a lot of Gooks in the room all the time.

Then Christmas came and it was the usual holiday deal. We always referred to it as a "BFD," which of course means "Big Fucking Deal." That was an in-joke because one of our guys had written a letter home saying

312

"The Vietnamese always give us a BFD, which he said "of course means a big fine dinner." I imagine his family got the drift.

So they put on the big feed this year and they had a Christmas program on the radio. This program had been done by Yanks. The guy that headed it up was Air Force Captain Quincy Collins. Quincy had a lot of acting and musical talent. He had put on shows and entertainment at Officer Clubs and elsewhere.

Quincy seemed obsessed with putting on shows and musicals. So he took the opportunity this year to do it. The show was their idea so he had to put in a few things the Gooks wanted in order to get to do it. One thing he did was a little skit about a guy who flew out of Da Nang and went to fly a mission. He didn't like the war, he didn't like the mission, and it kind of went like that. Quincy also played the piano and some guys working with him sang Christmas songs. They told jokes and a bunch of stuff.

The result for everybody in our room was it just about made us puke. So instead of "Quincy Collins," we referred to him as "Quincy Puke."

On Christmas Eve we went out to a quiz. We were about the last room to go out. In the quiz room were Chester and Marian the Librarian. There they sat in all their regal glory. Marian was so drunk he couldn't see straight and he was also pissed off. We sat down and he said something like, "Merry Christmas, Criminals." Then Chester poked him and made him shut up.

They had this stupid goddamn Christmas tree. It was the funniest thing I ever saw. We walked in and started laughing our asses off at it. It was some piece of shit the Gooks had gotten and tried to decorate. He asked what we thought of the Christmas tree. Bud Flesher said, "What Christmas Tree?" It went right over their heads. They also had a statue of the Virgin Mary sitting on a table and they asked us if anybody wanted to pray, that we were now allowed to pray. We declined the offer.

They had some candy and coffee on the table. We stole all the candy and drank all the coffee they had. We told them that we thought they blew rats! They didn't get that either. Then they told us to leave and go back to our room. That was Christmas Eve.

They threw our front doors open with a great flourish on Christmas Day. There were about 15 Gooks standing out there, including the overall camp commander we called "The Fox." We didn't bow when we went out to pick up our chow. We just ignored them and picked up our chow. They had the most pissed off looks you could imagine. Once again we had a gigantic, good meal, a true BFD. There was even a little bit of Gook wine.

313

They filled our cups up about a half inch high and that's all we got. It was almost like brandy, probably about 40% alcohol or so but it tasted like cough medicine.

On New Year's Day we had another decent meal. Then 1968 started off with more guard harassment. Bud Flesher was really beginning to get the heat put on him for all the crap he was giving the guards. The climax came one night in mid-February when the five of us were out in our courtyard washing. Bud was washing one of his blankets and he asked me to help him shake it out. So I got hold of one end, he got the other end and we began to shake the water out of his blanket. But we were shaking it too hard because it was an old blanket and it ripped, so we took it back inside.

Several days before Bud had been asking the Gooks for more blankets for the men in our room. He told them we didn't have enough to keep us warm. We were really freezing our asses off. It was a grim winter and we didn't have nearly enough clothing to keep warm. He also said, "At least give us replacement blankets if we can't have more because the ones we have are old and worn." Well, now Bud had ripped his blanket so he asked the Gooks for a needle and thread. Goose wanted to know why and Bud showed him that he'd ripped his blanket.

The Gooks just went ape shit when they saw that Bud had ripped his blanket. In no time at all Chester came around and they looked it. Then they brought him a needle and thread and he sewed it up. That night he went to a quiz and he came back about three hours later. They had asked him, "Why do you make plots against the Vietnamese people?"

This was the Gooks' devious thinking. They figured Flesher had been asking for blankets for us and had intentionally ripped his so we could get more. They thought that he had destroyed their valuable property, these old pieces of shit they called blankets. The next day they came in and moved him out and into The Zoo. Then they took Sima, Morgan, Fer and me to another room in The Annex where they left us for a few days. Then they took us out, one by one, to a quiz. They asked us about the blanket. It was just incredible! We told them we had just been shaking the damn thing out and it ripped. I told them Flesher and I had been shaking the blanket. We didn't have any plan or anything else. They said, "Well, all four of you will be punished for having helped Flesher in this plot."

So then they moved us out of that room and back into our original room. When we went back they had leg irons outside the room. They put us in them and we stayed in irons for about two days. Fer had dysentery so bad that he had to take a shit 47 times one day. He was a walking Zombie and he had these damn leg irons on. So he had to park himself by the bucket all night long. The next morning we "Bao Cao'd" (called) for the guards. The Goose came and I explained to him in hand signs and pigeon-Gook that Fer had bad diarrhea. I wrote down in the dust the number of times. Then Goose looked at him and his eyes got as big as saucers. He looked at me and said, "Okay, Bac Si." Bac Si means doctor.

He turned around and took off at a dead run. Honest to god, I think Fer would have died in the next couple of days at the rate he was going. They came back with a medic and Chester, the interrogator. One look at Fer and they took him out of the irons. But the rest of us stayed in. They gave Fer a bunch of pills to help stop the shits and put him on a sweet-rice diet. This, the pills and getting him out of those damn irons helped to get him squared away a little bit. They took the rest of us out a couple of days later.

We didn't hear from Flesher for the next 2½ or 3 years although we did hear where he was. In the spring of 1968 some guys came over to The Annex from The Zoo and told us about him.

They had taken Bud to The Zoo and put him in The Pig Sty. The first visitor he got there was "Fidel," a Cuban interrogator. Fidel and another Cuban interrogator we called "Raul" were sent to North Vietnam by the friendly Cuban government for one year. Apparently they were on loan to show the Vietnamese Cuban interrogation techniques and to experiment with American POWs. Fidel was running a horror-show program in The Stables.

Flesher was in The Pig Sty when Fidel came in and said, "You have a terrible attitude fellow, and we're going to change your attitude." Fidel was a big guy, probably six feet tall and 200 pounds. The guys said getting hit by Fidel was not like getting hit by a Gook. He was really a blood thirsty cocksucker and he spoke excellent English. We all thanked God that they didn't have more Cubans like Fidel to work on us. They would have made blithering idiots out of all of us and probably would have gotten more propaganda than by their own clumsy methods.

Fidel put Flesher through a submission program. He didn't really want to fuck around with him. All he wanted to do was make him submit, to tone him down. The Gooks had given Flesher over to him to settle him down a little bit. It only took Fidel about a week or so and sure enough he did get Flesher settled down. After that Bud just sat there, solo in The Pig Sty for six months where they left him alone. Solitary didn't mean shit to Bud Flesher. He was a very tough boy!

315

In February of 1968 we started having a lot of bombing raids nearby. They would come so close the plaster would fall out of the ceiling. One night in particular we had some really heavy raids and we were having them during the day too. We could look out through the cracks and see 105s going by. Jesus, the sky was just filled with flack and the whole damn ground was shaking from the anti-aircraft fire. This was thrilling for us. Somebody was trying to get us out of there. It was the greatest thing in the world for morale whenever we heard aircraft bombing and shooting. It was like being right in the middle of a western movie. It was terrific!

One night some Navy A6 attack planes came in low and dropped CBUs, bomb cluster units, along with some big bombs. The big ones sounded like 1,000 or 2,000 pounders. It was so close that half our ceiling fell in. Some falling bricks nearly killed Scotty because they came so close to him.

First thing the next morning the BDA, bomb damage assessment, team came through. It was Marian the Librarian, the Goose and another guard, and they had their little stove pot style helmets on. These helmets the Gooks wore reminded me of Nazi helmets. They came down low over the ears and had that same design. Something I might interject here too is when the Gooks marched in a dress parade they wore these helmets and goose-stepped exactly like the Germans did in World War II.

I mentioned before how stupid Marian the Librarian was. Well, he took a look at the room and then ordered all of us to get on our knees and hold our hands up in the air. He was so pissed off he walked around and slapped the hell out of us. Of course we had done absolutely nothing. Oddly, the other Gooks looked embarrassed. Goose, being the sergeant, was really embarrassed about the whole thing. Marian said something to Goose and they had a little conversation. Goose was obviously pissed off and we could tell he was reading Marian the riot act.

Finally Marian stomped out of the room. Then Goose signaled to me and made a little sign with his finger rotating on his watch. He said, "Four." (He held up four fingers.) In other words we were going to be on our knees for four hours.

Then he looked at me and said, "Okay, Bât?" They gave all of us Vietnamese names. Mine was "Bât," with a circumflex over the "a," and was pronounced like "But." Our names were too hard for them to pronounce so we all got something that sounded like the first syllable of our names.

I nodded and said, "It's up to you, Doc." Then he walked to the back of the room, closed the window shutters tight and pulled the latch down on it. Then he walked out the front, locked our interior doors and then locked our hatch. Then he walked outside and locked the outer doors. And then he walked out into the courtyard with loud footsteps, slammed the gate shut and was gone.

With that we all plunked down on our asses and sat around. Like I said before, there were always Gooks coming around to the back window. But we just sat there for four hours, ready to get back on our knees in case somebody showed up. But nobody came near our building for four hours.

Finally after four hours we heard loud footsteps coming down the walkway. Goose was particularly noted for his stealth and he could get a door open with a key faster than anyone could believe. It would only take him a second or two to have the door open from the closed and locked position. But this time he rattled around the court yard door, stomped up the walk and messed with the outer door lock for about 30 seconds. Then he did the same with the inner door like he was having trouble with it. Finally he opened it and looked in the room where we were of course all on our knees. He looked at me and said, "Okay" and gave us the down sign. It was the damnedest thing I ever saw. The old sergeant had his way and saved some face with us.

After this Chester got hold of the two young guards who had been pestering us so much and made them lay off. They'd only come around to the back window maybe once a day and when they did they were pretty quiet and didn't give us any shit. They'd get their little curtsy from us and then buzz on off. Overall, the guard harassment stopped for a little while.

On April 20th, my third anniversary, we were out in courtyard bathing. For some reason, probably a mistake, the guys next door were out in their courtyard too. They let them out to get their clothing or something and the guard had left the area for just a few seconds. Hayden Lockhart yelled over "Happy Anniversary, Phil." I said, "Roger Hayden, thank you and hey H, something always happens on my anniversary so keep your heads up."

Every anniversary I had there we'd always moved that day, or the day after, or some big shuffle had taken place. Well I'll be god-damned but we were all moved that very night over to room six. At first there was just Sima and myself together, and then Barry Bridger and Bill Shankel moved in. An hour later Al Lurie joined us. Al was an Air Force captain who had moved from The Zoo. He was the first source of information that we had gotten from The Zoo.

The Gooks were doing this in screwy stages instead of all at once.

317

They had these ridiculously complicated plans. In a very short period of time we got Scotty Morgan, John Fer, Dave Wheat and Hayden Lockhart added to our room, making us nine. There were two rooms in each of five buildings. Rooms one through eight all had nine guys in them. Rooms nine and ten had fewer. With all the moving around we finally had some information from The Zoo and also better contact among the various buildings.

There were a lot of new shoot-downs from 1967 who hadn't found out about the Tap Code yet. They didn't know how to communicate very well. But we got a good communication system going now with the old heads mixed in with them. We started flashing hand code among buildings from a vent in one building to a doorway in another.

These nine man rooms were terrific. It seemed like we had so much to talk about and there was always a conversation you could get into. Or you could ignore somebody else if you wanted to at that moment. It was a big morale boost and a hell of a lot better than living in a small room with one or two guys. Living for months and even years on end with maybe one other guy was a terrible thing for some guys as I said earlier. There were cases where guys who hated each other had to live together for two or three years.

Every POW memorized an extensive list of names. We updated our lists whenever we could get new names. We continued to do this right up to the very end when we had more than four hundred names. Guys were always comparing name lists. We also did this on the wall with other rooms. We would go through our entire list of 250 or 300 names, tapping back and forth, to see if "anybody knows so-and-so or did they think this name was a possible POW or was he somebody that was killed." The Gooks kept many names secret so we had to keep lists for our intelligence people after we were released.

1968 was the year of the infamous Tet Offensive in South Vietnam. It came in late February that year. The Gooks up in Hanoi were absolutely ecstatic and it was the wildest show we ever saw as far as the guards and the interrogators and camp personnel acted - they really went bull shit. They shot off firecrackers and had fun and games for about two weeks. They really enjoyed themselves and their morale was just about as high as it could have possibly been. They really thought they were winning the war.

They called some of my friends out to quizzes with officers from the Communist Party. The word they were putting out in these quizzes around Tet went something like this: "Our cadre is now moving into South

Vietnam. Soon we will have control of South Vietnam and Vietnam will be one. As soon as that has happened we will form a united front and march into Cambodia and Laos to take over those two countries. After that we intend to go into Burma and Thailand and control the entire Indochinese Peninsula. After that we will launch an invasion into the Philippines and then into Australia and New Zealand and when we are strong enough we will launch an invasion into the United States." I met a lot of people after I got back who thought the domino theory was pure bull shit. But that was the party line coming down through the camp.

After this big shuffle occurred and we filled up all the rooms in The Annex, we discovered everybody in the camp was an 02 or 03 grade officer. Most of the 04s were in The Zoo and the high rank 05s and 06s were being kept in The Hilton. The Gooks thought they could circumvent our senior ranking officers by selecting our SROs for us. They started doing this by putting whichever most senior officer they wanted in the camp.

In The Annex it turned out that our SRO was an Air Force captain named Konrad Trautman. Captain Trautman, Konnie, had been passed over twice for major. He was a very good man but not a strong leader in the beginning. Konnie was very conscientious. He did as good a job as he could and he eventually developed into a good leader. He was not a dynamic person and didn't give out inspirational leadership. But he was a very fine man who wound up doing a great job as our SRO.

At this same time the Gooks started another system to try to break up our military organization. They instituted what they called the "Room Responsible." Room Responsible was a man in your room who was appointed by the Gooks to be responsible for the room. If anybody in the room did anything wrong, the Room Responsible guy would pay for it. He would be the man punished. If you needed anything from the guard or the turnkey, the Room Responsible was the man who had to ask. If anything happened in your room the Room Responsible was called out to the quiz instead of the senior man in the room. The Room Responsible was always somebody junior. When the guard would open the door we would have to line up in two lines in front of our bunks. But the Room Responsible would have to stand in the center of the room.

This effort to undermine our military organization was a clumsy thing. It went on for a couple of years but it never worked. It just made us more dedicated and firmly convinced that our military structure was needed. However, there were many times we had to play their game, to use our Room Responsible, because we couldn't get things any other way.

319

Tom Sima was our room senior ranking officer but our Gook-appointed Room Responsible was Al Lurie. So the way we worked was Tom made all the decisions in the room and then he instructed Al what to tell the Gooks or what to ask for. As far as the Gooks were concerned, their Room Responsible program was working, while as far as we were concerned our military rank system was operating.

Later on when the heat came off and the physical brutality stopped we refused to operate with Room Responsibles. We just put up a stone wall to the Gooks. We would not allow their appointed Room Responsible to do anything whatsoever. Our senior men dealt with the Gooks. Whenever we couldn't get things from the guards or when they'd just ignore us then we'd just do without things. They played games with this Room Responsible system off and on after September of 1969. It just depended on what kind of mood they were in. But they didn't resort to the physical brutality after that time, just a little harassment. Sometimes they used it when they'd get a little pissed off at us or we'd raise a little too much hell. Then they'd start playing the Room Responsible game again.

They maintained up to the very bitter end that we were not Prisoners of War and we were never treated in accordance with the Geneva Conventions, nor was our rank structure ever recognized. But in the end, the last couple of years, we forced them to deal with our senior ranking officers simply because we refused to be dealt with any other way.

Sometime in April we got word that there was a request and a plan to commission the three enlisted guys, Bill Robinson, Art Cormier and Art Black, who were living with Ed Davis, a Navy Lt (jg) and four other junior officers. The officers in that room sent out a request to give these guys battlefield commissions "since they were doing the same work and suffering the same as all the officers." Something like this had never been done before in a POW camp so the request went all the way up to our most senior officers, who unanimously approved the plan. The five officers in the room then put the enlisted guys through "Officer Candidate School" classes, based on information they knew plus information that was tapped over to them. The courses in the room were completed and then, in a solemn ceremony, they were given the oath of office and sworn in as officers.

In late April and throughout May of 1968 there was some kind of peace scare going on again. During this time the food just went up to gangbusters. We were getting no side dishes but they would bring us a big pot of soup for nine men and it would contain potatoes, meat, vegetables and lots of good stuff. Sometimes we got bread and sometimes rice. For the first time, during this brief period, we were beginning to get enough to eat. We all began to gain some weight and we got a little healthier.

The bad dysentery and diarrhea also disappeared in the spring of 1968 and the medical treatment started to improve slightly. If we got a cut, scrape, ringworms or something like that they would bring blue medicine to put on it. This Gook blue medicine, which we called "sheep-dip," was the Vietnamese miracle medicine. It was good for everything from cancer to lumbago as far as the Gooks were concerned. Still, if we had a headache, toothache or something like that we couldn't get an aspirin.

This little peace scare and good food lasted until the end of May. The summer of '68 was fairly uneventful for us with one exception. That was the first release of three pilots. These guys had been disgustingly and sadly acting as volunteers for the Gooks over in The Zoo. Information had been passed over to us that two of them had signed amnesty statements. Shortly after that they were moved out of the camp.

Everybody in my room kept strong faith in our fellow Americans because we knew it was our life blood. We had faith in these guys – a blind faith – that the Gooks were shitting us and that the guys hadn't really done anything wrong. We hadn't discussed it any farther than that. We hoped that when they got home they would be able to give our government a long list of names and tell what was actually going on in Hanoi.

We heard through the grapevine that there was a camp being utilized for people who were possibly about to be released. This camp was called "The Plantation." Later I talked to POWs who had been at The Plantation, guys who had not been of that soon-to-be-released status. But such people were kept there and they were getting special treatment. They were getting better food, were allowed to go outside to exercise and play games and they had books and things to write with.

The Gooks made a big deal about having released three pilots and they told us that these guys had a very good attitude. They said if we had a good attitude we might be able to be released and go home to our families too. They made maximum bullshit propaganda out of that. They got reams of propaganda out of the release in other countries. The Gooks also stated that these men repented for their crimes and had signed amnesty statements.

I would say one more thing in relation to the release of the three guys and it goes back to Larry Guarino. Larry passed around a long message for the camp after the three guys were released. It was very wordy and had to come through a very complicated communication system of tapping and hand flashing.

Frankly, I thought it was a bunch of wordy gobbledy-goop that didn't say a thing. It was a bunch of mishmash about going home with your honor, and if you're sick and wounded, then go ahead and go home. It was really weak and didn't tell us a thing. It pissed us all off in our room. As a matter of fact we concocted a message of our own and we wanted to send it all the way back to The Zoo. We wanted to tell Larry to get off his ass and send us something we could understand, in just about those words too, SRO or no SRO! We cussed and discussed this thing in the room for about a week. Finally guys with a little more tact won the day and we didn't send the goddamn message over to him.

The summer of '68 was a long hot summer. It was a real bear. Living in those bastardly hot rooms with nine guys was really a cocksucker. Everybody had heat rash. It got unbelievably hot in there, especially at night. We'd lie down to go to sleep on our boards at night and have to fan ourselves constantly. The Gooks did, by the way, give each man a new fan once a year. It was just a little paper hand fan but boy that thing was worth more than its weight in gold because we really get max use out of it. We'd lie down and just fan ourselves till we fell asleep.

We would wake up with a stream of sweat running off us. It's just impossible to sleep under a mosquito net because that made it even hotter. We didn't wear anything in North Vietnam but a pair of shorts from about the end of April till the end of November. We couldn't stand anything else. It's just too damn hot!

In the fall of '68 something happened that just about entirely destroyed morale. It raised us up to a real high for a short period and then it wound up being a really crushing blow for most of us. That was the cease bombing and the opening of the Paris Peace Conference. The first thing we heard was the bombing had stopped. We knew the Gooks had said since February '67 that if we stopped bombing they would talk. Well now we had stopped bombing and it seemed like giving in on our part. Then they went through all this bullshit about the Paris Conference and how they were trying to decide whether to use a round table or a square table or highchairs or whatever.

We all said, "Whoopee." We thought that with the bombing stopped completely and not making war on North Vietnam it meant we would have to be home in 30 days, or at least something would have to be signed to get prisoners released.

Well 30 days went by and nothing happened with us. Then around the end of December we realized that we had been played as political pawns by President Johnson. Moreover LBJ hadn't run for President again but he wanted to get Humphrey elected so he sacrificed us. That was the way most of us felt; certainly the way I felt about the thing.

So we stopped the bombing and they started the Paris Conference and Hubert Humphrey lost the fucking election anyway. And they didn't do anything for us. They didn't even get any guarantees out of the Gooks for our well being. I guess they did get some sort of agreement to allow packages to be sent to us.

Our first packages came in February of 1969. We were excited about it. We had heard that so and so down the line had been called out to quiz and had gotten a package from his family. There was supposed to be one there for everybody and guys started going out to get a package.

Some of them were absolutely ludicrous. We just couldn't believe it. There were guys in the camp who went out to get a package that consisted of three or four packs of chewing gum. One of my roommates, John Fer, went out to get his package and it was two packs of playing cards and some chewing gum. Fer didn't play cards and his father knew it.

People were sending little tokens and pieces of crap because they were not sure whether or not we would get the stuff. But that was pretty stupid because our government could sure as hell afford to crank up some nice packages for the families. They could have sent them to us even if there was only a chance in a million that we'd get the damn things.

When I came home I found out that the U. S. government didn't pay for any of the packages that were sent to me. My wife paid for every one of them with the exception of things she would get at the base dispensary like vitamin pills and some kinds of medicine. The damn packages were expensive and I paid for them myself.

The fact is the Gooks stole about 80% of it and that was a real sore point for me. If our government had been smart they would have sent Red Cross packages instead of having our families send things that would probably get picked over by the Vietnamese before they got to us. At least then, with all the guys supposedly getting the same stuff, there wouldn't have been a lot of guys feeling bad because their families didn't send them something better.

The Gooks turned it into a big propaganda show, of course. They announced to the world that we were not prisoners of war, but "criminals being allowed by the humane policy of the Democratic Republic of

Vietnam to receive packages from our families. " They were not from any official source for prisoners of war like the Red Cross. That was just one more thing where our government let us down.

Then from this time on, when letters came to us, they were addressed to "Phillip Neal Butler, Camp of Detention, Democratic Republic of Vietnam." Now what kind of fucking way is that to send a package or a letter to a guy who is spending 24 hours a day trying to prove to the enemy that he is "LT Phillip Neal Butler, United States Navy, Prisoner of War?" But that's the way stuff came in and it just seemed to us that we were fighting the damn battle all by ourselves and that nobody was backing us.

That was some irony that we were finally getting letters from home and the envelopes are a downer like that. I'm sure most of the men were just happy to have gotten the mail no matter how it was addressed. But personally I would have rather not received any than to get it like that. That's how I felt about it and I had a lot of friends who felt the same way. I guess I have a more hard-headed attitude about this. The Gooks were doing all this for propaganda. If our government had stayed a little firm and sent all the letters in a standard way, I think the Gooks would have had to eventually relent and let people receive them that way. It would just have required our people back here at home to put up a little bit of a fight too, like the way we were putting up one.

So the packages started coming in and I was sitting there thinking, boy won't it be fantastic to walk down to that quiz room and get a package? When is my day going to come? I waited to walk down there and see my first American goodies from my family in almost four years. Finally I was called out and as I walked to the quiz room I was never more excited in my life. I was like a kid getting up at five o'clock in the morning to look under the Christmas tree.

I walked into the quiz room and there was a big shoe box sitting there and it was my package. The interrogator started taking all the stuff out and he laid it on the table, showing it to me. My wife had sent me an outstanding package. It had a lot of different medicines, vitamin pills, tooth brush, tooth paste – some real necessities and things we were really hurting for. I read the invoice. He let me read the invoice and everything was there that she had sent except for a few items that had been removed by the Gooks. These were a carton of American cigarettes, decks of cards and nail clippers. These were things that they wouldn't let us have. Who knows why?

Then the interrogator said, "This is your package from your family. You are allowed to have it. Sign this receipt form." I took the receipt form and it had the numbers listing each item and a place to sign for it at the bottom.

At the heading of the paper it said, "Due to the lenient and humane treatment offered by the Democratic Republic of Vietnam, I have been allowed to receive from the government of the Democratic Republic of Vietnam, a package from my family." I just about puked! I took that paper and shoved it back at the interrogator. I pushed all the stuff back towards him and said, "Take it and go fuck yourself with it." Then I stood up and walked back to my room.

I can't remember a time in my life when I'd been more pissed off. The rest of the guys in my room did the same thing. We told the Gooks to smack it. Some of the other guys in the camp had been offered the form to sign and they had signed it, thinking it was just a little chintzy piece of propaganda that wasn't worth while. The package had come through to them and they thought they ought to have it. Their families and our government wanted them to have it and I believe that was true. I didn't blame them for taking the packages and signing for them, then or now.

But for myself, it just made me sick to see that in writing and to see those little bastards being so cheap, after all those years, over a package. I just couldn't stomach it for myself so I turned it down.

They never let any American cigarettes come through. They gave us three Gook cigarettes a day. But never would they allow us to have American cigarettes. I guess they liked them too much themselves and took them. Later on they let us receive pipe tobacco. I managed to get a pipe in one of my first packages later on. But then later after that they had a huge raid and took all of our pipes away from us. Then later again they gave some of them back and I managed to get my pipe back. So we'd get pipe tobacco occasionally but we didn't have very many pipes to go around. It was kind of weird.

On Christmas of 1968 our whole room went out to a quiz together. We picked up a little package of goodies for each of us, some candy and shit like that. They had a Christmas tree there and that kind of crap. They gave Hayden and me a couple of letters. This was the first mail I received in over two years.

I went back to the room and looked at my three letters. One was from my wife and two were from William Butler's wife. Now we didn't have the name of another Butler and here was a letter to William Butler. I read this guy's mail and he had some pictures too. I memorized his letters; got them down cold. Then I told the guard to give them back to the interrogator and the interrogator came around the next day and said, "Why do you give this mail back?" I said, "It's not mine. It's for another POW." I said, "My name is not William Butler, it's Phillip Butler." He said, "Okay."

I met Bill Butler two years later, Christmas of 1970, when he was in a room near mine at Camp Unity. I stood up at the window and hand-jived with him in another window. I introduced myself, told him I received his mail two years ago. Of course they never gave him the letters. I asked if he would like to know what his wife had to say. So I hand-jived his letters over to him and he got a big kick out of that. The mail was a little old but he was still happy to hear about it. He had received some mail since then but the Gooks had never given him those letters.

1969 came and the big saying was "Across the Line in '69." It never came about. Some kind of slogan like that came around about every New Year's and guys would always laugh their asses off at them. The big news during the first part of 1969 was the Paris Conference. This went out over radio Hanoi Hannah constantly. It was an enormous blow job. The only thing the Paris Conference did was give the Gooks worldwide propaganda and a place to toot their horn.

It was absolutely worthless and LBJ had stopped the bombing for nothing. I personally had to assume they knew all along it was never going to amount to anything. The guy who was doing the talking for the North Vietnamese at the Paris Conference, Nguyen Tri, was nothing but a party hack. He had no authority whatsoever. He was just a mouth piece. So here was our senior diplomat talking to this low-ranking nothing, along with his sidekick a North Vietnamese Colonel. It was really frustrating.

In the early spring of 1969 around Tet the Gooks released three more Americans. This time it hit us hard and everybody's attitude was quite a bit different. Now we found ourselves at long-last faced with a situation that we truly were distressed about. That was over three of our fellow Americans - Low, Thompson and Carpenter. We felt deep hatred for these three guys. What they had done to gain their release was obvious. They had signed amnesty statements to begin with and they made three special tapes that the Gooks played to us.

James Frederick Low, and he lives up to his name well, had a reputation in the Air Force that other guys in the camp had known for a long time. He was said to always have been the kind of person who sacrificed other people for his own ends. There were guys who had flown with him in Korea and had known him throughout his career. He had gotten his wing man shot down in Korea to get a little glory for himself.

But he outdid himself this time. In his tape he told us that we should go along with anything the Vietnamese wanted. He said it was a rotten, stinking war that we had gotten ourselves involved in and we all had made a big mistake. He said now we had to look out for our own ass.

That's exactly what he said too. He said that's what he had done and he advised us to do the same thing. He told us to go into the interrogation room and tell the Vietnamese anything they wanted to know. He said we could give them anything we know because it would be kept in the strictest of confidence. We could be sure of that. Thompson and Carpenter's tapes were about the same. It was the most sickening, rotten pile of crap I ever heard come from an American voice!

Some people asked me later if I thought these guys weren't really coerced into saying what they did. We could always tell in almost every case. I realized that I had no proof they said this voluntarily, but when we listened to these guys on tape they sounded straight and they were convincing. They sounded like they meant it. Guys who had lived in The Plantation and another camp with Low, Thompson and Carpenter told us things they had been doing. They had been going to quiz two or three times a day. They were walking around outside in the camp with their arms around guards. These guys had even done things like lock up gates for the Gooks.

Some of the guys had seen Low ask the Vietnamese if he could have a large photograph of Ho Chi Minh to hang in his cell. The Gooks had gone along and allowed him to have it. So as far as I'm concerned these guys were genuinely opportunistic. They didn't really believe the shit the Vietnamese said because nobody educated in the United States who had been an officer in the armed forces could ever believe this crap!

But Low, Thompson and Carpenter spouted the whole line of bull shit out of how "we were the imperialist aggressors and the ruling circles in the United States government made all the policies and the large corporations owned the people." They were a verbatim parroting of their propaganda lines - the whole line of sickening bullshit! They played all three of their tapes to us repeatedly for several days.

About this same time we heard that guys over in The Zoo were getting art materials. The head of this group was Quincy Collins. Quincy had put up another Christmas tape in the Christmas of 1968. He had some musical instruments and he was teaching some guys to play the guitar. They were also playing a piano. Then the Gooks had them drawing pictures and paintings of camp routine. We saw some of them in The Auditorium when we went for our Tet or Christmas quiz.

Some of the guys were pretty talented. The thing is, the Gooks were getting propaganda out of them. They would take these pictures downtown and display them to show what American pilots were being allowed to do in a prison camp. About 90% of us, all except one room, were dead set against this drawing pictures thing. Larry Guarino put out the policy that it was okay to do art work and that he and Ron Byrne were doing art work.

This pissed us off royally. There was one room in our camp, a room of young guys, all of them O2s who were also playing around with art. So Konrad Trautman, our SRO did not put out an order counter to Larry Guarino. I kind of agree with him now and can see that if he had put out counter word this might have caused confusion and dissension in the lower ranks. That's probably why Konnie went along with Larry.

In the early spring of 1969 we had been moved to room eight. There were a couple of guys in room six who wanted to try to escape. They were John Dramesi and Ed Atterberry. These guys probably would have a different story to tell, but our perspective was very simple. There were two guys in that room who wanted to escape and six guys who did not want to. Nor did they want them to try.

The reason was that if they did try, they would fail and everybody in the camp was going to suffer. It was going to mean everybody's ass in a big way. There was absolutely no chance to escape from this camp in the middle of Hanoi. Everybody felt John Dramesi was a glory-hound type guy. He actually wanted to try this escape for his own glory.

They really didn't have a decent plan but we were all ordered to start working on it. Konnie detailed assignments for picking up certain kinds of gear and so forth. We stole black clothes and coolie hats for these guys. We manufactured better shoes that they could wear. We stole a couple cans of meat. They began to make preparations.

They hid all the stuff we had stolen for their escape in the attic of their room. They had gotten the wires over the vents loose, one by one, and crawled up in the attic where they stored this stuff.

At this time our communications with The Zoo were so poor that we really couldn't get the story over to Guarino. We physically couldn't get it to him. So Konnie was taking this whole thing on his shoulders. He was actually in the room next door to these guys, with good communication, so he had the whole burden. Konnie thought about this thing and got a consensus from others. What he finally came up with was that he felt it was his duty as SRO to approve an escape that was well planned. He turned down Dramesi and Atterberry on several occasions because he felt they were not well enough prepared and because he said they didn't have a good enough plan.

But finally he just gave in. Then one night in May they went. They went out through the roof, up into the attic and out through another hole in the roof. Then they let themselves down with a rope onto the ground. They crawled on their bellies through the camp and went over the wall. They made it a few hundred yards away to a river and were captured about six o'clock that morning.

The Gooks came around early that morning and checked the rooms after these guys were captured and found out what room they were missing from. Within a few hours they pulled out all the guys in that room and put them in solo cells around The Annex and The Zoo. They started interrogating these guys. They brought Dramesi and Atterberry back to The Zoo in a jeep.

Lots of guys in The Zoo were peeking out through their cracks and they saw Dramesi and Atterberry get out of the jeep and go into the interrogation room. Then the Gooks started a rein of terror!

They started pounding the hell out of the guys in their room. Then they went around and pulled out every room SRO in The Annex, even though they were not really responsible. Tom Sima was taken out of our room. They took these guys over to The Zoo. They brought out straps made from jeep fan belts and started whipping these guys with them and torturing them for information about the escape.

Then they worked on them for about 30 days, just beating the hell out of these guys. They extracted propaganda out of some of them. They got some tapes to show delegations. In other words they had them beaten down anyway so they used them for propaganda. They took Dramesi and Atterberry and Trautman back to The Hilton and gave them special torture treatment there.

Ed Atterberry never returned. It was the last time he was ever seen because they killed him. Naturally the Gooks only say that he died in captivity. Dramesi lived through it and he later came back. Konnie Trautman came back to The Annex after a month or so. Then they took all the room SROs and made up a room of nine in The Annex. They gave them some special bad treatment for a couple of months. They got irons, special confinement, reduced rations and what have you for several months. They also got more fan belt trips.

Then they started working on the rest of us in the camp. Our turnkey started down the bed line in my room. On the first day he got the first guy, the next day he got the second guy and so on around the room. They took us out to the quiz room and laid us out over a chair or on the floor and whipped us with this fan belt. It was excruciatingly painful. It raised huge welts and blisters. About ten of those and you almost lose your mind.

By cross-interrogating all these people they found out everything. Then they went around to all the rooms and sealed up the vent holes. They put metal plates across the vent holes that went into the attics. That meant nine guys lived in a completely sealed up room. We figured temperatures probably approached 150 degrees at times in the rooms and it lasted all summer long this way.

Off and on they were putting guys in irons and manacles. They were putting us in handcuffs too, but manacles locked our wrists together. They would manacle us with our hands in front and also put leg irons on. So then we just stayed in the clothes we were in for weeks and months on end. Our roommates had to help us take a shit and feed us.

About August of 1969 they really started getting ugly. They had a huge room shuffle. They took all the guys who were letter writers, those whose names had been released and had written letters in the past and they put us into one room. I was one along with Hayden Lockhart. At first it looked like the Gooks were going to torture us for some propaganda, some things they wanted us to say in our letters. It looked like they were going to write our letters for us. One of the things they had tortured Tom Sima, our SRO, for was, "How do Butler and Lockhart get information out to their government in their letters?"

Also around late summer of 1969, the Gooks got this thing going about money. They took a couple of guys over in The Zoo and tortured them at great lengths to write home and ask for money, which they did. And the wives sent money. This money was deposited in some Hanoi bank. It was fifty bucks or something like that! Anyway I think the idea was for them to see if they could get ransom for us out of our families.

They were also asking us questions in quizzes about insurance. The Gooks didn't know what insurance was. They figured if you had a $20,000 insurance policy then you could get your hands on $20,000. It's really weird they were so screwed up! They knew that we all had this $10,000 government insurance policy so they figured that was $10,000 dollars we owned. They obsessed over insurance and money. They'd ask how much pay we got. We never told them what we were paid but they had the stupid pay scale and knew how much we were being paid anyway. This obsession over money sort of faded out after awhile and they got into another program. They were always looking into anything they could with these new little programs.

So we letter writers moved into this room together. There was a bombing raid or two and we had some ceiling fall down so they used that as a reason to come in and put us all in leg irons, except Neil Jones. He had a broken arm. The bone had been completely severed since the time he was shot down. He'd been tortured that way and they had cut nerves in his arms so he lost partial use of it. Neil was fairly healthy with the exception of his arm. He had to be careful not to bump into anything because he had two bone ends that were loose. He had a little cast he wore around his arm and this gave it some support but it still didn't do him a hell of a lot of good, it was just kind of an excuse to throw us in leg irons. We stayed in that horribly hot room through August.

Then one morning in September, probably one of the most beautiful mornings of my whole life, we woke up and heard funeral music over the loud speaker. Later that day we heard that Ho Chi Minh had died. This began an entirely new regime with new policies and a whole new phase of treatment of POWs. The hellfire and brimstone years of my prison life were over.

21. Zoo Annex - Part II

On the morning of September 3rd 1969, we woke up as usual around 6:00. There was a funeral dirge playing on all the loud speakers around the camp, and presumably all over the country. Accompanying the funeral dirge was the Ho Chi Minh song. After that we could hear gun salutes. This was taking place downtown someplace but it echoed all around and went on repeatedly through the whole morning.

The turnkey didn't come around at the normal time that morning. About 9:00 o'clock the back window to our room opened up and one of the camp officers standing there with a long sad look on his face. He wore a black arm band. He told us on this day something very sad had happened in the country and that the entire camp and the entire country was in mourning and that we should all show a good attitude. He told us not to try to converse with the guards or to hassle them and that they would not do anything with us either. In other words he explained that we were to keep our mouths shut.

I can't remember who this officer was but it might have been Chester because he was our camp officer in charge at that time. He shut the doors and left. A little while later our turnkey came around and opened the door. He indicated the same thing. He was all dressed up and wearing his rank. The Gooks rarely wore their rank or insignia on their uniforms. This was part of their mantra that everybody was equal. But this day it was interesting to see that they were all wearing their ranks.

It appeared that all of the guards and officers were one rank below what they had been prior to the escape in May. So we began to understand a little bit about the heat that had been put on us and the revenge that had been taken by the camp guards and officers. Because of the escape they'd all been busted a rank or a rate. Not only that, the turnkey for the escape room and also our room had disappeared. He had obviously been cashiered for his negligence. That was fine with us since "Magoo," as we called him, was a particularly vindictive bastard.

That day, wearing their ranks and black arm bands, they also looked like they were about to cry. It was absolutely marvelous to us. The turnkey told us we were not going to bathe that day. A little while later the chow came and a couple of the guys were allowed to go outside and wash up the plates. The leg irons were taken off that day and then put back on that night. We went through the night with them on.

Then the next day a bunch of turnkeys came around and took off our leg irons. They also went around the camp and took leg irons and manacles off other people. Then they carried all that miserable paraphernalia out of the camp. And that was it for the leg irons and the manacles.

The funeral dirge and mourning went on for about a week. The format was pretty much the same. Our outside time was very limited for bathing. We just had enough time to go out and do it and then get back into the room. We were pretty much being ignored by the guards and officers.

Then after a week or two we began to notice a change in the pattern of things. First of all the food improved. It improved dramatically over the meager rations we had been receiving all summer as punishment for the escape. We began to get some good meals for breakfast. Instead of getting half a loaf of bread we were given bread that had been cooked in pig fat and had sugar sprinkled over it. We called it a "Greasy-Gut-Bomb."

Then one day the Gooks threw our door open and came in with big smiles on their faces. There was a pile of stuff out in the court yard. They said they had new materials to issue us. We each got a new, additional blanket. They also told us if any of us had old blankets with holes in them we could get them replaced. The turnkey took down the names of the people who needed replacement blankets. Well, this was really shit hot because the difference between being miserable and just uncomfortable was that third blanket in the winter time.

Then they came in with stuff that really astounded us. I don't know if I reported previously but they'd never let us keep any rags or anything to use as handkerchiefs. I constantly had a cold and drippy nose. They gave us each two handkerchiefs. Then they gave each of us a large, brightly colored, yellow and red bath towel. It looked like a "Real McCoy" towel you might see in a dime store some place in the states. The only thing we had before was a little white hand towel that wore out after a couple of months.

But the crowning glory on the whole business was a thing each of us got that we later referred to as "snake baskets." They were wicker baskets, about a foot deep and maybe nine inches in diameter. They were lined with padding and had a little lip. We had no idea what they were for until they showed us we were supposed to slide our water jug into this thing. It just fit. It was to keep our water warm. They like to drink hot water, no matter what the weather, and when they get tea they like to keep it hot. To us

Yanks it was ridiculous because throughout the hot weather we'd do anything to cool off the water so we could drink it.

After all this they came around and took an inventory of our clothing. Everybody got clothing replaced that needed to be and we were allowed to have more clothing than before. We each got two Gook T-shirts in addition. After all this we felt like rich men; like real capitalistic war-mongers at last.

We also noticed change in their policies toward us. The guards stopped harassing us. They no longer came to the windows for us to bow. They'd come around only to look in and get a head count. When they did pop open the window they'd get a head count and just buzz off with no contact or confrontation whatsoever between guards and Yanks.

Most significantly, there were no more interrogations. No one in the camp was going to quiz. We noticed that the two little Gooks who had been in the English Interrogator training program were just attending to administrative details, like letter writing.

Shortly after this a turnkey came around one day and stepped in the room. We all lined up like we always did and gave him half-ass bows. Our bows were getting more and more half-assed as each day went along because we were finding out no one was going to hammer us. He stood there with a big grin on his face and said, "No." Then he demonstrated a bow for us by nodding his head, just a mere head nod, and he said, "Okay." He went through this three or four more times. "Bow, no! Head nod, okay!" He was telling us bowing was finished and that they wanted us to nod heads. The Gooks did everything step-by-step. They were phasing out the bowing by having us just nod.

In October of 1969, one of my roommates, Daryl Pile, came down with hepatitis. The Gooks went berserk with the medical treatment. They came running and they were in and out of the room for several days with medics, camp doctors and more attention than we had ever seen in all the years we had been there. They brought Daryl eggs, sometimes six hard-boiled eggs. They said Daryl had a disease that was infectious and that they wanted to move him to another room by himself.

They moved him over to room eight which was empty but had a bunch of guys next door. Not more than a few days later Hayden Lockhart came down with the hepatitis. So they moved him in with Daryl. They stayed over there for two weeks. We didn't have much contact with them other than short messages like, "We are doing okay" and so forth. After a few weeks they came back to our room. Daryl had a big box under his arms. It seemed that just the day before he had received a package from home.

We were really amazed when Daryl opened it because it had all kinds of good things in it that the Gooks would have taken out in the past. We bitched at Daryl and Hayden because they had eaten a lot of the stuff the night before. But it was shared with the whole room of course.

We asked Daryl what he had had to do or sign to get his package, and he said it was nothing. It was just a standard receipt form that listed the items. He signed the release form saying he had been allowed to receive a package from his family and that was it.

A few days later we all started being called out, one by one, to the quiz room. We went through the half-ass head nod routine, sat down and signed for our packages and then went back to our rooms. We weren't getting much in the way of clothing but we were getting toothpaste, tooth brushes, soap and stuff like that. Later on all that stuff stopped but the no-interrogations policy continued.

Next the Gooks came around and said they were going to allow everybody to write. Anybody who wanted to could write home. The letter writing was to be standardized so we could write one letter a month. When all the guys started writing letters we thought it was a phony, put-up deal. The first couple of months they were still fiddling around and playing games by sending some letters home and some they weren't. But by about spring of 1970 they were sending everyone's letters out. At last they weren't discriminating anymore between people whose names were released and those whose names weren't released.

It seemed that everyone in the camp finally had their names released. Everyone was writing and mail was coming in both directions, albeit at extremely irregular intervals. But at least the outside world knew that all of us in the camp were alive. As far as the camp officers and the quizzers went, their only function seemed to be to take care of the letter writing. We did this by going down to the quiz room where we sat and first wrote a draft. Then we went back to our room and in a couple of weeks the draft came back with red censored lines in it. Then we copied what was left of our original onto a seven- line letter form and they supposedly sent it home.

Christmas of 1969 the Gooks did something they never did before. They brought in a Vietnamese version of pool. It was a little pool table about six feet long and maybe four feet wide. It was a game where you try to shoot a small ball against a peg and get it into a hole, with different holes giving different scores. They set it up in one of the quiz rooms. They also brought a couple of badminton rackets and a couple of birdies into the camp. They never did string up the net. But they did start letting us go out and fiddle around with the pool table. And they let us go out as an entire room to work outside, pulling weeds, chopping wood, carrying trash and moving rocks from one pile to another pile. They also had us cleaning out "Lake Fester," which is what we called the little man-made lake in the middle of the camp. We didn't mind the work, since it gave us more opportunity to go outside and the exercise was healthy.

Another big change was instead of obsessing about our communications, they just played ignorant. We still communicated covertly as we had always done – by hand signals, tapping, and note dropping – but the Gooks completely ignored the whole thing. We could be banging away on a wall and a guard would be wandering around in the hall outside but he'd just ignore us and keep on walking.

The vent-hole grates in the bottom of the rooms had been sealed up since the escape attempt. After September 3rd they knocked out the concrete and brick seals and they were open again. This was how we had been communicating to another building. We were flashing tap code out of these grates to a guy who had his head in one, watching and flashing back to us. We'd flash tap code with the little white lids that fit on top of our cups. But now the Gooks would not even look at those grates. They would walk by and never look. We'd be flashing along, and of course we'd stop when one of them came by, but they'd never look to see what was going on. Essentially they were just ignoring us.

Another big thing happened...probably biggest deal of all! Cigarettes went up from three to six a day. Wow! What a deal that was. In a room with six guys there were always a couple of guys that didn't smoke. There were some rooms with only a couple of smokers and guys were wolfing down a pack and a half a day. Smoking those strong Vietnamese things, we were really doing something! Of course cancer was not much of a threat. Being POWs, it wasn't something we worried about.

One day our room went out to pick weeds or shovel and we noticed that on the other side of the yard another room of guys was out batting a badminton birdie around. Here we were, two rooms out in full view of each other, and the guys in the other room waved over to us. These were guys we had never seen before. We had been talking to each other for years but had never been face to face. We still had a distance separating us I guess, maybe 40 or 50 yards, but at least we were in full view of each other. The guards just smiled and acted like there was nothing to it. This sounds small but to us at this time it was a really thrilling thing because it was a major breakthrough.

This continued the next few days. There always seemed to be another room purposely out when we were. Guards would leave court yard gate doors open so when we went out to a quiz room to write a letter or something, guys in another room would be out in their court yard bathing. They'd gang up around the door and wave to us and call out their names so we could get IDs on them. The guards would just smile and act ignorant. It looked like this was their first step-by-step, Mickey Mouse way to open up the camp so people could go out together during the day. That's what it looked like, but as it turned out it never came to pass in The Annex.

In the spring of 1970 they dropped that routine. They weren't really trying to prevent us from seeing other people but they just didn't give us the opportunity. Occasional opportunities came when we might be out working and the guard would leave the court yard door open. But when he finished his business outside our court yard he would shut the gate.

We noticed a big-official type guy in the camp on a couple of occasions. We called him the "GSO," General Staff Officer. He came twice in 1970. He seemed to be some sort of a policy liaison man between all camp personnel and the military staff in Hanoi that oversaw the prison routine. He was probably a Colonel although he never wore his rank. But he was obviously a VIG - a very important Gook. All the people in the camp would jump through their asses when he'd come around.

On a couple of occasions he called someone to come in and talk to him. It would just be somebody at random in the camp. I never did but I had roommates who did. He'd just ask about all the things that were going on in the camp and what our feelings were on this, that and the other. He would talk bullshit about how they could improve relations and all this kind of horseshit.

We told him time after time we didn't want any of their goodies. Just let us open our doors, write our letters home and we would take care of ourselves. We also told him we wanted better medical treatment and we bitched about the food all the time. So it looked like finally, after all these years, they were sending somebody down into the camp to find out what the hell was going on. It looked like somebody up high was taking an active interest in the POWs, or criminals, as they were still calling us.

Previously we had these obnoxious camp regulations. They plastered a copy in every room and they would have a copy plastered in the quiz room. Everybody would brush their teeth and shake out their tooth brush on the camp regulations in our room. If you felt particularly pissed off you might spit on it as you happened to walk by. One day they came in and took down the regulations, and they stayed gone for several weeks.

Finally they came back with a new set of camp regulations and posted them on the door. They were quite something to behold. They were a complete change, a softening of the line. This set of camp regulations didn't say anything whatsoever about communicating. They referred to us as "American Airmen detained in the Democratic Republic of Vietnam." They stopped calling us criminals but they didn't speak of us as prisoners either. All the business about "when being questioned by the camp officers you must give full information to the extent of your knowledge and you must tell everything" wasn't there. There was an item that said when any person was sick he must "Bao Cao" the guard. It noted that if we did not report being sick to the guard we would be punished. We also had to keep our room neat and clean and in order. It was more like a set of college dorm regulations than a prisoner of war camp.

Throughout the spring of 1970 there just weren't any confrontations with guards. As time wore along we even stopped nodding our heads. The guards bitched a little bit about not getting the head nods but they never did anything but just bitch and then leave. Nobody was being smacked around. One guy in our room, Air Force First Lieutenant Gerry Gerndt, had a confrontation with a guard in the spring of 1970. It was a pretty bad confrontation, I think he said "Fuck you" to the guard, which was a real no-no. They had learned that English word early on. So you just didn't do that.

If he had done that six months before he would have gotten his bloody head knocked off, taken to the quiz room, been strapped about 10 lashes, and then put into leg irons or manacles. All they did with him this time was take him out of the room and put him in a small solo cell that they had built for that purpose. It wasn't really any big deal. It was a small, single man cell. They left him there for about a week and then brought him back to our room. After what we had been through, it was nothing. Christ! We couldn't believe it!

Gerry told us the guard had come around and given him all his meals and water. He had even been allowed to get a fresh bucket of water to wash with.

The same thing happened later that spring and another guy got the same punishment. They let him cool his heels for a week in solitary and then brought him back to the room. Of course now we all wanted to have confrontations with the guard in hopes of being thrown into solitary for a week because it was a great chance to get the hell away from your roommates. It was literally viewed as a chance to relax for a week and to be alone for awhile instead of having arguments with your roommates all day long.

The food and everything continued to be good and then they started up a new program for propaganda. This was real soft line stuff. It was more a good deal than anything else. It wasn't the old hard line push they'd had before. It amounted to drawing and art work, but you could do it in your room if you wanted. The Gooks told us if we wanted to do this they would give us paper, pencils, crayons, paints and crap.

Everyone in our room told them to stuff it. All the other rooms in The Annex did the same thing except one. We still had a little bit of a problem because over in The Zoo where Larry Guarino was SRO, there were guys doing art work and Larry had authorized it. He was also still doing it himself.

There was one room of the youngest guys in our camp. They were all 24 or 25 years old. Two or three of them wanted to draw, they were artistically inclined and so they did. Then all the guys in that room were doing art work. This really hacked off the other rooms.

Next door to them was a room of eight or nine guys who a couple days before Christmas had moved into our camp from Son Tay. These guys were all the Catholics who had been bundled up and taken to the Son Tay camp. They had been asked if they wanted to attend church services and all of them had refused to go.

So this room of Catholics was living next door to the artistic guys. Their SRO was my old roommate, Smitty Harris. Smitty was jumping up and down over there. He was an old hard-liner, an old '65 reprobate like myself. He was telling these guys that he advised against doing art work strongly and he didn't think they should do it. He was firing messages over to Konnie Trautman telling him to knock off this soft-line shit. As it went through all the rooms we were adding our endorsements in agreement. But Konnie, in spite of all the strong feelings against the art work in the camp, decided he would not counter Larry Guarino's orders by giving stronger orders, thus superseding Guarino's.

The room Konnie was in at this time was all of our senior SROs who had been put together after the escape attempt. After September 3rd their punishment dropped off too but they remained together. Konnie and those guys had gone through quite a lot. They were still being careful, not scared but careful. They were "cooling it" as we termed it. They had all been beaten up badly so they were kind of playing it cool.

The Gooks were taking selected paintings downtown for the public to see. They were getting foreign correspondents and people to come take pictures of the shit so they would go out and spread bullshit stories about all the nice things Americans were allowed to do in the camps. Another thing they had been trying to push was the "camp magazine." The name of this piece of crap was "New Runways," a real cute little name for pilots. "New Runways" had art work and articles that were supposedly written by Americans. These things were printed up by the Gooks. I never actually saw one myself but I guess they distributed them out to the world. They were trying to get articles saying we were looking for new runways, choosing a better way of life for ourselves, not going along with American policies and that we realized the Vietnamese people had the right to control their own destiny. There were poems that had been written by Yanks. I guess there were four or five guys in the Hanoi area who were writing articles for it. This "New Runways" kick went on for awhile and then they dropped it. I don't imagine they printed more than three or so editions before they dropped the program. But I believe they did get some good propaganda out of it.

One thing we had started began to grow as we were able to communicate with more people. A great diversion for almost everyone became attending classes that were taught by POWs. We had guys that were experts in all sorts of things. Some of our teachers taught mathematics, engineering, electronics, history, geography, foreign languages and numerous other academic subjects. Men also gave instructions on other topics of interest like hunting, fishing, sports, bridge, and anything else they could remember. Guys also told lengthy stories in the evenings, plus movies. Movies were very popular as we got into the bigger rooms.

I had a fairly good background in Spanish so I began teaching it to cellmates and to other guys by tapping. I was able to improve my own courses by getting vocabulary and such from what others remembered. I loved telling movies, so later on in the big rooms I was usually a once-a-week feature. Again, I always added what I remembered about a movie with scenes other guys remembered as a preparation for my "show." I must admit adding a few flourishes of my own as well, especially of course for the sexy scenes. Those were popular, usually accompanied by many hoots and groans.

I benefited by learning a good bit of French and German from my own language teachers. My primary French teacher, Glen Daigle, was a

340

"coon-ass" from southern Louisiana so he was fluent in French. Well, sort of. (I got some interesting reactions from French people when I was in France on a European vacation just after I came home.)

There were always interesting debates and arguments about things people taught. Whenever there was a difference of opinion on the veracity of a statement or piece of information, we always referred to it as a "Hanoi Fact." That meant it was to be checked out later.

One day, in the early summer of 1970, we were out in the court yard mulling around, peeking through the cracks and holes we had bored in our walls, looking at our "TV" sets. I was looking over towards room nine when I saw the court yard door open there and there was a Yank in the court yard. This room had been empty so I called a couple of guys over and they all took a look. We were pretty excited about seeing a new solo Yank in the camp.

This guy appeared to have something wrong with him. He moved very slowly and was all slumped over. He looked skinny and he had black hair. He appeared to weigh 125-130 pounds so he was obviously not in good health. He was sweeping the court yard with slow, deliberate strokes, kind of acting like a zombie. None of us could recognize him until I got Burt Campbell to look and Burt said, "Jesus Christ, that's Cobeal."

So we had an ID on Earl Cobeal. We could not get any communication over there to him. The turnkey was taking care of him like the rest of us. He was getting the same food and everything else that we were but he was living solo. He stayed in that room almost two months. We would observe him whenever we could, when we were out in the court yard. On a few occasions we saw him when the turnkey would open the court yard door and take him out or something like that. He appeared to be semi-catatonic, like he was having deep mental problems. Then finally days went by and we never saw him again. So Earl Cobeal was there in The Annex in late spring and early summer of 1970. Sadly Earl never made it home.

About June of 1970 we got a medical inspection. "Mr. Peepers" came around. This was the old doctor who had been hovering around the camps off and on for a couple of years. Old Peepers had been a pretty good Joe. He was the guy who had come in, doctored me up and had gotten me off the hook when I was being tortured back in Little Vegas.

Peepers came into our room with a big smile, "How are you, okay, uh, okay?" He came down the line to each individual bunk. He had an officer to interpret and we could speak English or a little French to him. He spoke a small amount of English and understood a lot more than he spoke.

When he got down to my bunk he stopped and said, "Ah, Butler, how are you, okay?"

I said, "Okay."

He motioned for me to raise up my pant legs and he took a look at my knees. He had me take my shirt off and he looked at my battle scars. Then he had them take down notes on my condition. He remembered very well from Little Vegas all the places I had been banged-up. He looked in my ears and said "Um, yep, broken ear drums." He checked my teeth, "Yep, broken teeth."

He said, "Okay, eat?"

I said, "Yes, I eat like a horse."

He said, "Exercise?"

I said, "Yes, I exercise."

He said, "Sleep okay?"

I said, "I sleep okay."

He went over to Neil Jones and gave him an examination. Neil was the one with the broken arm. The bone in his upper arm was completely severed from when they first put him in the straps back in '66. They crunched those broken arms around and cut some nerves in his arm. Peepers had a big confab with Neil for about 45 minutes. What it amounted to was the Gooks wanted to give him an operation. They had approached Neil with a proposal for an operation in the spring of 1969. After a lot of thought Neil had decided against it because the operations these guys gave out were not the best!

They did things to guys like they did to Dale Osborne. They removed half of his forearm and then attached his hand and wrist almost to his elbow. They did some real bad shit to other guys and left them in miserable shape.

Mr. Peepers kept insisting that what they would do when they operated was graft a piece of bone there and put a pin in his arm to bring it back together. This pin would be a bar six to eight inches long. He said after the operation Neil would be in casts for six months or so. He said Neil would get several casts and they would be changed. And after it healed he would be able to use his arm again.

We didn't see any reason to believe we were going to be released any time soon, so we began to discuss it when Peepers left the room with the guards and medics. Finally Neil said he wanted us to think about it for 24 hours and then we'd have a room meeting where we would go around the room and everybody would give their opinion. The next day we did that. My opinion was I couldn't see doing any correcting surgery here since he wasn't in any real pain. I told him that if I were him I'd wait until I got home and let them do it where I knew I could get good work done.

Most of the other guys in the room voted the same way. I think there were only one or two guys who thought it might be a good deal to have it done. Then Neil thought about it for about another week or so. Finally one day he was called out to interrogation. He told them "Okay" he would let them do it. He came back and told us what his decision was and we were all behind him. We told him good luck.

A couple of weeks later they came and took Neil out of the room, to a jeep and to the hospital.

After he was gone our turnkey was always addressing Tom Norris as the SRO, though I was senior to him. This turnkey was always asking things of Tom so I told him not to give answers but just to point back to me in the back of the room.

The turnkey was a real good little guy we called "Howdy-Doody." Howdy was a pretty good buddy of mine, as far as guards went. We always got along well together. I liked to work outside with another guy in the room named Tom McNish and Howdy would come get Tom and me all the time. McNish is a huge guy and really strong. Howdy would come get us to do chores in the yard like hoeing weeds or carrying trash around. Tom and I could carry pretty heavy loads and Howdy liked to take us out when other Gooks were around the camp so he could let them marvel at how much shit we could carry at one time. Tom, the monster, would show them how he could lift a bomb-shelter cover and carry it by himself. These covers were round, about 3 to 4 feet in diameter, and they weighed probably 200 pounds. So Howdy and I were on pretty good speaking terms. Howdy taught me some Vietnamese words and I could communicate with him pretty well.

Howdy seemed pretty confused about this. Tom Norris kept directing him back towards me. This went on for about a day. Then the next day I was called out to an interrogation. I walked in and this was my first meeting with "The Elf." It seemed that now Elf had been transferred to be our officer-in-charge. I walked in and didn't head nod or anything. Elf just looked at me and told me to sit down. He started off real pleasant, just like the format since September 3rd, with "How are you?"

I said, "I'm fine."

He said, "How are your roommates?"

I said, "They are fine too. Lockhart has a cold and McNish has a headache. Why can't we get aspirin more often?" and I started off on my usual line of the chow is lousy, and why can't we get more bread and bitch, bitch, bitch about this and that.

He said, "Now stop, I bring you here for the first time. I want to meet you. I want you to tell me about yourself. Are you married?"

I said, "Yes."

He said, "Do you have any children?"

I said, "Yes."

He said, "You are in the Navy, is that correct?"

I said, "Yes, that is correct."

"What is your home town?"

And so it went with little bullshit things like that. Then he said, "Now do you have anything you want to tell me?"

I said, "Yes, I do. Captain Jones" – The Elf got a grimace on his face when I used Captain but he kept his mouth shut – "Captain Jones was taken to the hospital. As you know, Captain Jones was our senior ranking officer but now I am the senior ranking officer in our room. Evidently your guard does not realize this and I would appreciate it if you would instruct him to deal with me since I am senior to Captain Norris."

He sat there politely and listened to this ream of horseshit I was giving him. I went on and on about how being the senior ranking officer of my room, I was, of course, responsible for my men. With that he held up his hands and said, "Stop, Stop, Stop - you do not understand!"

The Elf had a particular manner of speaking that was very funny. Many guys spent hours mimicking Elf in our rooms.

He said, "You do not understand. You do not understand. Here in the Democratic Republic of Vietnam everybody is equal. Everyone is equal. Of course, you are a criminal. You are not a prisoner of war, and you all have the same rank. You are the same as all of your roommates, as all the prisoners here. Nobody is a senior officer. We do not recognize your rank at all. We do not deal with you. We deal with all of you as individuals because you are all equal. But - of course, since you are the senior ranking officer of your room, you will be responsible for your men." Then he smiled real big.

My head was spinning; it was typical Gook! With the smile planted on his face, he repeated, "Do you have any requests?"

I said, "Yeah, get out your pencil and paper."

He grimaced and said, "Just make them limited, just the major ones."

I said, "Okay, first of all, how is Captain Jones?"

He said, "Jones is doing fine. He is in the hospital and he is receiving good treatment."

I said, "When will he return?"

He said, "I do not know. I do not know. This is up to the doctors."

I asked, "Can you give us some indication whenever you find out he will return?"

He said "Of course."

I said, "Okay, about the health of the guys in my room," and I mentioned a couple of guys who had minor problems.

He said, "All right, I will send a medic. Any other questions?"

I said, "Yeah, about the chow, the food is really lousy."

He said, "Now you are receiving vitamin pills, right?"

I said, "Yes."

(Each guy was now receiving a vitamin pill everyday. We were getting them in our packages as they arrived. This is one thing the Gooks never really cut back, probably because they realized that this was cheap health insurance. It didn't cost them a thing since they were coming in our packages and they kept us a hell of a lot healthier than what we had been before. Most everybody's problems just cleared up about a thousand percent after we started getting vitamins.)

He said, "We try to give you what we can," and then he added some more excuses.

I continued with a few bitches about minor things.

Then he said, "If you're through you can go back to your room."

So Howdy came in with a big smile on his face and we sauntered back to the room together. The guys in the room were waiting to go out to bathe. Our time to bathe was to come when I got back to the room.

When we arrived, Howdy, at the door, said, "Bât, wash, okay?"

I said, "Okay." I made a motion to the guys and we all went outside and washed.

As we finished washing Howdy came in and got us all collected back in the room.

Standing at the door he said, "Bât."

I said, "What?"

He said, "Open window." He meant the window in the back of our room.

I said, "Okay," and one of the guys reached back and popped the window open. Then with a really big smile, Howdy shut the door and walked off.

It was amazing. Not only had The Elf heard me but he acted on it right away. Considering the way our "demands" had been ignored, and used against us all those years, this was quite something. For the next three or four weeks that I was SRO in the room, Howdy called me when he wanted anything done.

Then Neil came back and he told us all about the fantastic treatment he'd received at the hospital. He had been put in a room, a genuine hospital room, which was terrific by Gook terms although shoddy by our standards. Neil reported that the surgery had been done with a nerve-block anesthesia. He was awake the whole time but had no sensation whatsoever. He said the nerve block was just tremendous. He had watched and the surgery had been excellent. They put the pin in, sewed him all up and put him in a cast.

He had a guard with him in the room the entire time since Neil had gotten out of surgery. This guard had done absolutely everything for him. Neil was real weak after the surgery. His guard had helped him to the crapper, helped him wipe his ass, and just did everything for him.

Neil had done a lot of talking with this little guard and eventually the guy told him that he had been in the 1968 Tet Offensive and that he was an actual South Vietnamese VC. After the Tet offensive he had moved up north and become a guard in the camp. Neil and this guy got along really well and they were actually good friends for the rest of the time we were in The Annex. This guy would come around and open the back window when he was on duty and shoot the shit with Neil.

So Neil received top-notch medical treatment for Gook land. When he came back to us he was on an extra beefed-up diet, getting all sorts of good treats. We also made him eat all the meat and protein things we got in our packages. There again we told him he would eat it or we would shove it down his throat, so he didn't have much choice.

Neil was in an upper body cast through the summer. It got hotter than blue blazes and he got heat rash under the thing. The poor bastard was miserable. We used to take turns fanning him. But at least his arm was healing up. He came out of his cast six months later and began to use his arm. He could bend it at the elbow and use his hand well enough to close his fingers and bend his wrist inward. But he could not raise his hand nor could he open his fingers after he closed them.

The nerves that ran along the top part of his arm had been cut. The muscles had no movement in that direction. But now he had an arm that he began to use. I lived with Neil for the next couple of years, and there at the very end, when we were ready to go home, he could do 20 push ups. His repaired arm was about an inch and a half shorter than the other arm. But he had an arm that didn't look too bad, though it had some bad scars in the upper part of it. He could shuffle cards with his hand and do small things like that. It got stronger as time went along.

Neil Jones went through a lot of pain and misery with that arm for years but he was a real gutsy guy who kept standing tall. Also, he got lucky, got a good operation and some decent treatment at a good period of time in prison life. I expect that with certain restrictions he would be able to fly again with his new arm.

Nothing much eventful happened in the summer of 1970. It got hotter than hell and everybody suffered with heat rash. But everybody was much happier and our mental conditions began to improve noticeably. We started losing our intense hatred and bitterness, maybe reducing it down to just a normal amount of hate and bitterness towards the little slant-eyed cock-suckers!

Then on the afternoon of August 25th, 1970 we began to see a lot of activity in the camp and the word spread that there was an imminent move. The Gooks came around and gave everybody their packages. Normally they would store most of our stuff in the quiz room and only allow us to take parts of it back to our room.

But they had us all go to the quiz room and check out all of the stuff that belonged to us. There was also a big rush to get our August letters done. So from the little camp signs that we were always watching and our familiarity with everyday routine, we immediately sensed significant changes. It was impossible for the Gooks to hide them from us. So we all became aware that we were going to move on the afternoon of the 25th.

There was a lot excitement among the guards amidst the preparations. There were Jeeps all around and we could see guards loading up gear and getting ready. That night they came in and told us to roll up all of our gear. They put us on a bus with guys from other rooms. It was a normal bus with seats in it. We were not handcuffed, put in leg irons or even blindfolded.

We had more damn crap and paraphernalia than we could believe. We had all of our package goodies, our snake baskets and our bed rolls. We looked like bachelor officers moving from one station to another in a Corvette. The busses were loaded and full. To top it off the buses were open and we could look out. I remember it was a beautiful, moon-lit night. We got underway from the Zoo Annex and began the drive to a new camp that we would name "Camp Faith."

22. Camp Faith

8/25/70 – 11/25/70

We drove into the new camp area after a two hour trip where we saw a lot of barracks and Army troops stationed in the immediate area. It looked like an extremely large military complex. We drove up to the side of the camp itself and were let out. They walked us into a center compound area which was probably 300 by 100 yards. Several buildings were in the center of this large compound. Ringing this center area were five other prison compounds, two on the north, two on the south and one on the west side. Each of them was surrounded by high brick and concrete walls, probably 12 to 15 feet high with barbed wire on top.

We were moved into the compound on the north side of the complex. We walked in through a gate in the wall and there directly in front of us was a long building. We walked through a back door and into a room that was obviously going to be a quiz, or administrative room since there weren't too many quizzes taking place anymore.

We walked through this room and out the north side where we were split off into different rooms. There were 5 prison rooms in this building. I was taken to room four and found that eleven other guys were already there. They were all guys I had lived with or covertly communicated with in The Annex. It was a nice room as far as prison cells in the Hanoi area went. There were wooden bunks built down either side of the room. In the back was a large cupboard where we could put our crap like toilet articles and package items.

To my great surprise, there was a table with benches down either side in the center of the room. I couldn't believe my eyes when I saw this. This table would accommodate about eight guys so we rotated eating at the table when we got our meals. On the north and south side of the room were completely open bay windows. The windows were about three feet wide and eight feet high, with bars of course. Along the north side, in front of the building, was a porch that ran the length of the building. In front was a large yard area with a clothes line that ran down the center of it.

The yard extended past the length of the building on either side and out about 70 yards to the wall, which we assumed was the north wall of the complex. At the west end of the camp were four crapper stalls and a large open-bay shower room. It had a huge water tank that was about five feet deep and ten feet long. The tank had a spigot that filled it up. So when lots of guys were in there to bathe we could dip water with our buckets and shower ourselves. The floor of the shower room was concrete as was the floor in our room. It was by far the most beautiful set up we had seen since we arrived in Vietnam.

That night we immediately made contact with the guys in rooms five and three on either side of us. The next morning we were in contact with rooms two and one. There were a total of 56 of us. We were all of the people from The Annex with the exception of 12 guys who had been moved out earlier and were taken to a different camp some place. We didn't know it at the time but soon found out they also had come to Camp Faith, but had been moved into another compound area there.

Communication was duck soup here. We made contact with the other guys just by talking out the back windows to each other. Guards would come around and make some feeble attempt to tell us to shut up but then they'd just walk on and kind of ignore it.

The next day the Gooks started letting us out one room at a time to shower and so forth. It turned out that The Elf was going to be our officer in charge of the compound. He told us that we were going to clean up the prison yard and remove all the grass from it. They brought in some shovels, and dirt tampers made of concrete. We started to work, one room at a time. Then there were two rooms at a time. They kept us segregated from the rooms at the other end of the compound. We were not allowed to walk across a certain line so we could communicate with each other.

This Mickey Mouse business went on for a week or two. We started to have conflicts with the camp personnel because we were defying them by openly talking to each other. Then we began actually walking over to shoot the shit with each other. The guards were running themselves nuts trying to keep us from doing this, but what the Gooks were doing was this step-by-step, Mickey Mouse shit again. They were changing the policy gradually; though of course not fast enough for us.

Eventually, after a month or so, it finally evolved to where everybody in the compound was out together from about 8 o'clock in the morning till about 1:00, which was siesta time. Then we could go out from 2:00 until about 5:00 in the afternoon. We removed all the grass and made it look as slick as a baby's butt. We built a track that we could run on and guys started running. Some of our craftsmen made baseballs that were really as good as the major leagues. Okay, not that good, but they were good. They used a combination of rolled up socks and bread dough packed into a hard ball for the center core. They cut pieces of material to make the baseball wrapper. They sewed it with homemade needles. These baseballs were really beautiful. Only trouble with them was someone was always throwing one over the wall. Whenever that happened we usually wouldn't get them back because Gooks on the other side would collect and not return them.

All we were able to do was play catch, but that was tremendous. One thing we noticed was how screwed up our reflexes and reactions were after having not done anything like this for such a long time. At first it was difficult to throw with any coordination or accuracy. It was also difficult at first to catch a ball. We felt clumsy at it. After awhile we noticed our reactions improving and we were getting back into the old swing of things.

I met Navy Lt. Mike McGrath in this room which was very lucky for me. Mike was flying A4s out of NAS Lemoore, was shot down in 1968 and had known my wife so he had some personal information about her and my daughter Diane. Mike had been terribly tortured with his broken arm. His shoulder bone had been pushed up under his scapula from the ejection and the Gooks used it to torture him. He turned out to be a terrific artist and made clever things out of almost nothing. He also turned out to be one of my best friends.

In truth, considering our status, we were really enjoying life out there and it helped that it was sunny all the time. Guys were running around in their skivvies and we all got good sun tans. Everybody's weight started increasing and guys started looking pretty damn good. My weight went from 160 to 180 pounds in the three months I was at Camp Faith.

The first night there was a little confrontation in the room next door with Tom McNish and a guard. Tom was just sitting on his bunk, which happened to be next to a window, and he had his hands on the bars. Like I said before, Tom was a real monster of a guy. He has about a 50-inch chest and 18-inch biceps. He was really a bruiser. Tom was sitting there with his hands on the bars and the guard came by and started raising hell with him about it. The guard walked up and checked the bar. He wiggled it around and like most bars and windows in Vietnam you could wiggle them but you would never be able to break out.

The guard wiggled the bars around a little bit and then went running away. Tom didn't think anything about it. But about three hours later, around midnight, the Gooks came rampaging into the camp with the camp commander who was a two bar and star major. They all came storming into McNish's room, grabbed him up and put him into a solo cell for bad guys on the back side of the building. They put him into the cell and in leg irons. They said he had been trying to escape. Then they came around and inspected all our rooms in the middle of the night.

They left Mac back there in irons for about three days and then they took the irons off him. There were no real problems for him because he could talk to us. We named that cell "Uncle Tom's Cabin." Then after about three more days they put him back into his room. They were all peaches and cream after that.

Later on, after we moved to Camp Unity, we talked to other guys who had lived in other compounds at Camp Faith. We found out that the Gooks had done this same thing in all the compounds, on the same night, checking all the window bars. The camp commander's big idea was to show authority. It was typical of how the Gooks liked to operate. They let you do something and then they let you figure it out for yourself what you did wrong.

The camp commander was about average height and rotund. He had very smooth features, kind of beady eyes and the kind of hair that Vietnamese and a lot of Asians have that sticks out. His stuck out quite a bit so we nicknamed him "Bushy." I'd say he was probably 50 years old or so and had obviously been through lots of war. Bushy really wasn't too bad as far as camp commanders go. I also had him for camp commander up at Dog Patch later on. Of course he was screwed up as far as commie officers go but he wasn't too bad as a camp commander.

We noticed that the guards and camp people were all new. They were people we had not seen before. We had a bar and 3 star sergeant who was the overseer of the turnkeys. There were two turnkeys for the building. He also handled the gun guards. They had guard towers on all the corners of the camp that were manned at all times to watch the walls. The Gooks up there had submachine guns and walkie-talkie telephones. In case there was any kind of break they could call central headquarters. This bar and three star sergeant who ran the camp was really a terrific guy. If there was one Gook I'd like to bring back and enlist in the Navy it would be this guy.

He was an efficient and intelligent operator and he actually had a pleasant personality. He always had a smile on his face and he would come up to us and shoot the bull. He wasn't trying to be overly friendly but he was just a damn good sergeant. He kept his men in line. If we needed tools to repair anything or if we needed small items around the camp he would see that we got them in a jiffy. We just called him "Sarge."

Everyone just eased off. In general our mental and physical health improved dramatically. Everybody picked up weight and began to look like human beings again. The food was some of the best I had as a POW. They would bring a huge pot of soup and all the bread we wanted for each meal. We just told the guard that we wanted more and the next meal it would there. They'd bring the huge soup pot and somebody from our room would go out to pick it up and bring it in. It was the same with the big water pots. We had one of these huge pots in our room. They gave us tea once a day and water once a day. They would have given us tea twice a day if we asked for it but some of the guys pissed and moaned and didn't like the tea. Other guys pissed and moaned and didn't like the water. So our SRO, in utter frustration said, "God damn it. We'll have half and half."

Konnie Trautman was SRO for the compound and also a roommate. Our compound was pretty cut off from the other compounds so there wasn't really much communication with them. There was some a little bit later but for all purposes our compound was Camp Faith and Konnie was our SRO.

Konnie began to have a few confrontations with Bushy. Bushy would come into the compound and Konnie would go up and make a request for the entire compound and Bushy wouldn't talk to him. He would piss and moan because Konnie was trying to act like an SRO and wouldn't listen to him. But whenever there was a problem in the compound Bushy would be down there with Elf and they'd call Konnie out to quiz to ream his ass out instead of calling somebody else.

This was typical Gook behavior. They were saying they weren't recognizing our SROs but they did recognize them, mostly because we forced them to. This was a game we played up until the day we left. They had knocked off the "room responsible" thing for all intents and purposes after September 3, 1969 but they tried it again a few occasions later when they were having too much trouble with an SRO. Then to put pressure on him, they would assign some junior guy to be a room responsible and call him out and talk to him. This was one way they had to get an SRO to settle down and not raise too much hell. In other words they were saying "if you want to deal with us you have to be reasonable or we won't deal with you."

Nothing much eventful happened at Camp Faith until we had been there about four weeks. One day one of our more aggressive types, Bob Purcell, was outside in the yard and he decided to climb up in a tree to look over the wall. Percy had more guts than you could believe. There he was, up in a tree looking over in the next compound. It was a wonder he didn't get shot by some guard in a tower. He was looking over the wall and he noticed that in the next compound east of ours there were five guys living in a room. They were Gartley, Mayhew, Brown, Ingvalson and someone else whose name I forgot.

Percy had known Roger Ingvalson before he was shot down and they had been friends so he yelled over to him. Ingvalson saw Percy and gave him a big smile and a wave. Percy yelled for him to pick up a note on top of the wall. So we dropped a note there the next day and they picked it up.

We knew, from the stuff we had heard on the radio and from rumors, that these five had been playing ball with the Gooks. They had been segregated from other people from the first moment they walked into prison. None of them had ever been tortured and they had been given the real low pressure, low key, soft line by the Gooks. And they had pretty much bought it. They had been doing stuff for propaganda like going out to press conferences and they were getting extra special treatment.

But they had always been separated from the other guys and didn't know what was really going on. I think some of them had made statements and probably some of them also made amnesty statements. So Percy got contact with them and Konnie started sending notes and instructions over to these guys to stop playing ball with the Gooks. He told them they were on our team. And we told them briefly the kind of treatment we had experienced and the kind of torture that had gone on.

This sort of opened their eyes to what the hell was going on. They acknowledged all our notes and sent back a little information they had and what had been going on with them.

Rog Ingvalson was a guy I personally felt sorry for. He had been more or less playing soft with the Gooks. As I said, he'd been segregated ever since he came in and had never been with any other guys. He was an Air Force major and his wife had a terminal disease when he was shot down. I believe he had three children and he knew his wife was going to die.

It was a terrible thing for him to live with in prison, not knowing when and so forth. As it turned out she died in '69 or '70 and he found out about it in '71. It was really a tough go for the guy. As soon as he found out his wife had died he gave up hope of an early release and joined our team. He was a hard nut from that point on.

I don't think he ever did anything that was very bad. He did play kind of a soft line and he was hoping they would release him. Hell, I think if my wife had been the same as his I might have done the same thing if I thought I could do it and not completely give up my honor. I would have wanted to leave that shit hole to get home before my wife died too.

When we moved into Camp Faith, we hard-liners started in on Konnie from the first night we had room meetings. Some of these meetings lasted from after chow till nine o'clock at night. We just went round and round the room on every subject of prison life and prison policy. After three or four nights of this Konnie said he wanted to get a consensus from other SROs in the other rooms, which he did. They all took the same stand and he said, "All right, we're on our own alone out here and I'm it. My policies are to hold the line."

So Konnie started writing policies for us. There was to be no drawing, no going out to anything outside the camp, including church services, no decorating our rooms for Christmas, no going out to a Christmas Tree, even if it was Christmas Eve and even in the quiz room. Real hard line stuff. Anything we could do to take the propaganda weapon away from the Gooks. If anybody was in the yard and somebody walked in with a camera, or we saw anyone with a camera, somebody would yell "Hey, Rube!" With that warning we'd all buzz back into our cells. If they happened to be locked then we'd all stand and turn our backs to the cameras. We would stop what we were doing and counter the propaganda.

Of course there was to be no head bowing or nodding whatsoever. The Gooks saw we had gone to this and this prompted the political cadre and the camp commander to come around to each room one afternoon. They informed us through an interpreter that they did not want head nods from us. This was, of course, after we had stopped doing it. They said what they wanted was for us to simply stand at attention in front of our bunks and be counted when the guard opened the door.

Konrad told them, as did the SROs in the other rooms, that we would not stand at attention for enlisted camp personnel. We would stand by the bunks and be counted but not at attention. We would only stand at attention for a camp officer since we are officers. At that point the camp commander and the cadre kind of swallowed but they had to buy it. And that was the end of that Mickey Mouse.

We got the camp completely cleaned up and everything organized according to our military structure. All our normal room and camp-wide work details were organized as a military organization. Things were just going along nicely and we were in the process of constructing a roofed-in area. We were building this with timbers and were putting a hard-packed floor in it. We were going to make a ping-pong table room out of it. The Gooks had promised us they were going to give us a ping-pong table.

Then came November 25th. We were all sitting in our room peacefully.

We hadn't heard an airplane in months. All of a sudden the whole damn sky lit up and there were bombs going off and shit flying everywhere. There were lights in the sky and all kinds of action going on about 15 miles away. This turned out to be the "Son Te" raid where they were supposed to be rescuing us. We didn't know what was going on at the time. But Jesus Christ, when we did find out, that our U.S. commandos had missed rescuing us by fifteen miles, we were some kind of pissed!

The next day the Gooks were very upset. They were running around inside the compound with a double guard force. That afternoon they came roaring into the camp and told us to pack up our gear because we were moving. Holy Cow! We were really ticked off because this was tropical paradise compared to all the years before. We grabbed our stuff and all of us got on the trucks. We left Camp Faith and went back into Hanoi, to the Hilton again. Only this time we went to the east side of the Hilton, into the very large compound area we called "Camp Unity."

23. Camp Unity

On November 25th of 1970 we underwent a very rapid move from Camp Faith back to the Hilton. We were rushed out of our cells and into trucks that evening with no consideration given by the Vietnamese for keeping people separated or anything else. They just ran us out of the camp into a whole slew of trucks that were waiting with their engines running. We saw large groups of Vietnamese prisoners being moved into the Camp Faith area as we were being herded out. They were wearing prison garb just like ours, indicating they were not just normal North Vietnamese criminals or probably not political prisoners. They were most likely South Vietnamese prisoners of war.

The large fiasco that had taken place a few nights before turned out to be the Son Tay raid. The order from their high command probably came during siesta for them to move us out that night. So they had about six hours to get everything together. On the afternoon of the 25th the Gooks rushed into the compound area. They moved everything out of the quiz room and were obviously very excited. Apparently they were really scared that another raid was going to be staged the next night and we were going to be plucked out of the camp. We didn't find out what had happened until after Christmas.

We got into the trucks. Some people were handcuffed, some had their hands tied, and some were hand cuffed to each other. In one way or another we were all bound up and away we went.

We rolled into the front of the Hilton and they marched us through the Heartbreak courtyard area then out into the big compound. In a few days we would name it "Camp Unity." I was taken with my group all the way across the compound into room two. This was a very large room, about 60 feet in length and 30 feet in width. It had a concrete bunker located in the center of the room that extended all the way to the back wall. There was a narrow aisle about 3½ feet wide that ran the length of the room on either side of the bunker. There was also a small adjoining room, where there was a two-hole crapper, located next to the cell door.

When we walked into the room the rest of the guys were already there. They were all of the guys who had come from my compound in Camp

Faith, 56 of us, jammed into the room. Our bed was the concrete bunker in the center of the room. There were no bed boards or anything else at this time. We threw our mats on top of it and that's where we slept. A day or so later the Vietnamese brought in some large wood planks, bed boards, and we put them down on the bunker. We were sleeping elbow to elbow and some guys had to sleep on the floor in the aisle. It was extremely crowded.

When we walked in the psychological impact on all of us was tremendous. This was the first time we had been thrown into a large room with so many people around. Back at Camp Faith we were getting outside but we didn't mass together as a group. Here at Camp Unity we were faced with this situation where all of us were jammed together in one great big goddamn room together. It was like a huge cocktail party.

It was a very emotional experience for me yet also very uncomfortable being around so many people. There was a lot of noise and confusion. It had been five years or more since I had experienced being around this many people at one time and in such close quarters. I felt fear and claustrophobia. It was a most unusual experience for all of us. Making it worse was the obvious fact that the Vietnamese hadn't made any preparations whatsoever for our arrival. The room was filthy and there were no provisions for water, food or anything else.

We were in there for 30 minutes or so when the outer door opened up and The Elf, along with several guards and a couple of his junior interrogators showed themselves. The Elf made an announcement. He told us we had been temporarily moved into this camp. This would be temporary lodging for us and the camp authorities realized the conditions here were not good, like the conditions in the camp we had just come from. He said they wanted to make conditions here good for us but this was temporary due to unforeseen circumstances. That was because the American Imperialists had bombed the Vietnamese people near our camp. They, of course, had moved us out in a hurry to save our lives.

Then Konnie Trautman stepped up and asked The Elf if we could get some water. He said, "Yes, we will bring you some water." After a couple of hours or so they did bring in a couple of pots of water so we could at least get a drink after that long trip. Konnie called us all to attention as soon as The Elf left. Everybody stopped what they were doing, sat down and listened to Konnie talk. He gave a ten-minute spiel, telling us that these conditions were pretty bad. And since we were so crowded we were going to have to exercise maximum consideration for each other.

He said each of us was to just bunk down wherever there was a place for this night. We had to move in close to get everybody on top of the concrete bunker. He said tomorrow we would start getting our room organized. He called out for the next senior man who it turned was Dan Doughty. Dan was the executive officer for the time being. Konnie told us to refer our individual problems if we had any to Dan. Dan would report to Konnie and Konnie would deal with the Vietnamese. He told us that he didn't want anybody to talk to the guards and that he would do all the talking.

So we bunked down for the night. Most of the guys sat up and shot the shit all night long. But some guys managed to get a little sleep.

The next day Konnie called a meeting of the half dozen or so senior people. They talked over the problems at great length and decided to organize our room into flights. We had six flights, each flight had a flight leader with the flights numbered in Air Force fashion: A, B, C, D, E and F. We Navy guys were in the minority. A-flight leader was the third most senior ranking man in the room. The second most senior ranking man in the room was our "operations officer," or "executive officer" if he was Navy. Konnie was the room SRO.

After we had organized into six flights we shifted our bunks accordingly so flights stayed together in the same area of the room. Konnie took the first bunk next to the door and the executive officer took the one opposite from him, also next to the door. Then we began to organize our room into work details. These were tasks like picking up chow and carrying out dishes, picking up water, cleaning up crappers, cleaning up the room, washing dishes and numerous other details. We organized our room into a functional unit for everyday living.

We had a room doctor who was Air Force Captain Dave Ford, a guy who had been a veterinarian assistant while going through high school. He had the best medical knowledge of anyone we had in the room. In fact Dave did have pretty good medical knowledge and he served us well for the next couple of years. He had served in almost every room he was in as a doctor and did a fine job.

We also had a room chaplain who was responsible for Catholic and Protestant services on Sunday. And we had a room education and entertainment officer who happened to be myself. I had served in that capacity at Camp Faith for our compound. There were numerous other functional jobs. We also set up our organization for communications. We had a communications officer and he had a number of people who worked with him.

Back in the old days everyone had communicated all the time because it was necessary since we had such small units. Now with more people together not everybody needed to be a communicator. Our communicators became very expert at all the different codes we had and they were always the ones sending and receiving messages and advising the SRO on incoming and outgoing traffic from outside our room.

We became a very efficient unit. Our operations and communications became swift and effective. As the days, weeks, and months went along our communications became more intricate and complicated. We developed a number of different communication circuits, with different people responsible for a certain circuit. We had the normal information circuit from room to room. This was just normal traffic and information that was debriefed everyday.

Another communication circuit was what we called a "Flag Circuit." This circuit was a primary link between room SROs and the SRO of the camp. This was in order to give SROs of each individual squadron (room) a closed circuit that was not available to anyone else in order to communicate with the SRO of the camp. He could relay problems with some individual in the room or just leadership problems that he himself was having. Or maybe he might have a bitch with an SRO in another room where they couldn't agree on something. These issues would be taken up with the SRO of the camp via our Flag Circuit. Sometimes there would be small infractions of discipline within a squadron where the SRO of a room would send a flag message to the SRO of the compound asking for advice, his recommendation, or just reporting to him on action that he had taken.

We also had a number of top secret circuits. They were for planning and organizing in the case of direct bomb damage, escape plans and other things. We had a very highly developed, covert organization that hinged on our communications. Though we were many together and the Vietnamese weren't trying any longer to keep us from talking with each other, communications were as vital as they had ever been.

Sometimes it was necessary to send top secret information by tapping or notes. When this happened or when there was any possibility whatsoever of someone else receiving the information, we had a couple of methods we devised to encode and decode.

Two methods that we used frequently were "knot and slide." These really were simple systems involving the alphabet. We would take what day of the week it was, starting with a Sunday. Here is an example: Let's say it was a Wednesday, and Wednesday being the fourth day of the week if we wanted to send an "A" we'd send a "D" instead. There were various methods like this. We also had systems using days of the month. We had many different ways of encoding our communications. The important thing was to use a key that was not readily apparent to the enemy. We also had methods of sending that used what we called the clock code. For example we could put little marks where the numbers on the clock were to provide the key to a tap code.

These communications systems depended on all of the participants knowing what key was being used for which messages. We standardized our methods and whoever was working on that particular circuit knew what method was being used for a certain period of time. We also changed our codes frequently. We stopped one we had been using after a month or so and we'd start a new one that someone had dreamed up. In case of any interceptions the changes would keep them off balance because we were always shifting the types of code in use.

Another security measure was that only a small number of people were responsible for each top secret circuit and these people were purposely not known to the SROs. This was for security in case an SRO was tortured to divulge classified information.

We had communications with the rest of the camp SROs in less than 24 hours after our arrival. Guys were always pretty fast with comm. and it didn't take long for us to find out who was around and what was going on to get organized. We did it very quickly after years of experience. We found out that our SRO of the camp, Colonel Flynn, was located in room seven, and that all the heavies were in that room at the time. All the heavies and several other selected people had come from Alcatraz and various other shit holes. These were prisons where the Gooks had been keeping their thumb on people for years.

The heavies started getting together immediately and they began pumping out camp policy to us. I guess this is the reason they came up with the name "Camp Unity" because this is the first time we had ever been unified. There were over three hundred of us together in the camp at this time. It was a perfect opportunity for Colonel Flynn and other high ranking officers like Colonel Winn, Colonel Risner, Captain Stockdale, Captain Denton and others to get out straight, unadulterated truth that would stand and hold for us the rest of the time we would be prisoners.

They published what they called "Plums." Plum was a code word for policy. There were eventually seven or eight plums that were put out to us. They concerned all the facets of our behavior as prisoners of war. They

360

mandated how we should act as prisoners of war with each other and with the Vietnamese. They once and for all finished the idea any body had about going to a delegation, giving any information in interrogation or doing anything whatsoever in the way of propaganda for the Gooks. There would be no more drawing, painting pictures, outside church services, or trips outside the camp for anything other than a move of POWs from one camp to another.

Another plum was concerning early release. Essentially it was that we should not accept early release. It said that if were offered early release by the Vietnamese we should demand to speak face to face to the SRO who was Colonel Flynn. If denied the opportunity to do this then we should demand that we be released in order. That order was established by Colonel Flynn, the heavies and was strictly according to Geneva Conventions. It mandated that first to go would be the sick and wounded, then civilians, then enlisted personnel, then in order of shoot downs with the old timers going first.

If denied this opportunity and simply taken to an airplane – in other words we were going to be expelled from the country – then we should keep our mouth shut and say absolutely nothing. They made it plain that we were not to do anything to secure our own release nor were we to accept an early release if given a choice. When actually being released, we were not to wear fancy clothes nor carry lots of luggage and crap with us. We were to do it in a military manner and to maintain our military bearing as members of the Armed Forces, whether we were allowed the privilege of wearing our uniforms or not. We were certain at that time, and always had been, that we would not be released in uniforms. The Gooks would never allow that of course.

Another plum concerned the code of conduct. It was a very simple code. It is a very good guideline for a military person to follow while a prisoner of war. Part of the code stipulated keeping faith with our fellow prisoners and our allies. There was some flexibility in it because of the situation the Communists put us in.

As far as I personally was concerned as a prisoner of war in North Vietnam, our code of conduct was a beautiful guide line for me to follow and I did follow it to the best of my ability. However I think no piece of paper could be perfect when the unknown situation would arise, but in general the code of conduct is a good set of guidelines and we all tried to follow it.

No matter how hard all of us tried to maintain our military bearing there were certainly times when it broke down. There were moments when personal emotions overwhelmed every effort to maintain military bearing. One in particular happened to me in 1971 at Camp Unity.

At that time I had only received two letters from home, after years as a POW. Thinking about my wife and daughter was agonizing. Diane had been born on March 2nd of 1965 and I had been shipped out on March 4th, just two days later. I hadn't seen my child during those six critical years of her growing up. I virtually hadn't heard a word about her during that whole time. I didn't even know what she looked like.

One day the Vietnamese called some of the guys out to get letters from home. And lo and behold, I was one of the guys. I went outside and sat down at a table they had set up. The interrogator handed me a letter. I opened it up and there was not only a very short letter from my wife but also a photograph of Diane. As I read the letter and looked at the picture, a flood of tears started coming.

When I got up and walked back I was sobbing and couldn't talk to the guys. A lot of guys who were outside there saw what was happening. A lot of them started crying too when they saw my reaction to the letter and photograph that I had been given after all those years.

Diane was six years old in this picture. I had such a powerful emotional reaction. All those years as a prisoner. All those years away from my baby girl. It was all combined with the heartache of knowing I had been there so long, that I didn't know when I would ever get to go home and that I might not go home. It was just overpowering at that moment. I felt like my stomach and heart were going to come out of my body. It was so painful, and so terribly depressing.

While at Camp Unity we found out from Air Force Major Ken Hughey that the Vietnamese were keeping civilian captives in a separate camp. Ken had been shot down in 1967 and shortly after that he had been bugging the Gooks to allow him to have books to read. He was bitching for better food and so forth but in particular he bitched for books. For some unknown reason to us, though many of us had bitched for many a year, they took Ken away from the Heartbreak camp and put him into a camp no one else had been in. It was out in the country and we named it "Camp Charlie Victor". They put him in a building by himself. There were no other military personnel out there.

There was another long building some distance away from him that contained all the civilians who had been captured. There were also a few military personnel who had been brought up from the Tet offensive.

Among them was an Air Force Colonel Purcell. This camp had a low-key operation going. There were not too many interrogations and there was no head knocking. They were running their operation the way you would expect with civilians.

Then the Vietnamese started giving Ken books on Shakespeare and some novels. They let him live out there in the country by himself while he read these books. I think it was some little experiment on their part. They didn't get jack shit out of Ken but they let him read all these books.

There was a civilian living close to Ken named Manhart. One day Ken discovered he was there and he made contact by climbing up the wall and yelling at him. Then they started exchanging notes and Ken taught this guy everything we knew including the Tap Code. He got all the names of the other civilians that came up with him which Ken memorized. Later on the Gooks just moved Ken back in with us. And that's how we had the information on our civilians.

Throughout our confinement in Vietnam, starting in 1965, the civilians were always kept separate from the military with one exception. That was with Ernie Brace for just a short time when we moved into Camp Unity. Ernie was in a solo room in building zero, which was right around the corner from room one where the heavies were and they got contact with him.

Ernie was a CIA civilian who had been flying for Air America. He quickly picked up our communications and was just like any other military man in the camp. He took his orders from the SRO and was a communicating son of a gun, just like anyone else. Ernie had been brought in from the Dien Bien Phu area in the Truong Son Mountains, way out northwest of Hanoi. I believe he had been shot down in April of 1965 and he spent a very lonely first 2½ years in a cave and in leg irons.

From talking to some of our civilian POWs at Balboa Naval Hospital, I found out they did some of the same goddamn things we military did! They resisted and served with honor. What it said was that when an American is stuck with a bunch of Communist Gooks he's going to perform. It doesn't matter what kind of hat he has on. That's all there is to it.

Ernie, as an Air America CIA pilot, was pretty lucky to get out alive and fortunate to be moved in with other guys when he was. The Gooks told him he was shot down in Laos. They kept him with us at Camp Unity for seven months. Then they moved him and four other military guys who had been shot down in Laos off to another camp. They kept them separated from the main group until release time came and then they were released along with all of us. We called them the "Lu-Lu's" or the Laos Boys. They included Stischer and Bedinger who showed up in 1969 when they were brought into Little Vegas for awhile.

After the Gooks had jammed us all together into one big compound, they started putting bamboo screens over the windows so we couldn't see out. This was to interrupt our communications but it really just temporarily derailed them. They also started placing bamboo screens in the court yard so they divided each room off with its own separate court yard. They let rooms out one at a time so we couldn't communicate with each other when we were outside. Relative to the freedom we'd enjoyed before the Son Tay raid and relocation, this was a pain. But we were resourceful and reverted back to our old patterns of wall tapping, hand flashing, boring holes in screens and walls, passing notes, sweeping, coughing and spitting tap code. The word passed around via the old telegraph just as it always did, and in a hell of a hurry.

When we all got together on November 25th, after being penned up and separated for so many years, we had developed one hell of a lot of hostility and a lot of energy. Everybody was ready to do battle with the slant-eyed group. We were as aggressive and ornery as we could possibly be.

The Vietnamese were beginning to see that now they had their work cut out for them. They had about 350 some-odd, wild-ass and pissed off Yanks. The heavies in room seven were no exception. They had been penned up in Alcatraz, getting their asses kicked all those years, and they felt the same as the rest of us. So the room SROs began to bitch and raise hell for some of the things we didn't have, which were many. And we began to develop ways to harass the Gooks.

We established five "conditions of readiness." Condition five was "Normal Steaming" or routine. In other words it was to just treat the Gooks with disregard. Don't mess around with them and don't harass or give them any trouble.

Condition four was "Military Posture" where we pissed off the Gooks by forming up in ranks and marched outside.

Condition three was "Stare" where we would go out in the courtyard to bathe and we'd get groups of 25 guys or so to just stand around, stare and glare at the guards. This would really drive them up the wall.

Condition two was "Sing." This was where everybody would start singing a song like the "The Star Spangled Banner," or anything we could think of. We would make a hell of a racket.

Condition one was where everybody went on a hunger strike and we refused food from the Gooks for so many days, with the exception of the sick people.

These "Conditions" were designed to put pressure on the Gooks and to do battle with them. In a short time the Gooks tried to exert control in obnoxious ways and they became the ones doing the provoking. I think they were pissed off about the Son Tay raid so they started playing that silly game again of "Room Responsible." Also, the guards were obnoxious to the guys and they started using strong-arm tactics again.

One night in December all hell broke loose in the camp and it started with the room the heavies were in. Those guys started shouting that rolled from room to room around the camp. Gobel James, who had a magnificent tenor voice, sang "America the Beautiful" and that had an incredibly powerful affect on all 350 of us. We were locked in our rooms but it was a near riot. The Gooks really got scared and came storming into the camp in force. They must have brought several hundred armed guards into the compound.

I was pretty proud of this when I think about it because the little bastards had to keep all kinds of those little devils around to guard us. So we did manage to occupy quite a few guards while we there. That meant fewer Gooks available to be shooting at our buddies when they came flying over. Maybe it's a small thing but it gave us a good feeling to know that we were doing something in the goddamn war besides just sitting down there watching it.

That night the Gooks came armed and screaming into the camp, and they started grabbing out SROs right and left. They took all the heavies out and threw them in solitary cells over in building zero. They put the colonels into an area we called "Blue." Then they came around, issued new camp regulations and started putting pressure on the rest of us. For instance, they wouldn't let us out to bathe. They also took a couple of guys out and beat them around a little bit.

The day before Christmas they came rampaging into the rooms. We had all our package items and stuff guys got from home. Some guys had civilian T-shirts, towels, socks and sweat shirts for the cold weather. The Gooks came in and took every single article of American goodies we had. They took the snake baskets that nobody really cared about anyway. They took all our American soap, tooth paste and tooth brushes. This was a big loss. The Gooks just carried baskets and baskets of shit out of the room.

We sat out there in the court yard while guards had rifles on us and watched all these good things we had for the past year or so go right out the door. The Gooks stacked it in huge piles out in the center court yard of the camp. They left it there, let the weather rain on it, and then they threw it all on trucks and took it away. We never received any of this stuff back, with the exception of some socks and T-shirts and a few other clothing items.

From that point on we never received any intact packages. Packages arrived in a spasmodic fashion. When we did go out to get a package if we had, say a jar of peanut butter, the damn Gook would open it up and we could take as much of it as we wanted on a plate. We had to take it back in the room that way. We never received any toilet articles again. They were always removed from our packages. So getting a package was a frustrating experience from that point on. The 6.6 pound packages we were supposed to receive usually were something on the order of a pound and it was all primarily things to eat, probably things the Gooks didn't want.

That was our Christmas present from the Vietnamese on the 24th of December. We had made preparations for Christmas with paper and things to make decorations and a Christmas tree. The Gooks wiped all that stuff out. But some way, the guys got together that night and did it all over again with nothing. We used straw brooms to make a Christmas tree and we made decorations with articles of clothing.

Christmas of 1970 was truthfully one of the best in my whole life, including Christmases with my family in my younger days and as a married man. It was the most exciting Christmas I ever had. We organized an entertainment schedule that went for about 10 days through that holiday season. We had a choir, parties and guys made bathtub booze by fermenting fruit and sugar in our water crockery jugs. We had plays and skits and one guy, Rod Knutson, even dressed up as Santa Claus. He was terrific. Rod looked as much like Santa as any you would see on the street with all the dress-up junk he was able to collect. And somehow or other Santa Claus made a uniform again after the raid and we went ahead and had the whole shebang!

We developed our Christmas programs within each room. They weren't used by the Vietnamese for propaganda purposes. The only thing the Vietnamese did was come around and bang on the door to try to get us to shut up but they had no success whatsoever. As I said, it was the best Christmas I've ever had. Despite the attempt by the Vietnamese to wipe us out of everything we still felt we had everything because we were together for the first time. It was almost a mystical experience.

1971 started off slowly and most of the guys were pretty teed-off at the Gooks from all the years of frustration and from this latest action. The guards were acting like horses asses, which caused us to search for new ways to combat the little bastards. Lots of suggestions went up to the SRO.

Our high-ranking SROs had been moved out of room seven into solo and some dual rooms. They were in "Rawhide" and "Blue," two cell blocks in a different part of the camp. It really pissed off the rest of us that the Gooks had isolated our senior men. We were also angry that a couple of the guys had been slapped around and put into irons for a day or two. It was just a scare tactic the Gooks used on some of the more vocal members of our group.

They took Konnie away and there was some shuffling of guys among the rooms. Our new SRO wound up being Air Force Captain Bob Purcell, the same Bob Purcell who had climbed the tree at Camp Faith. Bob was an amazing guy. Back in the dark days of 1966 when they were rationing food to force guys to write biographies, Bob did something that became a legend among all POWs.

"Percy," as everyone called him, had lived next door to a new guy named Jon Reynolds, who was being beaten and starved. Somehow he managed to figure out how to climb up into the ceiling of his building. One night he took strips of bread from the loaf he had been given for dinner and tied them to a string made from a long thread out of his blanket. He climbed up into the attic of their building, then crawled across the attic over above Jon's room, loosened the light fixture and let the strips of bread down to Jon. As he did it, he sang, "Every time it rains it rains, pennies from heaven. Don't you know each cloud contains..." and so on. Now how classy is that? What a great POW story that was among us! Stories like that were the stuff that defined us.

Percy was our SRO and he was really good at it. He had a knack for settling guys down and getting us unified. He was also good at talking with the Gooks because they obviously respected him. He was practically on a first name basis with some of them just because they liked him. The Elf always called him "Percy." It was funny but helpful for us too.

People started talking about a letter moratorium because guys were really angry. This idea gained support and it got to where almost everybody was in favor of it. All of us knew the Gooks got some good propaganda out of the fact that we all were writing letters. They could tell the world we were all allowed to write and receive letters. They could show the world what great treatment we were getting. Finally, the suggestion went up from our room SRO to the camp SRO with most everyone in favor of a moratorium.

We decided to put pressure on them and make them look like dopes at the Paris Peace Conference. We were going to stop writing letters and let the Gooks try and explain that across the table to our people at the so-called peace talks. It would be interesting when our people back home started raising hell about the fact that we were not able to write because now they had become accustomed to receiving letters every month. We thought we'd kind of have them by the short hairs, so to speak. After some discussion by the senior ranking officers, Colonel Flynn, the camp SRO, put out the word that the letter moratorium would go into effect.

It started off with people going out to write their monthly letters in January. Instead of writing a decent letter, 50% of the men from each room would write letters that were only filled with camp bitches. The camp commanders would obviously never let these go out. Since everybody and every room in the camp did this it showed the Gooks we had good communication because it was synchronized.

That pissed them off even more and we got quite a reaction. The Gooks sent an officer around to every room to tell us we were trying to rebel against the Vietnamese people and camp authorities. They said if we did such things we would never be allowed to write letters again. They said it was our right to write a letter a month and there was no point in us doing this, and that the camp commander would refuse to read any letters that were so written, et cetera.

The next month, because nothing had changed in the camp, the SRO told half of us to do it again. This time we would go into a quiz room, write our letter and hand it to the interrogator there. He would just take one look at it and sometimes tear it apart on the spot and scream at us to go back to our room. We were really getting to them and we were just enjoying the hell out of it! We were writing stuff like "We are being separated from our fellow prisoners of war and these people are trying to treat us like criminals. They do not comply with the Geneva Convention articles of 1949. The food tastes like shit," and so forth. It was all true and they knew it, and they could do nothing about it.

Then came the third month and everybody did it. This was really a fiasco. We went in to write our letters and the interrogator would look over our shoulder. He'd see that we weren't toeing the line and he'd just snatch the paper away from us, rip it up and tell us to go back to our room. We had them really upset with us.

That was January, February and March of 1971. Then we went on a total voluntary letter moratorium program, where we wouldn't write at all for three months and possibly extend the moratorium to six months. That was our plan. But it was voluntary and there were three or four men of over 300 who decided not to go on a letter moratorium. They continued to write and this caused some hard feelings among some people.

One guy in particular who was pissed was the SRO for room six, Larry Guarino, who sent a clear channel message down so all hands in the room would be debriefed. It was his personal message and not a command. He sent word out that he thought the guys who were refusing to go along with the group were being traitors to our cause. He asked why in the Hell didn't they join in and be Americans?

It was the worst bunch of bullshit we ever heard in our whole lives! Tough guy, Larry Guarino, who had failed to take a hard line in The Briar Patch and The Zoo. It was obvious what was bugging Larry. He was feeling recriminations for being such a pussy in the past and now he was trying to show that he was tough, with all the guys around so they could see him operate.

It didn't matter. We went on with our letter moratorium for about three months. The Gooks obviously didn't like it. They tried to get guys to write by being nice to some of us and nasty to some of us. They tried trickery and everything they could think of but it didn't work. We still didn't write. We ran it for three months and then we extended it for the rest of the six months.

Now, after having been released, I found out the American public had gone bananas about not getting mail from us. Americans started a letter-writing campaign and flooded Paris with complaints. Hundreds of thousands of letters were sent to the North Vietnamese at the Paris Conference. They finally had to announce they would refuse to accept any more mail because their office was being entirely flooded and there was no way they could handle it all.

We in the camp and Americans at home made them look like asses in front of the world. Everybody wanted to know why we were not being allowed to write and there wasn't any way the Gooks could explain it to the world. It was really terrific!

Finally at the end of the six months we told the Vietnamese we would write a letter a month in exchange for receiving a letter a month. The Gooks agreed to this one-for-one. They said, "You will be allowed to receive your mail." This was the biggest thing we were bitching about, the way they were interfering with our mail and packages. So they said okay, one for one, but it was just a big lie. We knew it would happen that way and receiving letters stayed about the same.

I received five letters the first five years I was a POW and a total of 16 letters in the eight years. I got eight of the last letters a week before I was released in February 1973. They were all dated 1967 and 1968, five and six years old! This was fairly typical, except in the first five years not very many people received any letters and lots of my buddies never got a letter until they had been there five years.

In the late spring of 1971 I had come down with some "crotch-rot" fungus, something like ringworm all around my genitals. The hot weather seemed to bring this stuff on. One Sunday my old buddy guard "Squirt" was on duty. Normally we couldn't get anything on Sunday from the Gooks. We didn't even go out and bathe on Sunday. They only brought us two meals and it was a real quick and dirty make-shift schedule. We normally didn't see anyone around and we were just locked in all day.

For some reason I always had good rapport with Squirt. He had been one of the interrogator trainees at one time. Over time I would kid around with him and he got a charge out of it. By 1971 he would always come by to chat with me whenever he was on guard duty. He was a very small guy so we called him Squirt, a name I actually used when talking to him.

Squirt was on duty this Sunday and when he came around I walked over to chat with him. I said, "Hey, Squirt old buddy, how about some medicine for the crotch-rot?" I made it clear that the stuff was driving me nuts so he nodded his head, Okay and took off to the medic shack. I guess he had a key so he opened it, picked up some medicine and brought it back to me later when he brought the chow around.

It was a salve I'd never seen before, a white salve in a jar. He told me I was supposed to put this stuff on and rub it into the area. We had been using this blue medicine I mentioned before that sometimes worked for the crotch-rot. So I told him Okay, thanked him and took this stuff back in the room. I put some of it on my balls and after a few minutes, wow – big mistake! This stuff was liquid fire and it was obviously the wrong medicine! My buddy Squirt had made a big mistake.

My scrotum and penis started swelling up immediately, until they were nearly three time's normal size. I had grapefruit-size privates down there and it was tremendously painful. It burned like crazy in a matter of an hour or so. I washed all this crap off that I could but it was too late and soon I could even hardly walk. My buddies yelled "Bao Cao" for me and Squirt came. Our room SRO told him what the hell was wrong. Squirt came over and wanted to take a look and I showed him what had happened. His eyes got as big as saucers and he took off on a dead run. He found a medic, the camp doctor and an officer, and they all came to take a look at me.

They had a big discussion outside for awhile and then the officer came into the room with Squirt in tow and the medic bringing up the rear. The doctor was really pissed off at Squirt and he had chewed him out in front of us. Squirt had a hang-dog look on his face. Then the camp officer came in and said, "What did you put on?" I showed him the canister. The interrogator said, "The doctor says that is the wrong medicine. That medicine is too strong. It's to be used only on your feet for fungus of the feet and not supposed to be used on sensitive parts of the body."

I told him, "Well, don't blame the guard here. I should have waited until tomorrow. I realize today is Sunday and there weren't any medics or doctors around but I asked this man to get the medicine for me. He agreed to do so and he did the best that he could. And besides that, not knowing it was strong medicine, I put too much on. So it's my own fault. It is not the guard's fault. Don't blame him."

Well, when I said that Squirt just lit up like a Christmas tree. I'd really bailed him out because he was about to get his ass in a crack. The officer said, "Then you agree that it was your fault?" I said, "Yes, it was my fault, not this man's fault." Then the officer turned around and spoke to Squirt in Vietnamese, and he just beamed, turned around and left.

Squirt had sort of been my buddy up to that point, but after that I could do no wrong! From that point on I could get anything I wanted from that guy, day or night. It really paid off. I was able to use him for the rest of the time I was in North Vietnam, not necessarily for myself but for the SROs I was serving under. Whenever we really needed anything that was a little unusual I was told to go to Squirt and he would come up with it.

Looking back, I think this business about not being familiar with the enemy was generally true. Nevertheless, I feel that we should never intentionally try to piss off guards without a good reason. We should try to conduct ourselves so we maintain our military bearing, so they will respect us. That's the big thing. But if any guard ever does show genuine interest towards us by trying to be friendly, I say accept them but stay cautious. These guys could do a lot of things for us, especially if we happened to have a particular guard who liked us. My friendly relationship with Squirt turned out to be damn handy for me and my buddies too.

A wild eye disease was affecting millions of people in the Middle East and Asia during the early summer of 1971. It was a lot like Pink Eye but more severe and extremely painful. We first heard news about it over the camp radio. One day Hanoi Hannah said that in Saigon 80% of the population had been affected by an eye disease that had been brought about by toxic chemicals dropped from American aircraft in South Vietnam. She said this eye disease was sweeping South Vietnam and that the blood thirsty killers, the American Air Pirates, were dropping toxic chemicals throughout South Vietnam that were having this affect on everyone's eyes there.

We all listened to this and wondered what the hell was really going on. Then somebody got hold of a *Vietnam Courier* and a little article on the back page said something about an eye disease that hit India and was affecting millions of people. Just about the time we were connecting the two, wham! It hit us.

It started with one guy in our 50-man room, Marty Neuens. Marty got up one morning with itchy and swollen eyes. By that afternoon his eyes were swollen completely shut and he was in mortal pain. We yelled for a medic and pretty soon a couple of them came. The interrogator came around and said Marty had a contagious disease so they were going to take him out and put him in a solitary room. They took him over to The Zoo and put him in a cell there. They drove him in a jeep just to get him completely away from the camp but it was too late. The infection had already hit the camp and within the next couple of days everybody started coming down with it. The Gooks came around with some eye drops that were supposed to protect everybody from the disease. They were adamant and demanded that everybody take these damn eye drops.

Some guys, only a few in each room, refused to take the eye drops. A lot of SROs were pissed about this because they believed that if the Vietnamese offered medicine we should take it. If they offered inoculations or some kind of preventive medicine then all hands should take it and not refuse it. As lousy as their medical knowledge was, ours was lousier. Chances were it might do some good so we should take it. Also accepting the stuff encouraged the Vietnamese to provide us with more medical treatment.

I did accept the medicine but it didn't matter. Everybody who took the eye drops got the eye disease! I don't know whether the medicine had anything to do with it or not but we figured they were probably passing the damn disease from person to person with contaminated medicine or through faulty handling. Some of the guys who didn't take the medicine also got the disease but most of them who refused the medicine did not get the disease. That was pretty funny because they had the last laugh, sort of.

The disease lasted about 24 hours and we were in so much damn pain we thought we were going to climb the walls. Then as the pain would recede and our eyes would begin to open they looked like road maps. They were blood red and they stayed that way for a couple of days. Then it was over. The Gooks were very worried about it and had their doctors running around to check everybody while it was going on. When everybody's infection had run its course and their eyes were opening up they wouldn't let us go out in the bright sunlight for a couple of days. Then for a few days after that the guards would check people to see if their eyes were still blood red. If they were, they wouldn't let them go out and take a bath.

The Gooks did show quite a bit of concern over this stuff. But the world-wide news really blew their story about the toxic chemicals in Saigon causing all the people to have an eye disease.

The Gooks came around with some inoculations during the summer of 1971. This was supposed to be what they called an "All Purpose Shot." It was given just under the skin, with just enough serum to make a bubble maybe a third the size of a dime. According to them it was the serum for typhoid, typhus and tetanus, all in one shot. They zapped us with one of these little beauties and everybody went back into the room laughing their asses off. Another thing the Gooks had a habit of doing was they'd shoot ten or twelve guys with the same needle and the same tube of serum. Of course they were just inviting hepatitis. But we played their stupid games. Nobody got typhoid or typhus after these tiny shots but I don't think it had anything to do with their super serum.

Late in the summer of 1971 they moved some guys out of the camp. They collected all of the quiet, easy going guys out of our and other rooms. These were not guys who had ever played along with the Gooks. They were just soft-spoken and very quiet. One of them was my close friend, Hayden Lockhart. Hayden was what I called the strong silent type. He was just tougher than a cob and didn't have too much to say when he was around other people, especially when he was around Gooks. He just kept his mouth shut. He acted the way I would have liked to have acted sometimes. Unfortunately I'd blow my cork at the little bastards too often.

They took all of them over to The Zoo. They told them they were going to give them a gigantic good deal. According to Hayden they put them in four- and seven-man rooms. It only lasted a few months. The treatment there was a hell of a lot worse than in Camp Unity. What they said was a good deal turned out to be a dog-shit deal. Apparently it was another one of their little transient plans. I think the Gooks thought they might be able to get through to these guys and get them to do something for them. They weren't able to.

They also did some room shuffling with the rest of us. The guys in my room moved to room four which was a better room as far as the layout went. Instead of having the bunks down the center of the room it had the bunks on either side with a large floor space in the center. There was more room to walk, exercise, fool around, have classes and what not.

From time to time the Vietnamese showed us propaganda films. I saw my first movie, "Our Sons and Daughters," back at The Zoo. The next movie we saw was at The Briar Patch right after Christmas of '66. When I got to Little Vegas they showed two different movies there. One of them was a scene showing Doctor Benjamin Spock, the noted peace activist, and some other protestors in Washington, D.C. and other parts of the country. The other movie was a Gooks and Yanks shoot-em-up. It was a Vietnam version of Cowboys and Indians, one of their war flicks.

Later in the summer at Little Vegas they showed another movie but because I was under punishment I was not privileged to see it. Oh that really broke my heart! The guys who were not under punishment also got a banana every once in awhile. I was getting them too at this time but Shitty Slim was taking them from me. He would steal them from my chow and put them in his coat pocket so I never did get any. The next time we saw any movies was 1969 in The Zoo Annex. They herded us over to The Zoo auditorium. When we got to Camp Faith we saw a couple of movies out in the yard at night time. This time we sat together since they weren't trying to separate us.

At Camp Unity they started using room one as the movie room. It was smaller than the others – it might have held thirty guys – so they started using it as a movie room. We saw a couple of different movies there. In 1971 they showed us one movie about the 50th anniversary of the Russian Revolution. It was made in the USSR and featured their huge October '67 air show. We got to see all kinds of aircraft and formation flying. It was a shit-hot movie and we all enjoyed it.

A few months later they showed us another damn Russian circus movie. That was shit-hot too because it had some broads in it. God! The guys just went out of their gourds looking at some of these Russian women in the circus. Everybody had their favorite dolly and the guys didn't stop talking about this gal or that gal in the movie for months after that. What a bunch of horny bastards we were. Holy Cow! Plus they were the first round-eyes we'd seen in years.

Christmas of '71 rolled around and optimism started running rampant again. Everybody at Christmas of 1970 had said they were damn sure that was going to be the last Christmas in Vietnam. It had to be. Surely this thing was not going to drag out to be another hundred-years-war. But then again, people weren't too sure.

The Gooks pretty much left us alone that Christmas. We were able to have our skits, plays, celebrations and we did a little decorating in our rooms. Everybody refused to go to any church services outside. Of course the Gooks were trying to get people to attend the services as it would have made great propaganda for them. But nobody would go because we had the word from the SRO and we were unified.

We all refused to draw any pictures for the Gooks though they were still trying to get people to do that. Everybody told them to smack it. All through 1971 there were occasional conflicts like before. We were always trying in our weak little way to improve our treatment. But we all knew our treatment was predicated on outside pressures and not inside. There wasn't anything we could do but we always continued to try.

Sometime in April of 1972 the Gooks held a big shuffle in the camp and all of us in room four wound up moving to room six. We didn't get any new roommates. We just moved. We had gotten some new roommates earlier. They were 1968 shoot-downs, the first we ever had an opportunity to talk to face-to-face with. These guys had come from the old room one.

One of them was a guy who turned out to be a close buddy of mine, Terry Uyeyama. Terry was Japanese-American but didn't speak any Japanese at all. One of the humorous things that happened in that room was a bunch of us guys who had been to Japan got together and taught Terry some Japanese words and numbers.

At Camp Unity lots of guys had little specialties. Some guys were good with their hands, like making things. Guys made all kinds of things out of bread by mixing it with water. You come up with this gooey stuff and you could make a kind of a paper maché. Guys made poker chips, ash trays and other things out of that. Other guys made fountain pens out of bamboo. Some guys were good at making ink out of various things. My very close friend there, Mike McGrath, was excellent at this stuff. Plus he was a talented artist.

For some reason I had gotten interested in picking locks and stealing in 1966. So I practiced and began to get pretty good at it. Then I branched out into picking pockets. I would work with other guys who would distract the guards. We would cook up a plot to divert attention and steal whatever item we needed. We would talk to a guard or get him interested in something we were doing. Meanwhile we would pick his pocket or have someone steal something that was close by when he wasn't looking. I enjoyed that and got better as the years went by. At the very last, a week before we were going home when we all knew we were going home, it suddenly dawned on me that I enjoyed stealing from the enemy and that I was going to have to kick this habit. So I decided that on the last day in North Vietnam as I was leaving the damn shit hole, I would pick a guard's pocket and steal something from him if I had the opportunity. And that would be the last thing I would steal for the rest of my life. So as we were going out that morning to take a bath I spotted a guard clipping his finger nails with a set of nail clippers. I'm now the proud owner of those nail clippers. They have the number "444" engraved in them, indicating they were made from the 444th aircraft they shot down. Could be! That was the last thing I ever stole. I swear it's the truth.

I was assigned to be the education officer once again, which I enjoyed doing. My duties included organizing an education program. We had classes everyday in our rooms. We usually had only one period of the day either in the morning or the afternoon, depending on what our outside schedule was. During that period we would usually have one class and sometimes two. Typically they would be language classes – French, German, Spanish, or Russian – which were the languages guys had studied before they were captured.

All of our service academy graduates had taken a language and some were pretty good at them. We also had a native French speaker who was Cajun from Louisiana and a native German speaker from a small town in Texas. I started teaching Spanish classes at Camp Faith in 1970 and continued up until the end. I had taken two years of Spanish in high school and two years at the Naval Academy. I actually learned more by teaching the classes and by getting new words and phrases from other POWs. Closely associated with teaching Spanish was the grammar, so I taught Spanish and English grammar as well.

We also had classes on areas of interest like vacation, travel, or jobs that guys had held before in their lives. They would talk about the ins and outs of places where they had worked. Guys who had worked, say, in a laundry or clothing store, would give lectures on wardrobes and how people should or shouldn't dress.

Lectures were given on psychology, sociology, geography, mathematics, chemistry, and all kinds of sciences. Guys would give lectures on the care and raising of pets, or anything in the world they could think of.

There was almost always somebody among us who was an expert on some subject people might be interested in.

Guys would share their notes on different subjects, passing them from one room to another. We would send out a query if anyone had information on a certain subject, like automobile racing for example. Then we'd get information from people in other rooms who knew about it and then we could create a lecture series on the subject. It was very interesting because many of the guys were able to deliver good lectures.

We had after-dinner speaking clubs in which guys would improve their skills in that area. And we held debates on interesting questions and political issues.

One of the funniest things, at least to watch, was the dance club. I had taken ball-room dance lessons for two years in junior high school, back in the early 1950s when it was popular. We kids all went to "Skilly's School of Ball Room Dance," where they taught the Arthur Murray method. I was a volunteer dance instructor for a year during 9th grade. Guys in our room found out about that and insisted on learning. So I gave dancing lessons in 1971. It was a scream! I had 40 guys practicing various steps by dancing with each other. Male dance instructors are required to learn and practice the female part as well so I could instruct them. I taught Fox Trot, Waltz, Rumba, Samba, Tango and Swing Dance. The guys would practice the steps and then switch roles. The Vietnamese could never figure this one out.

We would also have "movies," usually four to five nights a week. This entailed guys presenting a film as they remembered it. We would announce that a certain movie would be presented that night and whoever the movie presenter was would advertise it big. He would talk to guys ahead of time to get parts of the movie they remembered. Then that evening guys would bring their blankets to sit on and "watch" the movie. The presenter would sit against the wall on some stacked-up blankets at one end of the room. Guys would lie around, smoke cigarettes and listen. These presentations sometimes lasted for several hours. I was one of the movie presenters and it was a great deal of fun.

Other guys would tell travel experiences. One guy, Daryl Pile, had made a year-long tour of South America when he was about 20 years old. He dropped out of college and bummed his way around much of the continent. He'd done all kinds of interesting things while he was there and it took him several weeks of lectures to tell it all.

Some guys had unbelievable memories for books. We had guys that would get up there for six or seven nights and tell a book. Some of the best movie guys were told by specialists. One guy told "Gone With the Wind" and another told "War and Peace." It took them five nights to both of those.

We'd have poker games going every night of the week. We always had two tables set up and we put our name on a list to play on a given night. We had a guy who ran the poker club. It was nickel, dime and quarter, low stakes poker. Guys were just having fun and trying to learn the science of the game. We kept a running total of each guy's winnings and losses. It was more about the competition than the money, but at the end we consolidated our debts and guys actually paid off what they owed after we returned from Vietnam.

We always had something going on and this helped a hell of a lot to pass the time.

We were only there in room six for a month or so when one day in May the US started bombing again. This time there were attacks in the North around Hanoi. The Gooks were obviously getting nervous. They intensified security, put more screens up and separated us more. They were particularly worried about what they were going to do with so many of us together in these big rooms with the air raids going on. Whenever a raid would begin, they'd put ladders up in our windows and send guards up these ladders with submachine guns to watch us during the attack. They seemed to think we might try to bolt when a raid was going. They just didn't know and they were plenty worried about it.

Then on May 25th they came around and told us to pack up our gear because we were going to move that night. This really pissed me off because I had a fresh batch of wine I had made in my water jug. I had more than a quart of this stuff, made with all the sugar rations I could collect for a month and some dried fruit I'd gotten from a package. It was suppose to ferment for 12 days and it was a few days too early. Another guy and I were thinking, "How in hell are we going to take this stuff with us on the truck?" Naturally we did the obvious thing that evening. We drank our jugs of wine, even though they weren't quite ready but anyway it tasted good. The bacteria had not fermented into alcohol yet so of course we got the screaming shits from drinking it too soon. So we climbed on the trucks that night with a case of the screaming-meemies! It was a bad truck ride.

That was it for Camp Unity. Our next stop was going to be far away from Hanoi. The Elf had told us that our stay there was only going to be temporary. But it turned out that temporary was nearly the duration of the war! We were there from November 25, 1970 until we were released in

378

1973, with one exception. Those damn Yanks started blasting the North with B-52's and upsetting the Vietnamese government so they moved 208 of us to a camp up north, near Lang Son, just a few miles from the Chinese border. We were to name that place "Dog Patch."

24. Dog Patch

5/25/72 – 1/24/73

At about ten o'clock on the night of May 25th 1972 they came to get us again. We were all packed up and ready to go. The guards walked us out through Camp Unity, through the Heartbreak arcade, out through the main courtyard and out the main gate of the Hilton complex. We loaded onto trucks and started the long journey north. This was an eighteen hour ride and it was an ass buster all the way. It was probably the worst truck ride ever in North Vietnam.

As soon as we got past the northern limits of Hanoi, out into the countryside, the roads got very rough. We traveled up Highway 4 and in very short order we damn near started going straight uphill. The roads were just paths with enormous chuck holes and they were beating us to pieces in the back of that truck. Everybody was handcuffed to somebody else so we were all in pairs and that made it a hell of a lot worse because we couldn't hang on to anything. We were just being thrown around into each other.

To make matters worse, these trucks had huge reserve gas tanks that were up behind the driver's seat and gasoline was spilling out around us. Being pilots and air crew members, we were not prone to motion sickness, but the guards with us were puking all over the place. It was really murder. The Gooks would stop about every three or four hours to get out of the truck, walk around, stretch their legs and take a siesta. But they left us penned up in the truck and we were never allowed to get out.

We continued on. We thought we were going to East Jesus because we kept going and going. Guys were peeking out and watching signs and so forth and we figured we were right up on the Chinese border. Matter of fact, we were only five miles from the northern border with China, near Lang Son.

This was not a surprise to us. About two days before we were to be moved the guards had held a big pow-wow session in the center courtyard. One of our guys, my old buddy Tom McNish, had been next to the bamboo fence near the guards. He had peeked out and seen six or seven guards being briefed by an officer over a map.

Tom was one of our best guys when it came to understanding the Vietnamese language. Somehow he figured out from the conversation and the pointing at the maps that they were talking about an area on the northern border. That information was flashed around the camp and all of us knew where we were going anyway. It was also confirmed with the road signs and everything that we saw while going there.

We were in Cao Ban province in the northern part of the country. It was cooler up there, cooler than any place in Vietnam I had been. That was the one saving grace of the place. When we got there it was cold and this was the end of May. During the day it would just get in the high 60's and at night it would get down to around 50. As far as I and most of the guys were concerned, after the heat at the lower altitudes, this weather was just beautiful!

The camp was made up of a series of roughly 20 buildings. It was nestled in a valley between some mountains. These mountains rose like sheer cliffs over extremely rough, jungle terrain. There was no way in the world we could ever get out of there. We would never make it through that crap, especially not with our thin clothing. If we did make it out, there were 800 miles to go before we got any place we might want to be. So from the Vietnamese point of view, it was secure!

We finally pulled in to the camp and they took us off our truck along with a couple of guys from another truck and put us all in one building. These buildings were about 40 feet long and 25 feet wide. They were permanent structures with tile roofs, much like other buildings we had lived in before. Most of the buildings contained three or four rooms where they could put eight or ten guys in two large rooms and there were also one or two solo cells in the building. The building I started off in had eight two-man rooms and one solo room. They put seventeen of us in this building and we did have several guys who wanted to live in a solo room. So we chose our roommates and moved into these rooms. My cellmate was Terry Uyeyama.

The routine there was our room doors were opened during the day from about seven in the morning to five in the evening. Then as soon as we had finished our dinner they came around and locked us into our rooms. This really pissed us off because it didn't really serve any purpose. They had security on the outside doors of the building itself but they were probably nervous about the way the war was going, so it was a good excuse to lock us up. We spent the damn nights staring at one other guy in a little room. The cells were too small to do anything. So we were back to boredom. It was pretty miserable in that respect, especially after what we had experienced in Camp Unity. We had gotten used to being all together and

381

having all that activity. Now we were back to zero again.

We were free to move about in the building during the day but there really wasn't anywhere to move about. My building had these nine cells and just a little hallway that was not more than three feet wide. We got out in a little court yard on the building to wash for half of the day. That was either in the morning or the afternoon.

After two days of settling in and getting our communication networks established, we learned that there were 208 of us in the camp. One of the first orders of business, as soon as we got good comm. going, was to get a camp name. Every building submitted several names they wanted and we passed them around on the communication system. Every building voted and we decided we were going to call it "Dog Patch."

We went through the summer at Dog Patch and one blessing about the place was nobody got heat rash. This was the first and only time I was in Vietnam that I didn't get heat rash during the summer. It was comfortable up there, at least until the winter came and then it got colder than a witch's tit. The temperature fell below freezing at night up there in the mountains.

One curiosity about Dog Patch was that the camp officers developed a "no-show" policy. That is, they never came around. Even an SRO couldn't get a guard to bring one to talk to. We went for months without ever seeing The Elf who was there with us. We had a turnkey who spoke English and we had to deal with him. But even when dealing with him, he would just listen and he wouldn't talk to us.

In other words they had adopted a policy of completely leaving us alone. They wouldn't pass the time of day with us or do anything. The guards were there to open our door in the morning, give us our food, and lock us up at night. Then they would turn their backs, run out the door and stay away from us. It was amazing!

Also odd, by now they had finally trained some of the personnel to speak the language of the people they were guarding. There were probably 20 guards at Dog Patch and they all spoke English. But since they went to such lengths to distance themselves from us, we couldn't develop relationships with them. So we didn't bother to name them very much.

One of the first exciting things happened to the guys who moved into the building that was to be named "Cobra." The night they moved in they found two king cobras and hence the name of that building. There were a lot of snakes up there. Guys also saw kraits on occasion. A couple times the snakes would sneak into people's rooms. A krait is a particularly ugly bastard. It was the one that came into our room at Briar Patch and damn near nailed me in the face. It's not a large snake, only about as big around as a finger, maybe three feet in length and kind of sluggish by nature. But they are also what we referred to as a "three stepper." That means when one zaps you, you've got three steps and you're dead! They are neuro-toxic and can kill a human in nothing flat. There was nothing they could do for someone bitten by a krait. And they were all over the place. The guards were even more afraid of them than we were because they had to go on patrol around the area at night. They were always petrified of the snakes and who could blame them?

We were also told there was a lot of wild animal life up there. There were tigers around the camp and also a lot of bears, so the guards on duty at night had their work cut out for them. I got a little warm feeling in my heart when I'd be in my bunk at night, even though it was hard and a lot of times uncomfortable, just thinking about the guards out there. It was a hell of a lot better than walking around outside in the middle of the night with a rifle on your shoulder. It was better to be the captive than the guard at times.

There was also the fact that we were going to go home to the land of the Big Base Exchange. While someday those little bastards were going to be eating rice and marching behind a water buffalo for the rest of their lives.

Not a hell of lot happened that summer. We didn't write any letters for several months. When we did start writing it was apparent to us that since they were not being censored at all, so they were not sending them out. The Gooks were very nervous about the USA finding out where we were, so they were not sending our mail out. We didn't receive any mail there until about July or August. Then only one guy in our building got a letter and that was pretty typical in all the buildings.

We didn't get any packages until August. I didn't get one, as about half of the guys got cut out of the pattern. We got a couple more packages while we were there. Some of the guys got two because they were from the previous four months. We were supposed to get one every two months. Getting skunked on packages was a real pisser.

Things were fairly normal until August 7th of 1972, four days before my 34th birthday. That morning when I got up I just felt kind of lousy, like I had the flu or something. By that afternoon I had a case of screaming shits, bad headaches and I felt sick to my stomach. The next day I was damn sick and the turnkey wanted to know what was wrong with me. The guys told him I was very sick. So they sent a medic around and he gave me some of those instant-cork pills that did absolutely nothing.

Then I started having really bad dysentery. In a few days I was starting to excrete blood. And then my weight began to go down drastically and I started excreting not only blood, but also pieces of intestinal lining. I was starting to get very worried as were my cell-block mates. My weight went down and down until finally in September I was down from 175 pounds to about 120 pounds.

Every time I had to eliminate it was extremely painful and I was having to go to the stool 12 to 20 times a day. I'd get on the can in the middle of the night and have tremendous surges of pain that made me dizzy. Then I would pass out and fall off the thing. My roommate, Terry Uyeyama, would catch me and drag me back in bed again. We kept telling the turnkey and the medics but they didn't know what to do about it.

Then in September a doctor came to the camp. I had never seen him before. He was young, about 27 or 28 years old. He didn't speak English or French which made it apparent that he had not been educated outside his country but probably just in Hanoi. They were cranking out doctors of sorts as fast as they could in Hanoi at this time. I told him my problems. He looked at me and decided then and there that I was pretty sick.

He told me he wanted to see a stool specimen so I ran back in my room, unloaded one and brought it back to him. I think it amazed him that I was able to perform on command. I showed him a large pile of blood and mucous membranes. He took one look at that and his eyes got as big as saucers. Then he grabbed the medic who was with him and the turnkey, and they took off at a dead run towards the medical shack. I went back in and collapsed on the bed.

In about 30 minutes a group of camp officers, the camp commander, doctor, and medics, and every Gook in the world came running down to our building. They threw open the cell door to my room and started firing questions at me through the interrogator. "How long have I had this? What were my symptoms? Where was the pain? How much weight had I lost?"

Then the doctor had one of the medics give me shots. Right there I guess they gave me five or six shots. They were vitamin B12, B1, C, and some other things. I don't even know what the hell they were. Then they gave me some pills. They gave me a handful of pills, told me to take them every four hours and then they left. From then on that doctor and the medics stayed on me like the plague. The doctor actually came around almost every day to see me for a period of about two and a half months.

And I got from four to eight injections almost every day for awhile.

The young doctor kept working on me like that. It took about three or four weeks before the dysentery finally went away. Then I started a very slow process of recovery. As a result of the attention, and the success, this doctor and I got on fairly friendly terms. I could use a little bit of French and a little English and make him understand. There was always a guard with him anyway, a turnkey who spoke English to interpret. The doctor turned out to be a pretty good guy. He never tried to give me any political horse shit, any Party-Line stuff. He seemed primarily interested in my health and in trying to do his job as a doctor.

I have to say I got good medical treatment at this camp. I also got a lot of attention from around the camp since from communications everybody knew what was going on with me every day.

About mid-way through this disease the doctor told me it would take a long time for me to recover. They would give me vitamin and glucose injections about three times a week to supplement my diet. They put me on a special diet and I got meat, a hell of a lot of it, from September till the end of January. The guys in my building were pumping stuff into me that they got in their packages. I hated to take that stuff because it kind of eats your heart out to have to take that from the guys. But there wasn't much I could do because it was just like the situation I had been in before with roommates of mine, so I understood.

They kept on with all this attention into December and January. Other symptoms I experienced were extreme swelling in my feet, ankles, face, hands, arms and abdomen. This was because my kidneys weren't functioning properly and it was dangerous because it put a real strain on the heart. On several occasions the Gooks had to give me diuretics to get rid of the edema. In general they did pretty well for me and in a period of several months they got me through the worst of it. I still had swelling in my feet and hands when I was released on February 12th 1973. And it still took two or three weeks afterwards to completely get rid of the swelling.

Sometime around the first of November I had an allergic reaction, probably to some of the shots they were giving me. They were trying different kinds of vitamins to see what I would react to best. One day they injected me with a reddish colored liquid that was labeled vitamin B of some kind. I'm not sure which one. After a couple of days I developed a severe rash all over my body. I knew I was having an allergic reaction to the medical treatment and I figured it out before the medic did. I told him to knock off that shot, which he did. But that rash plagued me for two months before it finally went away.

When I was released I still had some of it and the dermatologist at Clarke AFB hospital told me it was pretty common for an allergic reaction from an injection to hang on for a number of months and sometimes even longer. I guess that's what it was. I do know I was in total misery with the constant itching. I went without sleep night after night because I had so much itching.

There was one very sad note that took place in the early fall of 1972. It stills tears me up when I think about it. That was the case of John Frederick, Chief Warrant Officer, USMC, who was the back seat RIO (Radar Intercept Officer) and navigator for Howie Dunn, Major, USMC. He had been captured with Howie in 1965. This man was one of our strongest resistors and fighters. He was a huge man with a monstrous build on him; seventeen inch biceps. John had 31 years of military service and had fought as a Marine infantryman in WW II, Korea and in Vietnam. He had been a Vietnam POW for seven years. John also suddenly became very ill in the fall of 1972. He was running extremely high fevers and became delirious.

When the Gooks checked on him he couldn't urinate, defecate, or eat. So they loaded him up on a stretcher and took him out of the camp. The Gooks told the people in his building that John had contracted typhus, then later they said it was cholera. No doubt it was the same thing I had. They took him out and we kept asking about him all the time. They kept telling us he was taken to a hospital. But after we were released we found out the Gooks had listed him as having died in captivity.

Jesus Christ, I can't think of anything worse. There was a guy with over 30 years of service, who fought in three wars, spent seven years as a prisoner of war, and no more than a few months before release he died in captivity. I'd guess they did take John out to some kind of hospital in the local area and tried to treat him. But he didn't make it. It could easily have been the same for me except for the fact that John was 50 years old and I was only 34.

In October of 1972 the Gooks started having meetings, and what sounded like celebrations, outside the wall of our camp. They were just singing, yelling and raising hell out there. Terry Uyeyama, my roommate, and I said to each other "Christ, something big has happened!" Sure enough they were all smiles around the camp. A couple of days later they came around at night and told us to pack up our gear because we were going to move. We knew it wasn't going to be an out of the camp move because we hadn't seen them pack up the biographies and all the other transport stuff ahead of us. We figured it was going to be an intra-camp shuffle but we couldn't find out why they were so excited.

That night they opened our cell doors told us to roll up our gear to move out. I was having a little trouble walking because I was still very sick so Terry was carrying his stuff and sharing half the load with my stuff. I held on to the back of his shirt and he was giving me support to walk along. We started out but when Terry got out the door of our cell the guard slammed his arm down in front of me, broke me loose from Terry, and pushed me back into the cell and slammed the door.

I couldn't figure out what was going on. They took a couple more of our guys out of the building and I sat back down in my room. When the guard left everybody in the building started talking out the doors to find out who had moved. One of the bright guys in the building said, "Hey, guess what, the guys that moved out of our building tonight are all 1968 shoot-downs." Then about a half-hour later the Gooks came back and took some more guys out. When they left we figured out all those guys were 1967 shoot-downs. Well, son of a bitch! This went on through the night until they got down to the poor miserable old bastards like myself who were 1965 shoot-downs.

They took us old heads up the hill to another building called "Copper," where some of the guys had been living and where eventually there were 19 of us together. Every one of us in that building was a 1965 shoot-down. The building next to us was also 1965 shoot-downs and the other buildings in our area were 1966 shoot-downs. When we got our communications established around the whole camp again we found out that every building was segregated by date of shoot-down.

Since the Gooks had never done anything this organized before, there could only be one reason for grouping us according to shoot-downs. It was something that I and my cellmates had dreamed of for seven and a half years! That was the fact that release had to be imminent because that's the order they were going to release us. This corresponded with the Geneva Conventions and with the release program set up by our senior ranking officers. The rule of order was sick and wounded, civilians, military enlisted, and then officers by order of captivity. So we were pretty fucking excited!

We moved into this new building and it was a great thing for us because it had two big rooms and we were split between them. There were a bunch of guys mixed in with us whom we hadn't lived with before so there were brand new conversations, new movies to tell, and new experiences to exchange. The treatment improved and the guards started locking us up in our rooms at night at nine in the evening instead of five o'clock. We were out all day. In the evening we were in our building after dinner time so we could play poker or bridge, listen to movies and do all the things we had done in the bigger Camp Unity rooms before.

One day an officer and several guards came around. They read a big blurb to us. It said the Democratic Republic of Vietnam had issued a peace initiative to the United States and the President of the United States had approved it. This initiative covered the major points necessary for ending the war. It was to be signed within a few days by Henry Kissinger and Le Duc To. After that it was to be signed by our Secretary of State and their Foreign Minister.

This was exciting news, to say the least. It looked like the war was going to end in just a matter of a few days. Then they came around again and told us the United States had showed a bad attitude and had refused to sign the agreement. Shit! Crap! Morale plummeted. We were back at square one again because it all fell through.

Soon it became obvious that the Vietnamese had not lived up to their agreements because we started bombing them. We were bombing downtown Hanoi with B-52s and the Vietnamese were telling us all about it. We knew that if Uncle Sugar was rolling B-52s over downtown Hanoi it wouldn't be very damn long before the son-of-a-bitch war would end!

We were back up on top of the world. President Nixon was finally bombing downtown Hanoi with B-52s. This was after almost five years of the bombing moratorium, while we sat up there and rotted in prisons. We also believed the mining and blockade of the harbors and rivers of North Vietnam that started in May of 1972 had a dramatic effect.

This was the first time we experienced a complete stoppage of supplies into the prison camps. We couldn't get soap, tooth paste, or clothing and there were no imported, canned foods in the camp. Everything came to a screaming halt. That didn't just hurt us; it affected the guards and everybody. We were living off the land with whatever they grew up there. They were giving us local buffalo meat, which by the way was outstanding. It was the most meat we had seen. They were going out of their way to give us decent food because of the pressure of ending the war and impending release of POWs.

That fall I was getting double rations of buffalo meat and all kinds of other goodies because of my illness. They were trying to bring me back to health. But it all came apart again and so the Vietnamese came at us with another big propaganda push. They brought in a tape recorder and played tapes for us. Some of us refused to listen. These tapes had been made by real neat guys who came to visit North Vietnam and find out how wonderful prison life was for us.

One of them was Ramsey Clark, who was really a naive son of a bitch. He came and made a tape. I just couldn't believe that a man who had been Attorney General of our government could be that gullible. He came to Hanoi, talked to a couple of guys, Miller and Wilbur who were playing the early release game, and decided that everything was just fine with the prisoners. Then he reported that we were getting outstanding treatment in accordance with the Geneva Conventions. The other was Jane Fonda who went back to the United States and told Americans how great it was for us in North Vietnam.

This kind of stuff did a lot to run our morale down. When Americans like that would come up there and say those things, then the Gooks would throw it in our faces. We felt so damn helpless because obviously everybody in the world was being told by these supposed eyewitnesses how great it was in a POW camp.

After all our previous years of torture, suffering and sub-standard living, these people came over to take a look. Of course they were shown what the Gooks wanted them to see. Then they went back to tell everybody how wonderful it was.

Just before Christmas Day of '72 our SRO told the camp commander that we didn't want to decorate a damn Christmas tree, we didn't want to decorate a God damn quiz room and didn't want to do the square root of shit! We didn't care if they gave us a meal or what the hell they did. All we wanted to do was get together with our buddies in the other buildings.

The camp commander wouldn't have any part of this. He detailed some of his guards to go put a Christmas Tree in one of the quiz rooms and they decorated it themselves. It was hard to believe, the Gooks making a Christmas tree. I will never be able to figure out their screwy Gook mentality. One minute they were torturing and kicking the hell out of us. The next minute they were decorating a Christmas tree for us. Unbelievable.

But then on Christmas Day they let us out of our building and we all went down to a center area of the camp where there was just a hell of a crowd of 150 or so of us. We had an old home week there in the yard. We were meeting guys we had never met before. Meanwhile all the guards, officers and Gooks in the world were standing around us with automatic weapons in hand. They were nervous, which didn't make a lot of sense since one, there was no place to escape to, and two, everyone knew we were getting close to being released. So why would we start anything?

Anyway, we got to meet all of our buddies on Christmas Day. A couple of days later they had a movie for us in one of the bigger buildings and we were all allowed to sit together. Nobody paid any attention at all to the movie. Everybody just ran around and bullshitted throughout the whole thing. It was another one of those screwy Russian Circus movies. By this time it was about the third one we had seen. Everybody was sick and tired of circus movies. And we were especially sick and tired of Vietnamese shoot-em-up movies so nobody paid any attention to it.

Then they started opening the door to the courtyard in the morning and afternoon so we could go down to the area near the building we called "Monty" if we wanted to. I was still sick, but some guys pulled all the rocks out of the area between us and leveled it all off. They got a tamper, pounded it down level and made it into this beautiful volleyball court. They probably got about two volleyball games in when, go-to-hell if we didn't move and leave the camp!

Anyway we had visiting privileges during the day, and at the same time the Gooks brought us our first magazines and books. For the whole camp of 208 guys, we got one French book, one German book and one Russian book. They gave us paper and pencils, for the first time, to copy stuff. So we sent several representatives down to this building where the books were being kept to copy the information. They came back at night and guys would sit around and study this stuff.

This sounds like a small thing but to guys like us who had been teaching or studying these foreign languages all these years, it was really interesting to get the straight word and see what was "POW information" and what was real. As it turned out we really hadn't done too bad a job through just our memories. We just screwed up on little things but we had done a pretty fair job of getting the basics across from just our own knowledge.

The Vietnamese also came up with some magazines and we noticed they all had prisoner's names on them. They were dated 1968, 1969, 1970, 1971 and 1972. This really pissed us off because now here were all these magazines that people had been sending us. People had been sending subscriptions of magazines to us and we went all those years without seeing them. It was really sickening!

There were sports magazines. And Jesus it was just amazing to find out what all the new baseball and football teams were. The only name I recognized in the lineups was Willy Mays, the only guy left around from my time period.

We got a couple of "Stars and Stripes" but they had cut out articles that were counter to their propaganda bullshit! But in those few weeks we were able to find out some of what was going on in the world.

Then in January of 1973 all the trucks in the world rolled into camp and they didn't let us out that day to bathe. We were crawling up into the upper windows to peek out and we knew we were going someplace. We saw the biographies being packed up and loaded on the trucks and all the guards were loading their gear onto the trucks. That night they came in and told us to roll up our gear. Everybody in our building had already rolled up their gear anyway. We were all packed and ready to go!

We asked the guards where we were going. "Are we going back to Hanoi?" The guards just smiled and giggled like little girls. We knew damn well we were going back to Hanoi. We hadn't heard anything about the bombing raids so we suspected the bombing had stopped. Besides, they had been telling us all along that this northern camp was just temporary for us. They had also told us that when the bombing stopped in North Vietnam we would move back to Hanoi. They had even gone so far as to tell us that when we left this camp and returned to Hanoi we could expect to be released soon after that.

That was easy enough for us to figure out anyway. So we danced around, took nervous pisses, and smoked cigarettes. Everybody ran out of cigarettes, ideas and energy. I think that was the longest night of my life. Finally about four or five in the morning they came and told us to file out of the building and they put us on trucks.

They didn't handcuff us this time. They just put our bags and asses on the trucks. I went all the way to the forward part of my truck. I sat right behind the guard who was riding shotgun next to the cab of the truck. We sat around for an hour or so and all the Gooks were so excited with joy they just couldn't do enough for us. All we had to do was act like we wanted to smoke and somebody would throw a cigarette to us. They were going bananas!

Finally they started their engines and we rolled out of camp Dog Patch for Hanoi. It was January 24th 1973. We were headed back to Camp Unity. It would only be for a few weeks. But those turned out to be the best 19 days of my captivity. And it was to be my last confinement as a prisoner of war in North Vietnam.

25. Camp Unity

1/24/73 – 2/12/73

We started south for Hanoi on January 24th 1973. It was the same ride as before, only in reverse; instead of being all uphill it was all downhill. In more ways than one! It was the same long ride and ass buster with 20 of us to a truck, all jammed in. But it was a pleasure all the way. We knew it was the first leg in our journey home.

I was sitting behind a guard and as we rolled on down the road he was whistling a song to himself. It was a French song I recognized. After he finished that one he started whistling a couple of classical numbers, starting with Beethoven's Fifth Symphony and then a couple of bars from Tchaikovsky's First Piano Concerto. Being a classical music nut, and having known Gooks for almost eight years, it amazed me that this character was able to reproduce some of these sounds.

I punched him in the back and said, "Hey." Then I whistled a few bars back to him. He lit up with a big smile, pointed to me and said, in pigeon English, "You like this stuff?" I said, "Hey Man! I really like these sounds, you know." I came to find out that this guy listened to the radio every time he got a chance and whenever they'd put on any classical music he just sucked it up like a sponge. He didn't have a lot of opportunity to hear it much but when he did he clearly loved it.

We started having an interesting conversation on that trip. We talked about music, in between talking about his family, how pretty his gun was and what brave fighters the North Vietnamese were. I suppose I might have thought it something of a contradiction that a serious commie could appreciate classical music, but I played along to get information out of him. I found out we were going back to Hoa Lo and why.

He told me the bombing had stopped and that the parties had gotten together at Paris. They had agreed that we were going to be released. I asked him when we were going to be released he said he didn't know for sure, but within a few weeks for us because we were the old troops.

Nobody else had gotten any word like this. I just happened to get in good with this Gook on the trip back to Hanoi. He also propped open a curtain with his rifle so I could see out. Then he gave me the job so I sat there holding his gun to keep the curtain open for about 14 hours of the trip. I got to see the whole damn Vietnamese countryside all the way back to Hanoi, including downtown Hanoi. He pointed out the craters from bombs and told me what different bombs had done them. Some of areas by the Red River as we drove into Hanoi looked like the face of the moon. You could see that those 52s had done their work. It was fantastic! All that beautiful damage!

One interesting thing was that he only knew a few English words like why, when, where, and how to conjugate the verb "to be" in a rough fashion. He could say, "Why is?" and "Where are?" and use a Vietnamese word I understood. As we were driving through the area where the B-52s had leveled everything, where people's huts and living areas had been wiped out, he pointed and said, "Why, Why, Why?" I pointed back at his rifle said, "Nam-Vietnam." That meant South Vietnam. And I said, "Why, Why, Why?" He sat back and roared with laughter. This had totally changed his mood. He nodded his head and said, "Why huh? Okay." So it was tit for tat and that settled that question.

When we got back to The Hanoi Hilton it was home again, home again. We were completing the circle, returning to the old prison downtown. The gates looked the same and the mold was still on the prison walls with all the broken glass on top. They opened the gates and we walked back inside. We walked through The Heartbreak area and out into Camp Unity.

When we walked into Unity we couldn't believe our eyes. It was about ten at night and there was not a single bamboo curtain to be seen. The entire camp was wide open. All the cell doors were there, all the windows were there, but all the bamboo curtains were taken down. There were two rooms of guys hanging out their windows shouting and yelling to us. As we walked by we were shaking their hands as they indicated the room for us to file into. It was fantastic.

We walked into the room and laid our crap down on the bunkers. I went into room four, the one I had been in before. Then the guards came around and told us the doors would be open until midnight and that we could go out in the yard to bathe and get cleaned up. So everybody, the entire 200 of us, went outside, got into the water tanks, turned the water on and took baths. Then we just wandered around and shot the shit with guys in other rooms until midnight when everyone went in and hit the sack for the night.

They opened our doors the next day and everybody just waltzed out into the court yard, almost like we were a prisoner of war instead of a con. We had gotten so used to being a criminal and now here they were taking that pleasure away from us. Hah! They had a volleyball court set up in the center of the courtyard, and a ping pong table off to one side. They gave each room a couple of ping pong balls and the paddles were kept over by the table. Anytime we wanted to go play ping pong we could do it...if you could kick a guard off the table. We had to nudge them out of the way to get on. Shit!

I went over to play ping pong and found out I could hardly hit the ball any more because it had been so long since I'd done anything to exercise my reactions. It was pretty grim.

We also discovered that the old forms of surreptitious communication were no fun anymore because all we had to do was walk over and talk to somebody in another room.

They let half of us out in the morning and the other half in the afternoon because there were so many of us and it was so crowded in the yard. They switched back and forth so we'd go out in the morning one week and the afternoon the next. But when we were outside we could go to the other rooms and talk to guys through the windows so it didn't make any difference. It just kept the crowded conditions down because of the court yard space.

We played volleyball from morning till night. We got inter-room competitions going. They even had guys from each room who were the volleyball coaches that got up their teams. We not only had room teams but also age teams. It was kind of funny, too. We had the "kiddie men's team" which was age 25 to 30. The young men's team was ages 30 to 35. The medium aged men's team was 35 to 40. And then beyond that we had the "old farts team." Most of those old farts had been staying in shape by exercising for years so they were pretty damn tough and age groups didn't make any difference as far as the competition went. We could only find five guys out of 300 men who were between 25 and 30 when we started searching around for a kiddie team. Then it dawned on us that we had all been cons too long. Virtually all of us were over 30!

It was beautiful to see some of these room teams. For instance Robbie Risner, Jim Stockdale and all the O6 guys were in room 6. Air Force Airman Third Class Robinson, previously battlefield promoted to 2nd Lt., was also in that room. Robbie is a huge guy. Even as a POW he weighed 220 pounds at about 6' 2". Robbie was the leader of their Volleyball team and it was fun to go out and hear Robbie saying, "Hey, Colonel, you're playing too close!" "Get back over there!" "OK let's hustle guys." It was really funny to hear him speak to these Colonels that way!

That's the way it went the last couple of weeks. The Gooks just couldn't do enough for us. For the first time since we had been in North Vietnam we also handled our own cooking and meal preparation. They had one Vietnamese who supervised the cooking and we had a cook shack out in the center of the court yard. The meal preparation duty rotated around rooms by the week. We sent a cooking detail there and they worked from about 6:00 in the morning until about 5 o'clock in the evening. They didn't have to be there all the time but they were most of the time. They cooked all the food and distributed it to all the rooms. Then our normal room details picked up the chow and served it to the people in our room. That was all the same as it had always been before with food, clean up, bathroom and other work details. This was the only normal POW compound situation I ever experienced in North Vietnam and it lasted for just two and a half weeks.

We knew we were going to be released soon. One day a truck pulled into the camp and a whole bunch of guys watched as they started unloading a lot of stuff. They were carrying boxes and boxes of clothing items to a store room. We waltzed over and started helping the Vietnamese unload the truck, looking in boxes and screwing around. They were filled with civilian clothes, shoes and little handbags.

The Gooks who were unloading the truck were smiling, laughing and pointing to us. We were asking them, "Is this stuff going to be for us?' They said, "Hey, you're going to go home in that." So we knew it was imminent.

We were all arranged in rooms according to our arrival dates. The guys that were 1965 and early 1966 were in rooms four, six and seven. In rooms one, two and three, and also in Blue and Rawhide the guys were late '66 and early '67 shoot-downs. The '68s and later had gone to The Plantation.

There is always some confusion about my having been in the Hanoi Hilton with John McCain. The proper answer to that is John McCain was in the Hanoi Hilton with me. We always show proper deference to each other for time served as a POW. John got there 2 ½ years after I did. In fact we just shared some time there, but never space. I was never aware of being in the same camp with him. The only time I ever remember being near McCain was here at Camp Unity. He was in a cell all the way across the other side of the compound. We had piled a bunch of blankets and other items so that a communicator could stand on top of this pile, look out the window, and communicate through mute code across the camp. One day our communicator asked me, "Did you know John McCain's over there?"

I answered, "My God, tell the other communicator over there that I'd like to see him." Which he did, and in a moment he said, "Okay, John's up there now." We looked across at each other and his hair was white so I thought I would needle him a bit. So in very slow mute code, because neither McCain nor I were practiced at that system, I flashed over to him, "My God you look old." And he sent back to me, "Have you looked in a mirror lately?" We both got a laugh and that was the sum total of our communication during our shared time together in Vietnam.

The room that Colonel Risner was in had stayed put all through the Hanoi bombing so we got the full blow-out from those guys on the B-52s, and what those raids were like when viewed from the ground. They described night bombing with the incredible noise and the flack. They'd be watching out the windows and there would be enormous fire balls that appeared over the wall of the camp. These fire balls looked like atomic bombs going off. It would develop and build and then the next thing would be an enormous blast from the over-pressure.

Risner said the bars and walls would bend from this over-pressure. It would literally blow them out of the windows, the whole damn ground and buildings would shake, and then there would be a huge roar from all those bombs being put down by the B 52s. They said it was incredible and beautiful. And, of course, it scared the living daylights out of the Gooks.

They also told us that while they had been there the month before we arrived; the new shoot-downs were brought in and put in Heartbreak. Later they were put into room seven so the old guys in room six and the brand new guys in room seven were right next door to each other. Then they also started putting new guys in room four, which was the room I was in. The screens were still up at the time but they were able to get contact with these guys and teach them how to communicate.

They got reams of information from them about what was going on in the outside world. The new guys told about cars, short skirts, long haircuts, wild clothing styles, the drug scene and everything they could think of that was going on in the states. They said there was almost a national hysteria over the prisoners of war. This was fantastic news to us because we thought we were just semi-forgotten people. We didn't realize there was so much concern in the United States.

I think this in itself is a big lesson to be learned for guys who are in a future POW situation and that is they can thank their lucky stars they belong to a nation that thinks more of human life and suffering than any other nation of the world. If an American becomes a POW, there will always be a majority of people in the United States who are thinking about them, feeling for them, and who would do anything to get them back. That certainly is a warm feeling I don't think anyone from any other country in the world could ever have.

We began to get all this information and we marveled over it. Every day we would have a debriefing session and we'd pick up notes and written material in installments that were being passed to all the rooms every afternoon. We'd spend an hour while somebody would sit in the middle of the room and read it all out to us. It was incredible! The new guys did a beautiful job of briefing us and letting us know what was going on.

As time wore on closer to the release we found out our three rooms would be the first to go, along with the sick and wounded. Then just a few days before release they came in and took out the guys who were sick and wounded. These were guys who were sick from diseases and wounds. I had gotten over my illness, so I didn't fit into that category and I was glad because I wanted to go home with my buddies. Also the guys who were badly beaten up years ago and were now cripples went out.

The camp commander called all of us out into the courtyard a few days before our release. There were numerous Vietnamese officers and apparently high-ranking people with him. We knew this was something big. Our senior ranking officer, Colonel Flynn, was in front with our other high-ranking officers. When the camp commander came Colonel Flynn turned to us and said "Fourth Allied Prisoner of War Wing, Attention!" We all came to attention. Then he turned and saluted the camp commander, who saluted back. Then Colonel Flynn turned and gave us "at ease."

It was a truly incredible experience, standing there in military formation, having our rank structure acknowledged with our senior ranking officer standing in front. And to know that we were soon going to be released. The war was ending for us, but the camp commander was pretty clear the war wasn't ending for them.

At that point the camp commander began reading the orders for our release in accordance with the Paris accords. When he was finished, Colonel Flynn saluted him, turned and called us to attention and then said "Fourth Allied Prisoner of War Wing, dismissed." Then without a sound from anyone we all turned and went back to our rooms. None of us wanted to give those officers the pleasure of cheers. But there were plenty when we got back to our rooms. That was the way true POWs were supposed to be treated. It was sad that it only happened a couple of days before our release, after more than 8 years of harassment, torture and bullshit.

On February 11th 1973 I was called out to an interrogation about five in the afternoon. I couldn't figure out why but I put on my long clothes and walked over to the Heartbreak area in the quiz room next to Heartbreak Hotel. There were two Gooks who I had never seen before. One of them asked, "Is your name Phillip Neal Butler?" I said, "Yes". He said, something in Vietnamese to the guy sitting next to him and this guy opened a brief case, pulled out a ring and put it on the table. He said, "Examine this please and see if it's yours." I looked and it was my wedding ring — the wedding ring they had taken from me on April 27th 1965. I couldn't believe it!

I said, "Well, yes it's mine." He said, "Very well please sign this form to certify that you received it." I did and he said, "That's all. Go back to your room." I turned, marched out and stuck my wedding ring on my finger. It was a very emotional experience for me, as one might expect. As soon as I got back to my room they called out another guy. I guess there were probably around 20 of us who got our wedding rings back. It wasn't a very good percentage but I guess I was one of the lucky ones. They'd had mine the longest and I just couldn't believe they had been able to keep it that long.

That night the guys in my room were called out in order of shoot-down. I was in the first group to go and we went to that same room again where they had boxes and boxes of clothing. All sorts of Gooks were around and we tried on civvies. They got me all duded up in grey pants, a grey long sleeve shirt, a jacket and a pair of black shoes. I didn't take any of the socks they offered. I wore my own American socks that one of my buddies had given me from his package. The black shoes were light weight, cheap Italian-style like ones you might buy in Tijuana. They found a pair that fit me okay. They also gave us a little handbag; a little kit that had a couple packs of Dien Binh cigarettes, a towel, a comb, a razor and some soap. The soap was just the usual Gook laundry soap. Then they sent us back to our room.

Guys just sort of marched around the room and showed off their new clothes. Everybody got all dressed up that night. Then the guard came and told us we would be awakened at five the next morning to go outside and bathe and shave.

He was wrong about one thing. We were not awakened at five o'clock because we were all quite awake when he came to open the door, and we had been all night long. We went outside and took our baths. I rolled up all the American gear I had collected over the past year or so and all the other goodies I had that I didn't want to take out with me. The only things I wanted to take home with me were the three clothes pins I had made and a needle I had made from a chicken bone that I had been sewing with for over seven years. I also kept my cup and spoon that had been my only eating utensils for years.

That's all I brought out with me in the way of crap that I had from prison. I took all my clothes and goodies down to the next room where there were a bunch of guys who were going to be released in the next increment. I shoved it all through a window there to my old buddy Bud Flesher and told him to either use it or give it away to other guys who wanted it.

I went back to the room and looked over all my notes, French, Spanish, German and all the lesson plans I'd written and collected over the years. I had a box of matches the Gooks had given me with the cigarettes. They were the first matches I had ever been given in North Vietnam. I gathered all this stuff into a neat little pile in the center of the concrete floor and set it on fire. Then I sat there and watched it burn and I just God damn near cried because it represented the destruction of eight years of misery. I knew the next day I was going to walk out into a world where I could pick up a book or a magazine anytime I wanted and get straight information out of it. I don't think many people could possibly realize how wonderful it is to be able to do that.

26. Flying to Freedom

2/12/73

About 6:30 in the morning on February 12th we all gathered around and drank the last of our coffee that we had gotten from packages. As soon as we had gotten back to Unity the Gooks gave us a package, and everybody got one this time. Some of them were not very big but everyone got a package. Amazing how these packages had finally caught up with us. I guess that night before I had about 473 cups of coffee, about 911 cigarettes, pipes full of tobacco and boy was I nervous!

On the final day, when we had been given these clothes, everybody got into the new outfits and we had our little carry bags. They weren't large but we didn't have much that we called our own. But people were taking things they wanted to save.

They took us out by cells. They had arranged the cells of fifty or so guys in the order of their shoot down date. So I was with the old timers in my cell, and we were the first ones marched out. I was number seven in line. There were six guys who had been held longer than I had.

They marched us out into the Heartbreak courtyard and I was standing there, number seven in line, ready to go out the gate. We stood there and stood there and it seemed like forever. It was only 45 minutes and then finally they brought the guys out of the New Guy Village area who were the sick and wounded. They put them with us and then they put us all on a bus.

It was a real live brand new North Vietnamese bus! We got on this beauty with no blindfolds or handcuffs, no screens over the windows. We rolled our windows down on the main drag of Hanoi and there were a million Gooks watching us leave. None of them waved but none of them cursed. None of them did anything but I know they were happier than we were to see us buzz out of town. Well, maybe not quite as happy as we were.

Then we got the king's tour of town. We rolled through Hanoi and up over the hill toward Gia Lam airport. We pulled over and stopped about a half mile before we got to the airport. We pulled into this military compound area with an open bay building and we were told to go in there and sit down. Out in the yard they had a medic station set up were they were taking care of guys who were sick and wounded. We sat in that room while everybody was running around just excited and about to wet their pants.

We sat there all morning until finally about noon the word came around that there was some problem in the discussions between the Americans and the North Vietnamese. And we thought "Jesus Christ it can't collapse now!" They brought us a loaf of bread to eat and a beer to drink and that was the only thing we had to eat that day. It seems strange that on the last go there they were still so fucked up and disorganized that they couldn't crank up a meal for us. But they didn't. So we waited until about two in the afternoon when finally the big wigs, the Vietnamese brass, were running around and they said, "Okay, let's go!"

We walked out of the compound and got on buses again and drove down to the runway. When we arrived we could look up ahead and see a huge crowd by the terminal building.

Just about that time I looked out and saw a C-141 on final approach. I immediately got a big lump in my throat and the tears just started running down my face. That was the first time that I had cried like that over being released. But the sight of that American airplane was too much. Besides that it was the first C-141 I had ever seen and it was just unbelievable!

We sat there for a few minutes and then the buses rolled up to this big crowd of people. We got off the buses, they lined us up according to shoot-downs and we walked into this group of people. There were Vietnamese, Polish, Canadian, French, and other foreign-service officers. Then I looked up and I saw my first American uniform in eight years. It was an Air Force Colonel standing there with a big grin on his face.

Then they started calling our names out over the loud speaker. The first name I heard called was Everett Alvarez and when they got to me they said, "Lt. Commander Phillip Neal Butler." That was the first time I knew I had been promoted. I had Vietnamese officers on either side of me and they walked with me up to a gate. They opened the gate and I walked through, across the line, and there was an American Air Force Major standing there.

He snapped to attention and saluted me. I saluted him back. Then he grabbed me by the hand and said, "Welcome to Freedom, Commander!" Then two great big Air Force sergeants grabbed me, one on each side, and they walked me out to the C-141. I can't remember what these guys said to me or what I said to them. I think they were half carrying me as I walked out onto the tarmac because my legs felt like rubber.

We walked out to the airplane, to the back ramp that had been dropped down. I walked up this ramp with the two sergeants still helping me and then into the back bay of the Medical Evacuation C-141. Then the prettiest Air Force Nurse I ever saw grabbed me and hugged me. She said "Welcome home, Phil." I can't remember what this nurse looked like. I have a sort of fuzzy image of her in her Air Force nurse's uniform. But I can still remember what she smelled like. It was heaven. She was the first good thing I had smelled in over eight years.

The first thing I can remember about that airplane was the smell of her perfume. Other Air Force personnel there had on after shave lotion and deodorant like human beings in the world wear. Jesus! The smell was just overwhelming.

I went forward, sat down in a seat, and this nurse strapped me in. She put her arm around me, gave me a kiss and said, "Now, you sit right there and relax, Commander. We are going home." I did. I sat right there, but I couldn't relax.

Finally we all sat down and they closed the back bay. Then we began to taxi out to the runway. I recall looking out the window at the tattered airport facilities there at Gia Lam, my final view of North Vietnam.

When we got to the end of the runway, the pilots moved the throttles forward toward 100% power on those huge C-141 jet engines. Then I could feel them release the brakes and we began to roll, then accelerate, then roar down the runway toward takeoff airspeed. Nobody moved or said anything.

But when the wheels broke the ground everybody in that airplane let out a spontaneous roar. It was deafening. We were screaming and yelling and everybody was crying, including the Air Force personnel and nurses; everybody who was on the airplane. I guess the pilot and co-pilot, too. I don't know.

We were on our way to Clarke Air Force Base in the Philippines. And that ended the almost eight years of my captivity in North Vietnam, and began my return to freedom.

THE THIRD LIFE OF A WARRIOR

"Liberty means responsibility. That is why most men dread it."

EPICTETUS (55 AD - 135 AD), *Discourses*

Introduction

I can empathize with Rip Van Winkle. He woke up in a confusing new world, as did I. The social changes between 1965, when I left the civilized world, and 1973, when I returned, are legend. The Vietnam War was as much a war of values for the world outside as it was a killing war for those inside. During those eight years I had been deeply involved in the latter, but totally isolated from the former.

Americans had at first begun to get restless, then adamantly boisterous with regard to the war itself. The peace movement brought out tremendous confrontations between the "doves" and the "hawks." "The pill" brought enormous changes in sexual mores and attitudes toward relationships between the sexes. New notions of sexual equality surged into the public discourse and into personal relationships causing ubiquitous debates and conflicts. There was a ground swell of anger and dissent on racial issues that brought deadly and destructive events. A new culture of psychedelic and "feel-good" drugs came on the scene. With all of this turmoil came new and radically different literature, music, dress, grooming, language and social mores on almost every dimension.

We ex-POWs returning home had absolutely no idea how we would be received. WW II and Korean returning POWs were not especially welcomed. But for us, the American public went crazy over our return. We literally became instant, though temporary, military rock stars. We were the returning heroes everyone had longed for. Sadly, many of my returning Vietnam War brothers and sisters had fared poorly at the hands of the public. They were often ignored at best and sometimes even castigated or

403

demeaned for their service. We, on the other hand, were given the total red-carpet treatment. Everyone wanted to meet, hear and know you. That included, for myself and other newly-returned, ex-POW bachelors, women everywhere who wanted to love us - and I suppose, "make it all better."

We were loaned a car of our choice for one year by the Ford Motor Company. We received gifts, including invitations to a Presidential White House Gala, a ticker tape parade in Dallas, a free week stay in Las Vegas with show tickets, free transportation and a visit to Disney World, a lifetime credit card for two tickets to any Major League baseball game (excluding playoffs and World Series games – damn!), and many other perks and gifts from our adoring public. I received hundreds of cards and letters from people who wore my POW bracelet. To this very day, 36 years later, I still get a half dozen or more letters or emails from people who wore my bracelet.

Conversely we former prisoners of war, with our heads firmly stuck in 1965, were thrown into a new and incredibly different world. Needless to say it caused confusion, consternation and internal conflict in each of us as we tried to adjust to our new America. It seemed like nothing was anything like what we had known. Everything was different. For all of us, even our families were totally different. Many of us faced rejection and even immediate divorce from those whom we had loved and planned for during those long, dark years of incarceration.

For me, returning home was a euphoric time, pasted with deep disappointments and distress. It was an emotional roller coaster.

For awhile I would awaken in the middle of the night and go check the door, just to make sure I could indeed open it and walk out. People who jangled keys drove me nuts. I would always ask them to stop and even grab their hands at times. The demon of post traumatic stress was always lurking just around the next corner. My family life was a disaster with a wife who sued for divorce and a lovely eight-year-old daughter who was trying to understand me as I was her. Everything about my future was up in the air, to begin again with plans for a new life. I also had to remain attached to Balboa Hospital as a patient for eight months, due to the physical results from my eight-year maelstrom of incarceration.

Somehow though, my first-life preparation and my second-life experience as a warrior helped sustain and get me through to where I am today. There have been times in my third life when I might have wished to be more like the crowd. I've paid the price with the loss of old friendships from school days in Tulsa and the Naval Academy. I've suffered condemnation from former fellow warriors, and most sadly for me, from many of my former POW cell mates and friends. Being blessed, or cursed, with a warrior mentality has certainly brought costs and benefits. But somehow the warrior spirit continues to lie deep inside me even throughout my third life. It motivates me to try my best to do the right thing for people and our planet. So honestly I wouldn't have it any other way. This old warrior continues to try his best, having returned with honor, to live with honor.

In this section I hope to show my transition into a third life. Most importantly to me though is that my readers understand that my intentions are to give a *description* of my life changes and they are never intended to be a *prescription* for someone else. If something here appears to be a positive take-away or lesson learned that is useful, then fine. I'm honored to have so served.

1. Freedom at Last

The powerful C-141 jet engines wound up to 100% power and we accelerated down the runway. Seconds later the wheels broke ground and a deafening cheer rose up from all of us – former prisoners of war. Freedom at last! Guys were hugging each other, yelling, crying, waving their arms and just going crazy. Apparently none of us had our seat belts on. No need for that at this incredibly special moment.

Everyone was up walking around, talking to friends and looking out the windows at the beautiful blue Pacific Ocean. One by one the pilot and co-pilot had us come up into the cockpit and sit down for a quick visit with them as we flew from Hanoi to Clark Air Force Base in the Philippines. Clark AFB doesn't exist anymore because Mount Pinatubo exploded in 1991 and covered it with mountains of ash and debris.

I was in the first airplane out because I was the seventh longest-held POW in North Vietnam. The agreement was that we would come out in order of how long we had been incarcerated, with the sick and wounded also on the first airplane. It took several weeks to fly us all out. There were some civilian prisoners as well. They were composed of some foreign military, CIA, journalists, nurses and others captured for no good reason in South Vietnam, then brought north. The total was 802 prisoners brought out of North and South Vietnam.

Of the 802 Southeast Asia POWs (661 military, 141 civilians/foreign nationals), 472 of us were tortured and imprisoned in North Vietnam One, Everett Alvarez, was held longer than eight years. There were 230 from the South Vietnam jungle POW camps where one man, Colonel Floyd James Thompson, survived nine years to return. There were 31 captured and held in Laos and 31 in Cambodia. Included in the peace agreements were the return of five men from the Cold War who were incarcerated in China. Two of these men were held for over 19 years under sub-human conditions.

The flight from Hanoi to Clark AFB took maybe an hour though time didn't seem to matter that day. We landed at Clark, taxied up to the hangar area and the pilots shut down the engines. The crew chief opened the door and we were asked to walk down the stair, one-by-one, in order of time spent as a POW. I was number eight down the stair. They announced our names and rank over a loud speaker as we walked down. There was a huge crowd of people, TV cameras everywhere and military brass like I've never seen before or since in my life. Commander Denton was asked to speak at the microphone where he gave a few powerful words of appreciation "for all Americans who never lost faith in us." He concluded with the most memorable words - "God bless America."

Then we all got aboard shuttle buses for the one or two mile trip to the base hospital. We all were astonished to look out the windows and see both sides of the road for the entire distance lined with cheering people. Americans and Filipinos were waving and holding signs that said, "Welcome Home." Maybe everybody who was stationed at that base was lined up and down that road.

We pulled up to the hospital and got off one by one and as we got off they announced our names one by one. All kinds of high ranking people including the Chief of Naval Operations and other Joint Chiefs were there. And we were all saluting each other. Actually they were saluting us before we could give the honor first.

And then that's where I met Brian Kelly. Brian, a Navy Lieutenant in uniform, walked up and introduced himself to me. He said, "I'm Lt. Brian Kelly, your Air Intelligence Officer sir. My purpose is to be with you to offer assistance and to debrief you on your prison experience. But we won't worry about that now. We're gonna get you taken care of here in the hospital." Then he said, "By the way, check this out," and he handed me a *Playboy magazine*. The centerfold was a new experience – full nudity – just one precursor to the many societal changes I was to experience. Wow. I've been a *Playboy* subscriber ever since. It's been 36 years and counting. You will have to take my *Playboy* from my cold, dead, well – whatever.

I felt an instant bond of friendship with this guy. As we walked along, some doctors and various other people came up to us and asked me, "Is there anything that you require that you would like to do first?"

I said, "Yes. I would very much like to see a dentist before I do anything else." I had terrible pain from broken and impacted teeth and had suffered with it for years. One tooth, broken off at The Briar Patch in 1966, had caused me constant pain and swelling. I couldn't wait to get to a dentist.

I was immediately escorted into the dental clinic section of the hospital. They put me in a chair and I suddenly noticed that I had four Air Force dentists hovering over me. These guys acted like they were extremely nervous, engaging in medical/dental debates. They examined my tooth, in quadruplet, while continuing their nervous and excited analysis. I observed this spectacle for awhile and finally just told them, "Would you guys please calm down. You're making me nervous. Just fix the tooth please." That got them settled down and they informed me that I needed a root canal. I told them fine, get on with it. And by golly they did a root canal on the spot. What a relief! It was the first time in almost seven years that I had been without dental pain. I've never enjoyed anything more than that root canal – well, relatively speaking – because of the pain I had experienced all those years.

The way they treated this returned POW seemed a bit comical to me. I was sacred material. This was a big deal because they hadn't known what to expect from us. Were we crazy? Were we volatile? Were we dangerous to ourselves or others? They had no clue.

From the dental chair they took me into the hospital and showed me a room where I was to stay. They had me in a room with another ex-POW friend, Wes Schierman. They were smart not to leave us alone, especially after so many years as prisoners.

Our room was decorated very nicely, and not just in comparison to where we had been. We had comfortable beds and all of the amenities. There were doctors and people everywhere to take care of us and whatever problems we had. At Clark, guys were usually staying there only one or two nights and then they were flown home.

The first thing everybody wanted to do was not to eat but to take a shower. The hospital floor we were on had showers in the hallway. Guys would get in the shower and turn on the hot water and just stand there for an hour. It felt so good to experience a warm shower with sweet-smelling soap, and to get the prison slime and stink off.

There was a huge clothes hamper in the hallway where all of us were throwing the uniforms the Vietnamese had given us. Then we were all given uniforms commensurate with our respective rank and service to wear.

We went to the cafeteria that they had set up especially for us. There must have been dozens of entrees and salads. And they must have had twenty different kinds of desserts. I remember I ate five or six entrees at that first meal and everybody was doing the same thing. I ate desserts until I was just about ready to die. It was so incredibly good to taste real food. The medical people were scared to death. They thought we were going to make ourselves sick. But we surprised them.

One of the first things that happened was a Navy captain and a chaplain came into my room. They said they wanted to talk to me. I thought, "Uh oh. This can't be good." They asked me to sit down and the chaplain said, "We're going to ask you to stay here for a couple of days because your wife was skiing with her boyfriend and she broke her leg."

I said, "What? A boyfriend? She broke her leg?"

He continued, "She was skiing with her boyfriend at Mammoth ski resort in California and she fell and broke her leg. She had to have an operation and have some pins put into the bones. So she is in a cast and she is going to meet you. But she would like a few extra days before you come home."

He added, "And by the way, we think your marriage is in trouble."

They were honest with me. They had to be. I was coming home now in 1973 with my head and memories stuck right in 1965. What a terrible shock! I was devastated. My vision of our perfect marriage and all those plans for the resumption of our family relationship were shattered. So in accordance with her wishes, I remained at Clark while all my fellow, long-held POWs were being transported home. I stayed there at Clark hospital for a few days, watching the other guys leave for home.

Finally after about three days I told Brian, "This is it. This is bullshit. I'm going home. Get me on an airplane. I'm going home." So I boarded the next evacuation aircraft to Barbers Point Naval Air Station near Honolulu. From there I was flown with other POWs to San Francisco. Then I transferred to a Navy C-9 transport and was flown to Miramar Naval Air Station in San Diego.

There were media reporters, TV cameras and crowds of people cheering for us at every stop. When I arrived at Miramar, I walked out onto a red carpet that stretched for about 40 yards. There at the end of the carpet stood my wife, Karen, and my eight-year-old daughter, Diane. When Diane saw me she immediately ran down the carpet and jumped into my arms. That was as big a thrill as the first time I held her eight years before. She just stared at me the whole time I carried her down the carpet to where Karen stood. I reached out to embrace my wife and got a tepid kiss on the cheek and hug.

Then some Navy people directed us to a staff car that was to transport us to Balboa Hospital. We got in the back seat with Karen sitting as far on the opposite side as she could and Diane between us. As we began to drive to the hospital I said something like, "What's going on?" I remember she said "Phil I need to tell you now that I intend to get a divorce."

2. Karen

We were taken to a beautifully appointed and decorated private room in Balboa Naval Hospital. This would turn out to be my home for a couple of weeks.

Things were not going well on the home front. Karen told me she really didn't want me to come home to our house in Del Mar because it would be uncomfortable for her and her boy friend, an M.D. she had met some three or four years previously. It turned out that Tom was a doctor and they had a relationship for several of the last years while I was gone. When I came home they were still in a relationship with each other. She didn't divorce me while I was gone, which some women did. She waited until I came home, so she continued to receive my pay and allowances the whole time I was gone.

Anyway, it was some welcome home. We went to Balboa Hospital and that's where she said she didn't want me to come home because she didn't feel comfortable with me being there. But after remaining in my hospital room for four or five days I finally did anyway. I went to see the home in Del Mar.

I tried to visit Karen and Diane in our Del Mar home after a week or so but it was extremely uncomfortable. You could cut the tension with a knife. One day Karen told me I should move on and find another female relationship because ours wasn't going to work. That was probably the final cap on the issue.

As it turned out we were scheduled for marriage counseling. The people at Balboa certainly tried to be helpful. But we only attended one session. The counselor, a Navy psychiatrist, asked me if I wanted to put our marriage back together again. I said yes, absolutely. Then he asked Karen and she replied no. He asked if she was willing to attend further counseling sessions. She said no. Then he looked sadly at me and said there was nothing any counselor could do if both parties didn't want to cooperate to restore the relationship. A few days later I asked the base legal officer if it was possible for one person to consummate a divorce. He told me yes, that in California, a no-fault-divorce state; it only took one person to complete a marital divorce.

At that point Karen said she was going to file for divorce. I tried to talk to her in the days that ensued, saying, "Okay, if you're going to file for divorce, let's don't get lawyers. You can have half of everything we have. That's fine with me. And I will certainly see to it that Diane is taken care of."

But that wasn't good enough for her. She hired a lawyer so I was forced to do the same. So I asked to speak to the Navy Judge Advocate lawyer at Balboa Naval Hospital for advice. I got an appointment to talk with him and he said, "I can't do anything for you because all my work has to be military. But I know a guy I think can help you. He was in the Navy with me and he's really sharp. He's nice and he has a law business in San Diego."

I called the guy and got an appointment with him. It turned out that he couldn't take my case because he was too busy, so he handed me off to his partner, a fellow named Bill Corr. It turned out Bill Corr was not only an excellent attorney but also a really nice guy. He took my case and really saved me in that divorce.

Bill turned out to not only help me through the divorce process with an equitable settlement, but he also became one of my best friends. Sadly, only 15 years later, Bill died of AIDs.

When I came home there wasn't anything left of my pay and allowances. The military has a form that people going off to combat sign. It allocates 80% of their pay and allowances to their families, and holds back 20% for when they return. But while we were gone some of the POWs' families needed more money, so they appealed to their representatives. Then Congress passed a law that these women could withdraw monies from the 20% of pay held back, based on an emergency need.

But when I came home there was a record of thirteen emergency withdrawals of my money and so there was nothing left. Karen had purchased a small house in La Jolla when she moved from Lemoore to San Diego in about 1967. Then in the early '70s she bought another larger home in Del Mar, just north of San Diego. She had rented the La Jolla home out to a friend. So when we divorced I got the little bungalow in La Jolla and she took the house in Del Mar.

After a couple of weeks some officer friends who were Naval Academy classmates of mine picked me up and took me to Point Loma. They began to help me get started in life again. One of them let me crash on his sofa in his apartment. Then he connected me with the apartment complex manager and I signed on for a two bedroom apartment of my own. They took me to the NavyExchange and helped me shop for basics to stock an apartment. Then they helped me get moved in and settled. That was the beginning, the new beginning.

All the way through this Brian Kelly was with me too. He was incredibly helpful getting me back into the world. Little things like getting a driver's license, opening a checking account and even using a telephone were mysteries that Brian helped me with. His friendship and counsel were invaluable. He helped me get grounded again in a new and strange world. He was much more to me than just a Navy debriefer.

During that time Karen was very confrontational with me in general and with regard to Diane. She seemed to blame me for leaving her. I think that was the bottom line. I got the blame for leaving her for eight years.

When it would be my weekend to see Diane, sometimes she would just take her someplace else. It turned out after our initial court session that I had to file an amendment to bring her back in court again to make it firm that I had certain days to see Diane. I tried for 50% custody and the judge wouldn't allow it because I was a POW just back from Vietnam! Plus Karen was the mother, a policy that trumped everything in 1973.

So Diane was in Karen's complete custody, but I got her every other weekend, for two weeks vacation in the summer, and every other Christmas. It wasn't very much.

When we went to court for the "interlocutory" or property settlement, there was an interesting moment. There was a law dating back to World War II mandating that returned POWs get paid $5 a day for their time in captivity. It was figured at three dollars a day awarded for insufficient food and two dollars a day for inhumane treatment. So for my 2,855 days I got awarded five bucks a day per that law, a grand total of $14,275! When we were before the judge, Karen's attorney stood up and said, "I think that Mrs. Butler should have half of that."

The judge got so red in the face that if it would have been legal for him to swear in a courtroom, he would have. As it turned out, it was the perfect thing for her lawyer to say because the judge was immediately on my side. He said not only "No", but, "Absolutely not. That's the worst thing I've ever heard. Sit back down. This is just horrible that you would even ask for such a thing after what this man has been through."

But it was a decent and equitable settlement for both of us. At least it looks that way in hindsight. She got the Del Mar home and I took the small and less valuable house in La Jolla. I also agreed that she would get a condominium that she had bought in – yes – Mammoth Ski Resort. She kept all the furnishings and two cars while I only took mostly personal items of mine that were still left. Karen got spousal support for a couple of years while she completed her Master's Degree and Diane got child support until she was eighteen, the standard stuff.

I never completely understood how she was able to turn so angry and vindictive towards me, that she could treat me the way she did. I think it's possible that she was taking out her anger on me as a projection of her sense of guilt for having left me, found a new relationship, and used up all the money. That's just a guess. It was upsetting at the time, to say the least, but I got over it.

Ironically, I owe a huge debt of gratitude to Karen's sister for her unflagging support and help during that traumatic period. Judy Olson made no excuses about being there for me the minute I arrived. She and her fiancé, Bernie Luskin, actually delayed their Hawaii marriage to accommodate my homecoming.

Judy did everything from holding me when I cried to helping me shop for clothes. She and Bernie gave me much-needed support and a base of refuge at their home in Huntington Beach, only an hour drive from San Diego. I had of course known her since I was 17, dating her older sister when she was just 13. Judy was always a good friend to me, though she had a rocky relationship, and still does, with her older sister.

Judy became and still is to this day much like a sister to me. She has been in my life on a continuing basis since my return in 1973 and now is a close friend to both my wife Barbara and me. We both love her very much.

In hindsight I think I did alright. Karen is who she is. She's out there and I've had almost no contact with her over the years, and no need for any. As things turned out, I've told many people that Karen, no doubt, gave me the best gift of my life. It was brutal at the time, but something that resulted in a merciful euthanizing of our relationship. Life is strange that way.

Five years later, on February 12, 1978, at a five year POW reunion in San Diego, I met Barbara. And I got it right the second time around, proven by our 32 loving years together.

A recent note about Karen: She just joined the Peace Corps in 2009, at age 71, and was sent to Botswana. She is living in bare, third-world conditions and has even had to learn the Setswana language to communicate with people for her two year assignment. She is counseling and teaching people about how to prevent AIDs. The people of Botswana are being devastated by that disease. Life expectancy there is now down into the mid 30s. It is amazing that she is healthy enough and that she had the guts and the will to do that. She has a wonderful sense of service. Barbara and I sent Karen our congratulations.

I've had some final thoughts about Karen. Joining the Peace Corps and going to Botswana reminds me of the Karen Olson I married many years ago. She is a strong, stoic, congruent, straight-forward and responsible person. The four years we were married were really good years. But after eight years had elapsed we both had evidently become different people. It was also a different world. I couldn't understand that very well in 1973 because I hadn't lived through those changes. Her behavior at the time seemed merciless. But with the passage of time it turned out to be merciful because I was freed to begin a new life.

3. Return — Home?

I was suddenly and jarringly faced with some huge changes in my personal life. But it was also an extraordinarily transformational time in our culture. I had left my home in March of 1965 and now I was back, eight years later, in the fantasy world of 1973. For a while everything was totally confusing.

For instance, I remember riding in a staff car with Brian during the first few days. We would be driving around in San Diego and I kept pointing out cars to him saying "What kind of car is that? What kind of car is that?" Then I would say, "Now there's a new car. What is that?"

And Brian would say, "No Phil. That car is five years old."

Of course all of the mores, especially sexual mores, were completely different. The pill had had a profound affect on the population and AIDS hadn't come around yet so sexual relationships between men and women were certainly not the way they had been when I left home. And of course I had also been married for four years back then.

The way people were dressing was really a panic. I saw my first bellbottom trousers, great big checkered pants, goofy looking shoes, and guys with long hair. From the back you couldn't tell if it was a man or a woman. It was really wild. I remember going out early on to shop for clothes. My sister-in-law Judy came with me to help me shop for some civilian clothes. We walked into a shop and I just turned to her and said, "Judy, I have no idea of what I should be getting here." There were no wingtip shoes, button-down Ivy League shirts, or any other clothes that looked familiar.

I can remember being around Balboa Hospital, seeing women with pierced ears, and asking if they were gypsies or in some cult. Because women in the 1950s wore snap-on earrings. This was all totally new, little things like that were just amazing. And seeing women with no bras was pretty amazing, too. Not to mention exciting. There was not even a hint of such fashion before I left. The verbal expressions and the way people talked was so different. I needed a translator to understand what it all meant.

The music was really different. The music was actually wonderful when I came home. The soft rock and the various groups who sang soft protest songs were compelling to me. It was sort of a pick-up on the old ballads from the '30s and '40s. Unfortunately it didn't last very long. A

415

couple of years later this great music had been eclipsed by more modern, atonal screeching stuff like Iron Butterfly and acid rock. Later when I was dating I found out dancing had changed dramatically. People danced without touching each other now. Ball room dancing and all that romantic stuff of the past seemed to be ancient history.

The transition was easier for some returning POWs than others. In the beginning we naturally teamed up to help each other deal with the readjustment. We did what we had done in prison where we had built a cadre of support teams. When we came home, several other former POWs I had known were also being sued for divorce. We supported each other. Other than that, I would say that I got support from the people at Balboa Hospital where I stayed my first weeks at home.

Each of us had a personal visit with our assignment officer at Balboa Hospital. Mine offered me a choice of duty, which could include graduate school. After graduate school in a social or behavioral science I would incur another four year obligation. I was thinking a great deal about a second career, after the Navy, and all of this seemed to fit nicely into my life planning. This option would allow me to eventually get a PhD, my life goal at the time, and to finish my Navy career with 20 years service and a retirement income. I also had the opportunity to stay in San Diego where I could be with my daughter.

One afternoon I was sitting in my hospital room when this Navy nurse, Mary Ann, who had been taking care of me, came around. She stopped and we talked for awhile. I had gotten to know her name and we struck up a friendship. During our conversation that afternoon she said, "Phil. I understand you're hanging around here. Why aren't you going home?"

I explained to her what was going on with my soon-to-be ex-wife. She said, "Well, I get off at 4:30. How would you like to come over to my house tonight? I'll make you a home-cooked meal." I said, "OK, fine." It turned out Mary Ann fixed a lot of things for me that evening and night. She was such a dear woman and I will always remember her with gratitude.

Speaking honestly, I took to the new freer sexuality with a serious appetite for making up for lost time. I had many short-term affairs with women, but always with the intention of finding someone to be with monogamously. My dating routine for the next five years turned out to be a sort of serial monogamy style. My more enduring female relationships during that time tended to last anywhere from two months to a year.

I met Joni Myers, an English woman, after a few months. We had a good relationship for almost a year, until I started graduate school in early 1974. Joni was very sweet and caring. She really helped me get through my divorce. And I believe she also helped get me through some of my anger towards my Vietnamese captors as well as towards my wife. I was experiencing a lot of post traumatic stress that year and also a rapid transition back to the real world. Joni was so supportive during those first months home. I will always remember and be thankful for her love then.

I was promoted to the rank of Commander within a few months, on full active duty and flight pay. All the services adopted a policy of giving us our choice of first duty station upon return. My choice was to attend graduate school at the University of California San Diego, to get a PhD in Sociology. My orders were for two years there, with a supposed verbal agreement for two more years if needed. I was well aware of the likelihood that the "verbal agreement" would somehow disappear and I was right. So I immediately buried myself in studies of my new discipline, carrying course overloads and doing independent studies during the summer sessions, such that I managed to complete the course requirements for a PhD in two years.

I had a lot of catching up to do. The real catching up was in terms of reading to find out what had happened over my eight missing years. I was also catching up as a graduate student at UC San Diego. I lived in the library and soaked up stuff like a blotter. I was making up for the eight years of being without any reading or writing materials whatsoever. So I stormed through the PhD program because I was starved for information.

Needless to say, I was by light years the wealthiest graduate student in my class of 15 people. So there I was, a thirty-five year old Navy Commander, bachelor, and graduate student with a new Jaguar. It was an XKE Roadster, silver with red leather interior. There were maybe three dozen relationships with various women over the five years that I was single.

After that it was back to the real Navy, the Human Resource Management Center in San Diego. While serving there for three years I was able to complete my field research for my PhD. Then my final two years in the Navy were spent as a faculty member at the Naval Postgraduate School in Monterey where I was able to complete my doctoral dissertation and receive my PhD degree.

Another big change was television. When I left, television was not nearly as prolific as it had become by the time I returned. In fact, when I left for Vietnam, color television was just getting started. I don't think I had ever seen color television before I left.

Television was important back then. It might have been the vast wasteland, as FCC Commissioner Newton Minnow called it, but there were still some important programs to watch. For instance, everybody was glued to the television during the Watergate hearings, trying to figure out what was going on. Everyone wanted to know specifically, as Howard Baker put it: What did the president know and when did he know it? I remember it as a scary time. Were we going to be a democracy or what were we going to be? Nixon's idea was, "If the President does it, then its okay." Unfortunately it turned out to be a precursor to the Bush-Cheney theory of government years later.

When we returned, as I've said, this country was desperate for heroes, and we got that assignment. It was "Welcome Home POWs" everywhere we went. In the first year or two it was like being a rock star. People would even frequently recognize me when I would go out. I don't know how. It was unbelievable. It went on and on. And then there was the whole POW bracelet thing with people who purchased and wore a bracelet with a Vietnam POW's name, or in some cases the name turned out to be a guy who was missing or killed in action. I actually got letters from women I didn't know, and other POWs did too, but especially the guys who had become single. Believe it or not, some letters came with keys in them. Young women would send me a letter and say, "Please come visit me" and enclose their house key.

The response to us – making heroes of us – seemed like an effort by this country that was so desperately conflicted about the Vietnam War. Perhaps a key to this was a feeling of remorse for the sordid and ungrateful way many returning Vietnam veterans had been treated over the years before the war was finally over.

Also, I think both the left and right wanted to make sure that they didn't treat us the way they had treated returning Korean War POWs, as though they were traitors, as though they had crossed over to the other side. There were the false allegations that they had been brainwashed, disloyal, broken and weak because they had not been able to stay with name, rank, service number and date of birth. They were excoriated because ostensibly they had given up information that could be used as propaganda.

Those of us in the Vietnam prisoner of war camps learned all too well that we needed to have second lines of defense, to give up a little information for the sake of our survival. At the time that I went down we were all under orders of name, rank, service number, date of birth but eventually reality trumped the unrealistic rules. Amazingly the Department of Defense changed this stupidly hard-line policy during the Vietnam War, mostly as a result of finally realizing it was self-defeating. They eventually adopted the same policy we came to as POWs from our years of tough experience.

4. Debriefing

I had been in an information vacuum for eight years. I spent those eight years fighting the Vietnamese, maintaining a tough-as-nails, right-wing, militaristic posture so that they couldn't or wouldn't want to use me for propaganda. Then in addition to all my family issues and social confusion, I found myself in Balboa Hospital under orders to complete a debriefing with my Navy Air Intelligence Officer, Lt. Brian Kelly.

So I sat with Brian, day after day, doing this debriefing while my head was still in the fighting warrior mindset. I was still at war with our captors, filled with anger and bitterness – it couldn't have been otherwise – and I had all these other things going on around me.

There I was, almost a stranger in a strange land. Robert Heinlein would have been able to describe it perfectly for me. As I was debriefing with Brian, the facts came out but my true emotions were stuffed someplace. They didn't start to surface until more time had passed, many years later. So during this time, I virtually had to re-learn how to have feelings about myself and other people, about life around me because for so long, in order to survive, I had to give up those feelings. As for the content of my POW experiences, Brian was amazed at how complete my memories were. I had purposely memorized every date, event, person and move during those eight years. So Brian interviewed me for a total of 36 hours on the chronological history of my time as a POW.

While I was a prisoner of war we all had to be hard line in order to resist their insatiable quest for political propaganda. But that didn't mean we didn't discuss issues about the war in our cells when later on we had cell mates. We tried to understand, through discussions, why we were really doing this bombing and why we were in this war. Most of the guys who had been shot down were saying that most of their missions were "to bomb snakes and monkeys." Most of the time there weren't even any real, viable, military targets to be firing at.

This came up when I talked with other POWs and it came up during my debriefing, both times with my emotions stuffed. The whole Vietnam war and our being involved over there began to make less and less sense to me, just as it made less and less sense to people here in the United States.

But we couldn't afford for it to not make sense, especially with all that we had been through. Ultimately, the majority of the Vietnam veterans probably made sense of it by staying on the right side of the political spectrum. These were the lessons of our military indoctrination. And for POWs, they were the lessons we learned in order to become hardened to deal with the Vietnamese interrogators. The Vietnamese always referred to us as "criminals." So as we toughened up with their inhumane treatment, we began to proudly refer to ourselves as "Cons." In actuality we had become tough cons.

Vietnam veterans often take one of two courses to rationalize their service in that war. One direction, to the right, is to say they had done their job, done the best they could do, but that they had been betrayed by the political system and by the politics of the left-wing American people. They often say they should have been allowed to continue to fight and win the war but it was the politics that defeated us. We should never have allowed them to win the Vietnam War. We should have won, defeating the communists, so the Vietnamese people would now have freedom and democracy.

The other direction, I label "to the left," is making sense but in a different way. I've taken this path after considerable soul searching and study. It is that we never should have been there in the first place. The war was a disaster. It was a cataclysmic mistake for this country that we will carry with us in our culture for generations to come. Just like the way we have carried the effects of the Civil War throughout our society for almost 150 years, we will carry the effects of this war for decades, maybe centuries.

What we did to the Vietnamese people was horrible, insane and unconscionable. We killed somewhere between one and two million Vietnamese people, the vast majority of whom were innocent civilians. They still have over three hundred thousand MIAs. Their country has been environmentally devastated for many generations to come with Agent Orange and all the bombs, small arms and munitions we put in that place that will be exploding, maiming and killing for years and years. We did all that stuff because we warriors were sent over there to fight. But the bottom line for me is American warriors performed courageously, selflessly and loyally for their country. We did our very best and should be given credit as warriors for having done what we were sent to do.

In the end my sense-making of the Vietnam War has been to hate the war but to love and respect the warriors. Indeed, that's how I make sense of all the wars and interventions that the United States has been engaged in since World War II. There have been over a hundred of them. Now there are the senseless wars we've gotten ourselves into, Iraq twice and in

Afghanistan. We are living in a world that Chalmers Johnson calls military Keynesianism. We are bankrupting our society through our military adventurism. At last count we have military and quasi-military forces in more than 150 countries around the world.

That was the sense I was making out of my experience in Vietnam during the first couple of years I was back home. And it seems little has changed over the almost 40 years since my debriefing. So with my emotions hidden away for safe keeping, I gave Brian 36 hours, all of it data oriented. On this date I did this and on that date so-and-so did that. It was memorized content and regurgitated in chronological order as it happened, because I had tried so very hard to remember everything as I went along because I knew if I ever got out alive I would be asked to repeat this stuff. But my emotional baggage was still safely locked away somewhere in the recesses of my brain and heart.

Medical professionals have a diagnosis called Post Traumatic Stress Disorder, or PTSD. This condition from war experiences has been around a long time, under different labels and modes of treatment. During WW II and Korea it was commonly called shell shock. When you send normal people out to engage in combat, that experience runs so counter to anything they've ever experienced or been taught to believe in, it causes enormous internal stress. War is not like the movies or television. There is far more personal horror, loss, pain, carnage and chaos. Everything is up close and personal, unlike a video game.

Some people may have PTSD for just a few months or years while others have symptoms for life. Sometimes it happens immediately upon return from war and some people have recurrences many years later.

I experienced both the stress of being a POW and of being repeatedly tortured. When I first came home I was grinding my teeth so badly at night I had to be fitted with dental guards so I could sleep without tearing my teeth up. I also had a hair trigger temper that I fought to keep in control. I didn't like being in close confinement with a lot of other people. I had to slowly accommodate being around more people. For years I absolutely could not stand the sound of somebody rattling keys. The sound pushed me close to the edge, always reminding me of the fear promoted by guards coming down the cell block to take someone out for interrogation and torture. Now more than 36 years later I still find it irritating but it doesn't drive me up the wall as it used to when I first came home.

I also experienced a lot of flashbacks, especially in the early years. I would have flashbacks at strange times, like when I was doing something innocuous. I might be doing dishes in the kitchen or I might be sitting in a classroom, or working at my job, or just walking down the street or driving a car, and all of a sudden something will flash through my mind. Then I will feel that same irritation or even anger rise up inside me again.

I have had flashbacks ever since returning from Vietnam and I expect they will continue to visit me for the rest of my days. But now when I have them, they have lost much of their power. They are not as jarring as they used to me. Now they've become just part of me and who I am.

The Department of Veteran Affairs has been particularly helpful with my stress and also other physical remnants of being a POW. I tell people I should have been better to my body when I was in my 20s and 30s. That uncoordinated ejection from my A4C in 1965 resulted in seven compression-fractured vertebrae. I have heart, skeletal and neurological problems from malnutrition, Beriberi and the other diseases I had in prison. I have osteoarthritis and osteoporosis from years of malnutrition and physical abuse. And I live with constant tinnitus from multiple broken eardrums. My VA disability rating is now 100%. But thanks to wonderful VA care and a magnificently understanding and supportive wife, I'm just doing great these days.

My POW experiences were powerful and defining. They have caused me to define myself and others in ways related to those experiences. I have a tendency to rate people in terms of how I imagine what that person would have been like if they had been in a POW camp with me. I know it's not an objective or sometimes even fair way to size people up. But it is almost involuntary now and I have to be careful not to judge people too much accordingly.

PTSD manifests itself in our society because we have so many veterans from all our wars and interventions. I'm sure our prisons are full of people with post-traumatic stress disorder that has either gone undiagnosed or been ignored. Lots of homeless veterans are no doubt victims of it. They show their rejection of society with an inability to make friendships or other social bonds with people so they even become itinerant homeless people. Some of our Vietnam Veterans came home and went to live out in the boondocks, in communes or even in isolation just to get away from everything. New research on the subject suggests that people who experience being in a car or an airplane crash, or other violent experience, can also have post-traumatic stress.

I recognize today that all of these issues were underlying the way I expressed myself while being debriefed in 1973. All of my dates, times and facts were accurate. But the content certainly contains the anger and stress I was experiencing then, but was unable to articulate at the time.

5. Diane

I'm sure many men have talked about the first time they held their first child, those feelings are profoundly powerful. You hold this little thing and you know that it's part of you. It's just incredible. I had an instantaneous bonding with this little baby. Then two days later I left, and when I came home she was eight years old. That same feeling of her being a part of me instantly returned when I came home and I still have those feelings today, even though father-daughter bonds have been broken.

For six years we had a very good father-daughter relationship after I got back from those eight years in Vietnam, even though it was only every other weekend. I did everything I could think of for us to have a good relationship. We did lots of wonderful things together. We went to movies and the beach. We went snow skiing. Diane loved sports so we went to ball games, hockey games, and I went to her sports events at school. I took her on vacations to places like Yellowstone and Colorado, and I took her to Tulsa several times to meet her relatives.

I bought a townhouse with a VA loan in Pacific Beach, a community of San Diego near the ocean, in March of 1974 after being home a year. I set up a bedroom for Diane with her own dresser, desk, art and other fun stuff of her choosing. I also bought a Fox Terrier puppy we named "Skeeter." He was a small tornado of play and fun, thus a real hit with Diane. One summer we painted the outside of our townhouse together, whereupon Diane had a great time getting as much paint on herself as the house. I invested in an old, run-down duplex some months later. Diane helped me repair and remodel that place, learning skills she uses today.

I tried to interact as a parent with her school but they wouldn't let me because I didn't have custody. I even fought to get to know what her grades were but the school wouldn't let me know because I wasn't the person who had custody.

The good times lasted until 1979, when she was 14 years old. I received Navy orders to be on the faculty at the Naval Postgraduate School in Monterey. When my wife-to-be, Barbara, and I left for Monterey my interactions with Diane became less and less. It wasn't just the mileage between us. Diane seemed to be changing a lot at that time.

After graduation from high school I offered to send her to any college or university she could get admitted to, anywhere in the world. But she chose instead to go into a transient and hand-to-mouth life existence. This was most distressing because she is very intelligent. But she never seemed to have the motivation or the ability to get her act together and do anything with her life.

When she was a senior in high school she drove to Monterey and told me that she was a lesbian. She said I was the first person in the family that she had told. She said she wanted to tell me first because she knew I would understand. I certainly did, being a PhD candidate in Sociology. I encouraged her to understand that she was normal because human sexuality encompasses a normal curve of variations. But I also warned her that she would experience discrimination and sexism in her life.

Barbara and I reinforced our support for her by marching with her in the San Francisco Gay-Rights parade. I served on and chaired the board of the Monterey County AIDs Project. We were members of PFLAG, Parents and Friends of Lesbian and Gays. We also later attended and supported her wedding ceremony to a woman.

I tried to visit her in San Francisco several times but she didn't seem to want my company. Things began to deteriorate more in the 1990s. Then sometime in early 1993, she told me that she didn't want a father anymore. Since then, little by little, our relationship has become estranged. She has just drifted away from me until now we no longer have any interaction.

I've left messages and things for her but she won't return my phone calls. I get nothing in return from her. I've never received a Father's Day, Christmas or birthday card from her. Today she seems to be a moody, unhappy, angry and antisocial person who lives life estranged from everyone.

Of course it must have been difficult for her, and most confusing, not having a daddy for eight years. I don't know what Karen was telling her, but even if it wasn't bad things, certainly her mother's own feelings and her behavior must have had some effect. I thought with the six years we did have together, and had such a great time with each other, that whatever she might have gone through she would have gotten over it in time.

I don't know all of the details, but at this writing, I understand she's unemployed and living in her mother's house, taking care of it and her mother's dogs while Karen is in Botswana for twenty-seven months on her Peace Corps assignment. She recently returned, unopened, a package of photographs and a letter I sent her.

It must have been very complicated for Diane. She has her own experiences. But ultimately it's not all about me and my relationship with her. She has reacted pretty much the same way with everybody in her family. She is 45 years old now, and like all of us, responsible for her own behavior.

I don't take responsibility for her choices. I look back on the time that I was in San Diego when she was a child growing up, and I know that I did everything possibly I could. If I had it all to do over again I don't think I could do it any better. I have no regrets, and no thoughts that I might have done anything that was wrong for her. When I look back I think I did a really good job, especially considering the fact that I was a returned prisoner of war who went through eight years of hell. I had to put my life back together and set those experiences aside in order to try to be an exemplary father for her.

I do know of several cases with other people who've had children who were drug addicts and children who had got into trouble with the law. I have friends and a relative who have children that are parasitic, leeching off their parents. That makes me feel thankful. Barbara and I are truly grateful that the situation with Diane is at least what it is and that at least we're being left alone. We're not being harassed and pestered or getting late night calls from the bail bondsman.

Diane has been no trouble. She's just not there anymore. I guess you can't have everything in life. And I have been so blessed with good things since returning home that I don't deserve to have any complaints about anything. It's been a wonderful ride up to this point. Families don't work for a lot of people. But I do have a wonderful wife, sister, and a new brother and sister-in-law. All of them love and support me and I love them dearly. I try to focus on what I have, not what might have been. Life is never perfect. But I still love and will always miss my only child, Diane Butler.

6. Return Home to Tulsa

As much as I love Monterey and couldn't imagine living elsewhere, I do feel significant connections to Oklahoma. Tulsa is where I was born and grew up. I don't feel part of the culture. But I do feel connections to the place and the history I lived in my first life - my childhood of family, friends, activities, schools, neighborhoods and the community I knew.

Of course those days are all gone now, but the feeling of connection is still there, and it works both ways. I returned to Tulsa in March of 1973, a month after I left Vietnam. I wore my uniform because my sister had said the family would want to see me in my uniform. I flew home on an American Airlines flight.

When we landed and were in the gate, the pilot requested that, "Everyone remain in their seat because we have Commander Phillip Butler aboard, and he is going to get off the airplane first. I understand that there's going to be a reception for him outside." Then he announced that I had been a POW and some of my story.

The passengers applauded as I stumbled up the aisle on the airplane and got off to see all my relatives there waiting for me. My sister, aging grandparents, cousins, uncle and aunts were there to shower me with hugs, kisses and tears. Then we walked out of the terminal where there were thousands of people. Several hundred of my high school classmates were in a line, some holding banners that said "Will Rogers High School Class of '56 Welcomes Phil Butler Home." I made a few stumbling remarks for the TV stations and then I was escorted out to the street.

There was a little sports car, a Lotus Elite, that was loaned for me to drive while I was in town. My sister and I drove off between the throngs of people and cameras to her home and later to a family reunion at my aunt and uncle's home. That was the same Uncle Jim, Colonel, USAF, who had wanted me to go into the Air Force 12 years before. Maybe Jim had been right back then.

As we drove around town to visit old friends that week I saw that every movie theater marquee and business window in that town of 300,000 people had put up signs that read, "Welcome Home Phil Butler." The movie theaters had even taken down their movie advertisements to put up the welcome home signs. It was a very big deal and I was blown away!

So when people ask me where I am from, the answer is Tulsa!

Frederick Chopin was born in Poland but left for Paris when he was in his teens, never to return. His last dying request was to have his heart buried in Poland and the rest of his body in France. His magnificent Romantic piano music includes his "Mazurkas" and other compositions that reflect his Polish heritage. In some sense, maybe part of my heart is still in Tulsa too. But never mind those theatrics. Just scatter my ashes here on my beloved California Central Coast. I'm a true Californian, cognitively, emotionally, culturally, physically, and in every other way.

That trip back to Tulsa after the war was certainly one of the most important moments of my life. And in retelling the story, another important person must be described, a person who could have spoiled the entire experience had I not dealt with her my whole life before. That person was my mother.

Mother was just impossible. She didn't even come to the Tulsa airport in 1973 when all the rest of the family, and much of the city, were there to meet me. I had escaped her miserable and hurtful behavior by leaving Tulsa in 1956 after I graduated from high school. During my teens her abusive behavior had been intolerable.

But my poor sister Linda had to grow up with her and endure her abuse for many years after I left home. Mother harassed and abused Linda incessantly. The physical abuse stopped, like it did with me, when Linda was big enough to beat her back. But even after Linda left home, mother would call her up and leave filthy and profane messages on her phone-answering machine. Occasionally she would also come by and bang on the front door, just to annoy.

Our mother had always seemed to know how to gauge when there was something important to one of us, and then she would try to disrupt it. For example, at our high school graduation she would make a scene. Or, if there was a family affair going on she would try to disrupt it. So she was a great thorn in my side and another motivator to get out of Tulsa. But Linda didn't escape her torment until 2006 when mother finally died at age 90. She died on my 68th birthday, and Linda said it was the best birthday present anybody could give. I think she was right.

7. Linda

When Linda was a little girl I would go get her as often as I could just to get her away from our mother. I felt a responsibility for her, as I did my father. I was in high school then, dating and going to the drive-in movies, and I would sometimes have my little sister with me. Linda would take great joy in sitting between me and my date, the little devil. She was supposed to be in the back seat asleep but that rarely happened. She would always stay awake through the whole movie. She was only 10 years old when our father died at age 44 in January of 1960. After that I really became a surrogate father as well as her brother.

Linda left mother's house at age 16, but still managed to finish her senior year in high school. She and her boyfriend got married and that marriage lasted from 1966 until I came home in 1973. They had a daughter, Michelle, who ironically is also estranged from her mother today. Michelle has led a hand-to-mouth existence and is a notoriously irresponsible person who has taken to drugs at various times. Linda and I often muse over how we both managed to survive our miserable childhoods and become successful while both our daughters rejected every opportunity to succeed. Is it something in our genes that we passed on? What a strange world.

I don't know if Linda waited for me to come home to divorce her husband or if it had been brewing for some years. But just as I found myself getting a divorce, Linda decided to do the same with her husband Robert Johnston. We had some brother/sister bachelor fun together for about five years before we each found a new wife and husband. Sadly, her second marriage to Steve did not work out either, but she has remained independently and happily single for almost 20 years so far.

Linda is a very interesting woman, something I would say even if she weren't my sister. On her own, she managed to go to college and become a registered nurse. She worked as an intensive care nurse for awhile and then started a private investigation business. She's been a private investigator now for over 30 years. She is known throughout Oklahoma, the United States and other countries as a top female PI. She has also invested wisely in Tulsa real estate and is the owner of numerous rental properties. She takes after her grandmother Butler by being a strong, independent woman and a successful business person.

It's been very valuable to both of us to have such a very close relationship. Together we've made sense out of what we went through. Somehow both my sister and I have been resilient to overcome hardships. As a result we have very little patience for people we know in their sixties or seventies who are still complaining about their stern father figure or mother. Some people blame their parents all their lives – for their own failures. Linda and I know everyone has choices, for whom or what they want to be. She is indeed my warrior sister.

Phil in first uniform after return from Vietnam

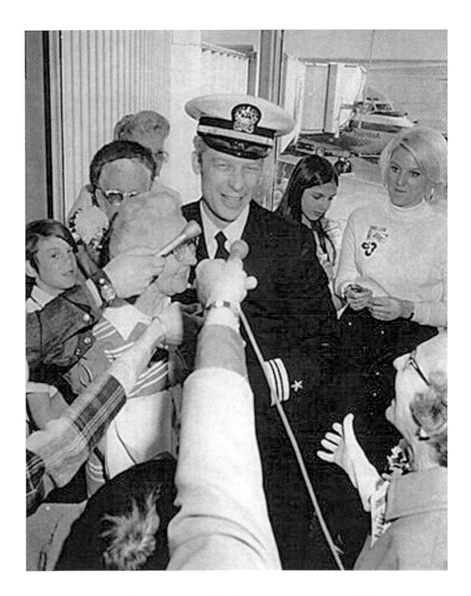

Welcome home at the Tulsa Airport, 1973, by Phil's family.

Phil with daughter Diane at Seaworld (1973)

Captain Phillip Butler (1981)

Phil and Barbara have been Point Lobos docents for 20 years

Phil's license plate. 2855 days, and nights, as a POW.

Phil and Barbara at Machu Picchu

Phil and Barbara with baby screech owl ready for release

8. Back on the Diving Board

"I never saw a purple cow
I never hope to see one;
But I can tell you, anyhow,
I'd rather see than be one!"

GELETT BURGESS, 1895

I didn't have much interest in flying anymore after I got my health back, which took about nine months after I returned from Vietnam. But I did get back into the cockpit for a short time. I went through instrument refresher-training in the TA4F & J, two-seat versions of the A4, at NAS Miramar. I needed to get my aviator re-qualification because as a qualified Naval Aviator I would continue to receive flight pay while on shore duty. So that was really important. I also wanted to get back on the diving board after all those years to prove to myself that I could still do it.

I and other returned POWs went through VT-4, Aviation Training Squadron 4, flying TA-4s. These planes had a little more powerful engine than the A4C I had flown. According to my log book, I had six re-orientation and nine instrument flights and I became recurrent on December 17, 1973.

I remember sitting around the pilots' ready room during this process. There I was, a Navy commander, ex-POW, listening to the young pilots who were where I had been eight years earlier. Only this was a time when our nation wasn't at war. These lieutenant jgs had just finished flight training and now were getting instrument qualified in the TA4 before joining the replacement air group and then their squadron. There was a lot of macho talk flying around the ready room and I just wanted to go slap them, the young idiots. They didn't know what the hell they were talking about. It was all about, "Getting out there and shooting guns and rockets and killing Vietnamese, killing Gooks," and "Oh, I can't wait."

I could see my previous self in these hot shots, talking all that nonsense just as we had. But they had no idea what it was like to be in combat, to see your buddies getting killed, to wind up being a POW and to watch some of your fellow POWs die. They couldn't understand the cognitive and emotional stress brought on by having fought and killed in a useless and disgusting war.

I believe this started a critical turning point for me. I had already been reading a lot about the war and had begun to question it all. Now this experience was just another catalyst that caused me to think seriously about what we had done to Vietnam and to the Vietnamese people. I began to understand the process of de-humanizing our "enemies" by calling them "gooks" that I had been subjected to. I suddenly realized how similar it was to all those before in my life who had called black people "niggers." It was a simply a sinister socialization process that legitimized the persecution and killing of other innocent people.

I was beginning to have serious second thoughts about all of that. I didn't feel part of it anymore and hearing those young pilots really started me feeling like Gelett's "purple cow" back in the Navy. That feeling only increased during the rest of what was left of my Navy career.

I wasn't angry at them. It really made me angry with myself. They were exhibiting the same mindless bravado that we did back then. It was the same Ready Room talk we had when we were out there flying combat. It's a way of rationalizing, of compensating for your fears, as an individual and as a group. It was like cheerleading yourself for what you were doing.

I think that kind of talk probably dissipated after awhile. Most of the guys I've since talked to, who were flying combat in Vietnam in the late 60s and early 70s when I was a POW, now see what a ridiculous enterprise it was. Most of them probably now realize how futile and stupid it was to be there doing this to Vietnam and to actual people on the ground. They always regret the loss of friends who were killed. But they had to do their duty, even if it was just bombing monkeys and snakes. But the truth is we were bombing and killing people, most of them innocent.

The American people finally got tired of the senseless slaughter. People were watching combat on their TV sets and seeing people actually get killed. They were watching the bodies come home in flag-draped coffins, and the American people, just little by little, got sick of it. Finally I think the doves began to outnumber the hawks and those who were in the anti-war movement became more predominant. As time went by they put more and more pressure on Congress and the Administration. But presidents Lyndon Johnson, Richard Nixon and their advisors were stuck in the quagmire. The times, they were a changing alright, but not soon enough. Not before cataclysmic slaughter and destruction had occurred.

In December of 1973 I interviewed with the department chair and faculty of the Department of Sociology at the University of California at San Diego. I was admitted to be one of 15 graduate students in my class, based on my Naval Academy record and my life experiences. Then I got the Navy orders I had requested. Instead of going to a squadron, I was sent to graduate school at U.C.S.D. At that point I left the aviation part of my life behind me. There were all those years of flying and the wonderful times I had as a kid with all kinds of airplanes. But now it seemed there were new adventures and things to do with my life. I had some of the greatest experiences in flying that anyone could have. But now it was time to do other things. It was time to make a positive difference in my life.

I have flown in various kinds of general aviation aircraft time to time since then. Several clients have flown in to pick me up in their airplane while I was a professional speaker. We'd fly off to some venue for my presentation. I was always invited to fly in the right seat of their airplanes. One time a client who had a Piper Cherokee picked me up in Monterey. We flew to Fresno where I gave a speech to a large audience. When we were making the pre-flight checks for the flight home, he said, "Why don't you take the left seat?"

I said, "Sure, okay," took the command pilot seat; he took the right.

A couple of his friends were in the backseat for the trip. I remember there was a big cumulonimbus thunder head sticking up in front of us on the trip home. One of the guys in the backseat tapped me on the shoulder and said, "Do you see that thunderstorm up there in front of us?"

I said, "No, where?" I still had my pilot sense of humor.

When we got home, I made a smooth-as-a-baby's-butt landing in Monterey and the owner said, "My God! Unbelievable! You can still really fly an airplane."

With flying, like riding a bicycle, you don't forget how to do it but you do lose your skills and your touch. I'm not as smooth on the stick. Suddenly it seems like there is a lot to do when I remember hardly thinking about flying the aircraft before. At first I found I was wandering on altitude a bit but pretty soon I got it nailed down. Nevertheless these experiences didn't reignite my interest in flying.

I flew great old airplanes as a kid. And I've flown missions off carriers that were incredibly complex, stimulating and exciting. So now to go up and grind around in a small plane again just seems boring. There are too many other things I would rather do at this point. I guess I've just moved on.

9. Military Data Gathering

The debriefing that comprises the central section of this book, my second life as a warrior, is probably still classified. It underscores the foolishness of how our government classifies everything but rarely gets around to declassifying anything.

No doubt our Department of Defense is honestly trying to learn from our experiences. And clearly they have. That has been proven by their rescinding the stupid policy of giving only "name, rank, serial number and date of birth."

They also have institutionalized an ongoing medical evaluation program that started in 1974 just after we came home. They are giving annual physicals to any of us former POWs who will come to a medical facility at Pensacola Naval Air Station. Our transportation and per diem expenses are paid, along with giving us a room in the Bachelor Officer's Quarters there. They are gathering medical data on us along with a comparison group. Each of us POWs has a comparison person who was not a POW. We're not supposed to know who our control group person is, but I do know that mine is a fellow who was a squadron mate and a Naval Academy classmate. He was a flier through the war – one who didn't get shot down.

The purpose of the continuing examination is to understand the physical, emotional and psychological affects of having been a POW. They already know a lot of things of course. They know the POW experience left us with skeletal, muscular, and neurological problems that people in the comparison group don't have. In my own case, having beriberi a couple of times has affected my heart and my vision, for example. I also had injuries to my spine from the uncontrolled ejection out of that cockpit in 1965. There are also the residual injuries and emotional scars from torture and beatings. And the effects of sustained malnutrition are being studied. They probably didn't know the long-term affects of these kinds of things until they had amassed data from the physical and mental testing of us through the years.

Most of us are also being cared for by the medical facilities of the Department of Veteran Affairs. I tell everyone that I'm the very fortunate recipient of socialized medicine. The VA delivers terrific care and does it more efficiently than any other health delivery system. My only question is:

Why doesn't every American citizen get this kind of medical care? Our country is definitely in the dark ages with respect to medical care. We are so far behind all the other industrialized countries, mainly because of the lies and distortions put out by lawmakers who are beholden to the pharmaceutical and insurance industries.

Brian Kelly, my debriefer, interviewed me in segments for a total of 36 hours. They were all tape recorded by reel to reel, the technology of the day. I obtained a copy of these tapes in 1973 and had them transcribed by a Naval Postgraduate School department secretary when I was on the faculty there in 1979-81. Unfortunately the transcriptions were full of errors and gaps. So about ten years later I started editing and correcting them. But it soon became apparent that I wasn't up to the task and they went back up on the shelf. When I decided to write this book, knowing that they would be a principal element, I began to go through the transcripts again.

It was very enlightening because there was so much I had forgotten about that had happened. Not surprisingly, since the debriefing chronicled eight years and was so detailed from my memory at the time. During my imprisonment, I made a very deliberate effort to remember everything because I knew the Navy would want to know what had happened. Also, there wasn't much to do most of the time, so keeping the experiences and observations sorted and updated was a good mental distraction to pass the time.

Brian didn't take the same flight I did from the Philippines. He came home on a different airplane but he was right there at the hospital waiting for me when I got off in San Diego. The debriefing started almost immediately after we both arrived.

The Navy wanted us debriefed immediately for good reasons. We would remember it all, and I think they knew we were still living that experience. In fact my head and heart were firmly stuck in the life of a POW while I was being debriefed. I must say now that I was still a very angry and defensive man, as I had been while a warrior POW.

But when the debriefing session was over, the socialization process of my third life began. I was walking around the hospital, seeing doctors and nurses, talking to people, going outside with friends and other POWs. Each of us had a private phone next to our hospital beds and I was getting dozens of phone calls from people whom I hadn't heard from in 15 or 20 years. I was going to the DMV to take a driver's test, learning how to write a check, and literally, learning how to use a telephone again. And as soon as the "machine" was turned off, Brian and I would go out into town together, to a bar or some place. I was starting to become Phil Butler in his third life.

I don't think I really began to understand a lot about my process and what I had been through until later. I learned more and began to put it together in a social-psychologically way when I went to graduate school in 1974-1976. That was a really great opportunity to put things into perspective and categories, and to better understand what had happened to me and to our society.

Brian Kelly did more than just debrief me. He was a life saver. The guy brought me back into present reality. He actually moved into my new apartment with me for a few weeks, even though his orders were to be with me for only a week. He was a friend who helped me recover not only from having been a POW, but from having been outside our culture at a crucial time. He helped me get through the trauma of my wife divorcing me. He became a friend and a guide for me to be reintegrated back into society.

As I mentioned before, when I stepped off the airplane at Clark Air Force Base, he walked out onto the red carpet to meet me. The first thing he did was shake my hand, introduce himself and then hand me a *Playboy*. He said, "Check this out, Phil; you've never seen a *Playboy* like this before." He had me pegged before he ever even met me.

10. Barbara

I met Barbara Baldock at the fifth San Diego area POW reunion on February 12, 1978. I was dancing with Joni Myers, former lover and now good friend when I spotted Barbara sitting alone at a table. She was there with her brother Chuck, his wife Terry and their parents. It turned out that she was going through a divorce. I couldn't take my eyes off her.

Finally Joni excused herself to go to the bathroom and I immediately made a bee-line rush over to Barbara. I introduced myself and we got to talk briefly before Joni returned.

After some discussion and hesitation on Chuck's part – after all his dear baby sister was going through a divorce and didn't need a womanizer like me to make things worse – Barbara and I finally got connected by telephone.

After several conversations, Barbara and I had our first date in May, at the fifth national POW reunion in Los Angeles. The first activity, after checking in to the L.A. Holiday Inn, was to visit ex-president Richard Nixon's home in San Clemente for a fabulous lawn party. We had all been invited because he really adored the returned POWs. Actually we all liked him too, at the time. We were then under the impression that he was responsible for finally bringing us home. And he had previously invited all of us to a White House bash back in 1973.

Great Mexican food and margaritas were on tables all over the place. And "Tricky Dick" was there on the lawn, holding court and telling stories. I grabbed Barbara by the hand and said, "Barbara, let's go over so I can introduce you to President Nixon.

She responded, "Oh No! I don't like him! I can't stand that guy." Barbara had been an active anti-war protester who advocated stopping the war to bring us all home. She had a dedicated peace and social justice philosophy.

I said, "No, come on Barbara" and I pulled her over toward the then dishonored-by-Watergate, ex-president. We were probably on our third margaritas, feeling no pain as we listened to Nixon tell stories. He was very funny and quite charming. I'll never forget the story he told about the Soviet leader Leonid Brezhnev coming to the United States and staying with him. There's a two-story guest home that we were standing near, and Nixon, well known as a good storyteller, regaled us with a humorous tale

444

about how Brezhnev's twenty-five year old secretary spent the night there too. Truth be told, Barbara and I had a good time. Maybe the margaritas helped too.

We were in Los Angeles together for three days and that's where our relationship and love began. We both fell hopelessly in love and everything just grew from there. We dated and moved back and forth between her house and my house in the San Diego area for a year, 1978-79. Then I got assigned to the Naval Postgraduate School in Monterey. When I told Barbara she said, "Fine! I'm going with you." She remembers it as my inviting her to go with me. Either way, it was fine with me.

So we both sold our homes and I got the Navy to ship our household belongings to Monterey. We came there a few weeks early because I had some teaching to do for a couple of days. Meanwhile Barbara went out with the realtors to look for a home. She found our perfect home, with a huge landmark Coast Live Oak in the front yard. We bought it together, moved in all our furniture and began life together.

Barbara was a TWA flight attendant at the time, flying the polar route from Los Angeles to London. She changed TWA bases to San Francisco after our move together. Those days she would be gone on trips for six or seven days at a time. A year later, we got married in the living room of our home, with her family and my family there.

Barbara lost her job with TWA in 1986 when the scurrilous Carl Icahn came in and ravaged the company, stripping all of the money out and essentially forcing the company into bankruptcy.

About that same time I was getting heavily into my second career of management consulting and professional speaking. So Barbara became my marketing director and that added another marvelous dimension to our relationship. Not all couples – probably not most couples – can work together in a business. But we thrived at it. Through all those years until probably early 2000 or so, one of us had to travel a great deal. But now we're both home together all the time and it's been very good. We've been together over thirty years and our relationship continues to grow.

Barbara and I think one of the paramount reasons our bond has remained so strong is that our values are so aligned. Incredibly enough, our values are absolutely in sync with each other as they were from the very beginning. It is striking that our outlooks on war, peace, military, politics, religion, nature and life-in-general are almost identical. That creates powerful glue for a relationship. Also we tell the truth. We deal immediately with the little issues that come up from time to time. We don't hold back and save up "red stamps" with each other. And it's also very important that we both have a good sense of humor. We have a lot of laughter. And we have tremendous love and respect for each other.

11. Chuck and Terry

Chuck Baldock, my brother-in-law, and I have been very close friends for a long time. We're probably like brothers actually, more than brothers-in-law. I knew him at NAS Lemoore even before I went to Vietnam. He was in the same A4 squadron that I had a cousin in. So I used to go over and see my cousin, Dave White, and I recall meeting Chuck and others in that squadron. Just five years after we came home I met his sister and we fell in love, to marry two years later.

Chuck got shot down in March of 1966. So when I introduce him to people I like to say, "This is my brother-in-law Chuck Baldock who was also a POW, but only for seven years." I never was in a cell with him, but we were able to communicate some. After we came home I went to the University of California San Diego graduate school and Chuck went to UCSD to complete his bachelor's degree in political science. He had entered Naval Aviation in the Navy Cadet program for guys who hadn't completed college. Chuck previously had completed several years at Penn State so our return was a good opportunity for him to finish his degree.

Chuck met and married Terry soon after our return home in November of 1973. They had a short dating period before deciding to wed but the match turned out to be perfect.

I didn't meet Barbara until almost five years later but that relationship has of course made mine with Chuck and Terry even closer. Barbara and I have taken a couple of two-week vacations together with Chuck and Terry every year for many years now. We almost always go to Hawaii together for a couple of weeks. We also spend ten days or so together at our house here in Monterey and the same at their house in Las Vegas every year. Just as Chuck and I are like the brothers we never had, so Barbara and Terry are like sisters. And my friendship with Terry has also grown into being like a brother/sister relationship.

Chuck got me started playing golf some thirteen or fourteen years ago and we both enjoy that together very much. It's a challenging and sometimes aggravating game, for which I will blame him the rest of my life. He's much better at it than I am but that's the way it goes. Chuck is a natural athlete and also a dedicated sports fan. I guess a "sports nut" would be a better term. He has an encyclopedic knowledge of sports facts and history.

After graduate school I requested and got the Navy assignment I had wanted. It was the Navy Human Resource Management Center in San Diego, to be a consultant team leader. The Navy had that program then that was essentially an internal, organizational -development consulting organization composed of trained Navy people. Our job was to visit different commands all over the world and basically do organizational development work, much like it is done for corporations. As a team leader, I had six to eight Navy HRM consultants working for me.

This was a program that had grown out of the Admiral Elmo Zumwalt era and it was perfect for what I wanted to do with my post-Navy life. First of all, it would let me get my feet on the ground for the new occupation that I planned for myself. And second, the three years as an HRM Consultant would serve as my field work setting for my doctoral dissertation in sociology. So I was able to do all of my field research while working as an HRM team leader.

Chuck called me one day while I was first on my new job and said, "Hey, I'm getting out of UCSD now. How do you like what you're doing?"

I said, "I love it, Chuck!"

He said, "Can you get me a job there?"

I said, "Sure, I'll talk to the CO."

And the commanding officer said, "Sure, I'll hire him. He can come here."

So Chuck joined my Navy command to become an Assistant Team Leader. He was there for several years with me and then one more when he retired from the Navy.

Chuck and I have never really been very interested in POW reunions. We have been to a few over the years, but our organization, "NamPOWs" has them practically every year now. My relationships with most of my fellow POWs are fairly situational, being mostly related to our time together as POWs. Besides Chuck, I still have some contact with a few of the guys who became good friends there and afterwards, including Hayden Lockhart and Mike McGrath. There are also a few others with whom I exchange e-mails occasionally. But we don't have face to face relationships because we live in different parts of the country.

There were 30 or 40 returned POWs still on active duty and living in the San Diego area when I first came home. We had a yearly get together there, usually just a dinner in the evening. When the fifth anniversary of our return came around, February 12th 1978, whoever was in charge of the group decided that we would have a dinner and dancing to celebrate. It was held at the Old Spaghetti Factory which was a really fun place to go in San Diego.

That's when I met Barbara. And that's when my life with Chuck and Terry began as well.

12. Second Career

I was conscious of wanting to build a second career for myself after the Navy when I came home in 1973. My first thought was to get out of the Navy, but then I was given such a great opportunity to get a graduate school education and training for a second career that I took it. One of my personal goals was to become an entrepreneur. Everyone in my family had been entrepreneurial business people so in a sense it was built into me from the beginning. But the Navy takes that out of you. Career military life tends to deconstruct all the entrepreneurial spirit you might have inside yourself.

Barbara and I were transferred to Monterey in 1979, where I became a faculty member at the Naval Postgraduate School in the Department of Administrative Sciences. NPS is a postgraduate school. That means people come to get Masters and PhD level, not bachelor degrees. Officer students who have already completed a bachelor degree come from our U.S. military, foreign militaries, and civilians from the Department of Defense and State Department. Students at the NPS are exceedingly bright and motivated, so being a professor there is a delight. It was a great assignment.

It was also an incredible opportunity for me to write my doctoral dissertation at the same time. My first submission was rejected but the re-write and re-submission the second time was accepted by my doctoral committee at UCSD. My dissertation title is "Engineering Organization Change: The Case of Human Resource Management in the U.S. Navy." It is a study that shows how the Navy wanted humanistic changes but approached individual and organization behavioral change like they would an engineering project. Of course it didn't work very well with that philosophy.

I went to my cap and gown graduation ceremony at UCSD in June of 1981 to receive my PhD, just three weeks before I retired from the Navy.

I was promoted to Captain, USN in October of 1980, one year ahead of my Naval Academy classmates and other officers in my year group. That was truly an honor but it presented me with a dilemma. Would I now get out in June of 1981 with a minimum-time 20 year retirement, or continue in the Navy since I had been put on the "fast track"? My decision was made more difficult because I needed to serve two years in grade as a Captain to retire at that rank, for of course more money. But by doing so I would have to agree to be transferred to Washington D.C. for a bureaucratic job at the

Office of the Secretary of the Navy.

I had already made plans for my new civilian career as a management consultant with my new skills and degree. In fact I had even started cultivating clients. Plus I didn't want to leave Monterey, especially for the boring job that would have been ahead. I didn't see much future in being a new Captain with a PhD, pouring coffee for Admirals and senior civilians at SecNav. So after some extensive soul searching, I decided to follow my heart and leave the Navy at 20 years. So I reverted in rank to Commander, USN retired, to begin my new life as a civilian business owner. It wasn't an easy decision, but in the end it was an honest one because I had been feeling so out of place those final years in the Navy. Following your heart is almost never the wrong decision in life.

The Navy was antithetical to the notion of someone building and successfully running his own business. The military is a hierarchical organization. There's no reason for creativity, imagination, and reflection, which are the keys to entrepreneurship. But during the time that I was training for the organizational development work in the Navy's HRM system, I learned a lot and developed valuable skills. My graduate training and PhD specialized in what is called "micro sociology" or social psychology. This education focused on the interplay of individual behavior in group settings. So my university education was perfectly aligned with my choice of a second career.

After leaving the Navy I also learned a lot by becoming a member of and trainer for "The National Training Laboratories," from working with the "American Management Association," and from becoming an experienced "Sensitivity Group," also called a "T Group," trainer for groups of business and organization executives. I specialized in team building with top-management groups in corporations and other organizations for over 20 years. That was satisfying work, to see people come together, learn to speak honestly with each other, take responsibility for their own behaviors and begin to work together to make good things happen.

In the course of working with client organizations I discovered that talking about my POW experiences was an opportunity for me to make more of a contribution. So I eventually started being called on to speak about my experiences to impart the lessons learned that were applicable to groups everywhere. Sometime in the mid 1980s I developed a motivational speech and began delivering keynote talks to large corporate audiences around the country. I enjoyed combining this work with my management consultations and training for close to 20 years. The act of giving other people some of the benefit of my life experiences was of enormous value for me. I found people everywhere seemed to get benefits from my experiences in Vietnam. In a sense, my POW experiences become a personal gift, one that I could pass on to others.

Unfortunately the physical requirements of constant travel became too onerous for me to continue. At the end of my active traveling career I became dependent on using a cane to get around and the stress of getting through airports and making connections eventually took a toll on my body. So I had to retire from those activities. But I have replaced them with interesting coaching and mentoring work here at home in the Monterey area.

The coaching and mentoring I do today is different in two ways. First, I work only here on the Monterey Peninsula. Second I have taken my social psychology training back to the individual level of analysis. I was working at a team level for corporate and organizational clients before. Now I'm working one-on-one with the processes that go on inside the individual. So clients have to be open and willing to talk about what's going on inside them, their own issues. My goal is to help them work on and solve their own problems.

It amazes me how many successful people come to a point in their lives where they wonder how they got where they are, why they're where they are, and why they're feeling so dissatisfied with where they are. They feel not only unhappy, but stuck. My work is to help people get themselves unstuck.

A lot of high-level corporate people have fallen off what I call "the rail of life." On one side of the rail are family, friends and activities of the heart. On the other side are the corporate or professional tasks that people do. Very often I see successful organization people who have fallen off the rail on the side of professional activities. They've left their families, friendships, and creative outlets so now they feel alienated, or they may even be divorced from their families because they've left them in the dust. Now they're looking back and wondering, "What have I done and how can I get myself out of this mess I've created by working eighty hour weeks? So what? Why am I doing this?" I like to tell everyone that during my eight years as a POW I never recall hearing another POW say something like "I wish I had worked more."

I have a positive belief in human potential. I was taken with the human potential movement soon after coming home. Certainly life deals serendipitous and tragic events to all of us, but I still believe we have a lot of control over the choices we make in our lives. We can choose, or not, to self actualize. I think most people have a great deal more control than they might imagine. Even if you've chosen a certain path that has prevented you from living up to your potential, you always have the power to change. We all encounter life-changing experiences and it's what we make of them that defines us. In that way we determine our next steps and even how the rest of our lives will play out.

So the good news is people can get their lives back when they are committed to doing so. If they're not committed, then it's just an exercise, just wallowing around in their own stuff. I've even come to believe that if a person isn't committed to something, then they haven't self actualized. They haven't quite grown up and joined the adult human race.

A life experience like being a POW, or any tragic experience, becomes a defining moment. For instance, if you've been in a horrendous automobile accident and lost loved ones in the crash, do you try to not think or not talk about it? That's the negative way. That way will eat you up. But if you write about it, talk and tell other people about it, you begin to make something positive for yourself and others. You can ultimately define it as a place to wallow and feel sorry for yourself, or you can turn it into a triumph. It can be a force for failure or a force for success. It's your choice. I call it turning a tragedy into a triumph. We all have the human potential to do it.

Leadership has been both a life experience and academic study for me. I had life experience in leadership at the Naval Academy, as an officer in the Navy, and then as a prisoner of war. My training in graduate school and in organization development also gave me an opportunity to study lots of different models of leadership.

I think by and large the leadership courses I took at the Naval Academy and in the Navy seem inadequate. They mainly relied on learning from the examples and personality characteristics of great men. But life experience has taught me that leadership depends on the situation, place and time. Different kinds of leaders and styles of leadership are required with different circumstances. There doesn't seem to be any such thing as a particular personality for optimum leadership potential.

Effective leadership styles are situational. The required leadership style at any given time is dependent how much the follower knows about the task. Is he or she an expert, novice or something in between? Also, how much emotional support does a follower need? This need changes from time to time with different situations.

To illustrate, we POWs were often on our own, especially when we were in solitary confinement, at interrogations or being tortured and abused. So Senior Ranking Officers needed to do a lot of consensus building before issuing any policies or orders. Emotional support and getting agreement on anything was paramount. Simple military "orders" out of the blue held no water with isolated men under duress.

It also became crystal clear from my POW experience that one of the biggest things a leader needs is empathy. Later on in my formal academic training I learned that listening skills are huge for being a good leader. If you're not a good listener, you're probably never going to understand people well enough to get them to work together and accomplish things.

When the person in the lead position is not a good listener and doesn't have empathy, he or she is likely to assign the follower a task they're really not capable of completing because they don't have the skills, or the confidence, or both to do it. Active listening is an important skill I taught for years in seminars. Listening to somebody is not just with your ears. You're listening with all of your senses and having empathy means listening with your heart. Empathy means to be able to put yourself inside their skin. Being empathetic doesn't mean being sympathetic. It's not about taking sides or feeling sorry. It means seeing, hearing, feeling and understanding the world the way another person does.

Finally setting the example can never be understated for being a good leader. Good leaders walk their talk. People who are followers or subordinates watch people who lead them like a hawk. So if you're in a leadership position, you have to know that every single thing you do and say is being closely observed. Therefore if you're not setting a moral, honest, legal and mature example, then all is lost.

Barack Obama showed himself to be good listener and an inspirational leader during his campaign. As a president, he has been effective in some areas of foreign policy. He has also accomplished quite a large number of things in a very short period of time during his first year. But the jury is still out on his leadership and presidency. It remains to be seen if he can govern as well as he campaigned. Politics has often been described as a contact sport, so the true test of his leadership will hinge on his continued determination to be a good listener, to understand complex situations, to set the example for Americans and the world's people and to lead with confidence and authority. In my opinion his accomplishments at the end of four years will rise or fall based on these same leadership fundamentals,

13. Nature

"The only species capable of stopping this catastrophe is the one causing it."

Jeff Corwin, 11/22/09

I have a deep and long love affair with nature. I lived across the street from a railroad track when I was growing up. Steam locomotives used to come by and we kids would go play across the tracks where there were open fields and little streams. There were a couple of little ponds where cows got in and drank. They were always dirty but we kids swam and fished in them anyway.

I collected snakes, box terrapins, "Horned Toads" and other lizards. I saw how all kinds of little animals lived. I often went camping overnight with friends. All we needed was a blanket or two and some hotdogs and marshmallows to roast. We fished for bass, crappie and catfish. Later on we'd have our rifles or our shotguns when we spent summer nights out in the woods. We also hunted rabbits and quail on winter mornings when the snow was on the ground. It was great fun. I was a Boy Scout for a period of time and went on some camping trips with my troop.

The fact that I spent a lot of time in the woods turned out to be a significant asset for me when I went down in the jungle of North Vietnam. I wasn't terrified of the outdoors. I was damn terrified of getting captured but I wasn't afraid of all the flora and fauna that were around me. So I was able to function, to give them a four day and night chase, being familiar with the woods. I wasn't afraid of the black night and funny noises, just the Vietnamese.

I'm very involved with nature today as a docent at Point Lobos State Reserve. Barbara and I have volunteered there for 20 years, giving nature hikes, staffing the information station and leading people through our Whaler's Cabin museum. I served on the board of the Big Sur Land Trust, an organization whose mission is "to preserve the significant lands and waters of California's Central Coast for all generations." I've also been involved with Barbara in the preservation and reintroduction of the California condor, and other endangered species, with the Ventana Wildlife Society. I have a philosophical relationship with nature that says we are all part of the universe. The atoms that make up our bodies were, are and will be part of life on our planet. Therefore all life should be respected.

It certainly has made my life richer that I married a woman who thinks the same way I do. Barbara has always been a nature and animal lover. So we're very compatible in that aspect too. Barbara was President of the SPCA board for four years and she's currently on the Board of the Ventana Wildlife Society. We have a deep and abiding love for our beautiful Central CaliforniaCoast, a very special place to live and pass on to others.

My love of companion animals has also continued to this day. Skeeter, the little rascal terrier, was my first dog when I came home. Then there was Abe, the sweetest and most lovable Golden Retriever ever. That guy would do anything you wanted, if he could only understand what you wanted. Abe loved to dive for rocks we would throw into streams and ponds. We called him our "rock dog." Jenny was our beautiful little cocker spaniel. She was practically joined at the hip to Barbara. We think she imprinted on her while still a puppy and saw Barbara as her mother. Bonny is our adorable little seven pound cockapoo. She loves people and never fails to provoke people into giving her pets when we are out. We've also had cats. Barbara joined me with her two Siamese-sister cats, Simba and Duma. They were the cat loves of her life. Afterwards we had Lady Griddlebone who had a fetish for sitting on my shoulder to groom my head. Tuxedo, our last cat was the consummate sweetheart who always wanted to be in your lap.

No doubt the greatest problem that our planet and all life as we know it have ever encountered is climate change. The scientific data are overwhelming in assessment that it is occurring at an unprecedented rapid pace and that the results will be disastrous on many scales. Pacific island nations are already losing their homes. Desertification, oceanic acidification and species extinction are accelerating. Beyond doubt we humans are the perpetrators of this coming cataclysm. But once again, commercial self-interests, religious fundamentalism and just plain ignorance are all in denial. Unfortunately they have been fairly successful so far at putting the brakes on solutions. I shudder to think what our posterity will experience and what they will think of us who left this legacy of destruction.

I should note that my attitude toward hunting and fishing changed when I got back from Vietnam. I collected up my guns among my personal affects when I returned. There was a Remington pump 22 rifle, an engraved Ithica over-and-under 20 gauge shotgun, an automatic 12 gauge shotgun and a beautiful collector's Winchester, lever-action 30-30. I had previously also owned a German 9mm Luger "Parabellum" that I had been using for my survival pistol. But the Vietnamese took that one away from me. I gave the rest of them away to friends when I came home. I have an abhorrence of killing anything now.

14. Music

"Before there was language there was music."

Arthur Conan Doyle

Tony, my interviewer, was asked who I thought were great men. My answer wasn't the traditional names like Teddy Roosevelt or Martin Luther King, Jr. Instead I picked a number of artists, particularly some composers. I was reminded the other day at a concert that we were listening to the work of Henry Purcell who only lived 36 years way back in the Seventeenth Century. Amazingly, his music is still appreciated by us 350 years later. I doubt that Purcell would have ever dreamed that his music would be inspiring people for 350 years and beyond. But it is. What a gift.

My mother introduced me to the piano when I was five years old. Two years later I took lessons from Mrs. Mayfield Huff for another five years and then Mrs. Helen Ringo for a year or two more. Then in 1951 at age 12 I quit. Stupid me.

But 23 years ago, in 1986, the thought of that tragic disengagement from music overcame me enough to answer a Monterey City adult education advertisement. So 35 years after the fact I checked in with a woman for three introductory piano lessons on a horrible old upright that was long out of tune. Lo and behold, I discovered that I still could basically read music.

In short order I bought a piano for my living room and signed up for lessons with a wonderful woman, Pat Ross. She brought me back to about where I had left off within a year and we advanced from there for a couple more years until she moved away from our area. But she handed me off to an incredible woman here in Monterey, Katie Clare Mazzeo. Katie Clare is a gifted piano teacher. She is also a celebrated professional performer and a wise teacher of humanities. I took lessons from Katie Clare until 2001 when I completed my lessons by giving a piano recital in my home. Now I love playing my piano at home for my own enjoyment and internal peace.

I always loved music from the baroque, classical and romantic periods. I'm especially fond of piano music, whether solo or with other instruments. My favorites are the works of Beethoven, Schubert, Chopin, Schumann,

Liszt and Rachmaninoff. Most of their compositions are beyond the skills of an amateur like myself. They are only to be appreciated when in the hands of a skilled professional. But many of them are accessible and I am always learning.

Maybe I pick composers as really great men and women because music engages me like nothing else can. It engages a different part of the brain from verbal and logical cognition. I think people who have been taught or seriously exposed to music in some form or another when they were children have gained a significant advantage in life. Neuropsychologists have been able to prove that people's brains develop differently, and affirmatively, when they have been introduced to music at an early age.

Today I can walk into my living room, sit down at the piano, take out some sheet music and start playing, maybe a Chopin nocturne. Before I know it, two or three hours can go by. The telephone can ring, my wife can call me, but they don't get through. Nothing seems to invade that space. My brain goes into a completely different order where I no longer think in words or of the time. Music takes over, blocking out all else. It's a unique human experience, one I'm very thankful to have available.

15. Fitness

Fitness has always been important to me. As a boy it was baseball, football, basketball, and riding bicycles. We kids were always outdoors, running around the neighborhood and playing physical games. No TV to distract us then. I didn't play sports in high school because I worked. But when I went to the Naval Academy, we engaged in all sorts of physical training and also sports, both of which were required.

I was in good shape when I was shot down. We squadron pilots used to go out and run up and down the flight deck of the Midway when we were at sea. Sometimes we were running into a 30-knot wind.

I was able to evade capture for four days and nights because I was in good physical condition. According to the map I carried and was navigating by, I managed to travel close to 75 miles by walking and running along pathways at night.

As soon as I was captured and put into solitary confinement I decided that I had to keep myself in good physical condition if I were going to survive. The spinal compression fractures I had suffered from the ejection were beginning to cause me a lot of pain. But I knew I had to exercise so I started doing push-ups against the wall because I couldn't stand doing them on the floor. In time, as I began to recover from my injuries, I was able to build up from that.

Word was out in prison that we should exercise in order to stay as healthy as possible and to keep our weight up. We found out that even if we exercised on reduced food rations it helped keep weight on. It was a matter of survival and of course it also helped keep us to stay sane and emotionally stable. Most POWs had a habit of exercising first thing in the morning. Later when we were in cells together we all worked out in our rooms every morning. Everybody would run in place, do pushups, sit ups and other exercises. I even learned how to walk on my hands and do hand-stand pushups to stay in condition.

When I got home I would get up every morning at five-thirty or six, work out in my apartment, and then go for a run of three to six miles.

When I was in graduate school at UCSD, all my younger classmates thought I was nuts because I enrolled in two physical education courses every academic quarter. I tried to explain that being physically fit is part and parcel of being mentally and emotionally fit. I knew all the Phys-Ed teachers and we became friends. I took basketball 101 and 102 several times. There I was at 35, running up and down the court with the 18 and twenty-year-old kids. I also took tennis, handball, gymnastics, and softball. I took anything they offered twice or more at UCSD, a small university of only 6,000 students then.

I started smoking when I was about thirteen or fourteen years old. It was one of the little gifts I got by copying some of my paperboy friends. Smoking was very much part of the culture back then and even though we did know it was harmful, the advertising easily countered that. I smoked all the way through high school, at the Naval Academy, afterwards as a pilot and then in prison after a time. They gave us three cigarettes a day in prison, a policy that varied as I explained in the "Second Life" section.

The Vietnamese had a strange outlook on smoking. They thought tobacco was as important, or sometimes even more important, than food. They were really addicted to smoking, big time. They gave their Army privates, their lowest enlisted guys, six cigarettes a day, and so to keep peace in the family they gave us prisoners three. Then later, in larger cells, we got cigs from guys who didn't smoke. Vietnamese cigarettes were strong and certainly not conducive to staying healthy. We used to rationalize by saying, "I'm a POW. Should I worry about cancer? I don't think so!"

I was smoking when I came home. Then I learned about the true health affects and that lots of people were quitting. So I thought about it for awhile and finally realized I was destroying my health. It was also apparent that smokers were rapidly becoming social pariahs. Even my eight year old daughter was urging me to quit. I tried to quit on my own unsuccessfully, a couple of times during the next two years.

Finally in 1975 I went through an organized eight week program called "Smoke Enders." It worked and I haven't had a cigarette since. That was probably my greatest lifetime gift to myself.

I have worked hard to stay physically fit throughout these past 37 years. I lived in San Diego until 1979. There I continued with my workouts. I played on the softball team for our Navy unit and also competitive racquetball. When I met Barbara we started doing morning calisthenics together. Then when we moved to Monterey we joined a health club where we continue to work out three to five days a week. I just marked 30 years as a member of our health club. Barbara and I are strong believers in physical fitness and keeping our weight in check. Because of my injuries I had to first give up running, then tennis and then racquetball. They have since been replaced with golf, but that's a separate topic of its own.

16. Golf

I blame my brother-in-law, Chuck, for getting me into golf. It's all his fault. Chuck started playing golf seriously early on when we came home. I absolutely abstained from it thinking it was a huge waste of time because I was busy with graduate school, then with my management consulting and training, then traveling with my professional speaking and, and, and....

When Chuck and Terry would come visit us in Monterey I'd occasionally let him drag me out to our local Navy golf course. We actually live next to a famous golf course, Old Del Monte, the oldest golf course west of the Mississippi River. In my running days I would run the three miles around Del Monte golf course twice early in the morning. And sometimes I would slog my way around it playing golf with Chuck. I'd rent some clubs and we'd bash around a little bit.

Then all of a sudden, it was around Christmas of 1995, Chuck came here and we played golf maybe twice. I got to thinking about it after he left. You know what? That was kind of fun. So I bought a cheap set of clubs for less than a hundred bucks and started playing with a group of older fellows who are still playing to this day, at least the ones that are still living. They call themselves the "Tuesday and Thursday seniors," aka "The Old Farts," and they play, as you might imagine, every Tuesday and Thursday at 7:30 in the morning at the Navy golf course, now known as Monterey Pines Golf Course.

That first year I tried to approach golf like baseball because I had been a baseball player. After all, don't you just hit a little ball with a club, and isn't it even sitting still? This does not work. So the Old Farts began to coach me, my first golf lessons. I was so screwed up from their advice after a year it was unreal. So I took some lessons, bought a decent set of clubs and got hooked. I date my serious golf bug to January of 1996. Thus I began this grand "game" at age 58. That's probably one reason why I'm not an excellent golfer. But now I love to play golf courses everywhere at any opportunity.

Golf is fascinating. What's always captivated me about golf is that it's really a metaphor for life. Every time I go out and play golf I meet myself. Golf brings out the best and worst in people. Whoever and whatever you are will be quickly shown on a golf course. Golf teaches and requires integrity. You know when you cheat at golf you have just cheated yourself.

You have to call infractions on yourself. No other sport or activity in life can compare. So I believe it is much more than just a game.

That's why in my coaching and mentoring I encourage people to play golf with me. Most of my clients are golfers, which makes the pitch easier, especially here where we have 23 golf courses, some of them world famous. I watch how they play and react to things because that gives me a lot of information about who the person is. Golf can be frustrating, no matter what level you play, and how you deal with it gives me clues as to who you are and how you behave in life. Golf also acts as a catalyst for getting my clients to talk about themselves. That's where we begin the mentoring process. Body language is loud and clear on the golf course. The set of one's shoulders, jaw and chin. People also really smile when playing well, getting a charge out of the game.

I find it fascinating to watch other people, to see how they play the game. There are different ways they deal with success or failure, keep score or don't keep score, are very rule-bound or make them up as they go along. Do they use the old "toe wedge," nudging the ball into a better place for bad lies? What qualifies to be a "gimmie" putt? Is it never allowed, a tap in, in the leather or ten feet? Conversely, some people are emotionally constrained to obey every single austere rule, and it makes them angry as hell when somebody else is not doing the same.

Then there are the guys who want to play your game as well as their own. That's what I call "white-man's disease," giving advice all the time.

Clients will sometimes admit that mentally they were back in the office while trying to play golf. And they come to realize that what they just did on the golf course is the same thing they do at home with their families.

Some people are so competitive they can't just relax and play golf. Every shot is crucial. Of course they are exactly like that in life. I played golf in a foursome recently, competing with other foursomes for just a $5 buy-in. One of my partners was a guy who got so angry he almost quit playing, and he's been playing golf forty or fifty years. So personally and professionally it's very instructive to watch how people respond to this sport.

I've applied the golf process to myself as well and have learned some important things. First, I started too late and will never be good enough at it to get beyond being a bogey player. I've had lessons from I don't know how many different professionals, and I've reached my limitation in golf. For that matter, in many ways I think I've reached my limitation in life. Finding and embracing my own limitations has been good for me.

Second, I have found out on the golf course that I don't focus very well on every shot. My attention drifts onto relationships with the people around me, the pretty day, the sunshine, the birds and the hills. I exhibit some minor attention deficit disorder symptoms on the golf course just as I often do in life. And even with all of my training, I can still experience frustrations in golf and can sometimes get angry at a shot. Then I have to bring myself back and ask, "What are you doing here and why did this piss you off?" My aggressive warrior instincts are always there, just below the surface, and they can sometimes get the best of me.

All the sports I played at the Naval Academy required me to give my best effort. We used to say give 110% in order to win. But in golf if you put in that kind of effort you will lose. Golf asks you to apply about 80% effort in a good swing. It demands a kind of restraint and focus that I don't think any other sport requires. No wonder it turns out to be such a practical tool for seeing into others, and into myself, what we can only describe as aggressive tendencies.

I have another enjoyable activity for my clients that is not dissimilar to the perspective I get of them on the golf course. I will often take them to Point Lobos State Reserve. It's a marvelous venue because the astounding beauty of nature let's people look inside themselves.

I have different experiential exercises that we do. We will sit on an ocean-side boulder where I ask them to close their eyes for several minutes to just listen. This is "sound without sight." Then I ask them to mentally shut out the noises and just observe everything then can for a few minutes. This is "sight without sound." When we compare what we heard or saw they usually find out how much they missed. That's because their attention has probably drifted back to work or someplace else. They have trouble "being here now." They learn lessons at Point Lobos about living life in the now and about really paying attention to their surroundings and to what people are saying to them.

By putting them in the outdoors at Point Lobos, or on the golf course, it's easier for them to escape problems and worries to concentrate on who they are and what they really want to do with their lives. Nature and Golf. Two incredible ways to explore within.

17. Atheism and Theism

There is some disagreement on the definition of atheism. Oddly, Christians in particular usually define it differently from the way most of us atheists do. They usually define us as someone who denies the existence of God. While I and most other atheists insist that atheism means something very different. We commonly profess to simply not believe in any gods. We don't make claims any broader than that an atheist is just a person who is not a theist. He or she is "a-theist." Thus we don't ascribe or assign theories of god or a creator to things that can't be proven.

Whatever might or might not have existed before or after the universal "big bang," some imagined life after death, putative miracles and the like are simply things I refuse to ascribe to God, Jesus, Mohammed, Yahweh, Santa Claus or the Tooth Fairy. I don't believe in the infallibility of a book, like the Bible, that contains some of the most inhumane and disgusting stories and directives imaginable. I don't believe in predestination, the previous existence of a Jesus Christ, rising from the dead, virgin births, miracles and so on. These are just outside what an atheist is willing to believe in because none have ever been objectively proven. I also know this old planet has been around for billions of years and we people have evolved from other forms of life over time.

I resent the fact that many Christians have tried to co-opt ethics, integrity, virtue and our legal system as having come from their own ideas. They try to make people in our country believe that if you're not Christian then you're not moral or ethical and so forth, which is ridiculous. Our modern notions of right and wrong, good and evil, legality and illegality do not in fact come from Christianity. They predate that religion by thousands of years, back to ancient Greece and before. Our modern morality and legal codes probably go all the way back to cave-people days when it was determined not good to go out and grab another guy's wife, or kill someone, because it would create a lot of conflict and problems. As an atheist I am a moral person. Since we don't believe in a heavenly after-life, most atheists are vitally concerned with making this life on earth as good as possible, even heavenly-like, for ourselves and everyone.

American Christians have long worked, successfully I might add, to particularly demonize atheists and atheism. They have been so successful at spreading stereotypes that atheists still remain the last bastion of prejudice.

Atheists are the only minority people who still cannot be elected to public office. We've outgrown our political prejudices enough to elect people from both genders, all ethnicities, gays, lesbians, trans-gender and the handicapped to any public office.

Theists have asked me how I can "prove there is no god." A rudimentary knowledge of logic is all that's required to know that it is impossible to prove a negative postulate. So my answer is always, "Prove to me that there is a god." This too can't be done, so I am content to not bother with believing in one.

I've been an atheist for probably more than 40 years. I say probably because my transition to that viewpoint came about gradually. Like most atheists, I was one before I realized it enough to call myself that. As I've said before in this book, my journey from theist to atheist actually began in my early teens. That's when I started rejecting the hard-shell and inhumane teachings of fundamentalist southern Baptism.

When people learn that I am an atheist, they sometimes will reprise the line that "there are no atheists in foxholes." This is no truer than the sad distortion that "we never leave our dead soldiers behind." There were prisoners for whom their belief in god was valuable. It seemed to help a lot of them. But I think POWs, on a scale of religiosity, were just like a normal curve of Americans with regard to belief, or not. We had everything from non-believers to people for whom religion was a huge part of their life. We had guys who would conduct Catholic services on Sunday in some of the larger rooms, and somebody would be the appointed chaplain of the room. While I think the majority of guys were probably religious to some extent many of them were pretty much apathetic about God.

I don't think that's at odds with most Americans. Apathy might be the dominant religion. Many say, "Oh yeah, I believe in God" because they don't know what else to do. They would be unlikely to profess agnosticism or atheism because that would seem too terrible. Once again, this is the demonizing of atheism at work. Many have probably never thought about it enough to really come out and decide the issue for themselves. For most people, religion, or lack of it, is something they picked up from their parents. Most probably accept their family's religion. Few ever ask, "Well, what's the deal here? What does this really mean?"

Humanists generally fall into two camps, secular and non-secular. Some do accept a few facets of religion, embracing notions of spirituality but not an organized "god" as such. Others are secular humanists, like myself. We want to make contributions to heaven on earth now because we can't count on any heaven afterwards. We want people to treat each other well – to be good to each other, to be peaceful, to not kill and to look out for each other – here on earth right now.

I'm a materialist who believes in the scientific method of rigorous proof and replication. Replication means any scientific discovery must be repeatable, again and again, before it can become an accepted fact. Darwin's basic concepts of evolution are a good example. Science can tell us there was a beginning, probably a "Big Bang," and that it was approximately 13½ billion years ago. As an atheist, I just have to say there are things I just don't know beyond that. And since I'm not a theist I won't assign theistic reasons for things I don't understand. I don't have to say, "Well, God must have done it or there must have been a god to do this or that." I just draw the line there and say: that's an unnecessary leap that requires a kind of faith I don't have and don't need.

18. America Today

It's not going to surprise anyone that I raised the issue of torture back in 2002 when it was first surfacing; but Americans were the perpetrators this time. I am really incensed, astounded, and massively disappointed in the American public, that Americans are so weak that they would tolerate the blatant violations of our Constitution, legal and moral order. They let a single event like Nine-Eleven, horrendous though it was, where we lost three thousand people, and make it seem like war was threatened against our entire country. They acted like we were in a full-scale war, like in Vietnam where two million or more people were killed during our American war with them. That Americans would react with such vindictiveness and buy into torture, which doesn't even work, just made me heartsick.

This is not the America I grew up in. My country then was brave and principled. But I'm afraid we've slipped and that Americans have gotten weaker. Maybe Americans have seen so much violence in the various media that they don't think the reality of torturing people has much importance. Maybe there are various cultural reasons for it, but whatever, it does seem to me that Americans have lost their moral compass. We've also lost our Constitutional way.

And it's not just we the people but it goes all the way up into the top of our legislature and the previous administration. Now I wonder if those responsible will be investigated and brought openly to justice. I know there is lots of resistance from CIA Director Leon Panetta and his predecessors who don't want the American people to know what took place and who set the policies. But that doesn't seem right to me. I think we should investigate everyone who was involved from top to bottom, those who wrote the memos, those who sanctioned them, those who gave the orders, and those who carried them out.

It is immoral to charge and convict Pfc Lyndie English and Sgt Charles Graner, her sergeant, when those who instigated their behavior were insidiously hiding in Washington. Their indictments didn't take care of the matter. They weren't the real bad apples. It all came down from Bush, Cheney, Rumsfeld, Rove, Addington and their cronies.

If we are to get America back on a moral track, there should be an independent investigation of the Bush Administration to show how involved they were in violating our Constitution. And if they are proven guilty, they should be punished for their criminal behavior.

But one thing we rarely see in American history is a president brought up on charges. It happened recently with Richard Nixon over the Watergate Affair, but he got pardoned by Gerald Ford. Bill Clinton got impeached for lying to a grand jury about his peccadilloes, but the Senate refused to convict. But what the Bush Administration did, with their lies to get us into Iraq and then the intentional torture of prisoners, has done tremendous damage to our nation. We owe it to history and our future to clear it up. What President Bush did went way, way beyond any of Clinton's "crimes," for sure.

I think those who did the actual torturing should be prosecuted as well. Certainly the officers who were responsible should be prosecuted, since they take the same oath of office as senators, representatives and cabinet members. All of us are sworn to uphold the Constitution and that's the bedrock of our whole legal system. Every member of our armed forces is also sworn to follow only legal orders. Torture violates international laws and treaties. That means, according to Article VI of our Constitution, ratified treaties rise to the level of Constitutional law. That's not to mention military laws and the civil laws of every state, county, city, town and jurisdiction in our nation that prohibit torture.

Ironically, we Vietnam POWs received moral encouragement and strength from telling each other that we were different from the Vietnamese. We took the moral high road in assuring each other that Americans would never torture prisoners the way they were torturing us. Sadly, and dangerously, that turned out to be not true. Now we know Abu Ghraib and Guantanamo weren't the only instances. There are CIA "black sites" where prisoners have been abused and tortured. And we've had a policy of renditioning our captives to other countries where they are tortured.

Goethe said that in every man there is a capacity for every crime. Americans, like all humans, are capable of the worst behavior that we have derided in others. No doubt any human is capable of the worst behavior in certain situations. Any nation's people are capable of torturing. But the ultimate responsibility falls on the nation or jurisdiction itself, to seek out, try and punish those who are guilty of nefarious behaviors like torture. A democratic and humane nation does not *institutionalize* torture. In North Vietnam, torture was institutionalized. That is to say it was OK with their legal and penal system. We fell to the level of institutionalizing torture, despite our laws, norms and moral order.

Those of us who flew over Vietnam knew that the dispersion of our bombs was wide enough to be killing civilians. In modern warfare, maybe 90% of the fatalities and injuries are civilian. That is inhumane by any standard. But we found out that with the determined enemy, civilian casualties didn't stop the war. Vietnam was a tragic example of that. They were determined to not succumb to the American aggression, despite the killing of literally millions of their people and the horrific destruction and environmental devastation of their country. They were determined to control their own destiny.

I think part of the problem with my fellow Americans is that they've never experienced that kind of death and destruction. They've never had to experience the wholesale slaughter, the napalm and Agent Orange, the leveling of every institution and building, including infrastructure, hospitals and schools that occurred in Vietnam. Or the kind of destruction that occurred across Europe during World War II, when armies rampaged across one country after another, ultimately killing more than 40 million people. I don't think Americans realize that in these terms, we've had it easy.

My experiences of war, incarceration, abuse and torture cause me to be hyper sensitive to our recent history. Why is it that Americans are not outraged at the brutality and killing done in their name? I think probably their attention is not there. Most Americans probably just don't care. They're concerned about their own TV programs, buying and consuming things. I must agree with those who say that Americans by and large have gotten soft.

Our educational systems have so degraded over time that Americans are becoming more illiterate, thus exacerbating the problem. Half our population isn't even functionally literate. They can't read and understand basic sentences, eighth-grade level newspapers, or even travel directions. They have a minimal vocabulary. This is deeply troubling because such ignorance and a lack of curiosity are being passed along, generation to generation. When I think back on my own childhood, I find it hard to imagine that there are a lot of ten year old boys and girls lying on the living room floor reading an encyclopedia. No doubt instead they are playing video games. And that doesn't auger well for a democratic republic.

It was amazing to discover during the 2008 presidential campaign that more than half of the Republican candidates didn't believe in evolution. And that over half of the American population doesn't believe in evolution either. Too many of our citizens are filled with religious dogma while being drained of the scientific or logical capacity to make reasonable decisions or come to sensible conclusions.

On the other hand I do come away encouraged when I deal with young college and university people today. I think we really didn't question our world as right or wrong when I was growing up in the 1940s and 50s. We assumed our government was right. Young people today do tend to question things more, and that's good. They don't seem to have that same self-assurance about their own futures and about the world in general. They've gotten a lot more information and they also don't think they are living in a safe or even sustainable world.

That's very different from the world in which I grew up. I can remember being eight years old, in 1946, and walking to grade school in Tulsa. I can remember weekends going out and riding a bus with my buddies to downtown Tulsa to see a movie. I can remember riding my bicycle everywhere in town at any time of the day and even in the evening, and there was never a thought of any danger for a kid whatsoever in that city of 200,000 people.

I can also recall that people in our community had a different, a stricter sense of responsibility. We didn't dare misbehave in town because every adult who walked down the street had the capability of being our mother or father if we acted up. So it was really a safer and more structured world for a lot of us.

That said, it was a very unsafe world then if you were a minority, particularly if you happened to be black. It was a much more dangerous world to live in for blacks back then. But for a white, middle-income kid the world felt and was safe, and we pretty much accepted everything that was going on as the right thing. Of course, that all got pretty much turned on its head sometime in the 1960s. Before I was blown out of the air in April 1965, I remember music coming out – Bob Dylan's songs and Peter, Paul and Mary – and that was the beginning of the protest for change in the '60s.

471

19. Guantánamo

Guantánamo Bay was first occupied in 1898, during the Spanish American War. President Theodore Roosevelt signed an agreement with Cuba's government soon after that. The lease for the bay, which was forced on the Cuban government, was for $2,000 per year. The "Platt Amendment," signed in 1903 granted the U.S. "the right to use and occupy the waters adjacent to said areas of land and water and to use the area as a naval station only." This lease was updated between the President Franklin Delano Roosevelt administration and the Cuban government in 1934.

The current Cuban government has always said Guantánamo should have been returned to Cuba in 1959 when the new revolutionary government took over. They maintain the main mission of the naval base has changed to spying on Cuba and now lately to the detention and torture of innocent people. The Cuban government has repeatedly demanded that Guantánamo Bay be returned to the Cuban people. The U.S. sends a yearly check for the $2,000 lease, but the Cuban government has never cashed them.

President Ronald Reagan admitted in 1985 that the purpose of the base was political: "...to impose U.S. presence, even if the Cubans didn't want it."

The agreement is admittedly complicated but the fact remains that the U.S. interprets it as an "open-ended duration" that can only be terminated by mutual agreement. To Cuba it means that Guantánamo Bay is "occupied territory." It's important to note that most other "territories held" throughout the world have been returned. For example, the Panama Canal was returned to Panama in 2000, Hong Kong was returned to China by the United Kingdom in 1997, and Portugal returned Macau Island to China in 1999.

In my opinion the only fair and honorable thing to do now is simply to pick up our belongings and give Guantánamo Bay back to the Cubans.

I guess as an alternative we could give the Cubans an equal-sized land port in southern Florida. That's said tongue in cheek, but the truth is that there is no logical, correct reasoning why we should remain at Guantánamo. We have no need of it, militarily or politically, and it's costing us huge sums to maintain.

As regards the 250 or so prisoners there at the time of this writing, they should never have been dragged half-way around the world from where they were captured in the first place. Perhaps they will all have been dispatched to other locations by the time this book is in print. Some will be sent to foreign nations we cajole or bribe to take a few here and there. And some will be brought to prisons in the U.S. We have plenty of maximum security prisons here for those who are the real killers that have been tried and sentenced. We have any number of terrorists incarcerated in our country and no one has ever escaped from a maximum security prison in the United States.

But now we have a big problem stemming from the illegal and immoral actions of the Bush Administration. Many of these people have been held for years without habeas corpus, being charged and brought to prosecution. And many have been tortured, making the bringing of evidence against them exceedingly difficult. We've gotten ourselves into another huge mess by violating our own Constitution and laws. We've also made ourselves out to be hypocrites around the world. So now we have to retrace our steps, bring the bad guys to trial whatever the problems therein, and release the innocents we snatched up on whatever pretexts. We made this mess. Now we have to clean it up.

20. Politics

I began my political life as a Republican, following the example and lead by my father. Dad always said "Republican is the party for business and Democrat isn't." I believe that probably summed up his understanding of politics because I never heard him utter any further clarifying remarks and I never saw him read a book or even a newspaper. He confined his reading and intellectual pursuits to the sports page.

I turned 21 just before my 2nd Class year at the Naval Academy in 1959. There was an election that next year, 1960, featuring the new, young, charismatic John Kennedy against the long-time California politician Richard Nixon. I was not swayed by Kennedy that year, so with a clear heart I voted for Nixon. Wow, that would turn out to be a blunder many years later! Of course Kennedy won a squeaker and was inaugurated on January 20, 1961.

As luck would have it, my 17th Company was the lead company in our battalion of four companies, and our battalion was chosen to march in review for Kennedy's inauguration parade. As a 1st classman I was second in command of our company, in the leading line abreast of about 600 marching Midshipmen. Neither our battalion commander nor our company commander happened to have resonating, loud voices. But I did. So I was tasked with the duty of giving the command "Eyes Left!" when we were to pass President Kennedy in the reviewing stand, standing behind his bullet-proof glass shield.

We marched down Constitution Avenue, drums banging, bands blaring a cacophony of sound and noise. Marching in step was hopeless. I believe we were marching to 600 different cadences; it was so noisy and confusing. It was snowing and we were trudging through ice and snow. When we got abreast the reviewing stand I raised my sword high, the other Midshipmen officers followed, and in my loudest and best effort, screamed "Eyes Left!" But I don't believe a cannon shot could have been distinctly heard, so later after we returned to Bancroft Hall at USNA, some of my friends in the back informed me that the hopefully synchronized turning of heads left occurred, yep, about 600 different times.

President Kennedy started to come on for me after his famous, "Ask not . . . " inaugural speech. This guy resonated with me. Then he came to our Naval Academy graduation and I got to hear him in person again. His speech was amazingly perceptive, though I was not as appreciative of it at that time as I have been these years later. My attention was more focused on throwing my cap in the air and getting the hell out of the Naval Academy.

Sadly, President Kennedy was assassinated in November of 1963 and Vice President Lyndon Johnson became president. I continued with my somewhat less conservative leanings until after Vietnam. In 1964 I voted for Goldwater because I was very suspicious of Lyndon Johnson's integrity. This suspicion was to be born out years later with the deception he exercised when using the Gulf of Tonkin "attacks" to get us into the Vietnam War.

When I returned in 1973, President Nixon invited all us former POWs to a White House gala dinner and event. It was incredible. And we returned POWs were pretty much in awe of him because we had been told, and believed, that he had courageously ordered the bombing of Haiphong and Hanoi to bring us home. This would turn out to not be so. Apparently Henry Kissinger was greatly responsible for the end-of-war bombing while Nixon dithered from 1969 to 1973 over how to end the war. He was a hawk of course and took retribution on anyone who opposed him to the point of being paranoid.

I think Watergate, just after that, was the big turning point for my political thinking. I had been reading a lot about the war and was in graduate school at UCSD where I was learning about American politics and society. But the Watergate affair really snapped me into a new way of seeing our political world.

I became a progressive, probably leaning strongly towards a party we don't have in this country. More like the European traditions of a democratic-social, or socialist-democratic party. Such parties are not socialist per se. They recognize the utility of both private and public institutions in society, and they emphasize the importance of citizen involvement at every level of political jurisdiction.

Through the years, especially after my retirement from the Navy in 1981, I became more politically active. I supported and campaigned for Gore in 2000 and Kerry in 2004. I helped lead the "Veterans for Kerry" campaigning in Monterey County. Today I sincerely believe the election of George W. Bush, twice, was one of the most tragic and destructive things that has happened to our nation, Constitution, rule of law, peaceful existence, environment and foreign perception in our entire history.

I told John Kerry after his unsuccessful campaign that I thought he should have been up front and proud of the fact that he had been a warrior for peace and justice after he came home from Vietnam. Sadly, he allowed his handlers to talk him into covering it up. I told him, "John, you and I both know that it took a lot more courage for you to stand up and testify before Congress against the Vietnam War than it did when you got your Silver Star. You know that and I know that. You got your Silver Star because of training, and the testimony before Congress took real moral courage on your part." His words back to me were, "Phil, you're absolutely correct."

I actively wrote, spoke and campaigned on behalf of Barack Obama. In so doing I wrote and actively spoke against my former Naval Academy company mate, John McCain. I would not have supported John if he had been my blood brother because I believe electing a president is just much too important to let family or friendships guide that decision.

Is Obama an outstanding president? The jury is probably still out. Only four years will tell us. But if nothing else, electing an African American to be President of the United States of America is a sea change in American history. Barbara and I cried throughout his inaugural speech. They were tears of joy, welling up from lifetime memories – memories of living with racism and prejudice. Finally, America had advanced one big step closer toward securing the blessings of liberty to all our people.

I received a lot of angry and abusive responses for my decision to oppose McCain and support Obama. Many of my former Navy friends and fellow POWs took such issue with me that to them I became their putative traitor. I'm afraid I lost some friends during that time. That saddens me. But in the end I realize they must not have been my friends anyway. They were just former friends and I didn't know it. At any rate, I have no regrets and would do it all over again. Standing up for what I believe, even in the face of castigation by those with whom I served, is part of what it means to be a warrior for peace and social justice and for me – to continue to live with honor.

21. Military Thoughts

What I went through has been a marker in my life, both for me and almost everyone who knows or meets me. It always seems like the first thing people know about me is that I was a prisoner of war for eight years. I've often told people it must be like being a priest or a cop. Whenever a Catholic priest walks into a room with his habit and collar on, or a cop in uniform, the conversations seem to suddenly change.

People in this country see a returned POW as something special. And they usually make assumptions from certain stereotypes. It's usually assumed that because I'm a former POW I must be Republican and in favor of the wars we are fighting, both of which are not true.

I sometimes meet men, informally or in business, who carry around a touch of guilt. They say things like their "draft number was 342" so they never had to serve in Vietnam. Now they regret it. My reaction to that is to immediately put my hand on their shoulder and say something like: "Well good. I am glad you didn't have to go there. It's important to me that you didn't have to go. So congratulations." Very often, they'll respond with something like, "Phil, yeah, but you know I feel like I missed something and I should have served."

Militarism is a powerful part of our culture and social order. We are so militaristic that many of those who haven't served in the military feel guilty about it. And even some of those who did serve but weren't in combat feel guilty. Huge numbers of men, some very influential, have been found to lie about military service and awards. The web site POW Network currently reports that over 1,750 men have been "outed" as phony POWs. That's enormously sad. It says a lot, not about those men but about our culture.

Americans have an inordinate need for credentials and military credentials count very high. Much more so, I would think, than in most other developed countries. Having been in the military here is a big deal, no matter what you've done afterwards. Americans have always admired people who serve in the military and especially those who won medals in combat.

But too often when our soldiers came home during Vietnam they were not treated well. That was a huge mistake and a tragedy. But by the time I was a returning POW, the United States was starved for heroes. So we were nominated. It was wonderful, and healing for us but certainly not fair to our warriors who came home earlier. Too many Americans made the classic mistake of "shooting the messenger."

I became a member of Veterans for Peace in 1991. That was the year our leaders got their war mojo back, after the Vietnam War, to invade another third-world country. I knew then that I couldn't stand idly by and do nothing. So I joined and have continued to be a member of VFP all these past years. I have served on their national board of directors and as chair of the board. VFP is an educational organization, consisting of veterans in over 100 chapters in the U.S. and Puerto Rico. It is also recognized as a United Nations non governmental organization. VFP members work to increase public awareness of the costs of war. We seek justice for veterans and victims of war. And we work toward the ultimate abolishment of war.

I'm no longer a warrior for war, but a warrior for peace and justice. But that doesn't mean I'm a pacifist. The fact is there are different kinds of wars. If we were to be invaded by some other nation or military entity, with bad guys coming toward my town, this old man would be one of the first to man the barricades. I'd have to borrow a gun though because I don't own one anymore.

There are lots of books on the complicated question of whether there is such a thing as a just war, and if so, what are the qualifications. My personal definition of a just war means a situation where one is defending oneself. Most of the peace and justice volunteers I know are comfortable with defending themselves as just. Some are pacifists, and I tip my hat to them. It would take a lot of courage to be and act a pacifist. Maybe more than I have. But it would be a wonderful world if we all were pacifists.

Another question I get from people when they find out that I'm a warrior for peace and justice, "Well, would you do away with the military?" I wouldn't, but I would certainly reduce ours to 20% to 25% of what it is now. For example, I don't see why we need 300,000 of our military in Europe right now. There is no Soviet Union or cold war anymore. Why have so many of our military in Japan and Asia? Then of course there are the questions of why we are making wars in Iraq and Afghanistan. The last I hear, our enemies that we try to defend from, Al Qaeda and their like, are in Pakistan, Yemen, Somalia, Sudan and most recently, eastern Kenya. Do we invade all these countries to root out these rogue terrorists?

I've been subjected to a lot of vitriol and anger from my former POWs, USNA, and veteran comrades. They came home but never changed. I did change. So I have had to experience many friendship casualties over my convictions and activities. But I am a warrior. And warriors have to accept casualties.

It's clear to me that militarism in the United States is extreme. It should be clear to anybody if you look at the figures that are fairly commonly known. The United States spends more on the military than all of the other countries of the world combined. That is an astounding but factual statement. Yet we are shamefully far behind other developed nations with health care, poverty, hunger, homelessness and a disintegrating infrastructure. Americans don't seem capable of connecting the dots between military spending at the expense of everything else. Meanwhile, Europe and Asia are passing us by while contentedly letting us be the gendarmes of the world for them. They haven't had such a burden of military spending. Why should they? No need. So they are able to exceed us on every other dimension.

We have been militarily bleeding our nation to death since World War II. The military-industrial complex that President Eisenhower warned us about has become much more monstrous and all-consuming than even he could have imagined. Our media, complicit in the conspiracy, has managed to sell this suicide as being necessary for national security. They have corrupted the people's understanding of what the military should be.

Since World War II, the U.S. has conducted hundreds of overt and covert, military and quasi-military interventions all around the world. The majority of America has been so dominated by the over-arching message of the mainstream media that we haven't come to terms with the fact that our wars are no longer about defending our nation. We are reaching our military around the world, stretching our resources to the breaking point, and only making our nation less secure.

Meanwhile we have been sending our best and brightest to be killed or broken in these insane grinders, always in the name of patriotism. Hundreds of thousands of families suffer the loss of beautiful young loved ones. Most recently veteran families are being forced to become lifetime caregivers to returning combatants with traumatic brain injuries.

Military contractors and businesses have virtually purchased the United States Congress, in a bipartisan fashion. So in recent years we see our Representatives and Senators spending hundreds of billions of dollars on military contracts that the Pentagon has neither requested nor wanted. What does that say about how the system works? The contractors make large political contributions and politicians pass legislation to buy what they are selling even though our military experts don't even want or need them.

479

Notwithstanding the enormous cost savings we would enjoy with a small military, we'd also be a lot safer. But American thinking has been so distorted with this excess militarism that they equate it with security when actually opposite is the case. Our interventions are making a lot of other people in the world angry at us. It is unfortunate that Americans have been propagandized into thinking "Militarism = Security."

There may be future times when we have to stop a threat that's outside our shores. I'd like to think that we could get things settled politically and diplomatically so we might start thinking of a world without war. At the moment, it's probably beyond the horizon. But we could at least begin by bringing the vast majority of our troops home from foreign countries. After all, home is where the real dangers for our citizens are. We have both home-grown and foreign terrorists roaming our land now so we really need to focus on good intelligence and protection here.

Our military involvement in countries around the globe is not limited to the 166 nations where we have American troops. For decades we have sponsored the School of Americas, now called the "Western Hemisphere Institute for Security Cooperation." It started off in Panama and now is located at Ft. Benning, Georgia. We have trained political operatives who are in governments through South America and other regions of the world. We have also trained tens of thousands of police and military for domestic security. We have taught them interrogation methods that easily cross the line of torture. This training, plus the ordnance and other tools of the oppressive trade, have kept the people down and dictators in control in dozens of countries around the world.

This is our degenerate view of spreading democracy. Our students have squelched the hopes of freedom for literally tens of millions of people, mostly in this hemisphere. Our arms manufacturers keep them outfitted with the latest weapons. Our Congress approves legislation whereby American taxpayers foot the bill for all this.

We have created a "Department of Defense" that is truly a Department of Offensive War. Americans will know they are truly secure when the whole world is able to depend on the United Nations for being the world's policeman instead of the U.S. But this isn't going to happen any time soon. We can start by providing more support to the peacekeeping capabilities of the U.N. It can be argued that The United Nations is structured and organized poorly such that it has difficulty getting things done. Unless China and Russia agree with the United States, Britain and France, the Security Council is paralyzed. It will take changes in U.N.

structure to alleviate these problems. It will also take a change in our global culture. And it will take more people actively advocating for peace and justice.

22. Nuclear Weapons

It's amazing and somewhat frightening for me to think back about our nuclear weapons delivery capability and flight missions in the single-place A4 airplane I flew. It was said that the A4 was actually designed around that capability, with long spindly landing gear that allowed space for a nuclear bomb on the centerline station.

We went through extensive nuclear weapons training in those days. We attended nuclear weapons school, where we learned about the bombs we might carry and the targets we would be assigned. There were frequent loading drills, uploading and downloading nuclear weapons, on the carriers. Some would take place during competitive exercises, during the day and night.

We practiced flying and delivery techniques with a dummy nuclear weapon called a "shape" which was essentially a 2,000 lb. solid concrete bomb with no explosive capability. We practiced a complex nuclear delivery technique called "over the shoulder." It involved running in on a target near Fallon, Nevada, at 500 knots and 50 feet above the ground. Immediately upon flying over the target we began a four "g" pull-up to inverted and then back down in a "split s" maneuver to make a run-out in the opposite direction. The dummy shape was released from our plane via an electric timing mechanism so its trajectory was straight up to an altitude of 5,000 feet or more and then straight down onto the target. Meanwhile we were miles away from the target going out on the original run-in line but in the opposite direction. A spotter on the ground some distance away would calibrate and radio our hit on the target. Of course anything within a few hundred feet was essentially a direct hit because we were practicing for the real thing which would be a one megaton or so nuclear bomb. It was very intense training. But I must admit it was a hell of a lot of fun to perform this maneuver too.

When we were on the ship, each pilot had two top secret targets that we worked on with our air intelligence officer. We made navigation and profile maps, called "strip charts" into the Communist country target we were assigned, either the Soviet Union or China. We were all assigned targets. So if the "whistle ever went," that is if the President of the United States ever activated nuclear war retaliation, then we would be launched with a nuclear weapon to our targets. Of course most of our targets were one-way trips. We were part of the nuclear weapons all-out-war capability of the day. It's very scary now to think of early 20-something lieutenant junior grades flying around with nuclear capability.

Most of the public in those days had the image of only the B-52s flying the failsafe routes when carrying nuclear weapons. But in fact our nuclear capability was very much spread out. The Navy had a huge component because every aircraft carrier had nuclear weapons to deliver with their attack aircraft. The fighters didn't carry nuclear weapons but all the attack community did. And of course, there were all our submarines with nuclear weapons, some of which were always out on station.

We had thousands of nuclear weapons pointed at places in China and the Soviet Union. It's truly some kind of miracle that we never accidentally got into some kind of nuclear holocaust with all the weaponry we had, all always at some degree of readiness. It speaks to the professionalism of military and political leaders on all sides, realizing how important it was to be sure everything was very carefully managed and made safely redundant. There were lots of safety features to the program of the day. But it still catches my breath to consider that during the more than six decades since Hiroshima and Nagasaki, some lunatic didn't detonate a nuclear weapon, or there wasn't some accident with the tens of thousands of warheads the nuclear powers had and still have.

Today I wonder if some sort of nuclear accident might just be inevitable. As long as there are so many nuclear weapons, the chances seem almost unavoidable. So my thinking leans toward the only sane answer which is to get rid of them all. We would need to start a phased downgrade with Russia and China. Then, having led by example, we could work together to begin de-nuclearising the other countries that now have a nuclear capability, including Britain, France, Israel, India, Pakistan, North Korea and possibly Iran at current count. We would have to run nuclear proliferation in reverse if we are ever to have a nuclear-free world.

It doesn't make sense to focus on the so-called rogue states since the major powers were the first proliferators. Nuclear weaponry has spread from the U.S. to the then-Soviet Union which is now Russia, then to China, Great Britain, France, Israel, India, Pakistan, North Korea and perhaps others. Where does it stop? How do we make sure no nuclear nation falls under the control of a lunatic dictator? That's what makes North Korea going nuclear so frightening. Or what happens if, as we saw in the films "Failsafe" and "Dr. Strangelove," some officer goes crazy? Or even more probable today, what if some terrorist group gets their hands on a nuclear device from some poorly-guarded stockpile or facility in any of these countries?

There doesn't seem to be a huge drive to gear down and get rid of those old nuclear weapons. Meanwhile we are developing more sophisticated weapons at Lawrence Livermore Laboratories and other places around the country. How counter productive is it to be developing new nuclear weapons when we already have the capacity to destroy all life on Earth? It's crazy, but our military industrial complex has such a powerful business component to war-making and militarism that new research and development is going on.

I don't see any other options to demilitarizing and denuclearizing our world. If we don't, I fear we're going to destroy ourselves. To accomplish it we must set the example by beginning that process. But I believe the overarching problem is we are really a very confused culture. As I note elsewhere, we equate militarism with security, and this precept goes virtually unexamined. It's part of the American psyche and has been built on through all of our war-making. It all began with our founding struggles, then on to our Mexican-American War, Civil War, War on Native Americans, Spanish-American War, the two world wars and all the undeclared interventions and wars since. The belief that if we don't have a strong military we're not secure is almost hard-wired into Americans by now. The frightening fact is that a massively powerful military actually invokes insecurity. First, just having it motivates its use. Second, I can't imagine why any nation would want to attack the United States. A terrorist group might, but you don't fight them with the most powerful and technologically advanced military in the world. Nor does it make any sense that we have to be the protector of everybody on the planet. Who elected us to be the world's policeman?

23. Post 9/11

The 9/11/01 attacks on the United States still seem to be widely misunderstood. We just reacted from those attacks by invading Afghanistan and then Iraq. The suicidal airliner crashes on our World Trade Center in New York City were perpetrated by radical zealots who were willing to die for a cause they believed in, no matter how distorted that cause. But their diabolically clever way of conducting the attacks with such success completely changed our world.

We lost a couple of huge buildings and 3,000 people were killed. In response we whipsawed into a punitive mode that brought on the invasion of Iraq when they had absolutely nothing to do with the 9/11 attacks. Most of the terrorists were from Saudi Arabia! We know President Bush and our intelligence people did have warnings but they didn't pay proper, if any, attention to them. We should have seen this coming. But sadly and disastrously, the people who were sworn to protect us were ill prepared and asleep at the switch.

The invasion of Iraq actually came about because President Bush and his neo-conservative advisors had been planning a war there for a long time, even before Bush's election. So the terrorist attack was used, once again, as a pretext for war much like the "sinking of the Maine" and the "Tonkin Gulf Attacks" were used to start WW I and the Vietnam War. We would hope to have leaders who are capable of keeping cool heads and thus responding appropriately and effectively, even when citizens are responding vindictively. But we didn't have level heads in the White House and Congress when the events of 9/11 happened.

I must admit that I was really conflicted at the time about invading Afghanistan. From experience and things I've read, I always tend to be suspicious of our intelligence operatives. But it seemed apparent from all I could find out that the Al Qaeda operatives were using Afghanistan, a failed state, for training and operational planning. Some of the Al-Qaeda people who had directed the World Trade Center attacks both times, in 1993 and 2001 were apparently there. So it seemed likely that it was the right thing to do, to attack and kill or capture the Al Qaeda.

I understand we pretty much had the Al Qaeda people surrounded soon after our invasion into Afghanistan. But the Bush-Cheney Administration was in such a hurry to go to war in Iraq, to control oil and so forth, that they pulled out the people we needed to finish the job in Afghanistan. So we wound up losing practically everything we had gained there. They lied about why we were invading Iraq, which had nothing to do with the 9/11 attacks, and took troops out of Afghanistan that we needed there.

Now we're in serious trouble in Afghanistan. I'll go ahead and use the word – quagmire – made famous during our war in Vietnam. Sadly, I see Afghanistan as another Vietnam. It's another tar baby that we can't get rid of. Meanwhile I'm afraid it's going to take Americans a long time to figure that out, just as it took more than ten years to get out of Vietnam. Once again, we are stuck in a hell of a mess.

Now President Obama is presented with the same dilemma President Johnson was in 1964 and 65. He's getting advice to send more troops to fight the Taliban, people who never attacked us nor do they even want to. Our purpose there is getting muddled with nation building, trying to make an ancient tribal society into something that approximates our own image. Meanwhile, the perpetrators, Al Qaeda, are in Pakistan, Yemen, Somalia, Sudan and lately in eastern Kenya. Do we have to invade there next?

Afghanistan, like Vietnam, is a political war, not a war that can be won with military. We lost Vietnam politically and that's why we lost it militarily. This will happen again in Afghanistan if we don't somehow help promote a stable government, even if it is Islamic or perhaps even Taliban in some provinces.

We do know that with the evolution of communications around the world, with the Internet and cell phones, it's probably inevitable that governments everywhere will gravitate towards more open and democratic forms of rule. It's inescapable when people can find out what is really happening and what they are missing. It is happening in Vietnam and China. You can see it happening all around the world because no government can totally block communications. And mass communication ultimately leads to mass motivation for a more democratic and prosperous life.

I believe we could easily be a catalyst for that change by basing our foreign policies on the promotion of human rights and self-determination of people everywhere. But first we have to start setting an example of mutual respect, rule of law and pursuit of dialogue with all nations. Worldwide peace and justice will never be gained at the barrel of a gun.

24. New Thinking

"It isn't enough to talk about peace. One must believe in it. And it isn't enough to believe in it. One must work at it."

ELEANOR ROOSEVELT

My perception of having lived three lives has quite a lot to do with what I thought and how I dealt with my worlds in each of those time periods. There was a transition in my big-picture thinking, what the Germans call a "Weltanschauung," a comprehensive conception or apprehension of the world, especially from a specific standpoint. Certainly my three worlds, first growing up in Oklahoma and becoming a warrior, second being a warrior at war as a POW for eight years, and now my life after the Vietnam War have each been remarkably different.

I radically altered my behavioral responses in the POW world to become a dedicated and angry warrior-soldier. My actions were both intentional and unintentional, on the one hand to survive and on the other to fight back. Then within the first year that I was home, my thinking changed and I became more liberal, humanistic and caring. That has continued to where I am today. Some of my life journey has been serendipitous and some came as a result of personal planning.

I learned a lot in that first year or two about my own life, the Vietnam War the military, our government and politics. My postgraduate school experience in Sociology at the University of California at San Diego no doubt helped me attain the third life change. I soaked up information with a vengeance at UCSD after being a prisoner of war for eight years and having never been allowed even a pencil and paper, much less a book or a magazine.

Graduate school was a mind opening experience. I made a transition from being a person who just accepted the orders and things I was told to becoming an intellectual, a person who questions things. That shift was a hallmark of my third life as a warrior. It meant taking responsibility in a new way. I wasn't going to be a follower any more.

I did take away a great lesson from my POW experience. Our motto "Return With Honor," has stayed with me and has now become an attempt to "Live With Honor." This motto has several components for me today.

Responsibility: I believe in taking responsibility for my own behavior. Sometimes it's tough to do and I sometimes catch myself blaming someone or something, instead of old number one. In my experience of leading hundreds of seminars and while mentoring individuals, I'm often amazed to hear mature adults blame "mommy, daddy, my boss, bureaucracy, hard knocks, bad luck," or whatever for things that are just their own damn fault.

Respect: In a way, respect probably follows responsibility. We really learned to have respect for each other as fellow POWs. It always becomes more prevalent and powerful among people who are put in a position of having to depend on one another. For me this value covers not just other people, but all life on our beautiful planet. Recent evidence is showing that we probably need to begin respecting our environment more if we are to continue living here.

Commitment: I've found a big need for commitment in my life. Having been given the gift of life, surviving death numerous times, I owe it to my world to commit to things that get me outside of myself, my own ego. It takes commitment to bring change.

Contribution: I feel strongly that I have a basic human responsibility to, in some way leave my world slightly better than I found it. So I've tried to make contributions by educating people about peace, justice and our environment. I've tried to give service where I could, on a dozen or more non-profit boards, and as a volunteer for numerous causes that promote better health and welfare to those less fortunate, and to nature.

I visualize having what I call an "internal gyroscope." It keeps me questioning societal norms, values, mores and all the information floating around us. Is this really true? Who benefits? Is this the right thing to say or do? How will this affect others? What will this do to our environment? Am I acting and living with honor?

25. Life with a Tin Cup and Spoon

The only utensils I ever had in prison were a tin cup and spoon. I became quite attached to them and so decided to bring them home with me on that wonderful day, February 12, 1973 when I left Camp Unity for freedom. I've always kept them on my bedroom dresser where I can see them every day. They take me back to remind me how fortunate I am now, to be thankful and not complain. They are a powerful memory aid that keeps me grounded.

My life here in Monterey has been exceedingly fortunate. I have a wonderful home and wife. We enjoy doing things together. I have a dear sister in Tulsa whom I can visit. We enjoy my dear brother and sister-in-law. We have a wonderful relationship because the four of us can see each other frequently. We aren't super wealthy but have enough to retire. Nowadays that is really a blessing. Our economy and the decrease in the average standard of living have snatched that opportunity away from many Americans.

People wonder how I have "made up," as they put it, for my torturous time in Vietnam. You can't exactly do that, but instead I've tried to take that experience and convert it, use it for some positive purpose.

I get a great deal of fulfillment from the peace and justice activities I'm currently involved in with Veterans for Peace, the Peace Coalition of MontereyCounty, and similar efforts. I have served on boards or volunteered for maybe twenty non-profit, community service organizations since 1980. I will note that some of these were learning experiences I would not do again because they took too much time and effort.

I returned in September of 2009 to Will Rogers High School in Tulsa. Our school was built in 1938, the year I was born, and three years after the famous philosopher died in a plane crash. They got things done promptly back then because the first graduating class was 1939. Since then the school has graduated over 40,000 students. Will Rogers High School is now on the National Register of Historic Buildings. It's an incredible Art Deco-style building that would cost who knows how many millions of dollars to build today.

The ceremony took place in the auditorium, central hallway, and library of the high school. On this occasion they inducted seven more people into the Will Rogers High School Hall of Fame making a total of seventeen members. I was honored to be one of those people inducted. They honor people for excelling in various life pursuits, including philanthropy, business, arts, music, government and the military.

About three hundred people were present. They had kids there who were seniors who led us out to the front row of the auditorium. We were honored with video presentations on each of us, then we were called up individually to be presented with a statuette copy of the original nine foot tall statue of Will Rogers in the hall of Congress.

I felt both very grateful and humbled at receiving such an honor from my old high school.

When I got up to say a few words after receiving my statuette, I thanked the committee that had selected me, and I put in a special thank you for my sister who was in the audience. Linda had worked selling POW-MIA bracelets during the time that I was a Prisoner of War. I thanked my classmates, the Class of 1956. I'd always had a really warm feeling towards them because when I came home in May of 1973, at Tulsa Airport, there were over a hundred of them lined up outside with banners that said "Welcome Home, Phil."

Since that time, when meeting and talking with classmates, I've found out I've become the class celebrity. I was anything but a celebrity as a kid at Will Rogers High School in 1956. Life is truly stranger than fiction. My life certainly has been anyway.

Prisoner of War wives began advertising our plight early in the war. They lobbied our Congressional representatives and were ever more visible in the news. Some of them formed a committee for the Prisoners of War and Missing in Action. They had bracelets made, each one of which had the name, rank and down date of the POW or MIA. They sold tens of thousands of these POW/MIA bracelets all over the country. The purpose was to bring awareness of us and to help support families of POWs and MIAs. Many Americans wore their bracelet for years and years through the war, and then when "their" POW came home, if he did, they could send the bracelet to him.

I received over a thousand bracelets with letters when I got home. I wrote a thank-you letter and sent a photo of myself to every one of them. In fact, to this day I'm still receiving probably four or five letters and emails a year from people wanting to send me "my" bracelet. It's amazing, all these years later, that people are still contacting me to send me a bracelet. As I did 36 years ago, I always reply and now tell them, "Please keep the bracelet in my honor. I have several hundred of them in a box in my office and I would be pleased if you would keep it."

After all the anticipation and planning during my eight-year incarceration, circumstances certainly turned out quite differently after I came home. The divorce turned out to be a good thing for me later. But to this day I feel cheated and saddened by what happened with Diane because when I came home I just loved her so much. I even made a career decision partially based on being able to live near her. But then later when Diane came into her late teens and early twenties, for some reason unbeknownst to me, she completely rejected me. She has refused to answer my calls or any attempts to communicate with her and now I haven't seen her in fifteen years.

Obviously from what I've been through and survived, I've had to be adaptable. So I have adapted to the sad situation with Diane. At various times she has lived almost itinerantly, and at this writing she is house-sitting her mother's home and caring for her dog while her mother spends two years in Botswana in the Peace Corps.

Diane is forty-five years old now. No matter what she has or hasn't done with her life, I just wish she'd relent and agree to have some kind of communication with her father. In a sense she rejects the idea of having a father. She refers to her mother as "Karen" and to me as "Phil." Nevertheless, the few times I have written to her of late, I've always signed off "Love Dad." For better or worse, I will always be her father and will always love her.

There have been little bumps along the way in the relationship with my sister, probably because we are both very strong and independent people. But we maintain a very close and loving relationship. My family, Barbara, Linda, Chuck and Terry are my joy in life. I consider myself exceedingly fortunate in that regard. I have a lot of perspective on it from all the family problems I grew up with.

There are of course some residual effects from the ejection from my A4C, combat injuries, malnutrition, various prison diseases, torture and beatings. But I am the extremely lucky recipient of the finest SOCIALIZED MEDICINE health care. I had to capitalize that because Americans have been terribly propagandized and brain washed by that term lately. My socialized medical care is of course delivered by the Department of Veterans Affairs, the VA. It turns out that every independent evaluation of their care rates them not only the highest in terms of medical care delivery, but also the highest in terms of monetary efficiency. I can only wonder: Why isn't this health care available to all Americans?

I recently summed up my life to the members of my local men's club. There are about 40 of us, all men who have achieved and made contributions to society in some field. We call ourselves "The Cavalry," though none of us even ride horses. The name came about whimsically so it doesn't represent anything militarily. Our habit at monthly meetings is for each of us in turn to tell a story, joke, or announcement. Our round-the-circle time is always educational, interesting and terribly entertaining. Then we have lunch together. They usually manage to extract a POW story from me, of which I have enough to last several lifetimes. One day a couple of years ago in our individual presentations, I told them the following: "All of us guys here are a bunch of lucky sons of bitches. But I'm afraid you guys have to take a back seat because I'm the luckiest son of a bitch here." My tin cup and spoon remind me of that every day.

Epilogue

Return with honor. What a powerful statement for a POW to live by. Our leaders in those prisons had it right from the beginning. More than anything else about that experience, today I'm thankful I took our motto to heart those many years ago and did manage to return with my honor intact.

Nowadays I think about my experiences in the context of the insanity of the war and the terrible disservice that we did to the country and the people of Vietnam. When you look at the tally at the end of the war, it's just hideous what we did to their country. We killed over two million of their people. They still have 300,000 missing in action and their country, North and South, has been environmentally devastated for generations to come. It was a really stupid, awful, deadly thing that we did to Vietnam and to the Vietnamese people. I would note too, that it seems they are quite able to run their own country by themselves today. They are doing so rather successfully without our help. It appears they didn't need our intervention after all!

I should note that many of us had these thoughts while we were prisoners of war. Of course being a POW was a different kind of situation because the Vietnamese were always trying to exploit us for political propaganda. So we always told each other, and reinforced with each other, that you had absolutely no choice when you went into that interrogation room. As we used to say, you had to appear to be a little bit to the right of Adolph Hitler when being interrogated in order to keep them from exploiting you for propaganda purposes.

The danger was not only the propaganda, but if we ever went soft, we would be endangering our fellow soldiers and pilots that were there. They were trying to use us as a weapon of war, and that's what we had to fight. It didn't matter what we thought about the war, and there were all kinds of thoughts among POWs about the war. We had to fight with everything we had inside so as to return with honor.

Communication is the essence of being human. We are all born into a society where we learn a language. And language gives us the capacity for abstract thinking, culture, history and reason. As John Donne said centuries ago, "No man is an island." The Vietnamese tried to strip us of our humanity through separation but we used clever and devious means to thwart them. We had to communicate to maintain our humanity, culture, history, reason and with it we were able to become a cohesive team that was a force to be reckoned with.

I think Americans in general have an innate ability to see humor and remain optimistic in trying circumstances. Certainly we POWs valued humor. Sometimes it was very dark, but humor greases things up so you can get through the tough times. And optimism was almost rigidly enforced. As I said, everyone always had a "go home date" in mind, but you dared not tell anyone yours was longer than a year. It wasn't very well tolerated.

Another factor that kept us determined and resistant was anger. Throughout the bad years from 1965 up through almost all of 1969, we were being abused and tortured so much that every one of us developed an intense hatred for the people who were our guards, interrogators and camp officials. We hated them with such an intense passion that no matter how we felt about the war we fought them with every fiber in our being.

This, I think, is a key lesson when it comes to interrogation and interrogation techniques, especially since the issue of "enhanced interrogation techniques" has come to the fore since we entered this war with Al Qaeda. It has been proven to this day, the same thing, that if you want to get something from a prisoner or a prisoner of war, the way to do it is to be decent and respectful and not do the kind of things they were doing to us. Nor what we apparently did to people we captured in Iraq and Afghanistan.

I don't suppose I should have expected the Vietnamese to be smarter about the way they treated us. But I was surprised that as intelligent human beings they didn't understand that they could have played it better to make us less angry and feel less hatred towards them and to the Vietnamese people. But I think that at the end, most of us POWs came to grips with the notion that when we came home we couldn't look back and obsess on the pain because we would just be further punishing ourselves.

When I came home I had an overarching feeling that for the rest of my life I wanted to try to do the right thing. I wasn't initially sure what that was but whatever that might be I wanted to try to do it. I thought that when I got home I not only wanted to return with honor but I wanted to live with honor.

Actually, I'd been thinking about that before I was returned to freedom, maybe a couple of weeks earlier, when our release was imminent. By the time I actually came home I was committed to it. With that thought in my mind, I studied and read what had happened in America while I was gone. Then graduate school fed my realization that I had to have a more open view of people and society.

I realized that my hatred of the Vietnamese guards, interrogators and officials was doing me no good. I especially became aware of how foolish it would be to condemn all Vietnamese for what this small group of individuals had done. During the weeks and months of my recovery, I began to sense the scope of the social change that began in The Sixties. I became aware of how radically transformed our society had become, whether everyone who lived through it was aware of it or not. With that increased awareness, I slowly became able to put away my old hatreds. I came to the understanding that it was senseless to ascribe the bad actions and attributes of a few select people to a group. It was just like racism, homophobia or any prejudice. Grouping people for blame is too easy and always wrong.

Many people think that we should stop looking for those listed as missing in action, but I disagree. I think that it's productive to continue to look for the MIAs, and in all of our war theaters. I understand there are about 2,000 MIAs from the Vietnam War, 8,100 from the Korean War and more than 48,000 from World War II.

For the families who are left, it really means something to find the remains. There's a sense of closure much more significant than the presumption that they are dead. While we don't spend a lot on the effort, I'm pleased that we do have a dedicated federal government unit that's composed of the different services that conducts searches all over the world for the missing. And every so often, though less often now, they find the wreckage of aircraft or the site of a battle.

It has always irritated me when I hear somebody say that the U.S. military doesn't leave our dead and wounded behind. That is utter nonsense. We sure as hell did, and still do, because usually it would have been insane to do otherwise. Wars are so chaotic that we do leave our dead and wounded behind.

So the least we can do is try to find as many remains of those left behind as we can. There are no prisoners of war still in Vietnam. That's just make-believe propaganda that the ultra-conservative crazies made up as a ploy to try to stop America from giving recognition to Vietnam. It was their perverted sense of vengeance for a war we lost, perverted because it kept alive some flicker of what was really false hope for the families of the missing. But we're through that now and we do have good diplomatic relations with Vietnam.

No matter what a person's politics, I think everyone who served in the Vietnam War had to make sense of it in some way. It's only human to create an explanation that will somehow justify the pain they went through. We all need to somehow justify our time there because if we don't, we wind up falling into the abyss. Unfortunately that has happened all too often. Guys came home and they became alcoholics, got addicted to drugs, abused their families or committed suicide. All of those things happened for guys who were unable to make sense of their experiences. This phenomenon isn't unique to Vietnam though. All wars grind people under after the war as well as during.

Probably due to the unique nature of that war, especially our failure in Vietnam, there are some common myths about Vietnam veterans. One myth is that half of us came home crazy, drug addicted, suicidal or later became derelicts on the street. Nothing could be further from the truth. Vietnam veterans are most often successful in their post-Vietnam lives. They are often the leaders and pillars of their communities.

The percentages of those badly damaged from the Vietnam War were no different from other wars we've been in. World War II, Korea and all our other wars have produced the same proportion of veterans who have had problems with drugs, alcohol, divorce, anger issues, homelessness and even suicide. The fact is that a lot of GIs at the very end of the Vietnam War got into drugs because drugs were available. Some of them weren't able to kick the habit when they came home. But in comparison with the rate for WW II warriors who came home to alcoholism, the numbers are comparable.

The same has been true of suicides. The myth that 50,000 to 100,000 Vietnam vets killed themselves is just that. The Centers for Disease Control estimate that number to be around 9,000 out of the 2,700,000 who served.

The Vietnam War did not discriminate against minorities by placing them in combat over and above their societal representation. You will find the statistics prove that every ethnic group suffered casualties or deaths in proportion to their percentage in American society at large. It's ironic, or at least curious, that these myths were perpetrated mostly by people on the political left. They set themselves up to be discredited when the truth about Vietnam was horrible enough. They say the first casualty of war is truth, and that's the truth!

I am frequently asked if I have any interest in returning to Vietnam, and the answer is very simply, no. I have several Vietnamese friends who have offered to take me on a personally guided tour. Other people along the way have also offered but I just have no need to do it.

It's not an antipathy or resentment against the country. I don't have anything I have to complete anymore with regard to my service there. I'm done. I'm complete with the whole thing. It just seems like an awful lot of trouble to get into an airplane and fly all the way back to Vietnam to see it. I don't like the weather there for one thing and I just love my life here.

I have a lot of veteran friends who have gone back. Some have gone back together in groups. Some ex-POWs have seen the old prison complex, or what's left of it. In fact, one of my good friends, Pete Peterson, a fellow Vietnam POW, was our first Ambassador to Vietnam, appointed by President Clinton. John McCain has gone back several times. John Kerry, who served courageously but wasn't a POW has been back many times in the service of diplomacy. Kerry and McCain are primarily responsible for our resuming diplomatic relations with Vietnam. We owe them our debt of gratitude for having the warrior courage to face the overwhelming opposition.

Veterans for Peace members and chapters have been involved with collecting medical supplies and money to send back to Vietnam. VFP and other organizations I've supported have also been involved in building medical clinics there.

What we did to Vietnam was beyond horrible. It was an illegal, immoral and catastrophic venture. But we have to honor and respect those who served there, just as we must for all the men and women who have served in other wars and interventions. It was never up to them to decide whether their war was good or bad. It was always up to the American people and those whom they elected. We should remember a big lesson from Vietnam, that it's not the warriors' fault. Don't blame the warrior for the war. You can hate the war. But always love and support the warrior.

The reports we are hearing now about both active-duty military and veterans of the Iraq and Afghanistan wars is not very encouraging. Many of our veterans are now returning home horribly disabled, veterans who would probably have died on the battlefields of Vietnam and earlier wars. The suicide rate is setting new records every year because of the prevalence of close combat and repeated deployments.

I've long advocated a universal draft which gets my left wing friends excited and upset. But I believe a universal draft for all young Americans, no matter what their physical ability, would be a good thing both for them and for our country. I think it should be a requirement for everyone when they become 18 years old. All would have to serve our country in some job of their choice, not just the military, for a minimum of one year, or better for two years. Because when they came back from those two years they would truly have, I think, internalized an identity as a United States citizen who's responsible for something and who's part of something, as opposed to just being alienated and out there flailing around.

There are so many different areas where young people can both make a contribution and expand their horizons. They could work with forest rangers, in health clinics, on various infrastructure projects or at senior centers. There are so many possibilities to get a sense of the country and the American people and to experience new situations. These public service ventures could lead to a rewarding profession. It could get kids focused even when they're not focused. It would give them the feeling that they have served their country and that it's their duty to continue to make contributions to society. They would make better college or university students and they would have learned to be responsible for something outside of themselves.

I have counseled, coached and mentored many people. One of the first things I ask is what they are committed to. Occasionally someone will say "I don't know, or maybe I'm not committed to anything." That's so definitive for me that I always tell them that's their problem. "You need to figure that out before we can work together because until you're committed to something, you are not a whole person."

I have physical disabilities as a result of my prison experience that are reminders every single day of what I went through. But as I've said, it was an experience that no amount of money or reward on this planet could get me to go through again, and by the same token, no amount of money or reward on this planet could pay to take it away from me. I know that some people can't understand it or wouldn't understand it, but those eight years were the most powerful and defining of my life. I am who I am as a result of that time. It's a rich experience because it brought about a lot of introspection that has been so valuable in my third life.

I have all kinds of other benefits from having been a prisoner of war. There is the enjoyment of turning a doorknob and walking through a door, something that nobody would think about unless they had had the experience of loosing their freedom by being locked up, to have all your actions controlled by armed and hostile guards.

I had several prison "epiphanies" but one especially deserves mention. One day, back at the Little Vegas camp, after I had been tortured for a month, a realization came to me. I remember being in leg irons and handcuffs and just starting to recover from my physical and emotional wounds. I began thinking back about my father, who had always criticized me about not being a sissy. Then it came to me that I had been carrying that part of my dad around in my psyche. And with that came the realization that he had probably been projecting his own insecurities out on to me. At that moment I suddenly felt an incredible "letting go" of all that pressure as I realized that I was a hell of a man after all.

That's when it occurred to me that I didn't have to continue going out of my way to make them mad. I leaned that a less hard-nosed approach could be successful and not so damaging. After those years of getting my noggin bashed it became clear to me that the one thing that was most important to the Vietnamese was to be polite. I finally found it was much better to just be polite and to resist in a softer way. That even turned out to be more effective than the hard-ass approach I had been giving them.

By whatever methods, we had to resist because they were trying to pick people they could break to use for political propaganda. Plus, we were working as a team in prison so the longer we resisted the more time other guys didn't have to go into interrogation. The Vietnamese had a limited number of interrogators and cells to interrogate people in, so taking up their time and space spared your buddies.

A key to my restoring my emotional sense was my daughter. Only eight years old, she was absolutely a sweetheart. I fell for her immediately, and I think she sort of started teaching me how to be a dad. We learned a lot about being ourselves together. Also I had girlfriends and that was huge help, to be around females, and not just macho males all the time.

I think the wall is mostly gone, but I'm still not quite like other people when difficult or bad things happen to me. I don't think I have as strong an emotional reaction to traumatic events as most people do. I still have strong defenses and I don't let myself experience the emotional pain as much as other people do. I ascribe that both to my Vietnam experience and to my childhood; living with an alcoholic father and an abusive mother. I learned how to protect myself emotionally and somehow to avoid the pain of what was going on around me. Ram Dass calls it "armoring your heart."

But I also learned how to be a good listener. Children of alcoholics, drug addicts and abusive parents usually come out being good listeners because they are always observing and watching to see what is going to happen next. Later on in life when I became a T-Group trainer, teaching interaction skills to group participants, I worked with executives in hundreds of sessions. My listening skills served me, and consequently them, very well.

I probably did a hundred of those week-long group sessions in various places, usually with ten to fifteen people. With all that practice I developed good antennas. I learned to see right through somebody and identify their true emotional set. No doubt I began developing that ability very early in life. People were often amazed at what I picked up on. I've had practice watching my mother and father, upper classmen at the Naval Academy and interrogators to see what was going to come next. Survival is a powerful teacher.

After my months in solitary confinement, one might think I couldn't stand to be alone, but when I got home I wanted to be alone more. It took me a while to want to be with people a lot. I certainly didn't want to be around crowds. Crowds of people built up a lot of tension in me. I still enjoy spending time alone today. My home office is downstairs where I can work by myself. I also enjoy just being out and doing things alone. My wife and I are both that way. She enjoys doing things by herself, too. We enjoy doing lots of things together but we give each other some separation as well.

Being a warrior means exercising courage in the sense of being willing to put your self on the line. There have been many people in our nation's history who have done so, from standing up for independence from Great Britain to stopping a school board from banning books. Many, many people I know have put more on the line than I have. I'm constantly amazed at the selfless contributions people make for us every day.

I've tried to make an extra effort in my third life to stand up for the downtrodden, those less fortunate than I have been. I guess I'm a sucker for the underdog. My POW experience has sharpened my innate sensitivity and concern for people who are kicked around in society, people who don't have any power or control. I admit there have been times when people could characterize my actions as tilting at windmills. Some of those times I knew full well it was true, but in my heart I just felt it was the right thing to do. For me this took some maturity, growth and courage because my dad, R.B., whom I loved and admired fiercely, was wrong about always being popular. It took a while for me to figure that out for myself but I'm thankful I did.

I see in my own transformations what I've observed in many people. That is we usually change our minds and evolve slowly. I'm acutely aware that all of us take a step forward from where we are standing, not from where someone else is. Some of us will allow ourselves small changes when we see incredible contributions others have made.

I've often noted that my fellow Americans give much more credibility to veterans than those who haven't served in the military. My peace and justice community friends often say they like to hear me speak or that they're happy to see me in a group because what I say or do carries a lot clout. Yet to me this is sad because many of them are the true heroes who should be heard. I know people who have spent their lives on the line in service of peace, justice, equality and the environment. Those warriors are my heroes.

It will be a long and difficult struggle to bring peace and justice to America, let alone the world. It will have to be a glacially gradual shift in consciousness, away from seeing war as an easy solution. After the atomic bombs were dropped in 1945 Albert Einstein said, "Everything is changed in the world except our way of thinking." He said we need a new way of thinking to a way of living peacefully with each other because we have created weapons that can never be used.

I'm afraid my fellow American citizens are often too easily convinced to lash out. They are too easily instigated to violence. I think Americans today, if pressed just a little, would probably support dropping atomic weapons someplace again, or invading another third world country on false assumptions again. They might even support sending Muslims to internment camps or deporting all Mexicans. Many would opt to trash our Constitution by passing laws that would require Christianity to be taught in all our schools. We also see Americans who are willing to kill the last of a species, pollute our environment or clear cut our forests for monetary gain.

So my reaction to this self-destructive craziness has been to speak or act out for the preservation of people and our planet. I have to hope that maybe some of the things I do will in a small way affect a few people here and there, and that maybe those people will affect a few other people, and so on.

The process of writing this book has rekindled strong memories of my prison experiences. Some of it has been difficult, especially going back through the debriefing notes, which brought up a lot of emotions. There were times when I would read through my debriefing notes, especially when I was cleaning up certain passages about an interrogation, beating or torture sequence, that were freshly distressing. I could feel the same fear rising up from those old gut-wrenching experiences I felt back there forty years ago. And I could feel the old anger and hatred rising up again. I discovered that even after all these years I could have a recurrence of PTSD. I have to say that it came back with a vengeance while I was editing and working through the events of my prison experiences. More than anything else that surprised and also disappointed me. I thought I was through all of that and had worked it out to completion. I thought I was invincible when it came to my own war experiences. Apparently not.

Writing this book has most importantly reminded me again of how thankful and incredibly fortunate I am to be here today. I have been blessed with a loving family, good friends, reasonably good health, an excellent and extensive education and a rich and interesting life. Because of that I'm motivated to help make a few things better for other people, animals, plants and this lovely blue marble we call earth. For all those I hope this testament of my three lives as a warrior will serve in some positive way. Perhaps it will motivate others to live with honor so things might become just a little better than while we were here.

INDEX

505

LaVergne, TN USA
21 October 2010
201782LV00008B/12/P